INTRODUCTION TO DYNAMIC
MACROECONOMIC THEORY

INTRODUCTION TO DYNAMIC MACROECONOMIC THEORY

An Overlapping Generations Approach

George T. McCandless Jr.

with Neil Wallace

Harvard University Press
Cambridge, Massachusetts, and London, England
1991

Library of Congress Cataloging-in-Publication Data

McCandless, George T.
    Introduction to dynamic macroeconomic theory : an overlapping
generations approach / George T. McCandless Jr. ; with Neil
Wallace.
        p.   cm.
    Includes bibliographical references and index.
    ISBN 0–674–46111–8 (alk. paper)
    1. Macroeconomics.   2. Equilibrium (Economics)—Mathematical
models.   I. Wallace, Neil.   II. Title.
HB172.5.M366   1991
339—dc20

90–27439
CIP

For Micaela

Contents

Preface

This book grew out of a series of lecture notes that we used at the University of Minnesota, University of Chicago, Universidad Central de Venezuela, and Centro de Estudios Macroeconomicos de Argentina. Our objective here is to provide relatively easy access to a wide range of basic issues in dynamic (or intertemporal) macroeconomics, yet to maintain the firm microeconomic foundation that is at the heart of almost all serious modern macroeconomic work. We use a single basic model throughout, the overlapping generations model under perfect foresight. Although this choice imposes some restrictions (for example, we do not consider economies with uncertainty), it enables us to use simple mathematics (nothing more advanced than calculus is required) and to concentrate on economic issues. In addition, we are able to illustrate each of our results with analytical derivations, graphically, and by working out examples. The exercises, an integral part of the book, are strategically placed and should be worked when encountered. Those marked with an asterisk are more difficult or more open ended than the rest.

Chapters 1 through 3, 5, and 6 construct the basic model and illustrate the methods for finding equilibria with different kinds of assets. The agents in all of the economies are selfish except in those economies described in Chapter 4, where some individuals care about their children. Chapter 7 proposes variants on the basic model that allow for equilibria with fluctuations. Chapter 8 adds a simple storage or linear production technology, and Chapter 9 modifies the basic model to generate the standard neoclassical growth results. Chapters 10 through 12 introduce money as an asset and explore restrictions that generate equilibria in which individuals hold both money and assets with higher rates of return.

The basic structure of the book was developed jointly. McCandless is responsible for the exposition and, at Wallace's request, this is reflected in the attribution. There is no portion of the book, however, that did not benefit from Wallace's detailed ideas and recommendations.

At Harvard University Press, Michael Aronson has been extremely supportive. We are grateful for the improvements in consistency and style that have come from Jodi Simpson's careful editing. Patricia Pitzele and Mustafa Koluman read and critiqued the entire manuscript. Barbara Belisle provided invaluable administrative support.

PART ONE

REAL ECONOMIES

Most questions in what has traditionally been called macroeconomics involve consideration of events at more than one date. For example, a decision to save is a decision to sacrifice current consumption for (at least the hope of) future consumption. There are two traditions in economics for dealing with intertemporal questions. One tradition attempts to study, simultaneously and explicitly, the entire time interval or time horizon that is relevant for the question at hand. This view was brought into prominence by Irving Fisher at the turn of the century (see, in particular, his *Theory of Interest*). The other tradition attempts to deal with such questions by focusing only on the present. It attempts to embed the future—or more precisely, present views of the future—by having them be one of the givens in the analysis. This tradition received its main impetus from John Maynard Keynes's *General Theory of Employment, Interest, and Money.*

We try to take Fisher's view of the world seriously, not only in terms of how we deal with time, but also by building our models entirely from microeconomic, general equilibrium fundamentals. We are explicit about the tastes or preferences of individuals, of the resources available to them, and of the technologies they can use. One advantage of this approach is that we can use the tools of standard welfare analysis for evaluating different policies. Models that use this type of analysis can quickly become very complicated, so we are forced to make certain simplifications.

One major decision we make is how long people in our models will live. Suppose we are interested in studying an economy from now to some date T units of time into the future. One way to model individuals is to assume that they all live for the entire time period. Another is to assume that some of them die and some new individuals are born during the period. We choose the second approach for several reasons. First, it is more interesting in the sense that it allows more kinds of outcomes. Second, it forces people to think about the future because they may be engaging in transactions with individuals who are not yet alive. Third, it allows us to deal with very long lived economies, ones that outlive any individual. The kind of model we use is called overlapping generations—new generations of people appear before all of the people from the earlier period die off.

We make other simplifying assumptions. Time is discrete; we label time periods by the integers. Each generation lives only two periods, so at each date there are some young and some old. In the next period the young have become old, the old have passed on, and a new generation of young have arrived. There is just one consumption good each period, and we will only consider very simple technologies for transferring this good from one period to another. All of the equilibria we examine are competitive, and individuals, except in the earliest chapters, have perfect foresight.

For the first nine chapters of this book, we deal exclusively with real economies; economies in which there is no money and all exchanges are barter exchanges, even exchanges that involve what we normally think of as assets. The kinds of exchanges we concentrate on are intertemporal exchanges. Individuals have claims to goods in a consumption pattern over time that is not necessarily their preferred consumption pattern, and we consider alternative objects that they might use to help them move closer to their preferred consumption pattern. We study how tastes, technologies, and time paths of income interact to determine interest rates, asset prices, and either growth or the price level.

We study a number of possible government policies: tax-transfer schemes that resemble social security programs, government borrowing and the effects of different maturity government debt, and different kinds of taxes (consumption versus income taxes). The economies we study will be able to exhibit fluctuations, from either real or endogenous sources. For most of Part One, we limit ourselves to endowment economies, where we do not allow storage or production, but eventually we relax these restrictions and get simple versions of neoclassical growth models.

The theory we present in Part One is not especially controversial. It comes from standard neoclassical economics. In Part Two we add a particular asset we call money. The use of overlapping generation models to model money is more controversial, so we have excluded that discussion from our examination of real economies in Part One and have placed it in Part Two.

CHAPTER **1**

Describing the Environment

There are at least two steps in constructing an economic model. First, one describes the environment in which the economic agents exist; and, second, one describes the kinds of social organizations that can be imposed on that environment and the equilibria that these organizations generate. Any given economic environment can permit a number of different social organizations for producing goods and allocating the goods that it produces.

For a group of individuals on some isolated island, the physical structure of the economic environment is simple to describe: it is the island, the quality of its land and the plants and animals that currently exist on it, the coral reef and the stock of fish that live there, the individuals themselves, their skills and ages, and the passage of time. There are many ways this tribe of individuals could organize an economy in their environment. They could choose one member to dictate work assignments and to allocate the produced goods. They could decide collectively how to assign work and goods. They could allow individuals to work independently and make trades with one another. Whatever organization they form, it must make work assignments and goods allocations and it must be able to do this beyond the life of any one member of the tribe.

In this chapter, we describe the economic environment that we will be using throughout the book. This environment is explicitly dynamic, so we begin with a description of time, how much of it we have, and how we keep track of it. We describe the lifetimes of the individuals who inhabit our economy. The seven ages of man get reduced to two:

youth and old age. Individuals have preferences for consumption over both of these periods of their lives. We define consumption allocations for this economy and Pareto conditions for comparing these consumption allocations.

In most of our models there is no production. The actions of interest are the exchanges, mainly intertemporal exchanges, that individuals choose to make with one another. Therefore, we endow individuals with quantities of goods and observe the exchanges they choose to make. We can safely study these *pure exchange models* because most of the results will carry over to economic environments with production.

Time

In a description of a dynamic economy one needs to be very specific about time. There are two possible ways of modeling time: time can be continuous, or it can be discrete. For the physicist this dichotomy is a serious problem, and there are physical theories of the world in which time is continuous and theories in which it is discrete (although the increments are very small).[1] We have chosen to make time discrete and index time periods by integers. We may be giving up some generality by doing so (and we may be losing some important characteristics of the real world), but we gain in expositional and mathematical simplicity.

All actions, decisions, and events occur at points of time, called periods or dates, which we denote by an index, t. The index can have values from minus infinity ($-\infty$, the infinite past) to plus infinity ($+\infty$, the infinite future). We use the convention of calling the current date (or equivalently, the initial period of the model) period $t = 1$, and we are interested in how the economy evolves into the infinite future. The *history* of the economy, that is, events corresponding to the t's from $-\infty$ to 0 (which is the most recent period already completed), is given and determines the initial conditions of our economy.

The fact that we are allowing time to go into the infinite future is important for some of the equilibria of our models. Even if no one believes that time will go infinitely into the future (the physicists say the universe will end, at least operationally, in finite time), the fact that this

1. John Barth in *Giles Goat Boy* pokes fun at this issue with a character who is trying to define ever more precisely when tick becomes tock.

date is far into the future and is unknown may be sufficient to allow infinity to be a good approximation of that future, unknown end point.

Starting at time 1 and taking history as given, we will be asking the following type of questions: How would this economy evolve under different types of policy rules? The question is carefully phrased. Note that it speaks of policy *rules*. We are interested in more than what the possible government policies will be in time $t = 1$. In fact, in some of our economies, we are not able to say what happens at time 1 without specifying what the policies will be in later periods. The notion of a *policy rule* that determines the policies at each period from now into the future is crucial to our discussions of policy.

The Population

At each time period t, a new generation appears (is born, if you wish). This generation, called generation t, is denoted by its date of birth.[2] There are $N(t)$ members of generation t. These individuals live for two periods. The members of generation t are alive in period t (when they are called the young) and in period $t + 1$ (when they are called the old). No member of generation t makes it into period $t + 2$; at the end of period $t + 1$ they all die.[3]

This construction of the evolution of the population is called overlapping generations, because there are two generations alive in any one period, the period in which they overlap. Figure 1.1 shows the life spans of several generations. This figure also makes it clear how the generations overlap. In time 0, for example, only the old who were born in period $t = -1$ and the young who were born in period 0 are alive. As time progresses to period 1, the old from generation -1 die and the young from generation 0 become old. A new generation (generation 1) is born and is young. This pattern repeats. Each generation overlaps

2. This practice is different from that used in universities, which denote each generation by the date of their "death" as students (or, as it is more commonly called, their graduation).

3. Kenneth Arrow has pointed out that one of the great economic problems individuals face is that they do not know the exact date of their death. This lack of knowledge prevents them from consuming the last bit of their income just before they die (suppose they consume the last bit of their income, thinking they will die during the upcoming night, but wake up the next morning alive and impoverished). We ignore that problem here.

generation	Time period					
	0	1	2	3	4	5
-1	old					
0	young	old				
1		young	old			
2			young	old		
3				young	old	
4					young	old

Figure 1.1

for one period with the previous generation and then overlaps for one period with the next generation. It overlaps with no other generations.

Figure 1.1 also allows us to find the number of individuals who are alive in any period. In period 2, $N(1)$ old are around and so are $N(2)$ young. [$N(t)$ is the population of generation t.] In any time period t, there are $N(t - 1)$ old and $N(t)$ young. The total live population at period t is $N(t - 1) + N(t)$. Population size can change, so $N(t)$ need not equal $N(t + j)$ for any $j \neq 0$. Both population size and length of life are exogenous and are not affected by any actions of any individuals. (The mystery of life shall remain a mystery here.) We are interested in studying economies in which the population grows, some in which it shrinks, and others in which it remains constant.

Total Resources

There is only one good in each period. This good is something that the members of the economy consume. It is the same good at different dates (although that is not crucial); but the date at which the good exists is important, so we denote the good by its date. The good that is around in time period 7 is called *time 7 good*. (You can think of this as time t bread, time $t + 1$ bread, time $t + 2$ bread, and so on.) In an important sense there are an infinite number of goods: one for each of the infinite number of time periods. Except in Chapters 8 and 9, no technology is available for directly converting goods at one date into goods at another date. For example, there is no storage technology that will allow each unit time t good to be transformed into some amount of time $t + 1$ good.

Let $Y(t)$ denote the economy's total endowment of the time t good. We are not going to worry about where this good comes from (for example, you can have an Israelites in the Sinai model of production and have manna fall from the sky). We are concerned, however, about who has claims to it and about how it gets used. The sequence $\{Y(t)\}$ for $t = 1$ to $+\infty$ describes the endowments of the economy in all current and future time periods.

When there is no technology for directly converting goods at one date into goods at another date, $Y(t)$ is also the amount of time t good that is available to the economy. In particular, either people alive at time t consume $Y(t)$ or it is wasted. For example, time 2 good is only available to those alive in the time 2 column in Figure 1.1 and can be consumed only by the individuals from generations 1 and 2.

Feasible Consumption Allocations

A *consumption allocation* describes who consumes what. Let $c_t^h(s)$ stand for the consumption of the time s good by individual h of generation t. The index h ranges over integers from 1 to $N(t)$. If there are 100 people in generation t, then it ranges from 1 to 100. Given that consumption only during one's lifetime is of interest, we assume that $c_t^h(s)$ can be different from 0 only for $s = t$ and $s = t + 1$. The expression $c_t^h(t)$ is the consumption of individual h of generation t when young, and $c_t^h(t + 1)$ is the consumption of the same individual when old. We use the notation c_t^h to represent the ordered pair of consumptions for individual h of generation t, so

$$c_t^h = [c_t^h(t), c_t^h(t + 1)].$$

A *time t consumption allocation* is given by the set of consumptions of the young at time t,

$$\{c_t^h(t)\}_{h=1}^{N(t)}$$

for all $h = 1$ to $N(t)$ members of generation t, and of the old at time t,

$$\{c^h_{t-1}(t)\}^{N(t-1)}_{h=1}$$

for all $h = 1$ to $N(t-1)$ members of generation $t-1$. A *consumption allocation* is the sequence of time t consumption allocations for all $t = 1$ to $+\infty$. It describes who consumes what for all time. A consumption allocation assigns c^h_t's for all individuals born in all time periods.

A *feasible consumption allocation* (or more simply, a feasible allocation) is a consumption allocation that can be achieved with the given total resources and the technology. The *total consumption at time t* implied by a consumption allocation is denoted $C(t)$ and is given by

$$C(t) = \sum_{h=1}^{N(t)} c^h_t(t) + \sum_{h=1}^{N(t-1)} c^h_{t-1}(t),$$

where we sum over the consumptions of all the young at time t and the consumptions of all the old at time t. Now we can state the following definition for economies without storage or production.

Definition   A consumption allocation is feasible *if the consumption path satisfies $C(t) \le Y(t)$ for all $t \ge 1$.*

The definition formalizes the idea that a given consumption allocation (independent of the mechanism by which it was chosen) can be achieved (and is therefore feasible) if the total consumption for every period is less than or equal to the total resources available in that period. Simply put, do we always have enough of the good around to allow people to have the particular consumption pattern we are studying?

The following four exercises should help familiarize you with some of the basic notions of our model. In all of them you are to show that a particular consumption allocation is feasible. These exercises also provide practice in the use of our notation. Try these exercises before going on. We work through Exercise 1.1 later, but try it first.

EXERCISE 1.1   Let $N(t) = N > 0$ and let $Y(t) = yN > 0$ for all t. Prove that if $0 < \alpha < 1$, then

$$c_t^h(t) = \alpha y, \qquad c_{t-1}^h(t) = (1 - \alpha)y$$

for all h and $t \geq 1$ is feasible.

EXERCISE 1.2 Let $N(t + 1)/N(t) = n$ and let $Y(t) = yN(t)$ for all t. Prove that if $0 < \alpha < 1$, then

$$c_t^h(t) = \alpha y, \qquad c_{t-1}^h(t) = n(1 - \alpha)y$$

for all h and $t \geq 1$ is feasible.

EXERCISE 1.3 Let $N(t - 1) = 2$ and $Y(t) = 2$ for all $t \geq 1$. Prove that the following allocation is feasible:

$$c_0^h(1) = \tfrac{1}{2} \quad \text{for} \quad h = 1, 2;$$

$$c_1^1(1) = \tfrac{1}{4}, \qquad c_1^1(2) = \tfrac{3}{4};$$

$$c_1^2(1) = \tfrac{3}{4}, \qquad c_1^2(2) = \tfrac{1}{4};$$

$$c_t^h(t) = c_t^h(t + 1) = \tfrac{1}{2} \quad \text{for } h = 1, 2 \text{ and all } t \geq 2.$$

EXERCISE 1.4 Let $N(t - 1) = 1$ and $Y(t) = 1$ for all $t \geq 1$. Show that the following allocation is feasible:

$$c_{t-1}(t) = (\tfrac{1}{2}) - (\tfrac{1}{2})^{t+1},$$

$$c_t(t) = (\tfrac{1}{2}) + (\tfrac{1}{2})^{t+1}, \quad \text{all } t \geq 1.$$

Exercise 1.1 considers an economy where the population is constant for all generations [$N(t) = N$, so $2N$ people are alive each period]. The total amount of the one good that is available each period is $Y(t) = yN$, where y is some quantity of the good per member of one of the generations (notice that Exercise 1.1 says nothing about who "owns" what). The consumption allocation we are examining is one in which each young person consumes some fraction, denoted α, of y. In each period, each old person consumes some fraction, denoted $1 - \alpha$, of y. You might think of these allocations as being determined by a social planner (a nice term for a dictator). There are N young each period and N old; so in each period the total consumption of the young is $\alpha y N$, and in each period the total consumption of the old is $(1 - \alpha)y N$. Summing the total consumption of the young and the total consumption of the old in each period, we find that

$$C(t) = \alpha y N + (1 - \alpha)y N = y N.$$

Total consumption each period is yN, which is equal to the quantity of the good that is available each period. Therefore, this consumption allocation is feasible.

Efficient Consumption Allocations

Definition *A feasible consumption allocation is* efficient *if there is no alternative feasible allocation with more total consumption of some good and no less of any other good.*

Remember that in this model the good is a time t good; and when we say that there is "no allocation with more total consumption of some good," we mean there is no allocation in which more of the one good can be consumed in one period and no less consumed in any other period. We need to check all (infinitely many) periods to show that an allocation is efficient.

In the following exercise, you are to show that an efficient allocation is one in which nothing is left over; that is, everything is consumed.

EXERCISE 1.5 Prove the following. A feasible consumption allocation is efficient if and only if it satisfies $C(t) = Y(t)$ for all $t \geq 1$.

In some endowment economies, it is not too hard to illustrate the set of efficient, symmetric, consumption allocations. *Symmetric consumption allocations* are those in which all members of all generations consume the same consumption pair. That is, they all consume the same amount of goods when young and the same amount when old, although consumption when young need not be the same as consumption when old. For a symmetric consumption allocation,

$$c_t^h(t) = c_s^j(s),$$

and $\quad c_t^h(t + 1) = c_s^j(s + 1),$

for any h and j belonging to generation t or generation s, $t,s \geq 1$. The second equation holds for members of generation 0. Note that for a symmetric allocation we require that members of generation t consume the same as members of generation $t + 1$, for example. We also require that all members of a generation have the same consumption pattern.

We consider two cases: In the first, the population is constant (the growth rate $n = 1$) and the total endowment of the economy, $Y(t)$, is constant. The second case is an economy where the population and total endowment are growing at a gross growth rate $n > 1$. The growth rate is defined as $N(t) = nN(t - 1)$. Total endowment follows a path such that $Y(t + 1) = nY(t)$.

In an efficient allocation, total consumption equals total endowment, so

$$C_t(t) + C_{t-1}(t) = Y(t),$$

where $C_t(t)$ is the total consumption of the young at time t and $C_{t-1}(t)$ is the total consumption of the old at time t. Because all members of a generation consume the same amount in a symmetric allocation, we can write the efficient allocation condition as

$$N(t)c_t^h(t) + N(t - 1)c_{t-1}^h(t) = Y(t).$$

If the populations of the two generations are the same, that is, $N(t) = N(t - 1)$, and the allocation is symmetric, that is, $c_{t-1}^h(t) = c_t^h(t + 1)$, then

$$c_t^h(t) + c_t^h(t + 1) = \frac{Y(t)}{N(t)}.$$

Figure 1.2 shows the consumption baskets, the set of c_t^h's, corresponding to the set of efficient, symmetric allocations for this constant-population, constant-endowment economy. The axes are consumption when young, $c_t^h(t)$, and consumption when old, $c_t^h(t + 1)$. The 45-degree line is this set of consumption baskets. The points where the 45-degree line touches the axes are points where the allocation gives all the goods to the young (the point on the horizontal axis) or all the goods to the old (the point on the vertical axis).

In Figure 1.3 we consider the economy of Exercise 1.2 for some $n > 1$. A possible symmetric allocation is one in which the old at each time t consume equally among themselves all of the goods available in each period t. If they do so, each old person consumes

$$c_t^h(t + 1) = \frac{Y(t + 1)}{N(t)} = \frac{nY(t)}{N(t)}.$$

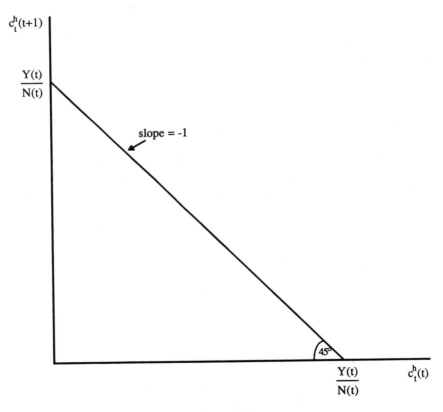

Figure 1.2

Another symmetric allocation is one in which the young consume everything. In that case, the consumption of each young person is

$$c_t^h(t) = \frac{Y(t)}{N(t)}.$$

The set of consumption baskets corresponding to feasible symmetric consumption allocations is the solid line in Figure 1.3.

The concept of efficiency gets more interesting in economies in which there is either production or storage. If goods that are not consumed today are inputs into the production process (help make more goods in the next period), then efficiency does not require that all the time t good

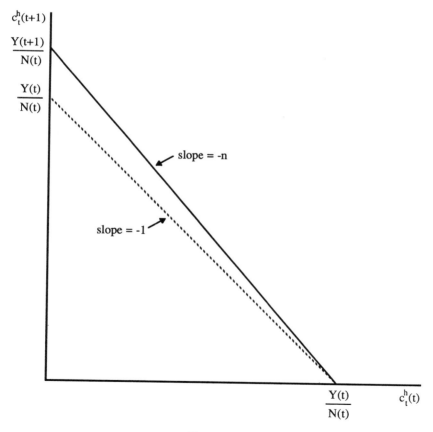

Figure 1.3

be consumed in time t. Efficiency allows a portion of the time t good to remain unconsumed at the end of period t if the remaining good is used in period $t + 1$ to produce some time $t + 1$ good and then is consumed as additional time $t + 1$ good. With production, one must examine the entire (infinite) sequence of consumption and outputs simultaneously to determine efficiency. A sequence where, for some t, $C(t) < Y(t)$ can still be efficient if there is either production or storage.

Preferences

We assume that we can express the preferences of each individual by a utility function. These utility functions can be illustrated by indifference curve sets that have "nice" properties; that is, they have the standard concave shape, and utility is higher on indifference curves to the "northeast."

Except in Chapter 4, the *preferences* of an individual are described by a utility function that depends only on the consumption of that individual when young and when old. When an individual is young and is planning lifetime consumption, both the consumption during that period (when young) and the future consumption (the consumption in the next period, when old) are taken into account. The *utility function* for individual h of generation t is written

$$u_t^h(c_t^h(t), c_t^h(t + 1)),$$

or sometimes simply $u_t^h(\cdot, \cdot)$, or even u_t^h. Let

$$[c_t^{h1}(t), c_t^{h1}(t + 1)]$$

be one consumption basket, which is made up of a particular amount of consumption when young and a particular amount when old. Let

$$[c_t^{h2}(t), c_t^{h2}(t + 1)]$$

be another, different consumption basket. If

$$u(c_t^{h1}(t), c_t^{h1}(t + 1)) \geq u(c_t^{h2}(t), c_t^{h2}(t + 1)),$$

then we say that basket 1 is *preferred* to basket 2. If

$$u(c_t^{h1}(t), c_t^{h1}(t + 1)) > u(c_t^{h2}(t), c_t^{h2}(t + 1)),$$

then we say that basket 1 is *strictly preferred* to basket 2. If

$$u(c_t^{h1}(t), c_t^{h1}(t + 1)) = u(c_t^{h2}(t), c_t^{h2}(t + 1)),$$

then we say that the individual is *indifferent* between these two baskets.

If the utility function is of a standard form, the consumption baskets for which the individual is indifferent will be connected and can be illustrated as *indifference curves*. Figure 1.4 shows sample indifference curves. Note that the axes of the commodity set are consumption when young, $c_t^h(t)$, and consumption when old, $c_t^h(t + 1)$. In that figure, the individual is indifferent between the points labeled c^1 and c^2, and the point labeled c^3 is preferred to either of the other two.

To get our "nice" indifference curves, we assume that the function $u_t^h(\cdot, \cdot)$ is strictly increasing in each of its arguments, is differentiable,

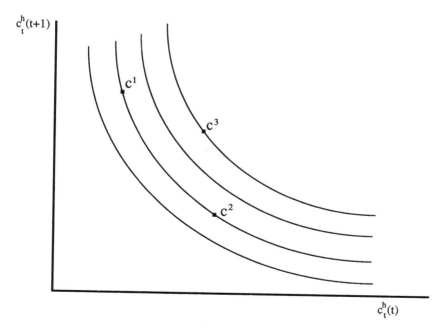

Figure 1.4

and is convex. The first assumption says that if an individual has the choice of consuming a fixed amount of the good in one period of life and of having more or less in the other period (young or old), then the choice of more consumption is preferred to the one of less. On the indifference curve graph, that assumption means that a movement either horizontally to the right or vertically upward puts one on an indifference curve with higher utility. Therefore, the first assumption means that points to the northeast are strictly preferred to points to the southwest.

Convexity is a little more complicated. Suppose that we choose any two of the many imaginable consumption baskets for individual h of generation t. We can denote these as

$$c_t^{h1} = [c_t^{h1}(t), c_t^{h1}(t+1)]$$

and $\quad c_t^{h2} = [c_t^{h2}(t), c_t^{h2}(t+1)],$

and we can choose them so that the utility level of the first is at least as high as that of the second. This choice is written

$$u^h(c_t^{h1}(t), c_t^{h1}(t+1)) \geq u^h(c_t^{h2}(t), c_t^{h2}(t+1)).$$

We want to describe, mathematically, all of the consumption baskets on a straight line between the consumption points c_t^{h1} and c_t^{h2}. If we let α go from 0 to 1 in the equation

$$c = \alpha c^{h1} + (1-\alpha)c^{h2}$$
$$= [\alpha c_t^{h1}(t) + (1-\alpha)c_t^{h2}(t), \alpha c_t^{h1}(t+1) + (1-\alpha)c_t^{h2}(t+1)],$$

then the path of c describes exactly the line we want. When α is 1, c is the first consumption basket; and when α is 0, it is the second consumption basket. As α goes from 1 to 0, c moves on a straight line between the two baskets. Convexity for the utility function means that all of the consumption baskets on the line we described (except possibly the other end point) have utility levels higher than c^{h2}. Written out formally, that statement is

$$u^h(c_t^{h2}) < u^h(\alpha c_t^{h1} + (1-\alpha)c_t^{h2}),$$

for α strictly between 0 and 1. Figure 1.5 shows two such straight lines on an indifference curve graph. Look at the line from the points marked c^1 to c^3. In this case c^3 is strictly preferred to c^1. All of the points on that line are above the indifference curve for c^1. Consumption baskets marked c^1 and c^2 are on the same indifference curve. However, all of the points on a line between them are on higher indifference curves. Figure 1.5 shows graphically what is meant by convexity of the utility function. Notice that the points on the line connecting points c^1 and c^2 would not be on higher indifference curves if the indifference curves had the shapes shown in Figure 1.6.

Once youth is passed, consumption when young does not matter. Once old, it is only the consumption when old that matters. The consumption of youth is history, cannot be changed, and is a constant. Because the utility functions are strictly increasing in either argument, an old person, when old, only cares about having as much consumption as possible in that time period. The old know that death awaits them and that nothing can be carried over to the next period. In particular, the old of generation 0 (those who are old in period 1, when we are

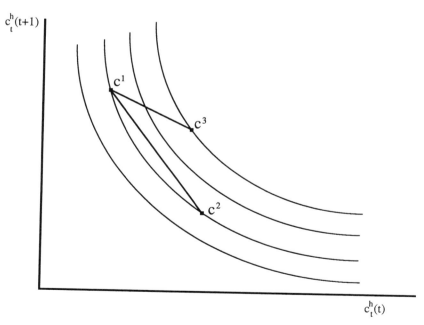

Figure 1.5

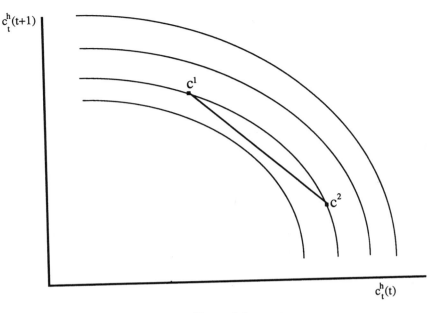

Figure 1.6

beginning our policies) are interested only in what they can get in period 1. The young of time 1 are interested in their consumption in that period and the next, for they will live to consume in period 2. An old person h at time 1 wants to maximize $c_0^h(1)$, and an old person h at any time t wishes to maximize $c_{t-1}^h(t)$. The only interesting planning problem is that of the young; the old just want to grab all they can get (in this model).

Pareto Optimality

To compare the consumption allocations that result from different assumptions about the economy, we use some standard notions from welfare economics. The first of these is Pareto superiority.

Definition *Consumption allocation* A *is Pareto superior to consumption allocation* B *if*
  (*i*) *no one strictly prefers* B *to* A, *and*
  (*ii*) *at least one person strictly prefers* A *to* B.

So, for one consumption allocation to be Pareto superior to another allocation, it must make at least one person better off and not make anyone worse off. What happens if someone is better off in one allocation and worse off in another? We will not allow ourselves to choose whom we will let be better off and whom worse. If a pair of allocations are like that (and such a case arises when allocation A is *not* Pareto superior to B *and* B is *not* Pareto superior to A), then we say that they are *noncomparable*. When we make the determination of Pareto superiority, we need to consider the utility level of all members of all generations (even into the infinite future); and, in particular, we want to include the old at time 1.

Consider this example economy. There is one person in each generation. Total endowment is 8 units of the time t good in each period, t. All individuals have the same utility function,

$$u_t^h = c_t^h(t)c_t^h(t + 1);$$

so utility is equal to the product of the consumption when young and consumption when old. Notice that this function generates indifference curves that are rectangular hyperbolas. Notice also that if consumption in either period of life is 0, then so is utility. Any small amount of consumption in both periods of life is better (for a person with this utility function) than no consumption in one period and any finitely large consumption in the other period.

First, consider the consumption allocation where each person (for generations ≥ 1) consumes the ordered pair,

$$c_t^h = [c_t^h(t), c_t^h(t + 1)] = [8, 0].$$

According to this consumption allocation, the one member of each generation consumes 8 units of the good when young and nothing when old. Suppose that each member of generation 0 (old when we start our model) consumes nothing. The utility for each member of each generation ≥ 1 is 8×0, which equals 0. For the old in period 1, all we can say is that their consumption is 0.

Consider a different consumption allocation. The total endowment in each period is still 8 units of the time t good; but now the consumption allocation states that for all members of all generations t, $t \geq 1$, the consumption ordered pair is $\hat{c}_t^h = [4, 4]$, and the consumption for the old of period 1 is 4. If the population is unchanged (suppose that there is only one person in each generation), then the same amount of the good is consumed (in total) each period. For each member of each generation ≥ 1, the utility is $4 \times 4 = 16$, so each of them is made better off by this new consumption allocation. The old of period 1 are now consuming 4 units of the good (rather than 0); and because more is better than less for them, they are also better off in the new consumption allocation. The [4, 4] allocation is Pareto superior to the [8, 0] allocation, because no one has a lower utility level with the [4, 4] allocation and at least one person has a higher utility level (in fact, everyone has a higher utility level). For a second example, a [3, 5] allocation is Pareto superior to the [8, 0] allocation but is noncomparable to a [4, 4] allocation. All members of all generations ≥ 1 are worse off (their utility level is 15 rather than 16), but the old at period 1 now have 5 units of the good rather than 4 units of the good and are better off. Because one person is better off while an infinite number are worse off, we must say that the two allocations are noncomparable.

EXERCISE 1.6 Let the utility function for all members of all generations (except the current old) be

$$u(c_t^h(t), c_t^h(t + 1)) = [c_t^h(t)]^{1/2} + [c_t^h(t + 1)]^{1/2}$$

and consider the set of Exercise 1.1 allocations. Specify two allocations, one of which is Pareto superior to the other. Specify two that are noncomparable to each other.

Now we can define the welfare criterion that we will use. This criterion is our definition of optimality.

Definition   *A consumption allocation is* Pareto optimal *if it is feasible and if there does not exist a feasible consumption allocation that is Pareto superior to it.*

In the example we gave above, among the consumption allocations that allot 8 units of the good each period and where there is only one member of each generation, the consumption [3, 5] is Pareto optimal. It is not the only Pareto optimal allocation: [4, 4] is one and so is [2, 6].

The consumption allocation [6, 2] is not a Pareto optimal allocation for this economy because, for example, another allocation, say, [2, 6], gives members of generations ≥ 1 the same utility level (2 × 6 equals 6 × 2), but the old of period 1 consume 6, which is more than 2.

EXERCISE 1.7 Prove the following. If an allocation is Pareto optimal, then it is efficient.

EXERCISE 1.8 Consider the resources, technology, and allocations of Exercise 1.1 and the utility function of Exercise 1.6. Prove that the allocation determined by $\alpha = \frac{3}{4}$ is *not* Pareto optimal.

EXERCISE 1.9 Consider the setup and allocations of Exercise 1.2 and the utility function of Exercise 1.6. Show that if $n = 4$, then the allocation determined by $\alpha = \frac{1}{2}$ is not Pareto optimal.

EXERCISE 1.10 Consider the setup and allocation of Exercise 1.3. Show that this allocation is not Pareto optimal if preferences are expressed by the utility function in Exercise 1.6.

EXERCISE 1.11 This problem is a generalization of the last exercise. Suppose that $u_t^h(c_t^h(t), c_t^h(t + 1))$ is the utility function of person h in generation t, $t \geq 1$. Let the marginal rate of substitution (MRS) for this person be defined by

$$\frac{u_{t1}^h(c_t^h(t), c_t^h(t + 1))}{u_{t2}^h(c_t^h(t), c_t^h(t + 1))},$$

where $u_{tj}^h(c_t^h(t), c_t^h(t + 1))$ is the partial derivative of the utility function with respect to its jth argument. Suppose h and h' are two members of generation t, for some $t \geq 1$. Prove the following. A feasible allocation that assigns positive first- and second-period consumptions to h and h' and implies different values for the MRS of h and h' is not Pareto optimal.

Exercise 1.7 shows us that efficiency is a necessary condition for Pareto optimality. We can illustrate why this must be so. If the allocation is not efficient, then there is some unallocated good in some period—because $Y(t)$ for some period is greater than $C(t)$ and the difference, $Y(t) - C(t)$, can be given to someone—and that someone can have increased utility by consuming that additional quantity of the good. Exercise 1.11 gives us a second necessary condition for Pareto optimality: the marginal rates of substitution must be the same for all members of each generation. We call this the *equality of MRS* condition. We can use an Edgeworth box to show why this condition must hold.

Before we use the Edgeworth box, we must discuss the concept of a marginal rate of substitution. It is defined in Exercise 1.11 as

$$\text{MRS} = \frac{\dfrac{\partial u_t^h}{\partial c_t^h(t)}}{\dfrac{\partial u_t^h}{\partial c_t^h(t + 1)}},$$

so the marginal rate of substitution is the partial derivative of the utility function with respect to its first argument (consumption when young) divided by the partial derivative of the utility function with respect to its second argument (consumption when old). We want to interpret this definition.

Consider an indifference curve. It is the collection of consumption allocations that provide an individual with the same level of utility and can be written as

$$\overline{u} = u_t^h(c_t^h(t), c_t^h(t + 1)),$$

where $c_t^h(t)$ and $c_t^h(t + 1)$ are consumption when young and when old, respectively, and $\overline{u}$ is the constant utility level of the indifference curve we are discussing. With normal conditions on the utility function, this function can be inverted and written as

$$c_t^h(t + 1) = f(\overline{u}, c_t^h(t)).$$

From that function, it follows that the slope of an indifference curve at each point is $\partial f / \partial c_t^h(t)$. We now want to show that the slope of the indifference curve at any point is the marginal rate of substitution at that point. Take the total derivative (using the chain rule) of the utility function at some fixed utility level with $c_t^h(t + 1)$ replaced by $f(\overline{u}, c_t^h(t))$. The total derivative of that utility function is

$$0 = \left[\frac{\partial u_t^h}{\partial c_t^h(t)}\right] dc_t^h(t) + \left[\frac{\partial u_t^h}{\partial c_t^h(t + 1)}\right]\left[\frac{\partial f}{\partial c_t^h(t)}\right] dc_t^h(t),$$

which can be rearranged to give

$$\left[\frac{\partial f}{\partial c_t^h(t)}\right] = -\frac{\dfrac{\partial u_t^h}{\partial c_t^h(t)}}{\dfrac{\partial u_t^h}{\partial c_t^h(t + 1)}},$$

so the slope of the indifference curve at any consumption point is the negative of the marginal rate of substitution at that point. In Figure 1.7 the slope of the indifference curve at point A equals minus the marginal rate of substitution at that point.

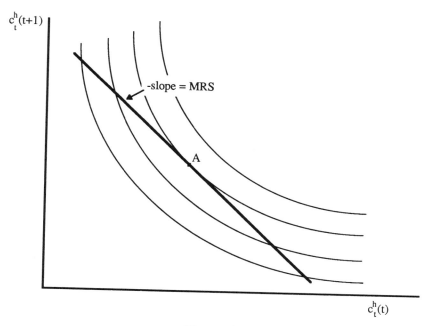

Figure 1.7

We now do Exercise 1.11. Let the given allocation be called allocation A. We construct a feasible Pareto superior allocation that we call allocation B. Let B be the same consumption pattern as A for everyone except individuals h and h' at date t. Figure 1.8 is an Edgeworth box with the origin for the indifference curve set for individual h of generation t (solid lines) in the lower left-hand corner and the origin for the indifference curve set for individual h' of generation t (dotted lines) in the upper right-hand corner (with utility for h' increasing in the southwestern direction). The width of the box is the total time t good to be allocated between h and h', and the height of the box is the total time $t + 1$ good to be allocated between these same two individuals by allocation A. Allocation A in the Edgeworth box is an allocation where the marginal rates of substitution for the two individuals are not the same. If the marginal rates of substitution were the same, the indifference curves would be tangent (for the slope of the indifference curve gives the marginal rate of substitution at that point). Look at the two indifference curves that pass through allocation A. If we move along the indifference curve u_3^h of person h to a point where it is tangent to an indiffer-

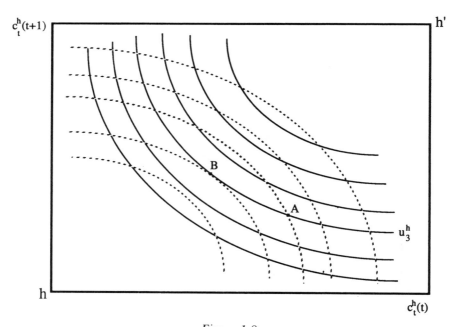

Figure 1.8

ence curve of person h', we get another allocation, B, that gives person h the same utility as allocation A and gives person h' a greater utility. Allocation B is Pareto superior to allocation A. The existence of the feasible allocation B means that allocation A cannot be Pareto optimal.

An allocation that is both efficient and satisfies the equality of MRS condition is not necessarily Pareto optimal. Try proving Exercise 1.12 before reading on.

EXERCISE 1.12 Prove that efficiency and equality of MRS are not sufficient conditions for Pareto optimality.

Exercise 1.12 can be proved by example. Here is a hint. Suppose that all of the members of generation t have exactly the same utility functions and the same consumption allocations. Then their marginal rates of substitution must be the same. Based on what you saw earlier about Pareto optimal allocations, find two efficient allocations for which everyone is better off in one than in the other. If you find such a pair, then the consumption allocation that has the lower utility is your example for the above exercise.

It is not easy to derive sufficient conditions for a Pareto optimal allocation. The physical environment, with the overlapping generations, is the source of those difficulties. It is possible, however, to suggest some additional properties of Pareto optimal allocations.

EXERCISE 1.13 Consider the setup of Exercise 1.1 and the preferences of Exercise 1.6. Prove that no allocation in the class described in Exercise 1.1 is Pareto superior to the allocation given by $\alpha = \frac{1}{4}$.

EXERCISE 1.14 Within the same setup as given above, describe all α's for which there does not exist a Pareto superior allocation among the class of allocations described in Exercise 1.1.

EXERCISE 1.15 Now consider the setup of Exercise 1.2 and the preferences of Exercise 1.6. Describe all α's for which there does not exist a Pareto superior allocation among the class of allocations described in that exercise.

From these exercises, we conclude that there is another necessary condition for Pareto optimality, namely, that the marginal rates of substitution be sufficiently high. This result comes from the double infinities of this model (infinity of periods and infinity of goods), and there is no direct analogue of it in finite models. We consider a model with a finite end point to illustrate this point.

Consider an economy like the one described in Exercise 1.13, where we are using the setup of Exercise 1.1 with the preferences of Exercise 1.6. First consider the Exercise 1.1 allocation where α is equal to $3/4$. We can show that this allocation is not Pareto optimal. If, in every time period $t \geq 1$, we take a little bit of the good from each young person and give that to an old person, we can make everyone better off. The lifetime utility for each young person under the $\alpha = 3/4$ allocation is

$$u_t^h = (3/4y)^{1/2} + (1/4y)^{1/2}; \tag{1.1}$$

and if we take as an example, $y = 16$, the utility for each young person is approximately 5.464. The consumption for the old at time 1 is 4 units of the good. Suppose that we take 0.1 unit of the good from each young person and give it to each old person. (We can do this in the economy we are studying because there are equal numbers of young and old each period.) The lifetime utility for each young person of generation $t \geq 1$ is

$$u_t^h = (3/4y - 0.1)^{1/2} + (1/4y + 0.1)^{1/2};$$

and using the same example as above, the utility for each young person is equal to 5.474, which is larger than the 5.464 for the allocation without the 0.1 unit transfer. Note also that the old at time 1 are now consuming 4.1 units of the good, thereby giving them higher utility than before the transfer (4 units). Everyone's utility has improved, so the second allocation is Pareto superior to the first. Therefore, $\alpha = 3/4$ cannot be a Pareto optimal allocation.

An important aspect of this discussion (which we have not stressed) is that our assumption that time goes to ∞ means there is always another young generation from which we can take the good to give to the old. Suppose that we all know that the world will end at time period T. In particular, the young of period T will not grow old and get a transfer from the young of (the nonexistent) period $T + 1$. In that case, an allocation with $\alpha = 3/4$ is Pareto optimal. A transfer of 0.1 unit from the young to the old will not make everyone better off. The transfer will make the young of generation T worse off. The transfer of 0.1 unit of the good reduces their consumption when young to 11.9 (down from 12). Because there is no next period, there is no compensating transfer from the next generation, and the young of generation T lose utility by the transfer. Because this one generation is made worse off, the second allocation is not Pareto superior to the first. The two allocations are noncomparable.

Let us return to the infinite horizon case. Suppose that the indifference curves in Figure 1.9 are generated by the utility function given in Equation (1.1) (these curves are not exact but are very close). The allocation with $\alpha = 3/4$ is shown at point A. The straight 45-degree line gives the allocations for all $\alpha \in [0, 1]$. First look at point B. This allocation ($\alpha = 1/4$) is on the same indifference curve for all generations t for $t \geq 1$ and gives the members of generation 0 greater consumption when old

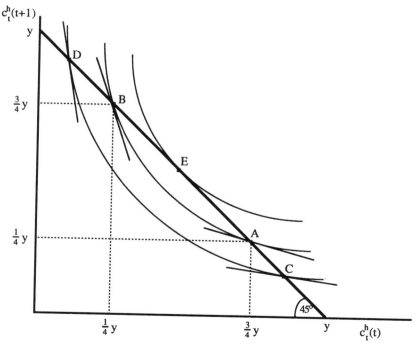

Figure 1.9

than does allocation A (α = ¾). Allocations C and D have the same relationship. Allocation D gives the same level of utility as allocation C for all generations t, $t \geq 1$, and increased consumption to the old of time 1 (generation 0). Consumption allocations D and B are noncomparable, because at D the old of period 1 are better off and everyone else is worse off than at B. A general pattern should be emerging. For α high enough, there exists a Pareto superior allocation. For low enough α, all other allocations are Pareto inferior or noncomparable.

Notice that for high α, the slope of the indifference curve is between 0 and -1. Because the marginal rate of substitution equals the negative slope of the indifference curve at points A and C, the MRS is less than 1. At the allocations with low α's, however, the marginal rates of substitution are greater than 1; and these are the allocations that are Pareto optimal. But why is a marginal rate of substitution of 1 so important?

Figure 1.9 can help us with that question. The y-to-y line gives all the efficient symmetric consumption allocations. The allocation that gives the highest utility to all generations t for $t \geq 1$ is the one just tangent to that y-to-y line. The tangency is at point E. At that point the marginal rate of substitution is equal to 1, which is the slope of the y-to-y line. For all allocations below that point, moving up the line toward E increases the utility of all future generations and also increases the consumption of the current old. This kind of movement is Pareto improving. Moving up the line beyond E increases the consumption of the current old but reduces the utility of all future generations. These allocations are mutually noncomparable. It is the tangency point of the efficient allocation curve with the indifference curve set that determines the beginning of the Pareto optimal allocations for this economy.

Reprise

We are working in an economy where time is discrete and where a generation of $N(t)$ individuals is born each period and lives through that period and the next. There is only one good at each date and, except in Chapters 8 and 9, there is no technology for transforming goods of one date into goods at another date. We call the good that is around in time t the time t good. Because there are no technologies for directly transferring consumption across time, feasible consumption allocations are limited to those where total consumption each period is less than or equal to the economy's total endowment for that period. Efficient allocations occur when the total consumption is exactly equal to that endowment.

Preferences are assumed to have properties that give us "nice" indifference curves. The utility of any individual born in period 1 or after is based on the consumption in both periods of life. For the old of period 1, only the consumption in that period matters, and more is preferred to less. Allocations are compared using the yardstick of Pareto superiority. A feasible allocation that has no feasible allocations Pareto superior to it is called Pareto optimal. Efficiency and equal marginal rates of substitution among members of the same generation are necessary conditions for Pareto optimality. For Pareto optimality, we also require that the marginal rate of substitution be high enough.

CHAPTER 2

Competitive Equilibrium

In Chapter 1 we developed a few basic notions about the structure of our economy. We have presented most of the information we need to describe an *environment*. A description of an economic environment must include information about the physical structure, preferences, endowment, and technology.

In the economies we are constructing in this book, the physical world is quite special. Ours is a world of discrete time periods filled with populations of agents who live only two periods (life is short if not exactly brutish) and whose lives overlap with those of two other generations. There is only one good and the individuals have preferences about their consumption of the good in both periods of their lives. The economy is endowed with some quantity of the good in each period and has no direct way of changing that good into a good of any other time period. That is, there is no technology for changing endowment at one date into goods at some other date (there is neither production nor storage).

This kind of description of the environment does not tell us much about what allocations will occur or how they are decided on. It states what the economy has, what people in it want, and what physical constraints it faces. Nothing has been said about the mechanisms for determining allocations.

There are many ways in which the economic environment described above could be organized. It might be organized like the Incan empire, where a dictator or a representative of the dictator determined exactly what each member of each generation contributed and received. No one except the Inca had rights to any goods and only the preferences of the Inca mattered in the distribution of those goods (although the preferences of the Inca most likely took into account the preferences of other members of the society). The discussion in Chapter 1 of Pareto optimal consumption allocations completely ignored the question of how any particular allocation might come about. In comparing allocations; we might have been the economists of the Inca who were recommending to him particular consumption allocations as being "better" for his subjects than others.

In this chapter we give each individual certain rights to control some portion of the goods that are available during that individual's lifetime. Individuals are permitted to trade the goods that they control for other goods. The rates at which they can trade one good for another (one time period's good for another time period's good) are the relevant prices. We are interested in the prices and quantities of consumption and trades that result from a competitive equilibrium.

Private Ownership

We consider economies where individuals have claims on, or rights to, quantities of the two goods that exist during their lifetime. These goods that they "own" are their endowment, and we denote the endowment of person h of generation t by the ordered pair

$$\omega_t^h = [\omega_t^h(t), \omega_t^h(t + 1)],$$

where $\omega_t^h(s)$, the *endowment* of time s good of individual h of generation t, is a positive or zero quantity of the period s good that individual h can use as desired. We call such an economy a *private ownership* economy.

In almost all economies, there is some private ownership. Individuals have rights to at least some portion of their own labor. This statement is true even in socialist economies where the capital stock (the machines) are owned by the state. It may seem that on becoming a slave one loses even the most minimal rights of ownership, even that of one's own labor, but that was not usually the case in practice.[1] This minimal quantity of

1. The Incan economy is interesting because there may have been no private ownership, not even partial ownership of one's own labor. For a discussion of the Incan economy, see Poma de Ayala (1613, translation 1978) and Murra (1980).

owned labor could be converted into consumable goods. With full rights to one's own labor, the quantity of goods one can produce and have the rights to is significantly larger. In our model we skip the production stage and give individuals rights to an endowment of the good.

We assume, for now, that the total time t endowment for the economy, $Y(t)$, is owned by individuals. That is, we assume that

$$Y(t) = \sum_{h=1}^{N(t)} \omega_t^h(t) + \sum_{h=1}^{N(t-1)} \omega_{t-1}^h(t).$$

The total endowment at date t is equal to the sum of the privately owned endowments of the young and the old who are alive at date t.

The important thing about economies where individuals have rights to goods is that they then can exchange those goods for other goods. Trade is not possible without ownership.[2] We are interested in the consumption allocations that individuals will choose given some initial allocation of goods. To do that we need to specify the constraints that the individuals perceive themselves as facing.

Competitive Intragenerational Trade

We observe many private loans being made in financial markets every day. Banks accept deposits (loans from individuals to the bank) and they lend these deposits to other individuals. In addition, a considerable number of loans are made by private individuals directly (in the form of bonds) to other individuals or agents (firms).

Even in the restricted world of our model, such loans are possible. Members of generation t can lend some of the good to other members of generation t at time t and get paid back at time $t + 1$. Because the individuals on both sides of the transactions are alive during both the borrowing and payback period, such transactions are possible. Such transactions are likely to occur if individuals of the same generation have different preferences or endowments. Trade is possible, for example, between a professional basketball player, who has a larger endowment when young, and a judge, who has a larger endowment when old. The

2. Sir John Hicks (1969) discusses the development of rights of ownership in a historical context. For Hicks, the rights of ownership are a precondition of trade.

physical endowment that makes the professional basketball player valuable disappears with age, whereas judges gain experience as they get older and then are likely to be more valuable. Trade would allow each of them to have smoother consumption paths than they would be able to have without trade.

Let $\ell^h(t)$ be the *lending* of person h of generation t. It is measured in terms of the time t good. It is possible for an individual to have negative lending; we call that *borrowing*. A young person who lends the quantity $\ell^h(t)$ of the time t good receives back when old the quantity $r(t)\ell^h(t)$ of the time $t + 1$ good. Likewise, a borrower of the quantity $\ell^h(t)$ of the time t good pays back when old the quantity $r(t)\ell^h(t)$ of the time $t + 1$ good. We call $r(t)$ the *gross real interest rate* at date t. It is measured in terms of the time $t + 1$ good per unit of the time t good.

The algebraic statements of the conditions of lending and borrowing are called *budget constraints*. The budget constraint for individual h of generation t when young is

$$c_t^h(t) \le \omega_t^h(t) - \ell^h(t). \tag{2.1}$$

Consumption when young for person h of generation t is equal to that person's endowment minus the lending that person makes. If individual h borrows, then consumption when young is greater than endowment when young by the amount of borrowing.

When old, the same person's budget constraint is

$$c_t^h(t + 1) \le \omega_t^h(t + 1) + r(t)\ell^h(t), \tag{2.2}$$

so consumption when old is equal to endowment plus the quantity of the person's lending times the gross rate of interest. If individual h borrowed when young, then $\ell^h(t)$ is negative and consumption when old is less than endowment when old by the amount of the time $t + 1$ good that goes to paying off the loan. Note that even though the interest is paid in time $t + 1$, we label it $r(t)$ because it is known by both borrowers and lenders at date t. This knowledge is similar to that of a credit card user, who knows the interest rate to be paid on a charge at the date the charge is made.

Although $r(t)$ is an interest rate, it is different in several respects from the interest rate one normally encounters. First, it is a gross rather than a net interest rate. Suppose that a loan of 100 sacks of time t wheat is repaid with 105 sacks of time $t + 1$ wheat. The net interest paid is 5 sacks of wheat or 5 percent per period. Our *gross interest rate* is simply 1 plus the net interest rate or, in this case, $r(t) = 1.05$. Second, because the loans are made and paid back in goods rather than in money, $r(t)$ is called a (gross) *real interest rate* rather than a nominal interest rate. The interest rate one normally encounters in a bank or in bonds is a nominal interest rate. Nominal interest rates appear in Part Two, where we introduce money.

We are assuming that individuals interact in competitive markets. This assumption means that individuals view prices as unaffected by their own actions, that is, by the amount they buy and sell. For the particular economy we are describing, the assumption of competitive markets means that all individuals take the gross real interest rate as unaffected by the amount that they, personally, borrow and lend. In the above budget constraints, person h treats $r(t)$ as given to them by the market and chooses consumption and borrowing or lending based on that $r(t)$.

Our objective is to describe the decisions that person h makes while operating in competitive markets and how those decisions depend on the person's preferences, on endowments when young and old, and on $r(t)$. This description of individual decisions is an important part of the description of a competitive equilibrium. We restrict the discussion to $r(t) > 0$.

We can combine these two budget constraints together and thereby look at the restrictions an individual faces when planning lifetime consumption possibilities. We divide Equation (2.2) by $r(t)$ and add it to Equation (2.1). We get

$$c_t^h(t) + \frac{c_t^h(t + 1)}{r(t)} \leq \omega_t^h(t) + \frac{\omega_t^h(t + 1)}{r(t)}. \tag{2.3}$$

When we weight consumption and endowment when old by the interest rate, weighted lifetime consumption must be less than or equal to weighted lifetime endowment. The lifetime budget constraint given in Equation (2.3) is expressed in terms of the time t good.

Equation (2.3) says that lifetime consumption expressed in terms of time t good is less than or equal to lifetime endowment expressed in the same terms. Because $r(t)$ measures the amount of time $t + 1$ good that one receives for giving up (lending) 1 unit of time t good, we can say that 1 unit of the good at time $t + 1$ has a value (price) of $1/r(t)$ in terms of the time t good. The left-hand side of Equation (2.3) gives the value of the consumption at time t in terms of time t good added to the time t value of consumption at time $t + 1$. In other words, the left-hand side of the equation gives the current or present value of the lifetime consumption. With a similar argument, the right-hand side can be shown to be the current or present value of the lifetime endowment. This notion of *present value* will reappear later.

Figure 2.1 shows all consumption pairs, $[c_t^h(t), c_t^h(t + 1)]$, that satisfy Equation (2.3) for a given endowment, $\omega_t^h = [\omega_t^h(t), \omega_t^h(t + 1)]$, and gross interest rate $r(t)$. Its upper boundary is the line through an individual's endowment with slope $-r(t)$. When the budget constraint holds with equality, we are on the budget line. Given an interest rate $r(t)$ and an endowment ω_t^h, this line gives the set of affordable consumption points.

We need to show that the consumption pairs that fulfill Equation (2.3) are equivalent to ones that fulfill Equations (2.1) and (2.2). We know,

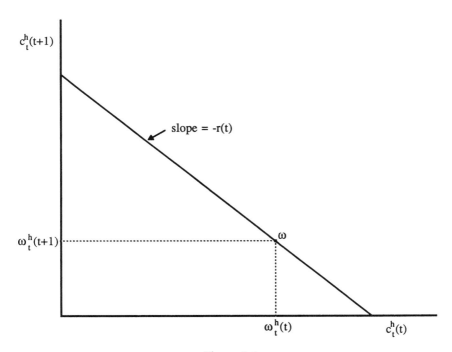

Figure 2.1

by construction, that for any consumption pairs for which both Equation (2.1) and Equation (2.2) hold, Equation (2.3) also holds. We also need to show that the equivalence works in the other direction. And, finally, we need to show how we find, for any pair of consumptions that fulfill Equation (2.3), the $\ell^h(t)$ that makes Equations (2.1) and (2.2) hold for those consumptions. Let $[\hat{c}_t^h(t), \hat{c}_t^h(t + 1)]$ be some consumption pair that fulfills Equation (2.3). Define $\ell^h(t)$ as

$$\ell^h(t) = \omega_t^h(t) - \hat{c}_t^h(t).$$

This expression implies that Equation (2.1) is satisfied. If this $\ell^h(t)$ allows Equation (2.2) to hold, then we are done. Substitute this equation into (2.3), giving

$$\frac{\hat{c}_t^h(t + 1)}{r(t)} \leq \ell^h(t) + \frac{\omega_t^h(t + 1)}{r(t)}.$$

This inequality can be rearranged to give Equation (2.2), the desired result.

Consumption Decisions

The competitive choice problem for individual h of generation t is to choose an affordable consumption basket to maximize utility. Specifically, individual h chooses a pair $[c_t^h(t), c_t^h(t + 1)]$ to maximize the utility function,

$$u_t^h(c_t^h(t), c_t^h(t + 1)),$$

constrained by the lifetime budget constraint (Equation 2.3),

$$c_t^h(t) + \frac{c_t^h(t + 1)}{r(t)} \leq \omega_t^h(t) + \frac{\omega_t^h(t + 1)}{r(t)},$$

with $r(t)$, and the endowments viewed as given. We have assumed that more is better than less for all individuals. That assumption implies that the above lifetime budget constraint will hold with equality. If at some consumption pair, the lifetime budget constraint holds with inequality, then there is another affordable consumption pair for individual h of generation t that permits more of each good to be consumed and, therefore, is strictly preferred to the original consumption pair. For a utility-maximizing individual, the lifetime budget constraint must hold with equality.

Graphically, the solution to the choice problem is illustrated in Figure 2.2. Given the budget constraint in Figure 2.1, an individual chooses consumption to get to the highest indifference curve possible. For an internal solution (one that is not at the point where the budget line meets the axes), the preferred point is on an indifference curve that is just tangent to the budget line. Point C in Figure 2.2 is the point on the budget line that maximizes utility.

This choice problem can also be solved by first using the budget constraint to express $c_t^h(t + 1)$ in terms of the rest of the variables. The expression is

$$c_t^h(t + 1) = r(t)[\omega_t^h(t) - c_t^h(t)] + \omega_t^h(t + 1).$$

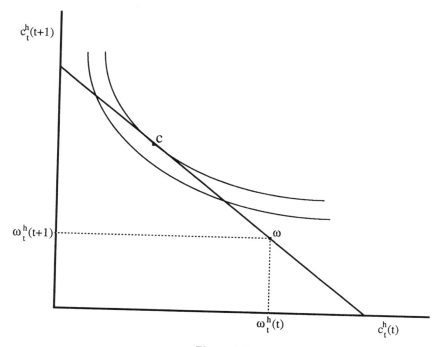

Figure 2.2

Substituting this expression for $c_t^h(t + 1)$ in the utility function gives

$$u_t^h(c_t^h(t), r(t)[\omega_t^h(t) - c_t^h(t)] + \omega_t^h(t + 1)), \tag{2.4}$$

in which the only choice variable for individual h is $c_t^h(t)$. Maximizing Equation (2.4) with respect to $c_t^h(t)$ means finding the value of $c_t^h(t)$ for which

$$\frac{du_t^h}{dc_t^h(t)} = 0.$$

Taking the total derivative of Equation (2.4) with respect to $c_t^h(t)$ and equating it to 0 gives

$$\frac{du_t^h}{dc_t^h(t)} = \frac{\partial u_t^h}{\partial c_t^h(t)} - r(t)\frac{\partial u_t^h}{\partial c_t^h(t + 1)} = 0.$$

The utility-maximizing choice for $c_t^h(t)$ satisfies

$$\frac{\partial u_t^h}{\partial c_t^h(t)} - r(t)\frac{\partial u_t^h}{\partial c_t^h(t + 1)} = 0,$$

or $$r(t) = \frac{\dfrac{\partial u_t^h}{\partial c_t^h(t)}}{\dfrac{\partial u_t^h}{\partial c_t^h(t + 1)}}. \tag{2.5}$$

The right-hand side of this last equation equals the marginal rate of substitution. A utility-maximizing choice for consumption when young (and therefore for consumption when old) occurs where the gross real interest rate equals the marginal rate of substitution.

Notice how similar the above intertemporal choice problem is to a one-period choice problem in which an individual is to choose quantities of two goods subject to a budget constraint. The main difference between the static two-good problem and our intertemporal problem is that the two goods in our formulation are different by the date at which they occur. In the static problem, the utility function describes the individual's tastes for the two goods. In our intertemporal problem, the utility function describes the individual's tastes for consumption of the one good over two periods of life.

Equation (2.4) suggests that it is possible to write a functional representation of an individual's consumption choice when young as a function of that individual's lifetime endowment and the gross real interest rate, where the function depends on the form of the utility function. For individual h of generation t, we denote the resulting *demand function for consumption when young* as

$$c_t^h(t) = \chi_t^h(r(t), \omega_t^h(t), \omega_t^h(t + 1)).$$

An Example

In this book, we work through a lot of examples that use a particular utility function, a Cobb-Douglas utility function; namely,

$$u_t^h = c_t^h(t)[c_t^h(t + 1)]^\beta.$$

We solve for the demand function for consumption when young that goes with this utility function by using the marginal rate of substitution condition we found in Equation (2.5). Taking partial derivatives of the utility function, we have that

$$\frac{\partial u_t^h}{\partial c_t^h(t)} = [c_t^h(t + 1)]^\beta$$

and $\quad \dfrac{\partial u_t^h}{\partial c_t^h(t + 1)} = \beta c_t^h(t)[c_t^h(t + 1)]^{\beta - 1}.$

Into Equation (2.5) we substitute the above partial derivatives and get

$$r(t) = \frac{c_t^h(t + 1)}{\beta c_t^h(t)}.$$

Substituting into the above equation the expression for consumption when old in terms of consumption when young from the budget constraint, we get

$$r(t) = \frac{r(t)[\omega_t^h(t) - c_t^h(t)] + \omega_t^h(t + 1)}{\beta c_t^h(t)}.$$

Solving for $c_t^h(t)$, we have the demand function for consumption when young of

$$
c_t^h(t) = \chi_t^h(r(t), \omega_t^h(t), \omega_t^h(t+1))
$$

$$
= \frac{\omega_t^h(t)}{1+\beta} + \frac{\omega_t^h(t+1)}{r(t)(1+\beta)}, \tag{2.6}
$$

and as mentioned above, consumption when young is a function of the gross interest rate, the endowments, and the β parameter of the utility function.

EXERCISE 2.1   Show that the demand function for consumption when young for the utility function

$$
u_t^h(c_t^h(t), c_t^h(t+1)) = [c(t)]^{1/2} + \beta[c_t^h(t+1)]^{1/2}
$$

is

$$
c_t^h(t) = \frac{\omega_t^h(t)}{1+\beta^2 r(t)} + \frac{\omega_t^h(t+1)}{r(t)[1+\beta^2 r(t)]}.
$$

Savings Function

Most of this book focuses on assets and on individuals' decisions about holding assets and about the equilibria that arise with different types of assets. With two-period-lived individuals, the logic of asset holding is simple: one acquires or sells assets when young to shift one's endowment pattern to a preferred consumption pattern. In the above sections, we summarized these decisions in terms of the demand function for consumption when young. For the economies in this chapter, once we know the demand function for consumption when young, it is easy to find the asset holdings. The only asset available is private borrowing or lending. An individual's demand for borrowing or lending is the difference between endowment and the individual's demand for consumption when young.

In the context of this chapter we can refer to an individual's demand for lending or borrowing as a demand for savings. An individual who has an endowment when young that is larger than desired consumption when young wishes to save. These savings are in the nature of an excess supply. Members of generation t who are demanding less of the time t good as consumption than they are supplied with as endowment have excess supplies of the time t good. Borrowing, or negative savings, is in the nature of an excess demand. Members of generation t who are demanding more of the time t good for consumption than they are supplied with as endowment have excess demands for the time t good. We define the *savings* of individual h of generation t as

$$\omega_t^h(t) - c_t^h(t).$$

Notice that desired savings of individual h of generation t can be expressed as a function of the gross real interest rate and of the individual's endowments when young and when old. The demand for consumption when young is given by the function

$$c_t^h(t) = \chi_t^h(r(t), \omega_t^h(t), \omega_t^h(t + 1)).$$

We can write the desired *savings function* of member h of generation t (the function that expresses the excess supply of or excess demand for consumption when young) as

$$s_t^h(r(t), \omega_t^h(t), \omega_t^h(t + 1)) = \omega_t^h(t) - \chi_t^h(r(t), \omega_t^h(t), \omega_t^h(t + 1)).$$

For the Cobb-Douglas utility function we used above, the savings function is

$$s_t^h(r(t), \omega_t^h(t), \omega_t^h(t + 1)) = \omega_t^h(t) - \left[\frac{\omega_t^h(t)}{1 + \beta} + \frac{\omega_t^h(t + 1)}{r(t)(1 + \beta)} \right],$$

$$= \frac{\beta \omega_t^h(t)}{1 + \beta} - \frac{\omega_t^h(t + 1)}{r(t)(1 + \beta)}.$$

For a case we will be using often, one where $\beta = 1$, the savings function is

$$s_t^h(r(t)) = \frac{\omega_t^h(t)}{2} - \frac{\omega_t^h(t + 1)}{2r(t)}.$$

Notice that we have expressed the savings function as either $s_t^h(r(t))$ or $s_t^h(r(t), \omega_t^h(t), \omega_t^h(t + 1))$, depending on the emphasis we wish to put on the variables that affect savings. Both of these methods of expressing savings are used in the rest of the book, the choice depending on the variables of interest.

We define an *aggregate savings function,* written as $S_t(r(t))$ to emphasize the importance of the gross interest rate in savings decisions, as the sum of generation t's private savings functions,

$$S_t(r(t)) = \sum_{h=1}^{N(t)} s_t^h(r(t)).$$

Recall the definition of the individual savings functions,

$$s_t^h(r(t)) = \omega_t^h(t) - \chi_t^h(r(t), \omega_t^h(t), \omega_t^h(t + 1)).$$

We substitute this definition of individual savings into the definition of aggregate savings and get

$$S_t(r(t)) = \sum_{h=1}^{N(t)} \omega_t^h(t) - \sum_{h=1}^{N(t)} \chi_t^h(r(t), \omega_t^h(t), \omega_t^h(t + 1)).$$

EXERCISE 2.2 Find the savings function for the utility function

$$u_t^h(c_t^h(t), c_t^h(t + 1)) = [c_t^h(t)]^{1/2} + \beta[c_t^h(t + 1)]^{1/2}.$$

EXERCISE 2.3 Find the $S_t(r(t))$ function for the following cases:

a. $N(t) = 100$; each h in generation t has the utility function

$$u_t^h = c_t^h(t)[c_t^h(t + 1)]^\beta,$$

with $\beta = 1$ and $[\omega_t^h(t), \omega_t^h(t + 1)] = [2, 1]$.

b. $N(t) = 100$; each h has the above utility function with $\beta = 1$, and

$$[\omega_t^h(t), \omega_t^h(t + 1)] = \begin{cases} [2, 1], & h = 1, 2, \ldots, 50 \\ [1, 1], & h = 51, 52, \ldots, 100. \end{cases}$$

Competitive Equilibrium

We begin with a general definition of a competitive equilibrium.

Definition   *A competitive equilibrium is a set of prices and quantities that satisfy the following two conditions:*

(i) The quantities that are relevant for a particular person maximize that person's utility in the set of all quantities that are affordable given the prices and the person's endowment.

(ii) The quantities clear all markets at all dates t.

In every time period, all persons are maximizing their utility subject to the prices they face [the $r(t)$ sequence is the only price we have yet] and the endowments they have (the ω_t^h's). This maximization behavior can be expressed as supply and demand curves (for savings or loans in this case) in every period. The equilibrium prices (there might be more than one) are those for which supplies equal demands in all markets in every period. When supply equals demand, the market clears.

To find an equilibrium, we follow a logic by which we impose conditions (i) and (ii) and see what conditions these imply for the sequence of prices and interest rates. We then search for sequences of prices and interest rates that fulfill these conditions. We can later check to see whether the resulting sequence of quantities generated by the sequences of prices and interest rates does indeed fulfill conditions (i) and (ii).

Both the demand function for consumption when young and the savings function for h in generation t describe the relationship between utility-maximizing choices and prices. The demand function for consumption when young is the demand curve for the goods market at each time t. The savings functions are both the excess demand and the excess supply curves for loans. To complete the description of a competitive equilibrium, we must describe the market clearing conditions.

We have only two markets in each period. There is a market for goods and a market for private borrowing and lending. Because a direct method for transferring goods from one date to another does not exist, clearing in the goods market means that total consumption in each period equals total endowment in that period. This *goods market clearing condition* is written as

$$\sum_{h=1}^{N(t)} c_t^h(t) + \sum_{h=1}^{N(t-1)} c_{t-1}^h(t) = Y(t) = \sum_{h=1}^{N(t)} \omega_t^h(t) + \sum_{h=1}^{N(t-1)} \omega_{t-1}^h(t),$$

which states that the sum of the consumption of the young and the old equals the sum of the endowments of the young and the old at each time t.

There is no reason for the young and the old of each period to engage in trade. They have the same good during the period their lives overlap, so there are no taste differences that might lead to trade. If the young had one type of good and the old another type and the utility functions of both groups depended on the consumption of each of these two types of goods in each period of life, then a goods trade would be possible and would most likely occur (with no trade restrictions). But, in this model, they have the same good. The only trades that are of interest are trading for consumption in different time periods. The discussion below shows why the young and old cannot trade in the current environment.

Suppose that some old person at time t attempts to make a trade with a (smart) young person. There are two possibilities at time t: (1) the young person could give the old person some of the good for a promise of future repayment; or (2) the old person could give the young person some good for a promise of future repayment. But in the next period (the future), the old person is dead. The young person could not collect a debt and the now dead old person could not enjoy a repayment. The timing is bad.

Therefore, no intergenerational trade takes place. If we sum Equation (2.1) at equality over the members of generation t, then we can write the total consumption of the young at time t as

$$\sum_{h=1}^{N(t)} c_t^h(t) = \sum_{h=1}^{N(t)} \omega_t^h(t) + \sum_{h=1}^{N(t)} \ell^h(t).$$

Because no intergenerational trade can take place, private borrowing and lending can only take place among members of the same generation. Because only the young participate in the market for loans, market clearing at each date t requires that the aggregate borrowing and lending of each generation must equal 0. Therefore,

$$\sum_{h=1}^{N(t)} \ell^h(t) = 0.$$

Given that aggregate private borrowing and lending of each generation equals 0, the total consumption at time t of the members of generation t satisfies

$$\sum_{h=1}^{N(t)} c_t^h(t) = \sum_{h=1}^{N(t)} \omega_t^h(t).$$

In equilibrium, the young at time t consume all of their endowment. From condition (i) of the definition of a competitive equilibrium, each person's consumption when young must equal that person's demanded consumption. When we combine these two ideas, we find that it must be true in equilibrium that, for all $t \geq 1$,

$$\sum_{h=1}^{N(t)} \chi_t^h(r(t), \omega_t^h(t), \omega_t^h(t+1)) = \sum_{h=1}^{N(t)} \omega_t^h(t). \tag{2.7}$$

All of the endowments are given to us as part of the environment, so the only variable in this equation is $r(t)$. For any equilibrium $r(t)$ sequence, Equation (2.7) must be satisfied at every date.

The equilibrium condition given in Equation (2.7) can also be described in terms of the aggregate savings function. Recall that we defined an aggregate savings function as

$$S_t(r(t)) = \sum_{h=1}^{N(t)} \omega_t^h(t) - \sum_{h=1}^{N(t)} \chi_t^h(r(t), \omega_t^h(t), \omega_t^h(t+1)). \tag{2.8}$$

The equilibrium condition of Equation (2.7) is equivalent to the condition on aggregate savings that

$$S_t(r(t)) = 0, \tag{2.9}$$

for all $t \geq 1$.

Using this result, we can restate, in terms of the aggregate savings function, the conditions on the $r(t)$ sequence for a competitive equilibrium in an economy where the only assets are private borrowing and lending.

Proposition 2.1 *If the quantities and the sequence $\{r(t)\}$ are a competitive equilibrium, then $\{r(t)\}$ satisfies*

$$S_t(r(t)) = 0 \qquad\qquad (2.9)$$

for every t.

Notice the logical direction of Proposition 2.1. It says that the sequence of gross interest rates in an equilibrium of an economy with only private borrowing and lending results in zero aggregate savings in every period. The condition expressed in the proposition contains both the utility-maximizing principle (in the construction of the aggregate savings function) and the goods market clearing condition (in that aggregate savings equals 0 in each period). We proved that this condition holds in the discussion leading up to it. The next proposition has the opposite logical direction. It says that for any $r(t)$ sequence that satisfies Equation (2.9), that sequence of interest rates and the resulting consumption quantities are an equilibrium. We prove this second proposition below.

Proposition 2.2 *If $\{r(t)\}$ satisfies Equation (2.9) for every t, then there exist quantities such that they and the $r(t)$ sequence are an equilibrium.*

We found the expression for an equilibrium in Proposition 2.1 by imposing the market clearing conditions and optimizing behavior as expressed by the functions for consumption when young and, therefore, by the savings functions. Following the same order of logic we used after the general definition of the competitive equilibrium, we impose the conditions in the proposition and see what conditions must hold on the sequence of gross real interest rates and prices. An equilibrium gross real interest rate sequence for the economy with only borrowing and lending must fulfill the condition that aggregate savings equal 0. To complete the discussion of the competitive equilibrium, we need to prove Proposition 2.2, that is, to show that *any* $r(t)$ sequence that fulfills the condition $S_t(r(t)) = 0$ generates consumptions that clear all markets and are utility maximizing subject to the budget constraints.

Consider some $r(t)$ sequence such that $S_t(r(t)) = 0$ for all $t \geq 1$. Given $r(t)$, individual h of generation t chooses a time t consumption to maximize utility. This utility-maximizing consumption choice is given by the demand function for consumption when young,

$$c_t^h(t) = \chi_t^h(r(t), \omega_t^h(t), \omega_t^h(t+1)).$$

The condition $S_t(r(t)) = 0$ and the definitions of aggregate and individual savings give

$$S_t(r(t)) = \sum_{h=1}^{N(t)} s_t^h(r(t)) = \sum_{h=1}^{N(t)} \omega_t^h(t) - \sum_{h=1}^{N(t)} c_t^h(t) = 0, \qquad (2.10)$$

for the $c_t^h(t)$'s determined by the function, $\chi_t^h(r(t), \omega_t^h(t), \omega_t^h(t+1))$. From the budget constraint of the young, we know that

$$\omega_t^h(t) = c_t^h(t) + \ell^h(t).$$

This definition and the result in Equation (2.10) mean that

$$\sum_{h=1}^{N(t)} \ell^h(t) = 0.$$

The market for borrowing and lending clears each period.

Because identical conditions hold on the consumption decisions the old made when young, their private borrowing and lending also sum to 0. Summing up the budget constraint when old (Equation 2.2) of the old at date t, we have

$$\sum_{h=1}^{N(t-1)} c_{t-1}^h(t) = \sum_{h=1}^{N(t-1)} \omega_{t-1}^h(t) + r(t-1) \sum_{h=1}^{N(t-1)} \ell^h(t-1).$$

Because private borrowing and lending made at date $t - 1$ by members of generation $t - 1$ sum to 0, the above equation states that total consumption of the old at date t equals the total endowment of the old at date t. Summing up these conditions we have on the consumption of the young and the consumption of the old at date t, we get

$$\sum_{h=1}^{N(t)} c_t^h(t) + \sum_{h=1}^{N(t-1)} c_{t-1}^h(t) = \sum_{h=1}^{N(t)} \omega_t^h(t) + \sum_{h=1}^{N(t-1)} \omega_{t-1}^h(t),$$

which states that the goods market clears at date t. The three conditions are fulfilled. The utility-maximizing consumption choices for any sequence of $r(t)$'s that fulfills the definition of a competitive equilibrium are quantities that clear the market in goods and the market in private borrowing and lending at each date t.

An Example of a Competitive Equilibrium

Let $N(t) = 100$, $[\omega_t^h(t), \omega_t^h(t + 1)] = [2, 1]$, and $u_t^h(\cdot) = c_t^h(t)[c_t^h(t + 1)]^\beta$, with $\beta = 1$ for all $t \geq 0$ and all h. We know from our previous discussion that the savings function for this utility function is

$$s_t^h(t) = \left(\frac{\beta}{1 + \beta}\right)\omega_t^h(t) - \frac{\omega_t^h(t + 1)}{(1 + \beta)r(t)}$$

$$= \left(\frac{1}{2}\right)2 - \frac{1}{2r(t)} = 1 - \frac{1}{2r(t)}.$$

Because everyone is alike, we can use the one savings function to get

$$S_t(t) = \sum_{h=1}^{100} \left(1 - \frac{1}{2r(t)}\right) = 100 - \frac{50}{r(t)}.$$

Equating aggregate savings to 0, we find

$$r(t) = \frac{1}{2}, \qquad \text{for all } t \geq 1.$$

The competitive equilibrium of this example is one where the gross interest rate is always $\frac{1}{2}$. That interest rate results in individual savings of

$$s_t^h(t) = 1 - \frac{1}{2(\frac{1}{2})} = 0.$$

Consumption in each period is the endowment of that period. In the following exercises the economies are more interesting.

EXERCISE 2.4 Describe completely the competitive equilibria for the following economies:

a. $N(t) = 100$ for $t \geq 0$. Each member of generation t, $t \geq 0$, has the Exercise 2.3 utility function with $\beta = 1$ and $[\omega_t^h(t), \omega_t^h(t+1)] = [2, 1]$ for all h and $t \geq 0$.

b. Same as a, except that $[\omega_t^h(t), \omega_t^h(t+1)] = [1, 2]$ for all h and $t \geq 0$.

c. Same as a, except that each member of generation t, $t \geq 0$, has the utility function

$$u_t^h = [c_t^h(t)]^{1/2} + \beta [c_t^h(t+1)]^{1/2}$$

with $\beta = 1$.

d. Same as a, except that for all $t \geq 0$,

$$[\omega_t^h(t), \omega_t^h(t+1)] = \begin{cases} [2, 1], & h = 2, 4, \ldots, 100 \quad \text{(the even)}, \\ [1, 1], & h = 1, 3, \ldots, 99 \quad \text{(the odd)}. \end{cases}$$

e. Same as a, except that for all $t \geq 0$,

$$[\omega_t^h(t), \omega_t^h(t+1)] = \begin{cases} [2, 1], & h = 1, 2, \ldots, 60, \\ [1, 1], & h = 61, 62, \ldots, 100. \end{cases}$$

f. Same as a, except that for all $t \geq 0$,

$$[\omega_t^h(t), \omega_t^h(t+1)] = \begin{cases} [1, 1], & t = 1, 3, 5, \ldots, \\ [2, 1], & t = 2, 4, 6, \ldots. \end{cases}$$

EXERCISE 2.5 (Pareto optimality) Prove that the competitive equilibrium of each of the following economies of Exercise 2.4 is *not* Pareto optimal: 2.4a, 2.4c, 2.4d, 2.4e, 2.4f. (You may find it helpful to review the material on feasible, Pareto superior, and Pareto optimal allocations.)

In Exercise 2.4d when 50 of each generation (the odd) have an endowment of $[1, 1]$ and 50 of each generation (the even) have an endowment of [2, 1], trade takes place. The savings function of the odd is

$$s_t^{odd}(t) = \frac{1}{2} - \frac{1}{2r(t)},$$

and the savings function of the even is

$$s_t^{even}(t) = 1 - \frac{1}{2r(t)}.$$

Aggregate savings are

$$S_t(t) = 50 \left[\frac{1}{2} - \frac{1}{2r(t)} \right] + 50 \left[1 - \frac{1}{2r(t)} \right]$$

$$= 25 - \frac{25}{r(t)} + 50 - \frac{25}{r(t)}.$$

Equating this expression for aggregate savings to 0, we get $r(t) = \frac{2}{3}$. The savings of each odd person are

$$s_t^{odd}(t) = \frac{1}{2} - \frac{1}{2(\frac{2}{3})} = \frac{1}{2} - \frac{3}{4} = -\frac{1}{4}$$

and of each even are

$$s_t^{even}(t) = 1 - \frac{3}{4} = \frac{1}{4}.$$

Each odd person borrows $\frac{1}{4}$ unit of the good from each even person when young and pays back $(\frac{2}{3})(\frac{1}{4}) = \frac{1}{6}$ unit of the good when old. The consumption of the odd becomes

$$c_t^{odd} = [\frac{5}{4}, \frac{5}{6}],$$

and the consumption of the even is

$$c_t^{even} = [\frac{7}{4}, \frac{7}{6}].$$

Notice that the utility of both the even and the odd has increased:

$$u_{\text{before}}^{\text{odd}} = (1)(1) = 1 \qquad\qquad u_{\text{before}}^{\text{even}} = (2)(1) = 2$$

$$u_{\text{after}}^{\text{odd}} = (1.25)(0.8333) = 1.042 \quad u_{\text{after}}^{\text{even}} = (1.75)(1.1666) = 2.042$$

As one would expect, when the members of a generation are not all alike, trade improves welfare.

If all members of a generation are alike in terms of preferences and endowments, then all have the same savings function and the restriction that total savings equal 0 means that each individual $s_t^h(r(t))$ also equals 0. Total savings, $S_t(r(t))$, are

$$S_t(r(t)) = N(t)s_t^h(r(t)) = 0.$$

When all $s_t^h(r(t))$ equal the same $s_t(r(t))$, then $s_t(r(t))$ must equal 0.

No trades are taking place, but an equilibrium gross interest rate exists. That gross interest rate can be found by solving for $r(t)$ in

$$s_t^h(r(t), \omega_t^h(t), \omega_t^h(t + 1)) = 0$$

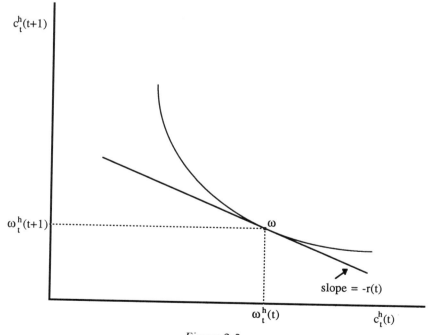

Figure 2.3

and is illustrated graphically in Figure 2.3. Point ω is the endowment point; and, because there is no trade, it is also the consumption point. Notice that an indifference curve is drawn passing through point ω. The equilibrium gross interest rate is given to us by the price line that passes through point ω and is tangent to the indifference curve at point ω. Because no trades take place in this economy, we would not be able to observe this price in the market; but such a price exists, and it is the one consistent with no intragenerational lending or borrowing.

Reprise

A competitive equilibrium is a sequence of prices (gross interest rates) and a consumption allocation in which all individuals maximize utility subject to their budget constraints and all markets clear in every period. Given the assets available in an economy, a competitive equilibrium must include a description of prices and all individuals' holdings of these assets. The budget restriction in these economies is determined by the prices that people face and their endowments of goods when young and when old. The price sequence in a competitive equilibrium is one in which all markets clear.

In the version of the model so far discussed, the only trade that occurs is intragenerational trade; that is, trade that occurs among members of the same generation. There are not enough objects in the economy to allow for intergenerational trade.

We find a competitive equilibrium by determining the savings functions for individuals and aggregating these savings functions into a total savings function for each generation (these could be different for different generations if the patterns of endowments and preferences change across time) and by equating the aggregate savings function to 0 at each date.

In general, a competitive equilibrium does not result in Pareto optimal consumption allocations. A competitive equilibrium does satisfy two necessary conditions for Pareto optimality—efficiency and equality of within-generation marginal rates of substitution. It can, however, fail to satisfy the condition that the marginal rates of substitution be high enough.

CHAPTER 3

Introducing
a Government

Government was an early invention of human beings. One of the advantages of governments over private individuals is that a government has a life longer than that of any single individual. Governments were not always able to take advantage of this characteristic, especially when the government was too closely associated with one particular individual (as in a kingship). Then government policies lasted as long as the king did and were likely to change with the new king. In the late medieval period, kings had great difficulty borrowing for exactly this reason. The debt of the king was often thought of (especially by the next king) as being a personal debt of the now-dead king, and the new government was no longer responsible for that debt. This attitude made kings a very bad loan risk, particularly if the loan was for financing a war and the king intended to lead the troops into battle.

We want to add a government to our model and consider the results of some of the policies that a government might follow. A government normally imposes and collects taxes and makes transfers. Governments often borrow to meet expenditures that they have chosen to make (rather than tax for them). The government of the United States in the 1980s borrowed an average of over $100 billion a year. We consider both the taxing and borrowing abilities of government, but we add them to our model in somewhat simplified ways.

A government policy exists not just at time 1, but for the future as well. In our models, once an economy has a government, it will continue to have a government for all future time periods. Policies of this government are a description of the actions of the government in all future time periods. There is some question about whether the government will or will not follow through on a policy that it has announced. This problem is called a time consistency question. It means that a currently optimal policy that a government announces and that includes a particular action for some time t might not be the optimal thing for the government to do when time t actually arrives. We both allow and force governments, in our economies, to commit themselves to a policy path. For more on time consistency issues, see Chari, Kehoe, and Prescott (1989).

Taxes

The simplest kind of *tax* to add to the model is a tax on endowments. Individuals are required by the government to give some portion of their endowment to the government. They may be required to give some portion of their endowment when young, when old, or both. Unless otherwise stated, individuals know when they are young how much of a tax they must pay in each period of their life. Individuals may also receive transfers from the government. A *transfer* is a negative tax in that the government gives an individual some additional endowment rather than taking it away. An individual h of generation t will face a set of taxes and transfers,

$$t_t^h = [t_t^h(t), t_t^h(t + 1)],$$

where $t_t^h(s)$ is the tax in the form of date s equals t or $t + 1$ good payable by person h of generation t and is positive if it is a tax and is negative if it is a transfer.

Suppose for now that the government does nothing but levy these taxes and transfers. In particular, it does not purchase and consume any goods. It follows that all taxes that the government receives get paid out as transfers. This budget constraint on the government means that for all time periods t,

$$\sum_{h=1}^{N(t)} t_t^h(t) + \sum_{h=1}^{N(t-1)} t_{t-1}^h(t) = 0,$$

or that the sum of transfers and taxes each period add up to 0. These taxes and transfers show up in the model by changing an individual's endowments. If the pretax endowment for individual h of generation t was

$$[\omega_t^h(t), \omega_t^h(t + 1)],$$

then the posttax and transfer endowment for the same person will be

$$[\omega_t^h(t) - t_t^h(t), \omega_t^h(t + 1) - t_t^h(t + 1)].$$

Solving for a competitive equilibrium in an economy with these kinds of taxes and transfers is fairly easy. Budget constraints now must include the taxes and transfers. The budget constraint of the young is now

$$c_t^h(t) \leq \omega_t^h(t) - t_t^h(t) - \ell^h(t),$$

and the budget constraint when old is now

$$c_t^h(t + 1) \leq \omega_t^h(t + 1) - t_t^h(t + 1) + r(t)\ell^h(t).$$

We solve the budget constraint on consumption when old for $\ell^h(t)$ and substitute that into the budget constraint on consumption when young. The combined (lifetime) budget constraint is

$$c_t^h(t) + \frac{c_t^h(t + 1)}{r(t)} \leq [\omega_t^h(t) - t_t^h(t)] + \frac{\omega_t^h(t + 1) - t_t^h(t + 1)}{r(t)}. \qquad (3.1)$$

Notice that this lifetime budget constraint is identical to the one we used in Chapter 2 (Equation 2.3) except that after-tax endowments when young and when old (in brackets) replace the endowments without taxes.

We can show graphically how the preferred after-tax consumption point is determined. The set of affordable consumption points for individual h of generation t is illustrated in Figure 3.1. The point ω is the initial endowment point. A line through this endowment point with a slope of $r(t)$ shows the set of affordable consumption pairs before any tax or transfer. Point $\omega - t$ indicates one of the many possible symmetric tax and transfer schemes for a constant population economy. It is symmetric in the sense that everyone receives as a transfer when old exactly the amount that they were taxed when young. The budget line

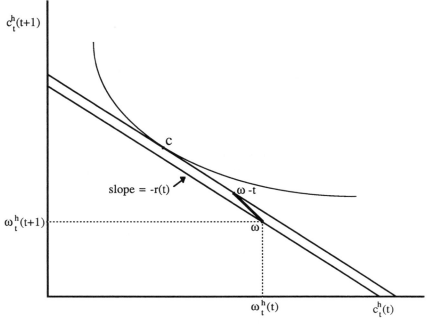

Figure 3.1

through this after-tax endowment point with a slope of $-r(t)$ gives the
set of affordable consumption pairs. Point c, where an indifference
curve is tangent to this budget line, is the preferred consumption point.

To find the savings function for an individual in the presence of taxes,
we first find the demand function for consumption when young and
then use that function to find the savings function. To find the demand
function for consumption when young, we follow the same procedure
we used in Chapter 2, but we use the after-tax-and-transfer endowments
instead of the original endowments.

Using the lifetime budget constraint, we get that consumption when
old is

$$c_t^h(t + 1) = r(t)\{[\omega_t^h(t) - t_t^h(t)] - c_t^h(t)\} + [\omega_t^h(t + 1) - t_t^h(t + 1)].$$

To choose consumption when young to maximize utility is to maximize

$$u_t^h(c_t^h(t), r(t)\{[\omega_t^h(t) - t_t^h(t)] - c_t^h(t)\} + [\omega_t^h(t + 1) - t_t^h(t + 1)]),$$

with respect to $c_t^h(t)$. Notice that in this equation, the after-tax endowments appear exactly as the endowments did in our earlier problem without taxes (see Equation 2.4). Taking derivatives with respect to consumption when young and setting that equal to 0 results in the condition that the marginal rate of substitution equals the gross interest rate. We can write the solution to this maximization as the demand function for consumption when young or as

$$c_t^h(t) = \chi_t^h(r(t), [\omega_t^h(t) - t_t^h(t)], [\omega_t^h(t + 1) - t_t^h(t + 1)]).$$

Following the logic we used in Chapter 2, we get the savings function for individual h of generation t equal to

$$s_t^h(r(t)) = [\omega_t^h(t) - t_t^h(t)]$$
$$- \chi_t^h(r(t), [\omega_t^h(t) - t_t^h(t)], [\omega_t^h(t + 1) - t_t^h(t + 1)]),$$

which is identical to the savings function we found earlier except that the after-tax endowment replaces the endowment without taxes. The aggregate savings function at each date t is found by summing up the savings functions of all members of generation t. Therefore,

$$S_t^h(r(t)) = \sum_{h=1}^{N(t)} s_t^h(r(t), [\omega_t^h(t) - t_t^h(t)], [\omega_t^h(t + 1) - t_t^h(t + 1)]),$$

where each of the individual savings functions are functions of after-tax endowments.

Consider an example economy where $N(t) = 100$ for all t, individual pretax endowments are $[2, 1]$ for all individuals of all generations, taxes and transfers are $[\frac{1}{2}, -\frac{1}{2}]$, and all these individuals have the utility function,

$$u_t^h = c_t^h(t)[c_t^h(t + 1)]^\beta, \tag{3.2}$$

with $\beta = 1$.

The savings function of individual h of generation t is

$$s_t^h(r(t)) = \frac{\beta[\omega_t^h(t) - t_t^h(t)]}{1 + \beta} - \frac{\omega_t^h(t + 1) - t_t^h(t + 1)}{(1 + \beta)r(t)}.$$

Substituting in the values of the parameters in this example gives

$$s_t^h(r(t)) = (1/2)(2 - 1/2) - \frac{1 + 1/2}{2r(t)} = \frac{3}{4} - \frac{3}{4r(t)}.$$

The aggregate savings function is

$$S_t^h(r(t)) = 100s_t^h(r(t)) = 75 - \frac{75}{r(t)}.$$

The general definition for a competitive equilibrium holds for an economy with taxes and transfers. In a competitive equilibrium, individuals are choosing quantities that maximize their utilities given the constraints they face, including the taxes and transfers; and all markets clear. The main addition in this section is that the government's budget constraint must also hold.

Summing the budget constraints of the young, we find that aggregate consumption of the young at time t equals

$$\sum_{h=1}^{N(t)} c_t^h(t) = \sum_{h=1}^{N(t)} \omega_t^h(t) - \sum_{h=1}^{N(t)} t_t^h(t) - \sum_{h=1}^{N(t)} \ell^h(t);$$

and because no intergenerational borrowing and lending is possible,

$$\sum_{h=1}^{N(t)} \ell^h(t) = 0.$$

Rearranging the aggregate budget constraint and substituting for the individual savings function, we get

$$S_t^h(r(t)) = \sum_{h=1}^{N(t)} s_t^h(r(t)) = \sum_{h=1}^{N(t)} [\omega_t^h(t) - t_t^h(t) - c_t^h(t)] = 0.$$

In an equilibrium, aggregate savings equal 0 for every generation t.

We can find the equilibrium gross interest rate for the above example economy. We found that the aggregate savings function equals

$$S_t^h(r(t)) = 100s_t^h(r(t)) = 75 - \frac{75}{r(t)} = 0,$$

which gives an equilibrium gross interest rate equal to 1.

Figure 3.2 shows the initial endowment-consumption point at [2, 1], labeled ω, and the price line, denoted by $r(t) = \frac{1}{2}$, tangent to the indifference curve passing through that point. The tax-transfer scheme described in the example economy above moves individual consumption to point c, where the price line (at the equilibrium gross interest rate, $r(t) = 1$) is identical with the set of efficient symmetric lifetime consumption baskets. The tangency of the indifference curve at point c means this is the best among all such baskets for members of generations $t \geq 1$. (It is not the utility-maximizing tax-transfer scheme for members of generation 0. A tax-transfer pair of [2, -2] would be preferred by them.)

The type of tax-transfer scheme we gave in the above example is not very different from the kind of "social security" that is in place in the United States. The young are taxed each period to provide for transfers to the (poorer) old. In the following exercises, you are to study several other economies with similar social security systems. Exercise 3.2 (which is marked with an asterisk because it is one of the more difficult exercises) is about the differences between consumption and income taxes.

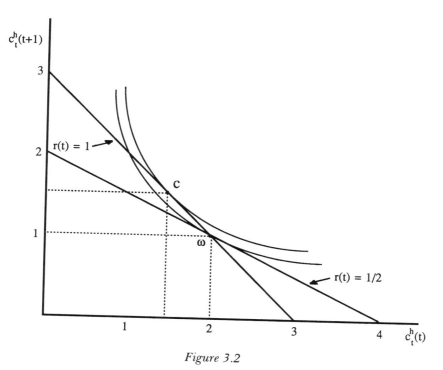

Figure 3.2

EXERCISE 3.1 (Taxes on young, transfers to old; or "social security" schemes) Here we consider only balanced budget schemes, those for which the taxes collected from the young at any date t equal the transfers at that date to the old. Assume throughout that people when young know and take into account the transfers they will receive when old.

a. Consider the Exercise 2.4a economy and consider a scheme in which each person when young is taxed 1 unit and each person when old receives 1 unit as a transfer. Describe the competitive equilibrium and show that it is Pareto superior to that obtained in the absence of the scheme.

b. Consider the same social security scheme within the context of the Exercise 2.4d economy. Compare the equilibria with and without the scheme.

c. Consider the Exercise 2.4a economy but with $N(0) = 100$ and $N(t) = 2N(t - 1)$ for all $t \geq 1$. If each person when young is taxed 1 unit, then what is the maximum that can be given to every person when old? Compare the competitive equilibria with and without this scheme.

d. Consider the Exercise 2.4a economy but with $N(0) = 100$, $N(t) = 2N(t - 1)$ for $t = 1, 2, \ldots, 10$ and $N(t) = N(10)$ for $t \geq 10$. Describe some alternative social security schemes for this economy. Relate the "difficulties" that arise to those that currently plague the U.S. social security system.

*EXERCISE 3.2 (Consumption versus income taxes) To get started, we write versions of Equations (2.1) and (2.2) that include a flat-rate consumption tax, z_c, and a flat-rate income tax, z_y:

$(2.1')$ $c_t^h(t) \leq (1 - z_y)\omega_t^h(t) - \ell^h(t) - z_c c_t^h(t),$

$(2.2')$ $c_t^h(t + 1) \leq (1 - z_y)[\omega_t^h(t + 1) + r(t)\ell^h(t)] - z_c c_t^h(t + 1).$

Show, without making any particular assumptions about preferences or endowments, that all nonnegative pairs (z_c, z_y) satisfying $(1 - z_y)/(1 + z_c) = g$ for a given, constant g satisfying $0 < g < 1$ are equivalent. As part of your answer, define *equivalent*. (Hint: What is the constraint an individual faces when making consumption decisions? How does $r(t)$ enter into that constraint?)

Suppose that a government is interested in choosing an optimal tax-transfer scheme for its economy. By optimal, we mean tax-transfer schemes that result in Pareto optimal symmetric allocations. In particular, we are looking for the smallest symmetric tax-transfer scheme that will give a Pareto optimal allocation. Tax-transfer schemes that take more from the young and give it to the old at time $t = 1$ may also be Pareto optimal allocations. Let us restrict ourselves to competitive equilibrium (with constant population and identical individuals) and try to find an optimal tax to take from (or give to) the young and to give to (or take from) the old. With constant population, we can imagine that the government will pair up young and old each period and enforce a transfer between them. What is the optimal amount of such a transfer and in which direction will it flow?

Suppose that all individuals in this economy have the utility function given in Equation (3.2). Let $t*$ stand for the transfer that we want to maximize the welfare of the citizens. If everyone is identical, then there are no private loans; so the only thing that could make consumption different from endowment is the transfer. For each individual, consumption when young will be

$$c_t^h(t) = \omega_t^h(t) - t*, \tag{3.3}$$

and consumption when old will be

$$c_t^h(t + 1) = \omega_t^h(t + 1) + t*. \tag{3.4}$$

If $t*$ is a tax on the young, it will be positive; if it is a tax on the old, it will be negative. Substituting Equations (3.3) and (3.4) into the utility function, we get a utility function where the only choice variable is the transfer, $t*$. We want to maximize utility with respect to $t*$, so we take the derivative of $(\omega_t^h(t) - t*)(\omega_t^h(t + 1) + t*)$ with respect to $t*$ and set that equal to 0. For an economy where endowment is [3, 1], the above equation is equal to $3 + 2t* - (t*)^2$, and the derivative with respect to $t*$ is $2 - 2t* = 0$.

This last equation can be solved for an optimal transfer from the young to the old of $t* = 1$. This amount is the smallest symmetric tax and transfer that results in a Pareto optimal allocation. Notice that if the endowment had been [1, 3], the initial allocation is already Pareto optimal. A transfer of $t* = -1$ would be required to get members of generations $t \geq 1$ to the best symmetric consumption allocation. This transfer of $t^* = -1$ would make everyone in generations 1 to ∞ better off, but the old of generation 0 would be made worse off.

Government Borrowing

Suppose that we allow the government to borrow from the young (it cannot borrow from the old). Initially, we let the government issue *one-period bonds* that are sure (safe or certain) claims on 1 unit of the good in the next period. The government in this model will honor its commitments and will always pay off its bonds.

The revenues that the government must raise to pay off or redeem the bonds can come from several sources. If the government issues $B(t)$ units of bonds in time period t, it will need to pay these bonds off, in period $t + 1$, with $B(t)$ units of the time $t + 1$ good. Here, bonds are always measured in terms of the quantity of the good they will pay off at the due date. So in period $t + 1$ the government needs $B(t)$ units of the good. It can get this quantity of the good by

1. taxing the young of period $t + 1$ a total of $B(t)$ units of the good;
2. taxing the old of period $t + 1$ a total of $B(t)$ units of the good;
3. issuing $B(t + 1)$ units of new bonds that raise $B(t)$ units of the time $t + 1$ good;
4. some mix of (1), (2), and (3) that adds up to $B(t)$ units of the good.

The government faces a budget constraint each period. Because, in our current model, the government transfers all income received from one group of individuals to some other individuals and does not keep any, we can write the *time t budget constraint of the government* as

$$\sum_{h=1}^{N(t)} t_t^h(t) + \sum_{h=1}^{N(t-1)} t_{t-1}^h(t) + p(t)B(t) - B(t-1) = 0,$$

where $p(t)$ is the price of one government bond at time t. One can see that this government budget constraint incorporates all of the above four methods of redeeming government bonds that were issued at time $t - 1$ by setting the appropriate elements of the government budget constraint to be equal to 0.

The government's budget is *balanced* when

$$\sum_{h=1}^{N(t)} t_t^h(t) + \sum_{h=1}^{N(t-1)} t_{t-1}^h(t) = 0,$$

that is, when the revenues from taxes exactly equal expenditures. The government runs a *deficit* when the right-hand side of that equation is negative and a *surplus* when it is positive. When the government is running a deficit, the time t budget constraint of the government indicates that it must borrow to pay for the deficit.

These definitions of deficit and surplus are slightly different from those used in the National Income Accounts of the United States. In the U.S. accounts, interest paid on government bonds is counted as a transfer, and a budget is called balanced if tax revenues cover expenditures and interest payments. In our description of a balanced budget, which might be called a balanced budget net of interest payments, interest payments on old government bonds do not count as a government expenditure. The interest payments on each old bond of $1 - p(t - 1)$ are covered by new bond issues under our definition of a balanced budget.

Before illustrating that the way the government chooses to pay off its bonds affects the consumption allocations generated by a competitive equilibrium, we need to show how these government bonds fit into our model. One-period debts of the government have the same risk characteristics as do the one-period private (intragenerational) borrowing and lending. Both of these are assumed to be perfectly secure, so a lender will get what is promised in either case. Because these bonds are identical in their risk characteristics, they must offer the same rates of return [gross interest rate, $r(t)$] as do the private loans. To see this, consider the budget constraints of some member h of generation t. With both private borrowing and lending and government bonds available, the budget constraints are

$$c_t^h(t) = \omega_t^h(t) - t_t^h(t) - \ell^h(t) - p(t)b^h(t), \tag{3.5}$$

when young, and

$$c_t^h(t + 1) = \omega_t^h(t + 1) - t_t^h(t + 1) + r(t)\ell^h(t) + b^h(t), \tag{3.6}$$

when old. Here $p(t)$ is the price of one government bond at time t and $b^h(t)$ is the quantity of government bonds purchased by individual h of generation t. We have included taxes in the budget constraints, using the same notation as earlier. A bond is purchased at a price $p(t)$ at time t and pays back 1 unit of the time $t + 1$ good, so the rate of return of holding one bond is equal to $1/p(t)$. Combining these budget constraints by substituting out $\ell^h(t)$ gives

$$
c_t^h(t) + \frac{c_t^h(t + 1)}{r(t)}
$$

$$
= \omega_t^h(t) - t_t^h(t) + \frac{\omega_t^h(t + 1) - t_t^h(t + 1)}{r(t)} - b^h(t)\left[p(t) - \frac{1}{r(t)}\right].
$$

(3.7)

The lifetime budget constraint is the same as in Equation (2.3) except for the subtraction of individual h's holdings of government bonds times the difference in the price of the bonds and the inverse of the gross interest rate (the last two are within the square brackets). The sign of the portion of this equation within the square brackets depends on the values of $p(t)$ and $r(t)$. If $r(t)$ is greater than $1/p(t)$, then it is positive. If $r(t)$ equals $1/p(t)$, then the portion in square brackets is 0. If $r(t)$ is less than $1/p(t)$, then it is negative. We wish to show that the interest rate on private borrowing and lending, $r(t)$, must be equal to the rate of return on government bonds, $1/p(t)$. We consider what must be true if it is not.

When $r(t)$ is greater than $1/p(t)$, then the return on government bonds is less than the return on private borrowing and lending. Individuals would want to issue their own government bonds. If individuals could issue their own government bonds, then an infinite profit could be made selling government bonds and using the revenues from those sales to lend in the private borrowing and lending market. Everyone would want to do this, which cannot be an equilibrium because no one would be buying the government bonds. As it is, we impose the restriction that individual holdings of government bonds be nonnegative; so the smallest that $b^h(t)$ can be is 0. The case in which the government is selling bonds and no one wishes to purchase any cannot be an equilibrium.

When $r(t)$ is less than $1/p(t)$, the return on government bonds is greater than the return on private borrowing and lending, and every agent wishes to borrow as much as possible (an infinite amount is desired) in the private borrowing market and to use the revenues from the borrowing to purchase government bonds. A profit of $1/p(t) - r(t)$ is made on each purchased bond that is financed by borrowing on the private loan market. Each additional bond purchased by borrowing adds $1/p(t) - r(t) > 0$ to the endowment side of the lifetime budget constraint. Each individual desires to borrow an infinite amount in the private market for borrowing and to purchase an infinite number of government bonds. Because there are no lenders in the private market and the number of government bonds is finite, this case cannot be an equilibrium.

The remaining case is where $r(t) = 1/p(t)$. When this occurs, the portion within the square brackets in Equation (3.7) equals 0, and the rate of return on government bonds is equal to the return on private borrowing and lending. Individuals are indifferent between private lending and lending to the government (purchasing government bonds). The present value of a government bond, discounted by the interest rate on private borrowing and lending, is equal to the price of the bonds.

We summarize the above result. An individual will desire to hold bonds equal to

$$b^h(t) = \begin{cases} 0 & \text{if } r(t) > 1/p(t), \\ \infty & \text{if } r(t) < 1/p(t), \quad \text{and} \\ ? & \text{if } r(t) = 1/p(t). \end{cases}$$

Because neither $b^h(t) = 0$ nor $b^h(t) = \infty$ can be an equilibrium, $r(t)$ equals $1/p(t)$ must be an equilibrium condition.

This condition, called the *present value condition*, implies that the lifetime budget constraint given in Equation (3.7) collapses to the same lifetime budget constraint that individuals faced in the economy with taxes and transfers but with no government bonds (Equation 3.1). Because both private borrowing and lending and government bonds pay the same gross interest rate, they are identical from the point of view of any individual. In the budget constraint of the young at time t, Equation (3.5), both private lending and government bonds appear. The particular mix of lending and government bonds that an individual chooses cannot be determined from the budget constraints, only the net position. It is quite possible that an individual is a borrower and then uses the loan to purchase government bonds. The exact amounts of private loans and of government bonds that any one individual holds are indeterminate. This indeterminacy means that we cannot write out individual demand functions for particular assets, although we can write out demand functions for net asset positions. Because private borrowing and lending in each generation sum to 0, we are able to say something about the demand for government bonds from each generation.

To find the conditions for an equilibrium, we sum the budget constraints of the young at time t (Equation 3.5). This summation gives

$$\sum_{h=1}^{N(t)} c_t^h(t) = \sum_{h=1}^{N(t)} \omega_t^h(t) - \sum_{h=1}^{N(t)} t_t^h(t) - p(t) \sum_{h=1}^{N(t)} b^h(t).$$

Rearranging this equation, we get

$$\sum_{h=1}^{N(t)} [\omega_t^h(t) - t_t^h(t) - c_t^h(t)] = p(t)B(t),$$

or, from the definition of savings when there are taxes,

$$\sum_{h=1}^{N(t)} s_t^h(r(t)) = p(t)B(t).$$

The left-hand side of this equation is aggregate savings at time t, $S_t(r(t))$, so we claim that the equilibrium condition is

$$S_t(r(t)) = p(t)B(t). \tag{3.8}$$

The old at time t consume all that they get. Summing the budget constraints of the old (Equation 3.6), we get

$$\sum_{h=1}^{N(t-1)} c_{t-1}^h(t) = \sum_{h=1}^{N(t-1)} \omega_{t-1}^h(t) - \sum_{h=1}^{N(t-1)} t_{t-1}^h(t) + B(t-1).$$

Summing the consumption of the old and the young at time t, we have

$$\sum_{h=1}^{N(t)} c_t^h(t) + \sum_{h=1}^{N(t-1)} c_{t-1}^h(t)$$

$$= \sum_{h=1}^{N(t)} \omega_t^h(t) - \sum_{h=1}^{N(t)} t_t^h(t) + \sum_{h=1}^{N(t-1)} \omega_{t-1}^h(t) - \sum_{h=1}^{N(t-1)} t_{t-1}^h(t)$$

$$- p(t)B(t) + B(t-1).$$

From the government budget constraint, we have that

$$\sum_{h=1}^{N(t)} t_t^h(t) + \sum_{h=1}^{N(t-1)} t_{t-1}^h(t) + p(t)B(t) - B(t-1) = 0.$$

Clearing the elements of the budget constraint out of the above equation gives

$$\sum_{h=1}^{N(t)} c_t^h(t) + \sum_{h=1}^{N(t-1)} c_{t-1}^h(t) = Y(t) = \sum_{h=1}^{N(t)} \omega_t^h(t) + \sum_{h=1}^{N(t-1)} \omega_{t-1}^h(t),$$

which states that the goods market clears at time t. Equation (3.8) is equivalent to the condition that the goods market clears at each time t.

From the present value condition, we can write $p(t) = 1/r(t)$. Substituting this result into the market clearing condition as expressed in Equation (3.8) gives one equation in one unknown, $r(t)$, namely,

$$S_t(r(t)) = \frac{B(t)}{r(t)}.$$

The above equation captures the requirement that total private savings at date t are equal to the time t value of outstanding government debt at time t, both measured in units of the time t good and the requirement that government debt and private debt earn the same return.

Suppose that in period 1 the government wishes to borrow 5 units of time t good and transfer it to the old from generation 0. It will pay off this debt by taxing the young of generation 2 and will issue no new debt after that. Let $N(t) = 100$, and let the endowment be (for all t)

$$\omega_t^h = \begin{cases} [2, 1], & \text{for } h \text{ odd,} \\ [1, 1], & \text{for } h \text{ even.} \end{cases}$$

The utility functions for all individuals h of all generations t are

$$u_t^h = c_t^h(t)[c_t^h(t+1)]^\beta,$$

with $\beta = 1$. The savings functions that are generated from this utility function and these endowments are

$$s_t^h(t) = \begin{cases} 1 - \dfrac{1}{2r(t)}, & \text{for } h \text{ odd,} \\ \dfrac{1}{2} - \dfrac{1}{2r(t)}, & \text{for } h \text{ even.} \end{cases}$$

The aggregate savings function is

$$S_t(t) = 50\left[1 - \frac{1}{2r(t)}\right] + 50\left[\frac{1}{2} - \frac{1}{2r(t)}\right] = 75 - \frac{50}{r(t)}.$$

For equilibrium, this expression is equated to 5 for $t = 1$. Solving the equation for $r(1)$ gives $r(1) = 5/7$; and the savings of the odd and the even of generation 1 are

$$s_1^h(1) = \begin{cases} 1 - \dfrac{1}{(2)(5/7)} = 0.3 & \text{for } h \text{ odd,} \\[2ex] \dfrac{1}{2} - \dfrac{1}{(2)(5/7)} = -0.2 & \text{for } h \text{ even.} \end{cases}$$

The even individuals are each borrowing 0.2 unit of the good from all odd individuals. At the gross interest rate $r(1) = 5/7$, there are additional savings by the odd of 0.1 unit of the good for each of them. There are 50 odd individuals; so the total savings by the odd that are not taken by the even are equal to 5, which is the amount of borrowing by the government. Notice in this example that government and private borrowing coexist.

Because the debt is paid off by taxing the young of generation 2, the payoff scheme does not affect the decisions of generation 1. They know they will get paid for the loans and that someone else will pay for it. The only thing that matters to them is the intragenerational borrowing and lending and the additional borrowing by the government. The total amount of taxes that must be paid by the young of generation 2 is equal to $B(t)$, which we have not calculated yet. Because $B(1)/r(1) = 5$ in this example and $r(1) = 5/7$, we can substitute that interest rate into the above equation and get

$$B(1) = 5r(1) = \frac{25}{7} = 3\,4/7.$$

To get the 5 units of the good to transfer to the old of generation 0, the government needs to issue $3\,4/7$ bonds in period 1 and tax the young of period 2 a total of $3\,4/7$ units of the time $t + 1$ good to pay off those bonds.

EXERCISE 3.3 (Endowment taxes versus government borrowing)   Consider the economy of Exercise 3.1a. Assume there is a government that will raise 25 units of time 1 good and transfer these units to members of generation 0. Compare the following ways of financing this scheme.

a. The government collects $\frac{1}{4}$ unit of time 1 good from each member of generation 1.

b. The government at $t = 1$ sells securities that are titles to time 2 good (one-period bonds). At $t = 1$ it also announces that the members of generation 1 will be taxed equally at $t = 2$ (when they are old) to pay off the bonds. (Hint: Show that the equilibrium under scheme a is also an equilibrium under this scheme.)

c. The government at $t = 1$ sells securities that are titles to time 2 good (one-period bonds). It sells enough to get 25 units of time 1 good. It will tax the members of generation 2 equally at $t = 2$ to pay off the securities it sells at $t = 1$.

Ricardian Equivalence

The equilibrium in Exercise 3.3a is also an equilibrium in Exercise 3.3b. This equivalence is a particular instance of a general result that often goes by the name of *Ricardian equivalence*. This result is named after David Ricardo, an early nineteenth-century English economist. The general result, which we prove in the appendix to this chapter, follows.

Proposition 3.1   *Given an initial equilibrium under some pattern of lump-sum taxation and government borrowing, alternative (intertemporal) patterns of lump-sum taxation that keep the present value (at the initial equilibrium's interest rates) of each individual's total tax liability equal to that in the initial equilibrium are equivalent in the following sense. Corresponding to each alternative taxation pattern is a pattern of government borrowing such that the initial equilibrium's consumption allocation, including consumption of the government, and the initial equilibrium's gross interest rates are an equilibrium under the alternative taxation pattern.*

Consider the simplest possible case of the kind of tax changes suggested in the proposition. Suppose that the government imposes taxes equal to 0.1 unit of the time 1 good on everyone in generation 1. For simplicity, all members of generation 1 are identical, so there will be no private borrowing and lending among members of generation 1. Suppose as an alternative that the government borrows 0.1 unit of the time 1 good from every member of generation 1 and taxes each member of generation 1 in time period 2 whatever is required to pay off the bonds. Setting private borrowing and lending equal to 0 and imposing the equilibrium condition that $1/p(1) = r(1)$, the budget constraints for member h of generation 1 are

$$c_1^h(1) = \omega_1^h(1) - t_1^h(1) - b^h(1),$$

$$c_1^h(2) = \omega_1^h(2) - t_1^h(2) + r(1)b^h(1).$$

When a tax of 0.1 unit of the time 1 good is collected (and no tax is collected from this generation in period 2), the consumption pattern for members of this generation is

$$[c_1^h(1), c_1^h(2)] = [\omega_1^h(1) - 0.1, \omega_1^h(2)].$$

When the government borrows 0.1 unit of the time 1 good from each member of generation 1 and then taxes them whatever is required to pay off the bonds, the taxes for person h of generation 1 in period 2 are

$$t_1^h(2) = r(1)b^h(1) = r(t)(0.1).$$

Notice that the present value of the tax liability for person h does not change. In the first case, the tax is 0.1 and, in the second case, it is $r(1)(0.1)$ paid in period 2; $r(1)(0.1)$ has a present value of 0.1.

In this second case, consumption is reduced by 0.1 unit of the time 1 good, because person h spends 0.1 unit of the time 1 good to buy government bonds. Consumption in time period 2 is still equal to the endowment, because the taxes are returned to individual h in the form of payments on the bond. The consumption pattern when the government issues 0.1 bond per person is

$$[c_1^h(1), c_1^h(2)] = [\omega_1^h(1) - 0.1, \omega_1^h(2)],$$

just as it was with the tax in period 1. Recall that an equilibrium condition requires that the marginal rate of substitution (MRS) be equal to the gross interest rate (Equation 2.5); and for time period 1, this condition is

$$r(1) = \text{MRS} = \left[\frac{\partial u_1^h(c_1^h(1), c_1^h(2))}{\partial c_1^h(1)}\right]\left[\frac{\partial u_1^h(c_1^h(1), c_1^h(2))}{\partial c_1^h(2)}\right]^{-1}.$$

Because the consumptions are the same in both cases above, the marginal rates of substitution will be the same, and so must the interest rates be the same. The equilibrium with the bonds at time 1 and a tax on members of generation 1 at time 2 is the same as the one with the tax on members of generation 1 at time 1. We repeat that the present value of the tax is the same in both cases.

The proposition says that if the government wishes to make some level of purchases and decides to borrow now and tax later instead of taxing now, the change of policy will not change any prices or any consumption patterns. This proposition is true as long as the change from taxes now to borrowing and future taxes does not change the present value of anyone's income. Notice that the proof of the proposition in the appendix assumes nothing about the kinds of preferences, endowments, or taxes that the economy had. The crucial hypothesis is the one concerning the present value of taxes on each individual. In Exercise 3.3, the parts a and c result in different present values of taxes. Ricardian equivalence does not hold for these two types of policies. In particular, if one possibility is to borrow from one generation and tax another and the other possibility is to tax the first generation, these policies result in different present values of taxes and equivalence fails. In an economy where individuals care only about their own consumption, if a government borrows today and taxes future generations to pay off those loans, that is quite different from taxing today. In Chapter 4 we look at Ricardian equivalence in cases where generations do care about one another.

Rolling Over Government Debt

Suppose that the government chooses each period to pay off old loans by issuing new ones. This practice is called *rolling over debt* (a popular practice). We will see that some such schemes are possible and others are not.

Consider a scheme in which the government wishes to borrow by issuing government bonds at date t and by taxing the young of date $t + 2$ to pay off these bonds. To do this, the government issues bonds at date $t + 1$ and uses the revenues from these new government bonds to pay off the bonds issued at date t. It then taxes the young at date $t + 2$ to pay off this second issue of one-period bonds.

As an example, assume that the government wishes to raise 10 units of the good to transfer to the old at time t. The usual equilibrium conditions for a problem of this kind are

$$S_t(r(t)) = \frac{B(t)}{r(t)} = 10.$$

This equation can be solved for the gross interest rate at time t, $r(t)$; and because $B(t)/r(t)$ equals 10 and we know $r(t)$, we find the number of bonds that must be issued at time t to get 10 units of the time t good. We now know $B(t)$, which is also the amount of revenues that the government must raise by an issue of new bonds at time $t + 1$. (Recall that the young of time $t + 2$ will be taxed to pay off the borrowing at date t.) The equilibrium conditions at date $t + 1$ are

$$S_t(r(t + 1)) = \frac{B(t + 1)}{r(t + 1)} = B(t),$$

where $B(t)$ is the number of bonds that were needed to raise the 10 units of the good at time t. This equation can be solved for $r(t + 1)$ and then for $B(t + 1)$. The young at time $t + 2$ must be taxed a total of $B(t + 1)$ units of the time $t + 2$ good to pay off the government borrowing.

EXERCISE 3.4 (Borrowing forever) As in Exercise 3.3, the government sells enough securities at $t = 1$ to get 25 units of time 1 good, which it transfers to members of generation 0. However, instead of taxing the members of generation 2 at $t = 2$, it sells enough new securities (new one-period bonds) to pay off the securities it issued at $t = 1$. At every subsequent date, it keeps doing this; it sells enough new securities to pay off the securities that come due. As completely as you can, describe the competitive equilibrium under this scheme for the Exercise 2.4a economy. Is the equilibrium under this scheme Pareto superior to the competitive equilibrium in the absence of any policy? Is it Pareto optimal?

EXERCISE 3.5 Analyze the financing scheme of Exercise 3.4 for two other economies: the economy of Exercise 2.4b and the economy of Exercise 2.4d.

Consider an economy where everyone has the utility function of Equation (3.2) and an endowment of [2, 1]. The population is constant with $N(t) = 100$ for all t. The savings functions of individuals in this economy are

$$s^h(t) = 1 - \frac{1}{2r(t)},$$

and the aggregate savings function is

$$S(t) = 100 - \frac{50}{r(t)}.$$

Suppose that the government wishes to issue bonds in the first period and to give the revenues from those bonds to the current ($t = 1$) old. Taxes will not be collected in period 2, but the government will issue more bonds to pay off these first bonds. This borrowing will continue forever. We want to determine the quantity of borrowing the government will need to do each period as a function of the quantity of goods it wishes to raise by borrowing in period 1.

Suppose that the government wishes to raise 50 units of the good in period 1 and give them to the current old. (You will soon see that this number 50 was not chosen accidentally.) The government wishes to issue $B(1)$ bonds so that the equilibrium gross interest rate that results yields $B(1)/r(1) = 50$. To do this, find the gross interest rate, $r(1)$, such that aggregate savings equal 50.

$$S(1) = 100 - \frac{50}{r(1)} = 50,$$

gives a gross interest rate, $r(1)$, of 1 and a bond issue, $B(1)$, of 50. The
government will need to issue enough bonds in period 2, $B(2)$, to raise
50 units of the good to pay off the old bonds. Notice that each period
the government will need to borrow 50 units of the good to pay off the
50 units of the good that it borrowed the time period before. Each old
person from generation 0 gets to consume 1.5 units of the good. Each
member of each generation is saving 0.5 unit of the good and getting
0.5 unit of the good back. The consumption allocation that results from
this rolling over of the debt is always [1.5, 1.5]. In Figure 3.2, this best
symmetric consumption point is on the highest indifference curve that
can be reached on a budget line that allows for any division of the total
lifetime endowment of 3 units of the good.

Suppose that the government chooses to raise just a little less than 50
units of the good by borrowing in period 1. Suppose that the amount
it chooses to borrow is 49 units of the good. We can follow the path of
borrowing that results from this initial policy and rolling over the debt
each period. We use the same aggregate savings function as above, but
now $B(1)/r(1)$ equals 49. Therefore, we have

$$S(1) = 100 - \frac{50}{r(1)} = 49.$$

The solution for $r(1)$ is 0.98 and $B(1)$ is approximately 48 (we will call
it 48). In period 2 the government needs to borrow 48 units of the good
to pay off its bonds. Therefore, the equilibrium $r(2)$ must satisfy

$$S(2) = 100 - \frac{50}{r(2)} = 48.$$

The solution for $r(2)$ is 0.9615 and $B(2)$ equals 46.15. The quantity of
bonds the government needs to issue is getting smaller each period. The
path of bond issues and gross interest rates (rounded off a bit) are
shown in Table 3.1.

Notice in Table 3.1 that the quantity of bonds approaches 0 and the
gross interest rate approaches 0.5. In this economy, if the amount of
the time 1 good that the government borrows is less than 50, the government needs to issue fewer and fewer bonds each period and can eventually pay off all of its debt with a very small tax on some generation's
young. In this economy all individuals of all generations are worse off

Table 3.1   Path of government bond issues and gross interest rates when
              $B(0)$ is 49

Period t	Number of bonds issued $B(t)$	Gross interest rate $r(t)$
1	48.00	0.98
2	46.15	0.9615
3	42.85	0.9285
4	37.49	0.875
5	29.98	0.8
6	21.41	0.714
7	13.62	0.6362
8	7.88	0.5788

than if the government borrowed 50 units and rolled that borrowing over. The old at time period 1 get less, and the utilities of all other individuals of all other generations are less as well. In this economy the borrowing forever of 50 units of the good is Pareto superior to borrowing and rolling over any smaller amount.

What happens if the government attempts to borrow more than 50 units of the good and to roll those bonds over forever? Suppose that the government announces that it will borrow 51 units of the good in period 1 and roll over forever the bonds that it issues for that debt. For this scheme, the equilibrium condition is

$$S(1) = 100 - \frac{50}{r(1)} = 51.$$

The solution for this equation is $r(1) = 1.02$. The number of bonds that the government needs to issue is 51 times 1.02, or $B(2) = 52$. Solving for period 2, we find that $r(2) = 1.043$ and $B(3) = 54.2$. Table 3.2 shows the time path of the required borrowing to keep rolling over this debt.

In the example economy, if the government attempted to roll over the sequence of government bonds beginning with 51 units of revenue at time t, the sequence would grow each period. Eventually, the amount of bonds that are required to pay off the previous period's bonds are more than the young of that period wish to save at any interest rate. A path of borrowings that lead to this infeasible borrowing for some date t is itself not a feasible rolling over policy. This path could not be an

Table 3.2   Path of government bond issues and gross interest rates when $B(0)$ is 51

Period t	Number of bonds issued $B(t)$	Gross interest rate $r(t)$
1	52.00	1.02
2	54.20	1.043
3	59.30	1.093
4	72.86	1.2286
5	134.21	1.8421

equilibrium path, and we cannot predict what would occur if such a path were proposed. Part of the proposed path might be feasible if the government stopped rolling over the bonds and taxed the young (of generation 5, in the above example) to pay off the bonds.

Some economists have called paths like the one illustrated in Table 3.2 bubbles. A *bubble* is an unsustainable price path for an asset. These economists believe that these paths might exist for a while, but the basic unsustainable nature of them means that eventually the prices collapse. They view asset price booms such as tulipmania (a price explosion in tulips in Holland in 1636–37), the Argentine land boom of the 1870s, and the U.S. stock market booms and crashes of 1929 and 1987 as examples of temporary occurrences of just such bubbles. Their argument is that, because these types of bubbles cannot continue, they must eventually burst. In our model economies, bubbles can never appear. Price paths that lead to what might be bubbles simply are not equilibrium price paths.

Equilibria like the ones just discussed are sometimes called *knife edge equilibria*. In this type of equilibria, there is one value for a particular variable that generates a stationary state. A *stationary state* is an equilibrium in which the same values appear in each period. For the example economy above, stationary states occur only when the government chooses in period 1 to borrow either 50 units of the good or 0 units of the good. (The reader should be able to verify why 0 also produces a stationary state.) All other amounts of initial borrowing and rolling over yield changing interest rates and changes in the amounts of government debt. Figure 3.3 illustrates the time paths of the three economies we solved above. We have connected the separate time periods in Figure 3.3 to better show each time path. The paths really should be points at the integer time values. Notice that if in this economy the government bor-

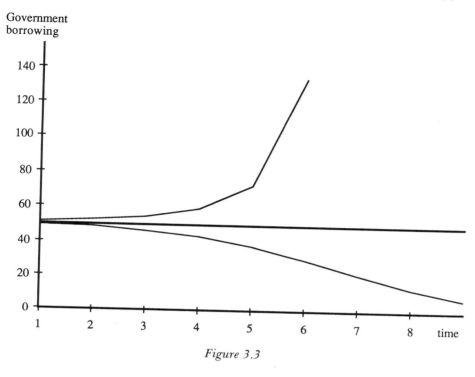

Figure 3.3

rows some other amount less than 50 (excluding 0), the same type of
path is followed as was followed in the 49 example. If any amount above
50 is borrowed, the same type of explosive path as was followed for 51
occurs. Only 50 and 0 are stationary state borrowings in this economy.

In an economy in which all individuals are identical in preferences
and in endowments, stationary state equilibria occur whenever the gross
interest rate and the consumption pair are the same for every member
of every generation (except the current old, for whom we may not know
the consumption when young). This statement is true even if the economy is growing. In the next exercise, you are asked to find the stationary
state equilibrium for a growing economy.

EXERCISE 3.6 Consider an economy where all individuals h
of all generations t have the endowment $[2, 1]$ and the utility
function

$$u_t^h = c_t^h(t)[c_t^h(t + 1)]^\beta$$

for $\beta = 1$. The population is growing with $N(1) = 100$ and $N(t) = 1.5N(t - 1)$. Find the amount of government borrowing and the number of bonds that the government must issue and continually roll over to generate a stationary state equilibrium for this economy. The absolute number of bonds the government needs to issue each period will grow. In solving this exercise, find the stationary state gross interest rate and the consumption pair that everyone has.

Equivalence between Equilibria with Bonds and Tax-Transfer Schemes

In our economies with bonds, the government operates under a budget constraint. With no direct government expenditures,[1] this budget constraint is

$$\sum_{h=1}^{N(t)} t_t^h(t) + \sum_{h=1}^{N(t-1)} t_{t-1}^h(t) + p(t)B(t) - B(t - 1) = 0.$$

We define a *balanced budget tax-transfer scheme* as one in which there is no government borrowing. This balanced budget condition is expressed as

$$\sum_{h=1}^{N(t)} t_t^h(t) + \sum_{h=1}^{N(t-1)} t_{t-1}^h(t) = 0.$$

In economies with bonds, we usually set taxes to 0 and found the allocations that could be achieved using these one-period government bonds. The following proposition gives an equivalence between equilibria with bonds and equilibria that can be obtained using balanced budget taxes and transfers. This equivalence is of interest because it allows us to restrict our attention to those economies with balanced budget taxes and transfers and be able to make statements about both types of economies. We use this proposition in Chapter 4.

---

1. That there are no direct government expenditures is not crucial. They are left out for expositional simplicity.

Proposition 3.2 *An equilibrium with bonds can be duplicated (in terms of consumption allocations) with a tax-transfer scheme that balances the government's budget at each date and has no government borrowing at any date.*

The government is issuing some quantity, $B(t)$, of one-period bonds at time t. It uses the proceeds either to pay off some old one-period bonds it had issued in period $t - 1$ or to give the revenues to the time t old. It will tax the young of time $t + 1$ to pay for these bonds or it will roll over the bonds by issuing new one-period bonds at time $t + 1$. Assume that if it chooses to tax, then it will tax the young of time $t + 1$ exactly the amount that they would have spent on bonds if the bonds had been rolled over. Notice that the total time $t + 1$ revenue from either of these methods of extracting goods from the time $t + 1$ young is the same. The relative welfare effects on the time $t + 1$ young of the two methods of collecting revenue depend on what tax-transfer policies are followed by the government in time $t + 2$. Now we concentrate on members of generation t.

The equilibrium for time period t in the economy with one-period bonds occurs at the gross interest rate that solves

$$S_t(r(t)) = \frac{B(t)}{r(t)}.$$

Let $\mathbf{r}(t)$ stand for the equilibrium gross interest rate for the economy with bonds. The budget constraints for individual h of generation t are

$$c_t^h(t) = \omega_t^h(t) - \ell^h(t) - p(t)b^h(t) - t_t^h(t),$$

and $$c_t^h(t + 1) = \omega_t^h(t + 1) + \mathbf{r}(t)\ell^h(t) + b^h(t) - t_t^h(t + 1),$$

where $\ell^h(t)$ is private borrowing and lending at time t, $b^h(t)$ is lending to the government, and $t_t^h(t)$ are taxes that are set equal to 0 in the economy with bonds. Figure 3.4 shows the choice problem for an individual h who makes private loans at time t. In an equilibrium with bonds,

$$\sum_{h=1}^{N(t)} \ell^h(t) = 0,$$

and $$p(t) \sum_{h=1}^{N(t)} b^h(t) = \frac{B(t)}{\mathbf{r}(t)}.$$

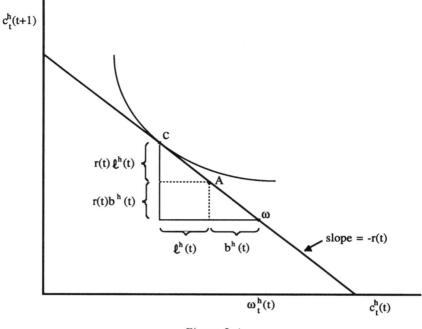

Figure 3.4

To find the equivalent equilibrium without bonds, but with taxes, set

$$t_t^h(t) = b^h(t),$$

$$t_t^h(t + 1) = -\mathbf{r}(t)b^h(t),$$

and set bond holdings to 0 for all members h of generation t. The total government revenues are the same as with bonds, because all members of generation t are now paying taxes equal to their bond holdings in the bond equilibrium. The return on the paying of taxes (the transfer they receive in time $t + 1$) is the same as the return they received on bonds. In Figure 3.4, the portion marked $b^h(t)$ should now be marked $t_t^h(t)$ and the portion marked $r(t)b^h(t)$ should be marked $-t_t^h(t + 1)$. Individual h is still on the same budget line as before and, with the same amount of private borrowing and lending as in the bond economy, will arrive at the same consumption point. If the private bond market cleared (as it did) at the old equilibrium gross interest rate, $\mathbf{r}(t)$, then it will clear in this economy with taxes and transfers at the same gross interest rate. This clearing occurs in Figure 3.4, because the individual h whose decisions it illustrates views endowment as being at point A (the after-tax point) and is trading to point C from there.

EXERCISE 3.7 Consider an economy with $N(t) = 100$, where all individuals h of all generations t have the utility function

$$u_t^h = c_t^h(t)c_t^h(t + 1),$$

and the endowments of

$$\omega_t^h = \begin{cases} [2, 1], & \text{for } h = 1, 3, 5, \ldots, 99, \quad \text{and} \\ [1, 1], & \text{for } h = 2, 4, 6, \ldots, 100. \end{cases}$$

The government issues 30 one-period bonds at time 1 and taxes the young of time 2 to pay off these bonds. Find a tax-transfer scheme (without bonds) that gives the same equilibrium consumption allocation and the same gross interest rate as the equilibrium with bonds.

Reprise

We add to our model a government that can tax, transfer, and borrow. Although we have not shown this generally, it is the case that, if a competitive equilibrium without a government is not Pareto optimal, then there exists a government tax-transfer policy that produces a Pareto superior allocation. In a stationary environment, the stationary competitive equilibrium without a government will not be Pareto optimal if the endowment and preferences are such that the marginal rate of substitution at the endowment point is less than 1. The tax-transfer scheme permits cross-generational transfers that cannot be achieved in a private economy without additional assets.

The government can also borrow. The concept of Ricardian equivalence says that it does not matter whether the government taxes the young today or borrows from them today and taxes them when old to pay off the debt. As long as the different options of borrowing and taxing do not change the present value of anyone's after-tax endowment, neither the consumption allocations nor the gross interest rate is changed by selecting different taxing or borrowing options. If the borrowing and taxing scheme shifts the tax burden to other generations, then the concept of Ricardian equivalence does not hold. Passing on taxes to other generations does change the consumption pattern and the gross interest rate that occurs in the economy.

It is possible for the government to borrow in one period and then to borrow again in the next period to pay off the one-period bonds that it issued in the first period. This rolling over of debt provides the government with several options. It is possible that the debt *never* gets paid off; that the debt gets rolled over forever. In fact, certain equilibria with this feature provide the members of the economy with higher utility levels than economies without government debt (and without tax and transfer schemes). The infinite horizon borrowing can mimic the social security system that provides the highest utility for members of generations $t \geq 1$. Infinite horizon rollover schemes have a knife edge feature. There is only one stationary state borrowing level for our economies. Borrowing levels smaller than that stationary state level follow a path where the amount of government debt diminishes over time. Attempts at borrowing more than the stationary state amount with a policy of rolling over in a perfect foresight economy will fail because the necessary amount of borrowing eventually (and quickly) becomes greater than the resources of the economy. If people know that the policy will become unsustainable, why would they ever lend the government the initial amount? (Why did the bankers who lent money to Latin American governments initially do so and why do they continue to do so?)

Appendix: Proof of Ricardian Equivalence

Proposition 3.1 *Given an initial equilibrium under some pattern of lump-sum taxation and government borrowing, alternative (intertemporal) patterns of lump-sum taxation that keep the present value (at the initial equilibrium's interest rate) of each individual's tax liability equal to that in the initial equilibrium are equivalent in the following sense. Corresponding to each alternative taxation pattern is a pattern of government borrowing such that the initial equilibrium's consumption allocation, including the consumption of the government, and the* *initial equilibrium's gross interest rates are an equilibrium under the alternative taxation pattern.*

Proof. The budget set of individual h of generation t, $t \geq 1$, with taxes included is

$$c_t^h(t) = \omega_t^h(t) - t_t^h(t) - \ell^h(t) - p(t)b^h(t) \tag{3.A1}$$

$$c_t^h(t + 1) = \omega_t^h(t + 1) - t_t^h(t + 1) + r(t)\ell^h(t) + b^h(t). \tag{3.A2}$$

Combining these, as we usually do, by eliminating $\ell^h(t)$, we get the single budget constraint for individual h of generation t of Equation (3.A3) plus $-b^h(t)(p(t) - [1/r(t)])$, which, because the last line equals 0 in equilibrium, constrains consumption by

$$c_t^h(t) + \frac{c_t^h(t + 1)}{r(t)} = \omega_t^h(t) + \frac{\omega_t^h(t + 1)}{r(t)} - \left[t_t^h(t) + \frac{t_t^h(t + 1)}{r(t)} \right]. \tag{3.A3}$$

The budget constraint for the government at time t is

$$G(t) + B(t - 1) = \sum_{h=1}^{N(t)} t_t^h(t) + \sum_{h=1}^{N(t-1)} t_{t-1}^h(t) + \frac{B(t)}{r(t)}.$$

This government budget constraint says that current government consumption, $G(t)$, and paying off the bonds from last period, $B(t - 1)$, are covered by the taxes on the members of both generations (this could include transfers to some individuals, where transfers are negative taxes) and by the revenues raised by selling new one-period bonds, $B(t)/r(t)$. This constraint holds in every time period $t \geq 1$.

Consider some initial equilibrium (indicated by bold letters) where

(i) For each generation t, the consumption pair, $[\mathbf{c}_t^h(t), \mathbf{c}_t^h(t + 1)]$, maximizes h's utility subject to the budget constraint (3.A3) when the gross interest rate is $\mathbf{r}(t)$ and the taxes paid by h are given by $[\mathbf{t}_t^h(t), \mathbf{t}_t^h(t + 1)]$.

(ii) All outside lending goes to government bonds, so

$$\sum_{h=1}^{N(t)} b^h(t) = \mathbf{B}(t).$$

(iii) The government budget constraint holds for some sequence of government consumptions, which will be kept fixed throughout the proof, of $\{\mathbf{G}(t)\}_{t=1}^{\infty}$.

Now consider some other (any other) tax pattern that for each h satisfies

$$t_t^h(t) + \frac{t_t^h(t+1)}{\mathbf{r}(t)} = \mathbf{t}_t^h(t) + \frac{\mathbf{t}_t^h(t+1)}{\mathbf{r}(t)}, \tag{3.A4}$$

for $t \geq 0$, which is the condition that the present value of the new set of taxes be the same as the original set of taxes.

If the interest rate stays at $\mathbf{r}(t)$, it follows from the one-equation version of the budget constraint, Equation (3.A3), that each individual h can afford the same set of consumption bundles under the new taxes as under the original (in bold) taxes. The part in brackets in Equation (3.A3) is replaced by a new set of taxes that has the same present value. Therefore, at the original interest rates, $\mathbf{r}(t)$, the same set of consumptions, $[\mathbf{c}_t^h(t), \mathbf{c}_t^h(t+1)]$, are again the utility-maximizing consumption bundles.

However, to get this same consumption with the original interest rate and the new tax pattern, h must lend to the government a different amount than before. In particular, Equation (3.A1) implies that the new level of lending to the government, $b^{*h}(t)$, is related to the original lending, $b_t^h(t)$, by

$$\frac{b^{*h}(t)}{r(t)} = \frac{b^h(t)}{r(t)} - [t_t^h(t) - \mathbf{t}_t^h(t)]. \tag{3.A5}$$

Summing the new lending of all h in generation t and using condition (ii), the condition that all outside lending goes to government bonds, we have

$$\sum_{h=1}^{N(t)} \frac{b^{*h}(t)}{\mathbf{r}(t)} = \frac{\mathbf{B}(t)}{\mathbf{r}(t)} - \sum_{h=1}^{N(t)} [t_t^h(t) - \mathbf{t}_t^h(t)]. \tag{3.A6}$$

Now we must show that this new level of total lending by the members of generation t clears the market in loans. Because the market clearing condition requires that outside private lending equal government borrowing, we must show that the right-hand side of Equation (3.A6) is the new level of government borrowing at t implied by the new taxes with government consumption unchanged.

The new level of government borrowing at each date $t \geq 1$ must satisfy the government budget constraint at the new taxes, so

$$\frac{B(t)}{\mathbf{r}(t)} = \mathbf{G}(t) - \sum_{h=1}^{N(t)} t_t^h(t) - \sum_{h=1}^{N(t-1)} t_{t-1}^h(t) + B(t-1) \tag{3.A7}$$

must hold. Because the government consumptions are the same in both the government budget constraints, we solve for them in Equation (3.A7) and substitute that into the original government budget constraint. We get that

$$\frac{B(t)}{\mathbf{r}(t)} = \frac{\mathbf{B}(t)}{\mathbf{r}(t)} - \left[\sum_{h=1}^{N(t)} t_t^h(t) - \sum_{h=1}^{N(t)} \mathbf{t}_t^h(t) \right]$$

$$- \left[\sum_{h=1}^{N(t-1)} t_{t-1}^h(t) - \sum_{h=1}^{N(t-1)} \mathbf{t}_{t-1}^h(t) \right] + B(t-1) - \mathbf{B}(t-1). \tag{3.A8}$$

If we can show that the second line of this equation equals 0 for all $t \geq 1$, then the first line of the equation gives us the result we need and the market for bonds clears each period at the original set of interest rates, $\mathbf{r}(t)$, $t \geq 1$.

Consider members of generation 0. At time $t = 1$, individual h of generation 0 has a budget constraint of

$$c_0^h(1) = \omega_0^h(1) - t_0^h(1) + \mathbf{r}(0)\ell^h(0) + b^h(0).$$

Because we are considering only changes in the taxes that do not change the present value of the taxes for any generation and because only the tax when old is of importance to the members of generation 0, then for this generation it must be that

$$\mathbf{t}_0^h(1) = t_0^h(1).$$

The number of bonds generation 0 is holding is also a given, so

$$\mathbf{B}(0) = B(0).$$

For generation 0, both the taxes and the number of government bonds are the same in the original and the new tax policies. Therefore, for time 1, the third line of Equation (3.A8) is

$$0 = - \left[\sum_{h=1}^{N(0)} t_0^h(1) - \sum_{h=1}^{N(0)} \mathbf{t}_0^h(1) \right] + B(0) - \mathbf{B}(0),$$

and the rest of Equation (3.A8) at time 1 is

$$\frac{B(1)}{\mathbf{r}(1)} = \frac{\mathbf{B}(1)}{\mathbf{r}(1)} - \left[\sum_{h=1}^{N(1)} t_1^h(1) - \sum_{h=1}^{N(1)} \mathbf{t}_1^h(1) \right].$$

We now prove by induction that the above equation must hold for all $t \geq 1$. (Recall that in a proof by induction we first show that some relationship holds for some initial t, $t = 1$ in this case. Then we assume that this relationship holds for some arbitrary $t - 1$ and prove that it then holds for t. Because we demonstrated that the relationship was true for some initial $t = 1$ and that it is true for any t if true for $t - 1$, it must be true for $t = 2$, then 3, then 4, and so on.)

Suppose that for time $t - 1$,

$$\frac{B(t-1)}{\mathbf{r}(t-1)} = \frac{\mathbf{B}(t-1)}{\mathbf{r}(t-1)} - \left[\sum_{h=1}^{N(t-1)} t_{t-1}^h(t-1) - \sum_{h=1}^{N(t-1)} \mathbf{t}_{t-1}^h(t-1) \right].$$

Because we have assumed that all changes in taxes maintain the present value of the tax bill for every individual, for members of generation $t - 1$ it must be the case that

$$t_{t-1}^h(t) - \mathbf{t}_{t-1}^h(t) = \mathbf{r}(t-1)[t_{t-1}^h(t-1) - \mathbf{t}_{t-1}^h(t-1)],$$

and summing over all h of generation $t - 1$, it must be the case that

$$\left[\sum_{h=1}^{N(t-1)} t_{t-1}^h(t) - \sum_{h=1}^{N(t-1)} \mathbf{t}_{t-1}^h(t) \right]$$

$$= \mathbf{r}(t-1) \left[\sum_{h=1}^{N(t-1)} t_{t-1}^h(t-1) - \sum_{h=1}^{N(t-1)} \mathbf{t}_{t-1}^h(t-1) \right].$$

Substituting this result into the condition we assumed held for time $t - 1$, we get

$$B(t - 1) - \mathbf{B}(t - 1) = \left[\sum_{h=1}^{N(t-1)} t_{t-1}^h(t) - \sum_{h=1}^{N(t-1)} \mathbf{t}_{t-1}^h(t) \right].$$

Substituting this result into Equation (3.A8), we get the desired result for time t, namely that

$$\frac{B(t)}{\mathbf{r}(t)} = \frac{\mathbf{B}(t)}{\mathbf{r}(t)} - \left[\sum_{h=1}^{N(t)} t_t^h(t) - \sum_{h=1}^{N(t)} \mathbf{t}_t^h(t) \right].$$

The proof by induction is finished and we have established that with the new taxes that maintain the present value of the tax bill for every individual, the original interest rates clear the market for bonds at every time period t. Therefore, there is no change in the equilibrium interest rates, consumptions of individuals, or the consumption of the government with these new taxes.

This completes the proof.

CHAPTER 4

Bequests

In the preceding chapters we have assumed that individuals are selfish, that they care only about their own utility and do not care about the utility of anyone else, either of their own generation or of any other generation. The only connections we have allowed people to have are through the market, by borrowing or lending, or through the government by tax-transfer schemes in which one generation is taxed in order to give transfers to another generation.

In this chapter we wish to change that and allow for caring. We continue to assume that members of the same generation do not care about one another in the sense that the utility of one member of generation t does not directly affect the utility of another member of generation t. This assumption means we are ignoring both within-generation altruism and what is commonly called romantic love (although some theories of romantic love say that it is selfish). We do, however, assume some intergenerational caring. The utility of members of generation t will depend, to some degree, on the utility of a particular member of generation $t + 1$. This assumption is meant to represent the kind of relationship that might occur between parents and their offspring.

Caring may give rise to bequests. For us, a *bequest* is a gift from some old person (the parent) to some particular young person (the child) without expectation of any return payment. This gift may not look exactly like the transfers normally called bequests, which are received only after the giver has died. The model we are using precludes those types of bequests because no goods survive across time periods. We approxi-

mate conventional bequests by allowing gifts to the young while the old
are still alive.

The size of these bequests is likely to depend on the kind of tax-
transfer scheme that the government has put into effect in the economy.
Recall that tax-transfer schemes provide for the intergenerational transfer of goods and that an intergenerational transfer of goods is the object
of bequests. It may even happen that the way the bequests depend on
the tax-transfer scheme is such that these gifts completely neutralize the
effects of the tax-transfer scheme.

We are interested in the effects of intergenerational caring in economies where either tax-transfer schemes or government borrowing policies (or both) are in operation. We showed at the end of Chapter 3 that
the equilibrium that results from any policy with government borrowing
can be replicated by some tax-transfer scheme without any borrowing
at any date. This being the case, we restrict the analysis in this chapter
to government policies without borrowing and remember that the results also apply to cases with government borrowing.

Analyzing bequests in a general framework where utility functions
are very general (but include the utility of some member of the next
generation) and where every member of every generation cares about
some member of the next generation can become very complicated
mathematically. Instead of this general framework, we look at three
classes of examples that illustrate the main points of the general framework. The first of these three classes is the simplest, and the other two
are variants in which specific complications are allowed. Keep in mind
that the only government policy that is allowed are tax-transfer schemes
(but, as shown earlier, these include policies that are equivalent to ones
with government borrowing).

Class 1 economies   *In these example economies, everyone except the members
of generation 0 (the time 1 old) is selfish. The population $N(0)$ equals $N(1)$, and
each member h of generation 0 cares about member h (junior) of generation 1.
There is no diversity within generations in either endowments or preferences.*

Class 2 economies   *This class is made up of economies much like those in
Class 1, except that diversity is allowed among members of each generation.*

Class 3 economies   *There is no diversity within generations and all generations have the same population size. In general, each member h of generation t*

cares about member h of generation t + 1. We limit the analysis here to cases where the utility functions have a particular kind of separability in preferences that keeps the analysis simple.

Generation 0 Cares about Generation 1

Let us consider Class 1 economies. Because only the members of generation 0 care about anyone else, the economy from time 2 and onward (when the members of generation 0 have all died off) is identical to the selfish economies we have looked at already. For this reason, we concentrate, here, on what happens only at time 1.

Members of generation 1 have a utility function of the usual sort:

$$u_1^h(c_1^h(1), c_1^h(2)),$$

where only their own consumptions determine their utility. The utility functions for members of generation 0 are of the form

$$u_0^h[c_0^h(1), u_1^h(c_1^h(1), c_1^h(2))],$$

so the utility of member h of generation 0 at time 1 depends on the consumption of that individual when old and on the utility that member h of generation 1 achieves. Notice that person h of generation 0 is not imposing his or her own values on the consumption of person h of generation 1. The utility of person h of generation 0 depends on the utility of person h of generation 1 as person h of generation 1 sees it. These parents want to make their children happy, but they are not imposing their view of what is best on their children. The parents are happier if their children are happier, whatever it is that makes these children happier.

To simplify the analysis, assume that from time 2 and onward, there are neither taxes nor transfers. Because all members of the same generation are identical, the equilibrium for time $t \geq 2$ is the competitive equilibrium with no borrowing or lending and with consumption in each period equal to the endowment in that period. This assumption is not essential, and we could allow other tax-transfer schemes. The assumption merely simplifies the analysis.

We begin by writing the budget constraints of the old at time 1 (members of generation 0). The old can give bequests to their children and can pay taxes or receive transfers from the government. The budget constraint for member h of generation 0 is

$$c_0^h(1) = \omega_0^h(1) - b^h(0) - t_0^h(1),$$

where the only new symbol, $b^h(0)$, is the bequest of member h of generation 0 to member h of generation 1 and is constrained to be greater or equal to 0. The old cannot demand gifts from the young. Consumption of the old at time t is equal to their endowment minus their bequest minus any taxes they might pay. Transfers are negative taxes and would add to the amount of goods available to be consumed or given in bequests.

The young at time 1 can receive bequests from the old. By assumption, they will not give any bequests to the next generation, nor will they pay any taxes or receive any transfers when they are old. They may pay taxes or receive transfers when young. Because all are identical and, in equilibrium, will receive identical bequests, there will be no borrowing or lending in equilibrium among members of generation 1. Therefore, their equilibrium consumption will satisfy

$$c_1^h(1) = \omega_1^h(1) + b^h(0) - t_1^h(1)$$

when young and

$$c_1^h(2) = \omega_1^h(2)$$

when old. Notice that members of generation 1 consume their endowment, and only their endowment, when old. The bequest that they receive contributes only to their consumption when young.

The government is required to balance its budget each period. That constraint means that

$$\sum_{h=1}^{N(0)} t_0^h(1) + \sum_{h=1}^{N(1)} t_1^h(1) = 0.$$

Because all members of each generation pay the same tax or receive the same transfer, it follows that

$$t_0^h(1) = -t_1^h(1).$$

Solving the utility maximization problem for the old at time t (generation 0) is now an interesting problem. In earlier chapters, these individuals only wanted higher consumption. The more they consumed at time 1, the better off they were. Now that their utility depends on the consumption of some young person as well as their own consumption, they have choices to make about the amount of bequest, $b^h(0)$.

The utility function of the old is

$$u_0^h[c_0^h(1), u_1^h(c_1^h(1), c_1^h(2))].$$

An equilibrium condition is that members of generation 1 when old can only consume their endowment. Incorporating this into the utility function of members of generation 0 gives

$$u_0^h[c_0^h(1), u_1^h(c_1^h(1), \omega_1^h(2))]. \tag{4.1}$$

Thus, the members of generation 0 at time 1 control, at most, only their own consumption at time 1 and the consumption of their "child" at time 1. Because these are the only two variables that can be affected, we should be able to analyze the choice problem for a member of generation 0 in the $[c_0^h(1), c_1^h(1)]$ plane.

The budget constraint for the old and the equilibrium conditions on the results of bequests can be used to find constraints on the relevant consumptions and to draw those constraints in the $[c_0^h(1), c_1^h(1)]$ plane. Consumption at time 1 of a member of generation 0 is determined by the taxes they pay and bequests they choose to give. This constraint is

$$c_0^h(1) = \omega_0^h(1) - t_0^h(1) - b^h(0), \tag{4.2}$$

where bequests, $b^h(0)$, are the only decision variable. Consumption at time 1 by members of generation 1 is determined by the taxes they pay and by the bequests they receive. This equilibrium condition is

$$c_1^h(1) = \omega_1^h(1) - t_1^h(1) + b^h(0). \tag{4.3}$$

Each member h of generation 0 chooses a bequest, $b^h(0)$, that maximizes the utility function given in Equation (4.1) subject to the budget constraints of Equations (4.2) and (4.3). Because, in this economy, all members of every generation are identical and have no assets, the consumption allocation determined by the choice of a bequest is the equilibrium allocation. We now show how this allocation is determined, first graphically and then analytically. The analytical solution is used to find the bequest given in an example economy.

Figure 4.1 shows the consumption pairs at time 1 of member h of generation 0 and member h of generation 1 implied by different nonnegative bequests, $b^h(0)$. Equations (4.2) and (4.3) show that a bequest of 1 unit of the time 1 good results in a reduction of 1 unit of consumption by member h of generation 0 and an increase of 1 unit of consumption by member h of generation 1. The 45-degree line extending northwest from the time 1 after-tax endowment point,

$$[\omega_0^h(1) - t_0^h(1), \omega_1^h(1) - t_1^h(1)],$$

describes the consumption pairs that can be chosen by member h of generation 0 by choosing the size of a (nonnegative) bequest. We can think of this line as the budget line that member h of generation 0 faces

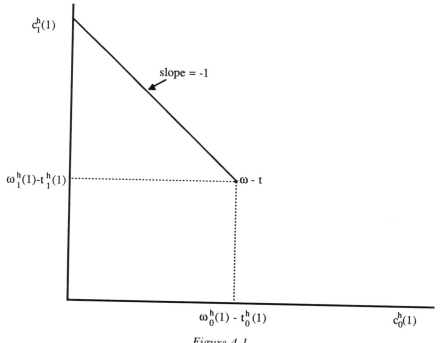

Figure 4.1

in determining how large a bequest to make. Recall that bequests are restricted to be nonnegative, so no points to the right of the after-tax endowment point can be reached.

The utility function for members of generation 0 at time 1 can be used to find indifference curves in the $[c_0^h(1), c_1^h(1)]$ plane. Once the equilibrium condition on consumption of the members of generation 1 at time 2 has been incorporated into the utility function, it is

$$u_0^h[c_0^h(1), u_1^h(c_1^h(1), \omega_1^h(2))].$$

Because $\omega_1^h(2)$ is given exogenously, utility for individual h depends on his or her choices of $c_0^h(1)$ and $c_1^h(1)$. Indifference curves are found by determining the sets of consumption pairs for which the above utility function has a constant value. Figure 4.2 shows an example set of indifference curves for a utility function of an old person at time 1.

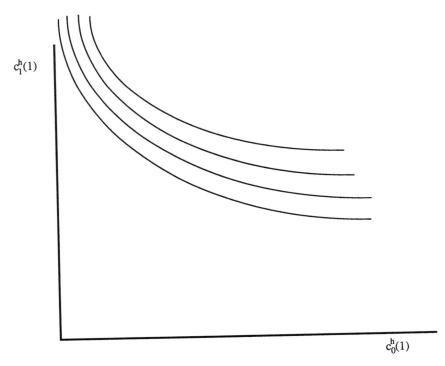

$c_1^h(1)$

$c_0^h(1)$

Figure 4.2

The utility-maximizing consumption point is found at the point on the Figure 4.1 budget line that achieves the highest indifference curve. Depending on the shape of the indifference curve set and the budget line, there may be an internal solution to the utility maximization problem or there may be a corner solution. Figure 4.3 illustrates a case where the utility-maximizing consumption point is internal. It occurs at a point of tangency between the budget line and an indifference curve at point c.

Figure 4.4 illustrates a case where the utility-maximizing consumption point is at a corner. The preference set is such that the preferred consumption point is at the lower end of the budget line. Individual h of generation 0 would prefer to consume at a consumption pair that would require receiving a transfer from a member of generation 1 and consuming at a point to the right of the endowment point. Such a transfer

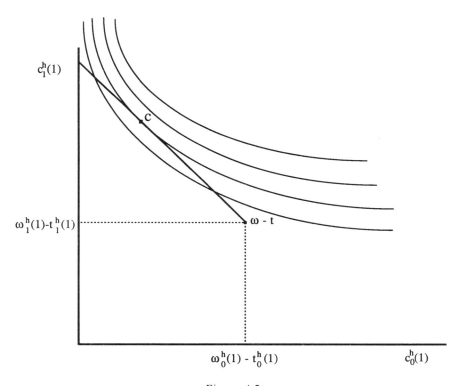

Figure 4.3

would entail a negative bequest, which we have specifically ruled out. The right-most point on the budget line is the after-tax endowment point, and this is where individual h will choose to consume. No bequest will occur with this corner solution.

In an economy such as the one illustrated in Figure 4.3, a small enough change in taxes and transfers will not change the equilibrium consumption allocation. The equilibrium illustrated in that figure is one in which bequests are being given under the initial tax-transfer scheme. As mentioned above, the tax-transfer scheme in an economy with identical individuals and with symmetric taxes and transfers means that

$$t_0^h(1) = -t_1^h(1).$$

Therefore, a small change in the tax-transfer scheme means that the end point of the budget line of Figure 4.1 moves slightly up the

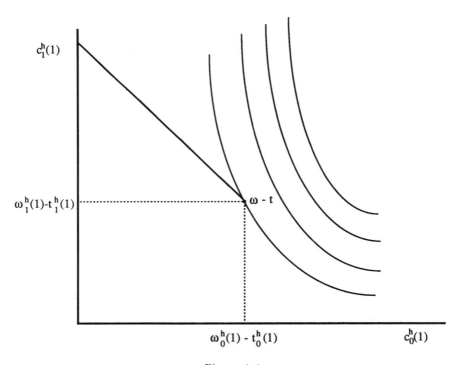

Figure 4.4

45-degree line to the left. If the change in taxes and transfer is small enough so that the after-tax endowment point is still below the pre-ferred consumption point, then the bequest will be adjusted to exactly compensate for the change in taxes and transfers. For this result to hold, there must be positive bequests both before and after the change in taxes and transfers.[1]

Figures 4.1 through 4.4 illustrate the general method of finding a solution for this situation. This equilibrium can be found directly by solving the maximization problem of member h of generation 0 at time 1. Substituting the budget constraints (Equations 4.2 and 4.3) and the equilibrium condition that $c_1^h(2) = \omega_1^h(2)$ into the utility function, we have

$$u_0^h[\omega_0^h(1) - b^h(0) + t_1^h(1), u_1^h(\omega_1^h(1) + b^h(0) - t_1^h(1), \omega_1^h(2))]. \quad (4.4)$$

This equation has one unknown: the bequests, $b^h(0)$. Given the endow-ments of the old and the young, and the taxes that the government chooses to impose, the old choose a bequest, $b^h(0)$, the only choice vari-able, to maximize their own utility. Notice that the balanced budget aspect of the taxes is already in the utility function, because we replace the transfer going to the old by the negative of the taxes that are being paid by the young. Recall that we have restricted the bequests $b^h(0)$ to be greater than or equal to 0. If a general solution to this maximization problem results in a negative bequest being the preferred one, then the restriction that bequests be nonnegative implies that the bequest must be 0 and the equilibrium is the corner solution where consumption equals the after-tax endowment.

To find the bequest, take the derivative of the utility function (4.4) with respect to $b^h(0)$ and set it equal to 0. This manipulation gives

$$\frac{-\partial u_0^h}{\partial c_0^h(1)} + \left(\frac{\partial u_0^h}{\partial u_1^h}\right)\left(\frac{\partial u_1^h}{\partial c_1^h(1)}\right) = 0. \qquad (4.5)$$

1. It is possible that this result holds if bequests in one of the tax-transfer schemes is 0. If the preferred consumption point is at the after-tax endowment point and the mar-ginal rate of substitution is 1, then a change in the tax-transfer scheme that moves the after-tax endowment point to the right will result in the same consumption point being chosen and bequests being made to completely compensate for the change in taxes and transfers.

From Equation (4.4), we can see that the utility function (and therefore its derivative) is a function of the bequest and of the bequest alone. We can solve this equation for $b^h(0)$. The resulting $b^h(0)$ is the general solution for the utility-maximizing bequest if it is not negative. If the solution is negative, it indicates that the tangency occurs at a point to the southeast of the after-tax endowment point along a line with slope -1. Given the shape of the indifference curves, a negative solution implies that the maximum, subject to the bequest being nonnegative, is at $b^h(0) = 0$, the after-tax endowment point.

Now let us determine the equilibrium bequest for an example economy. We assume that the young at time $t = 1$ have utility functions

$$u_1^h = c_1^h(1)c_1^h(2),$$

and endowments of $[2, 1]$.

The old at time $t = 1$ have a utility function of

$$u_0^h = \ln(c_0^h(1)) + \delta u_1^h,$$

where $\ln(\cdot)$ is the natural logarithm and δ is a positive constant. The time 1 endowment of the old is 1. From Equation (4.5) we find that the utility-maximizing choice for individual h of generation 0 occurs when $-1/c_0^h(1) + \delta \omega_1^h(2) = 0$, because, for this example economy,

$$\frac{\partial u_0^h}{\partial c_0^h(1)} = \frac{1}{c_0^h(1)},$$

$$\frac{\partial u_0^h}{\partial u_1^h} = \delta,$$

and $$\frac{\partial u_1^h}{\partial c_1^h(1)} = \omega_1^h(2).$$

Substituting the budget constraint for $c_0^h(1)$, we get

$$\omega_0^h(1) - b^h(0) + t_1^h(1) = \frac{1}{\delta \omega_1^h(2)},$$

or $$b^h(0) = \omega_0^h(1) + t_1^h(1) - \frac{1}{\delta \omega_1^h(2)}. \tag{4.6}$$

Assume that for individual h of this example economy, the tax-transfer scheme is $[t_1^h(1), -t_1^h(1)] = [\frac{1}{2}, -\frac{1}{2}]$. Then Equation (4.6) is

$$b^h(0) = 1 + \frac{1}{2} - \frac{1}{\delta},$$

and for $\delta = 1.2$, $1/\delta = \frac{5}{6}$ and the bequest equals $\frac{2}{3}$.

EXERCISE 4.1   In the above example, if there were neither taxes nor transfers, what would the size of the bequests be? What would the size of the bequest be if δ were to equal 0.8?

Notice that, when the consumption point is not at the end of the budget line, small changes in taxes and transfers will not cause changes in the consumption points of the young or the old. Suppose that the government chooses to tax the young more and, therefore, to give more to the old. This choice shows up in Figure 4.3 as an extension of the budget line to the right beyond the point of tangency of the indifference curve set and the budget line (point c). Because the point of tangency between the budget line and the indifference curve set is unaffected by this change, the preferred consumption point does not change. The bequests from the old to the young increase by exactly the same amount that the taxes increased. In this case, the bequests completely neutralize the effects of the changes in taxes.

EXERCISE 4.2   Suppose that the consumption point is exactly at the right-most point of the budget line. Suppose that taxes paid by the young increase. What happens to the preferred consumption point? Suppose that the taxes paid by the young decrease. What happens to the preferred consumption point?

EXERCISE 4.3   Suppose that the young at time 1 care about the utility of the old at that date but that the old do not care about the utility of the young. How would you model this situation?

Diversity within Generations

In this section we describe equilibria of the Class 2 economies we described at the beginning of this chapter. In these economies we drop the assumption that all individuals are identical. The group of interest consists of the members of generation 1, who, if they are different, can borrow and lend to one another. This new assumption changes the model in one very important way. Up to now, the consumption when old of the members of generation 1 has been constant. There has been no way for these individuals, once they are old, to consume anything other than their endowment. Therefore, changes in consumption when young could not have effects on consumption when old.

Allowing diversity within each generation causes bequests to affect consumption, when old as well as when young, of those who receive the bequests. Private borrowing and lending occurs because members of generation 1 are different and want to trade with one another. Changes in bequests change wealth for members of generation 1 when they are young and, through the effects on borrowing and lending, change consumption when young and when old. This economy is more complicated than the Class 1 economy, but we can still solve for equilibrium bequests. In this section we set taxes and transfers to 0. Taxes and transfers could be put into the model in exactly the same way as in the preceding section. We leave them out here, because we want to concentrate on the effects of private borrowing and lending.

There are N members of generation 0 and of generation 1. Each member h of generation 0 cares about the welfare of member h of generation 1 (his or her child). Members of generations $t \geq 2$ are selfish and only care about their own consumption. As above, the equilibrium for generations $t \geq 2$ is the same as it was in the comparable economy with everyone selfish, so we concentrate on generations 0 and 1.

The endowment that matters to member h of generation 1 is the one that they have after the bequest has been granted to them by their "parent" from generation 0. In other words, the relevant budget constraints for person h of generation 1 are

$$c_1^h(1) = \omega_1^h(1) + b^h(0) - \ell^h(1),$$

and $\quad c_1^h(2) = \omega_1^h(2) + r(1)\ell^h(1),$

where $b^h(0)$ is the bequest that person h receives and $\ell^h(1)$ is the amount of loans that this individual wishes to make. We combine these two budget constraints and find that the single lifetime budget constraint for a member of generation 1 is

$$c_1^h(1) + \frac{c_1^h(2)}{r(1)} = [\omega_1^h(1) + b^h(0)] + \frac{\omega_1^h(2)}{r(1)}. \tag{4.7}$$

This expression is exactly the lifetime budget constraint we found in Chapters 2 and 3, except that endowment when young is now the after-bequest endowment. Because the bequest is viewed as exogenous by individual h of generation 1, after-bequest endowment in this case is treated exactly the same as the endowment was treated in the earlier chapters. Maximization of utility with respect to this lifetime budget constraint can be expressed by the demand function for consumption when young,

$$c_1^h(1) = \chi_1^h(r(1), \omega_1^h(1) + b^h(0), \omega_1^h(2)),$$

or by the savings function

$$s_1^h(r(1), \omega_1^h(1) + b^h(0), \omega_1^h(2))$$
$$= \omega_1^h(1) - \chi_1^h(r(1), \omega_1^h(1) + b^h(0), \omega_1^h(2)).$$

To find an equilibrium, we require that all individuals maximize their utility and that all markets clear. The only market is for private borrowing and lending, and it clears when aggregate savings equal 0. We have been expressing this market clearing condition as

$$S_1(r(1)) = \sum_{h=1}^{N(1)} s_1^h(r(1), \omega_1^h(1) + b^h(0), \omega_1^h(2)) = 0.$$

Let $\mathbf{b}(0)$ be the vector of bequests by generation 0 to generation 1. This vector of bequests is

$$\mathbf{b}(0) = \{b^1(0), b^2(0), b^3(0), \ldots, b^{N(1)}(0)\};$$

it describes the amount of bequests that each individual h of generation 0 is giving to each individual h of generation 1. This vector will affect the aggregate savings function, $S_1(r(1))$, because element $b^h(0)$ affects the after-bequest endowment of individual h of generation 1. Once the vector $\mathbf{b}(0)$ is given, the market clearing condition can be solved for the one unknown, $r(1)$. Because changes in bequests change the perceived endowment and can change the amount of borrowing and lending that individuals wish to make, we can think of a function $\rho(\cdot)$ that describes the equilibrium gross interest rate for the economy as a function of the vector of bequests, $\mathbf{b}(0)$. We express this function as

$$r(1) = \rho(\mathbf{b}(0)).$$

We wish to find this $\rho(\mathbf{b}(0))$ function for an example economy. Consider an economy where all members of generation 1 have the Cobb-Douglas utility function,

$$u_1^h = c_1^h(1)c_1^h(2).$$

Given the lifetime budget constraint of Equation (4.7), this utility function results in a savings function of

$$s_1^h(1) = \frac{\omega_1^h(1) + b^h(0)}{2} - \frac{\omega_1^h(2)}{2r(1)}.$$

Let $N(t) = 4$, $t \geq 0$. The odd-named individuals ($h = $ odd) have an endowment of $[2, 1]$ and the even-named individuals ($h = $ even) have an endowment of $[1, 1]$. Suppose that we also limit the bequests so that the odd-named old give bequests of b^{odd} and the even-named old give bequests of b^{even}. The vector of bequests, $\mathbf{b}(0)$, is

$$\mathbf{b}(0) = \{b^{odd}, b^{even}, b^{odd}, b^{even}\}.$$

The savings functions of the odd are

$$s_1^{odd}(1) = \frac{2 + b^{odd}}{2} - \frac{1}{2r(1)};$$

and the savings functions of the even are

$$s_1^{even}(1) = \frac{1 + b^{even}}{2} - \frac{1}{2r(1)}.$$

The market clearing condition for this example economy, in which there are two even-named individuals and two odd-named individuals, is that the aggregate savings of generation 1 equal 0, or that

$$2\left[\frac{2 + b^{\text{odd}}}{2} - \frac{1}{2r(1)}\right] + 2\left[\frac{1 + b^{\text{even}}}{2} - \frac{1}{2r(1)}\right] = 0,$$

which, when solved for $r(1)$, gives

$$r(1) = \frac{2}{3 + b^{\text{odd}} + b^{\text{even}}}. \tag{4.8}$$

It should be clear from the above equation that the interest rate depends on the size of the bequests made to different members of generation 1.

We have done only about half the work required to find the equilibrium for this economy with diversity. Because the old at time 1 are interested in the utility of the young, and the utility of the young depends on the interest rate that they face, the bequest that each old person will make depends on the interest rate that exists at time 1. We showed above that the interest rate depends on the amount of the bequests. Now we need to determine the amount of bequests that each old person will make as a function of the interest rate. We assume that the old take the interest rates as given and do not choose bequests in order to influence the interest rate (we are assuming competition).

We have been assuming that the utility functions of the old depend on their own consumption and the consumption of some particular young person. The utility of the young at time t depends on the size of the bequest that they receive, their endowments, and the interest rate, which determines the amount of private borrowing and lending they make. We need the utility of member h of generation 1 in order to find the utility of member h of generation 0. For the utility function of members of our example economy, we have already written out utility as a function of the market gross interest rate. In general, this function of utility would be

$$U_1^h(r(1), b^h(0))$$

$$= u_1^h[\omega_1^h(1) + b^h(0) - s_1^h(r(1)), \omega_1^h(2) + r(1)s_1^h(r(1))],$$

where we have replaced the consumption when young and when old by the budget constraints with savings included. The functional notation,

$U(\cdot, \cdot)$, denotes the utility of a young person as a function of the interest rate and the bequest.

Each member of generation 0 is choosing a utility-maximizing bequest. The utility function that is maximized is the same as the one in the preceding section; that is,

$$u_0^h[c_0^h(1), u_1^h(c_1^h(1), c_1^h(2))].$$

But we want to substitute into the above function the utility of the young and the budget constraint for the old. This substitution gives

$$u_0^h[\omega_0^h(1) - b^h(0), U_1^h(r(1), b^h(0))].$$

We find the bequest for each member h of generation 0 by maximizing the above utility function with respect to $b^h(0)$. Note that these choices of bequests are functions of the gross interest rate, $r(1)$. For an economy with N members of each generation, there are N functions, one for each member of generation 0 that gives the bequest that this person will make at each gross interest rate. Let the bequest function for member h of generation 0 be denoted

$$b^h(0) = \mathscr{b}^h(r(1)).$$

The vector comprising these bequests for all members of generation 0 is

$$\mathscr{B}(r(1)) = [\mathscr{b}^1(r(1)), \mathscr{b}^2(r(1)), \ldots, \mathscr{b}^{N(1)}(r(1))].$$

For the case where the utility of the young is the product of the consumptions in the two periods of their life, the utility of person h of generation 1 as a function of the gross interest rate is

$$U_1^h(r(1), b^h(0)) = [\omega_1^h(1) + b^h(0) - s_1^h(r(1))][\omega_1^h(2) + r(1)s_1^h(r(1))].$$

The utility function for old person h at time $t = 1$ is (for the example we have been using)

$$u_0^h = \log(c_0^h(1)) + \delta U_1^h(r(1), b^h(0)).$$

Writing that utility function so that it is clear that the bequest, $b^h(0)$, is the decision variable, we get

$$u_0^h(b^h(0)) = \log(\omega_0^h(1) - b^h(0)) + \delta U_1^h(r(1), b^h(0)),$$

or $\quad u_0^h(b^h(0)) = \log(\omega_0^h(1) - b^h(0))$

$$+ \delta[\omega_1^h(1) + b^h(0) - s_1^h(r(1))][\omega_1^h(2) + r(1)s_1^h(r(1))].$$

Old person h maximizes this utility function with respect to the bequest, $b^h(0)$. We take the derivative of the utility function with respect to bequests and get

$$\frac{\partial u_0^h}{\partial b^h(0)} = \frac{-1}{\omega_0^h(1) - b^h(0)}$$

$$+ \delta\left[1 - \frac{\partial s_1^h(r(1))}{\partial b^h(0)}\right][\omega_1^h(2) + r(1)s_1^h(r(1))]$$

$$+ \frac{\delta r(1)\partial s_1^h(r(1))}{\partial b^h(0)}[\omega_1^h(1) + b^h(0) - s_1^h(r(1))]$$

$$= 0.$$

The savings function, $s_1^h(r(1))$, for members of generation 1 of our example economy, equals

$$s_1^h(r(1)) = \frac{\omega_1^h(1) + b^h(0)}{2} - \frac{\omega_1^h(2)}{2r(1)}.$$

The partial derivative of $s_1^h(r(1))$ with respect to bequests, $b^h(0)$, is

$$\frac{\partial s_1^h(r(1))}{\partial b^h(0)} = \frac{1}{2}.$$

Substituting this expression into the first-order condition (the equation above where the derivative of utility is set equal to 0), we get the quadratic equation

$$0 = r(1)[b^h(0)]^2 - \{r(1)[\omega_0^h(1) - \omega_1^h(1)] - \omega_1^h(2)\}b^h(0)$$

$$+ \frac{2}{\delta} - \omega_0^h(1)[\omega_1^h(2) + r(1)\omega_1^h(1)].$$

The solution to this quadratic equation is

$$b^h(0) = \Big(\{ r(1)[\omega_0^h(1) - \omega_1^h(1)] - \omega_1^h(2) \}$$

$$\pm \Big[\{ r(1)[\omega_0^h(1) - \omega_1^h(1)] - \omega_1^h(2) \}^2$$

$$- 4r(1) \Big\{ \frac{2}{\delta} - \omega_0^h(1)[\omega_1^h(2) + r(1)\omega_1^h(1)] \Big\} \Big]^{1/2} \Big) (2r(1))^{-1}.$$

The above equation is a bit ugly, but the main point is that the bequest is a (fairly simple) function of the endowments, of δ, and, what is most interesting, of the interest rate, $r(1)$. Notice that at least one of the solutions of the quadratic equation will be negative and cannot be an equilibrium, because we have restricted bequests to be positive. It is possible that both the solutions to the quadratic equation are negative; in that case, we have a corner solution, and no bequests are made.

We now consider our example economy where the endowments of members of generation 0 are 1, of the odd-named individuals (h = odd) are [2, 1], and of the even-named individuals (h = even) are [1, 1]. Let $\delta = 1.2$. In that case,

$$b^{\mathrm{odd}}(0)$$

$$= \{ -(1 + r(1)) \pm [1 - (2/3)r(1) + 9r(1)]^{1/2} \}(2r(1))^{-1}, \qquad (4.9)$$

and $\quad b^{\mathrm{even}}(0) = \{ -1 \pm [1 - (8/3)r(1) + 4r(1)]^{1/2} \}(2r(1))^{-1}. \qquad (4.10)$

In Figure 4.5, we show the graphs of the above expressions of $b^{\mathrm{odd}}(0)$ and $b^{\mathrm{even}}(0)$ as functions of the gross interest rate, $r(1)$. The solid line includes in it the restriction that $b^h(0)$ cannot be less than 0. The dashed lines below 0 are the solutions to Equations (4.9) and (4.10) that are outside of that limit and are dropped. The curves that are used in finding the equilibrium are the solid ones that have the nonnegativity constraint built in to them.

There are two interesting, and slightly unusual, features of these curves. One is that the curves are upward sloping. This slope means that at higher interest rates the parents give more to the children than at lower interest rates. (These are the interest rates that the children

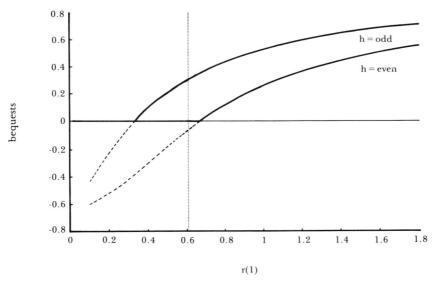

Figure 4.5

face, because the parents will be dead when it is time to collect at that rate.) Another is that at each gross interest rate, the bequest to the young people with the larger endowments when young (the odd) is greater than the bequest to the young people with the smaller endowment (the even). The parents in both cases have the same amount of endowment, and it might seem counterintuitive that the parents of the richer children give them more. It is the particular structure of the utility function of the parents that give rise to both of these results. At both higher interest rates and with larger endowment when young, a member of generation 1 will plan to consume more when old. Because the utility functions of members of generation 1 are

$$u_1^h(c_1^h(1), c_1^h(2)) = c_1^h(1)c_1^h(2),$$

an increase in consumption when old increases the marginal utility of each additional amount of consumption when young. At higher consumptions in the second period of life, a small increase in consumption when young has a larger impact on total utility than at lower second-period consumptions. Because the old are weighting their own consumption against the utility gained from consumption of their children, increased marginal utility from a transfer for the young means that the old will be willing to give up a little of their own consumption to gain utility through the increased utility of their children.

All the information required for finding an equilibrium for this economy is contained in Equations (4.8), (4.9), and (4.10). These equations are

$$r(1) = 2[3 + b^{\text{odd}}(0) + b^{\text{even}}(0)]^{-1}, \tag{4.8}$$

$$b^{\text{odd}}(0)$$
$$= \{-(1 + r(1)) + [1 - (\tfrac{2}{3})r(1) + 9r(1)]^{1/2}\}(2r(1))^{-1}, \tag{4.9}$$

and $$b^{\text{even}}(0) = \{-1 + [1 - (\tfrac{8}{3})r(1) + 4r(1)]^{1/2}\}(2r(1))^{-1}. \tag{4.10}$$

In a more general setting with N members of generations 0 and 1, we would have $N + 1$ equations. The first, like Equation (4.8), gives the gross interest rate as a function of the entire vector of bequests, $\mathbf{b}(0)$, which comprises the bequests of each of the N members of generation 1. The other N equations, the members of vector $\beta(r(1))$, give the size of the bequest of each member h (for h equal to 1 to N) of generation 0 as a function of the gross interest rate. We set $\mathbf{b}(0)$ of the equation $r(1) = \rho(\mathbf{b}(0))$ equal to $\beta(r(1))$ and get the equation $r(1) = \rho[\beta(r(1))]$. To find the equilibrium gross interest rate, we solve for the one unknown in this equation, $r(1)$, and then use it to find the equilibrium bequests from the vector $\beta(r(1))$.

The example economy we are using has four members of each generation; they come in only two types, so our model can be expressed in terms of the behavior of each of the two *types* of young. Equation (4.8) takes into account the fact that there are four individuals. To find the equilibrium, we solve the three equations given above for the three unknowns: $r(1)$, b^{odd}, and b^{even}. One way to solve this system is to find the bequests at each of the gross interest rates (as we did in Figure 4.5). Then, we use the vector of bequests at each gross interest rate in Equation (4.8) to find the gross interest rate that would occur from that vector of bequests. Notice that at each gross interest rate we find the vector of bequests that the old would make if that were the gross interest rate. We then use that vector of bequests to find the gross interest rate that would clear the market for private borrowing and lending.

Figure 4.6 shows the gross interest rate to gross interest rate curve (heavy line) that we described in the preceding paragraph. The two kinks in the curve occur at the points where the nonnegativity constraints kick in on the bequests function. The 45-degree line crosses the interest rate to interest rate curve at the one (in this case) gross interest rate for which the resulting bequests clear the private borrowing and lending market at the same gross interest rate. This *fixed point* (as we call such points that return the same value) is the equilibrium interest rate for which we have been searching. For our example economy, the fixed point (the equilibrium interest rate) occurs at $r(1) = 0.605$.

To find the amount of bequests that each member of generation 0 gives to his or her child, we must turn back to Figure 4.5. The bequest for the odd is found where a vertical line at $r(1) = 0.605$ crosses the odd-named person's bequest curve. In a similar fashion, the bequest for the even-named person is found where that same line crosses the even-named person's bequest curve. Notice that the nonnegativity constraint is in effect for the even-named person, so, in this equilibrium, no bequests are given from the even-named old to their children.

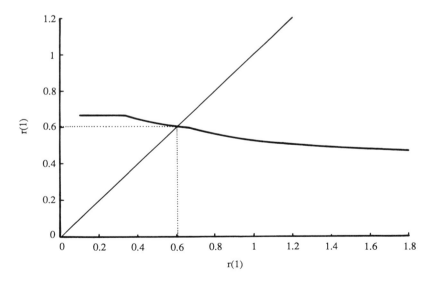

Figure 4.6

EXERCISE 4.4   Find the function for bequests as a function of the gross interest rates for an economy where the young have a utility function of

$$u_1^h = c_1^h(1)c_1^h(2),$$

and the old have a utility function of

$$u_0^h = \ln(c_0^h(1)) + \ln(u_1^h).$$

Endowments are [2, 1] for the odd-named young, [1, 1] for the even-named young, and 2 for the old.

EXERCISE 4.5   Find the equilibrium gross interest rate for the Exercise 4.4 economy.

All Generations Care about Their Children

In the Class 3 economies we assume that there is no diversity, so all members of all generations have the same preferences and utility functions. We also assume that member h of generation t cares about member h of generation $t + 1$, for all $t \geq 0$. The assumption that every generation cares about its young makes the world much more complicated because all generations become connected. If the utility of person h of generation 10, for example, depends on the utility of person h of generation 11, then so does the utility of person h of generation 9, for whom person h of generation 11 is a grandchild. This sequence of relations means that there exists a member h of generation 0 who needs to take into account the utility of person h of generation 11 in determining the amount of bequests to give to person h of generation 1. In fact, person h of generation 0 needs to take into account the utility of all the persons h of all generations. We can show this explicitly.

The utility of person h of generation 0 depends on his or her own consumption when old and on the utility of person h of generation 1. We write that as

$$u_0^h = u_0^h(c_0^h(1), u_1^h).$$

But the utility of person h of generation 1 depends on consumption when young and when old and on the utility of member h of generation 2. The utility function of person h of generation 1 is written as

$$u_1^h = u_1^h(c_1^h(1),\ c_1^h(2),\ u_2^h), \tag{4.11}$$

so the utility function of person h of generation 0 must now be written as

$$u_0^h = u_0^h[c_0^h(1),\ u_1^h(c_1^h(1),\ c_1^h(2),\ u_2^h)].$$

The utility of person h of generation 2 depends on his or her own consumption when young and when old and on the utility of person h of generation 3. We write that utility function in the same form as Equation (4.11) but with all the subscripts increased by one. Substituting this second utility function into the equation for the utility of person h of generation 0, we get

$$u_0^h = u_0^h[c_0^h(1),\ u_1^h[c_1^h(1),\ c_1^h(2),\ u_2^h(c_2^h(2),\ c_2^h(3),\ u_3^h)]].$$

We keep repeating this procedure, and the utility function of person h of generation 0 becomes a function of the consumption of the time 1 good that this person gets and of the consumptions of all future individuals named h. If we assume that all individuals care about their children, then they also care about all the future generations of their family.

To make this formulation somewhat more manageable, we are going to assume that the utility function of person h of generation t, when young, takes the form

$$u_t^h = \sum_{i=0}^{\infty} \delta^i u(c_{t+i}^h(t+i),\ c_{t+i}^h(t+i+1)), \tag{4.12}$$

where $0 < \delta < 1$. The *subutility function*, $u(\cdot, \cdot)$, is the same for all members h of all generations and depends only on the consumption of that individual during life. The consumptions of future generations enter the utility function through the discounted (by δ) subutilities of their own consumption.

Because there is no diversity in generations, there is no private borrowing and lending in equilibrium. Therefore, consumptions depend on endowments and bequests in a very simple way that is only a slight generalization of Class 1 economies. Changing our notation a bit, we define $b^h(t)$ as the bequest *received* at time t by member h of generation t (received from member h of generation $t-1$). Let $t^h(t)$ be the tax levied on person h of generation t at time t. Because the government's budget must balance each period and all individuals are identical, the tax on member h of generation t at time t is given as a transfer at time t to member h of generation $t-1$.

It follows that equilibrium consumption of individuals alive at time t is given by

$$c_t^h(t) = \omega_t^h(t) + b^h(t) - t^h(t), \tag{4.13}$$

for the young, and

$$c_{t-1}^h(t) = \omega_{t-1}^h(t) - b^h(t) + t^h(t), \tag{4.14}$$

for the old. We impose, as before, the restriction that bequests can only go from the old to the young, so $b^h(t) \geq 0$, for all t. The government chooses the taxes and transfers, $t^h(t)$, and they are taken as exogenous by all members of all generations. Given these restrictions, the budget constraint that an old person at time t faces is the same as the one in a Class 1 economy and is illustrated in Figure 4.1.

We would like to be able to draw indifference curve sets on the same axes as the budget constraint to find the equilibrium just as we did in the Class 1 economies. Even with the specification of the utility function in Equation (4.12), the preferences in this plane can be quite complicated, because, in general, they depend on both the consumption of the current old when they were young, $c_{t-1}^h(t-1)$, and on the consumption of the current young once they become old, $c_t^h(t+1)$.

There is, however, a class of functions, $u(\cdot, \cdot)$ for which these complications do not arise. If $u(\cdot, \cdot)$ is *additively separable*, it is of the form

$$u(c_t^h(t), c_t^h(t+1)) = f(c_t^h(t)) + g(c_t^h(t+1)),$$

where, as indicated, $f(\cdot)$ and $g(\cdot)$ are each functions of one variable, consumption when young and consumption when old, respectively. Given the above additively separable subutility functions, the utility function of person h of generation t is

$$u_t^h = \sum_{i=0}^{\infty} \delta^i[f(c_{t+i}^h(t + i)) + g(c_{t+i}^h(t + i + 1))]. \tag{4.15}$$

Equation (4.15) can be rewritten to emphasize the consumption that is taking place at each date. That is, the utility function of person h of generation t can be written as

$$u_t^h = f(c_t^h(t)) + [g(c_t^h(t + 1)) + \delta f(c_{t+1}^h(t + 1))]$$

$$+ \sum_{i=2}^{\infty} \delta^{i-1}[g(c_{t+i-1}^h(t + i)) + \delta f(c_{t+i}^h(t + i))]. \tag{4.16}$$

The first term on the right-hand side of this equation is the utility that comes from consumption at date t. The second term, the one in the square brackets, is the utility that comes from consumption of person h and child at date $t + 1$. The term on the next line contains the components of the utility function that occur in periods $t + 2$ or later. We wish to argue that the time $t + 1$ bequest is made by considering only the middle term of the above expression, namely,

$$g(c_t^h(t + 1)) + \delta f(c_{t+1}^h(t + 1)). \tag{4.17}$$

At the date that individual h of generation t is making a bequest, the first term of the right-hand side of Equation (4.16) is already determined. In addition, because it enters the utility function additively, its magnitude does not affect the consumption from time $t + 1$ on that maximize Equation (4.16). If one sequence of consumptions for date $t + 1$ on yields a higher value for utility than another sequence for some $c_t^h(t)$, then that sequence yields a higher utility for any other $c_t^h(t)$. Because this outcome is true at every date, it means that individuals acting at date $t + 2$ and later will make bequest choices that do not depend on their consumption when young. Therefore, any bequest at date $t + 1$ will have no effect on bequest choices at dates $t + 2$ or later. Neither does an individual making a bequest at date $t + 1$ need to make predictions about future consumptions, because those enter into the utility function additively. The third term of Equation (4.16), the term that includes the summation sign, does not matter in the time $t + 1$

bequest decision. Any bequest choice that gives a higher utility for some value of the third term of Equation (4.16) will give a higher utility for any other value of the third term.

The preceding discussion means that a bequest at time $t + 1$ that maximizes Equation (4.17) is also a bequest at time $t + 1$ that maximizes Equation (4.16) and therefore the utility function of Equation (4.15). Following identical logic, we find that the optimal bequest at time t by maximizing

$$g(c_{t-1}^h(t)) + \delta f(c_t^h(t)), \tag{4.18}$$

subject to the budget constraints given in Equations (4.13) and (4.14).

With identical individuals all of whom have an additive utility function, we can find the optimal bequest in each period by the same kind of graphical analysis we did for the Class 1 cases. The budget constraints of Equations (4.13) and (4.14) result in a time t budget line identical to the one in Figure 4.1. The time t indifference curves come from Equation (4.18). Graphically, we solve each period's equilibrium exactly the same way we solved the time 1 equilibrium in the Class 1 case—by finding the preferred nonnegative bequest at that date.

We solve the entire equilibrium by advancing from period to period and solving for the optimal nonnegative bequest. It does not matter whether the taxes or transfers or the endowments are constant through time. It does matter that all members of each generation are identical, in endowments, preferences, and the taxes and transfers they pay.

This version of the economy gives the same final result we got in the Class 1 case. If maximizing Equation (4.17) subject to the budget line of Figure 4.1 leads to a positive bequest at all dates, then sufficiently small changes in taxes will not result in any change in individuals' consumption patterns. Bequests will change to compensate for the changes in the taxes.

EXERCISE 4.6 Consider an economy in which all members have the utility function given in Equation (4.15), with

$$f(c_t^h(t)) = \ln(c_t^h(t)),$$

and $g(c_t^h(t + 1)) = 2 \ln(c_t^h(t + 1))$

with $\delta = 0.8$, and with an endowment of $[2, 1]$ for all generations $t \geq 0$. Taxes are equal to $t^h(t) = 0.6$. Draw the budget constraint faced by an old person at time t. Find the equilibrium bequests at time t.

Reprise

The results of this chapter show us that, if the utility of a member of the next generation matters to each member of the current generation, then there is an optimal amount of bequests that will be made from the current old to the young. For a given economy, there can be a range of tax-transfer schemes that result in the same equilibrium consumption patterns. The addition of diversity does not rule out these results but makes the models more complicated.

Ricardian equivalence tells us that any set of taxes and transfers that keeps the present value of an individual's tax liability constant results in the same consumption allocation and the same gross interest rate. If the government sells bonds at time t and then taxes the old at time $t + 1$ to pay for them, this practice results in the same consumption allocation as if the young of time t had been taxed.

One result of the addition of bequests is that the Ricardian equivalence can be extended across generations. Assume the government borrows from the young at time t and taxes the young at time $t + 1$ to pay off these government bonds. If there exists an equilibrium without bonds, where the members of generation t were taxed when young and where the old at time $t + 1$ made bequests to the young of that date, then (in economies with separable subutility functions) the old will increase their bequests to exactly compensate for the increased taxes paid by the time $t + 1$ young. Ricardian equivalence holds across generations.

A paper by Bernheim and Bagwell (1988) calls into question the kind of preferences studied above, the kind that underlie the extended Ricardian equivalence idea. They built a model in which families are interconnected (or linked) by descent (parent-child linkages) and by marriage (called operative linkages). One of their first propositions is to show that with everyone linked to everyone else, the "caring for one's children" hypothesis becomes a "caring for everyone" result. This extension of caring results in everything becoming neutral, so that small changes in taxes, bonds, prices, wages, and most anything else, are compensated for by gifts between members of the one giant human family.

The point of the Bernheim and Bagwell paper is that the implications of the kind of preferences underlying Ricardian equivalence when extended to take into account family formation seem absurd and can be fairly easily rejected by even casual observation of the real world. On the other hand, we certainly see bequests and lots of other examples of intergenerational caring. The resolution of the paradox posed by these observations is a subject of ongoing research. We do not pursue it further here; and for the rest of the book, we return to two-period-lived people with selfish preferences.

CHAPTER 5

Long-Term
Government Bonds

The government bonds that we analyzed in Chapter 3 were all one-period bonds. The government promised to tax (or use some other method) to raise enough of the time $t + 1$ good to pay off the bonds it issued in time t. Casual observation of the world reminds us that there are bonds with different maturity dates; that is, bonds that come due in different periods. The United States government issues Treasury bills, notes, and bonds. The Treasury bills come due in 3 months, 6 months, 9 months, or 1 year. Treasury notes have maturities from 1 to 10 years. Treasury bonds have maturities of more than 10 years.

We want to include in our model bonds of maturities of more than one period. We introduce k-period bonds. A *k-period bond* is one that is issued in period t and will be paid off at 1 unit of good per bond in period $t + k$. For example, the government might wish to issue enough bonds today (time period 1) to raise 25 units of the good. One kind of bond that the government might issue are claims on the time 3 good. We use these bonds primarily as a way of introducing you to the notion of a perfect foresight competitive equilibrium. Holders of bonds that mature in periods after they die need to sell the bonds to members of the next generation. In order for the holders to determine how attractive these bonds are at the time of purchase, they need to forecast what the price of these bonds will be when they will want to sell them.

k-Period Bonds

We need to introduce some notation for these bonds. We let $B_k(t)$ stand for the number of k-period bonds that exist in period t, each of which is a title to 1 unit of the time $t + k$ good. If these bonds are held for one period (to time $t + 1$), then we refer to them as the $k - 1$-period bonds of period $t + 1$. This number of bonds is written as $B_{k-1}(t + 1)$, and they promise to pay off that quantity of goods in $k - 1$ periods. As we pass from one period to the next, the k-period bonds become $k - 1$-period bonds, which become $k - 2$-period bonds, and so on, until they come due. Notice that we add the subscript $(k - 1)$ and the argument $(t + 1)$ to get the date at which the bonds mature $(t + k)$. The government then pays them off at 1 unit of the time $t + k$ good for each bond. We assume that the government never defaults and always pays off the bonds as promised.

This kind of bond is called a *zero coupon bond* because the issuer—in our case, the government—promises to make a payment only at maturity rather than promising to make a series of payments—coupons—and then a final payment at maturity. Bond holders are sometimes called coupon clippers, because some bonds have a number of coupons physically attached to them and each period the owner of a bond clips off a coupon and sends it in to the issuer of the bond. In return the bond holder receives a check in payment for the interest due. The multiperiod bonds we allow in the model do not explicitly pay out interest each period. Rather, they sell at prices at different dates that yield the appropriate interest rate.

We will represent the number of k-period bonds held from time t to time $t + 1$ by person h of generation t as $b_k^h(t)$. We require that the quantity of bonds that an individual can hold be nonnegative. Individuals can neither go short on bonds nor issue their own government bonds (which would be counterfeiting).

Selling short means to sell something one does not own. By the phrase "to sell something one does not own," we do not mean illegal transactions like selling the Brooklyn Bridge or a stolen car radio. When one sells short, one sells something one does not currently own but promises to deliver at some date in the future. However, one agrees today on the price that will be paid on the delivery date. This agreed-on price is called the *short sales price*. In these *futures contracts*, one purchases the good before the date of delivery and delivers these goods to the person to whom one sold the futures contract. The seller of the futures contract is guessing that the price of the good will be lower than the short sales price before delivery comes due. If so, the good can then be purchased at a price lower than it was sold for. The difference, of course, is the profit from the transaction. If the price of the good is higher than the short sales price at delivery, then the seller of the futures contract takes a loss. If someone sells government bonds short, this individual is betting that the price of the government bonds in the future will be lower than the short sales price.[1] In any case, we do not permit short selling in government bonds in our model.

We let $p_k(t)$ be the time t price, in units of time t good, of a bond that comes due in period $t + k$, a bond that pays 1 unit of the time $t + k$ good.

If we are in a world in which the future is not exactly known, people do not *know* what the price of this bond will be in the next period. The other people who will buy the bonds from them—the young of generation $t + 1$—are not around yet. The best that the current young can do is to form guesses or *forecasts* (also called *expectations*) of the price of the bond at time $t + 1$. These guesses or expectations can, conceivably, be different for different individuals, so we express the expectations at time t of person h of generation t of the price in time $t + 1$ of a k-period bond as $p_{k-1}^{h,e}(t + 1)$.

How this expectation is formed, we do not yet know. We simply assume that each individual has formed a subjective expectation of this price. It is possible that all of the individuals at time t have the same expected price, but such a restriction is not necessary. We treat the expectations at time t of person h of generation t as if they hold with certainty. This expression means that this individual believes that $p_{k-1}^{h,e}(t + 1)$ and only $p_{k-1}^{h,e}(t + 1)$ will be the price of the k-period bond in the next period. This assumption about certainty of expectations means (in a world that might ordinarily be thought of as being risky) that all of the probability falls on that number. None of the standard kinds of probability distributions that one might normally encounter apply when speaking of expectations. We make this *point expectations* assumption for simplicity. The model could be expanded to include other types of probability distributions around expected prices.

---

1. President Eisenhower, who was a military man and not familiar with the business world, had never heard of selling short until he became president. When he was told how selling short worked, he could not believe that it was legal. He viewed such betting that other people will do badly as somehow immoral.

We can now write the budget constraints that individual h of generation t faces in an economy with private lending and long-term government bonds. The budget constraint for consumption when young is

$$c_t^h(t) = \omega_t^h(t) - \ell^h(t) - p_k(t)b_k^h(t). \tag{5.1}$$

Consumption when young is equal to endowment when young minus the private loan made and minus the price paid for each k-period bond times the number of those bonds bought. When individual h of generation t is old, the budget constraint is

$$c_t^h(t + 1) = \omega_t^h(t + 1) + r(t)\ell^h(t) + p_{k-1}^{h,e}(t + 1)b_k^h(t). \tag{5.2}$$

Consumption when old is equal to the endowment when old plus the returns from the private lending (the amount of private lending times the gross interest rate) plus the gains from the sales of the k-period bonds that were bought when young. The consumption when old, expressed by Equation (5.2), should really be called expected consumption when old because it is the planned consumption that is determined, in part, by an expected price for k-period bonds. The budget constraint in Equation (5.2) is the budget constraint that the young person expects to face when old. For that reason, the expected price on the bond is included and not the actual price that occurs in period $t + 1$. The young person makes plans based on maximizing utility of consumption constrained by the budget constraint when young and the expected budget constraint when old.

Facing the budget constraints of Equations (5.1) and (5.2), the young person chooses a consumption pair, an amount of private lending to make and an amount of k-period government bonds to purchase. The individual takes as given the endowments, the gross interest rate, $r(t)$, the current price of the bonds, $p_k(t)$, and the expected price of the k-period bonds in period $t + 1$, $p_{k-1}^{h,e}(t + 1)$. We will not worry, for the moment, about where the expected price came from.

Equations (5.1) and (5.2) can be combined by solving (5.1) for $\ell^h(t)$ and substituting that into Equation (5.2). The result can be written as

$$r(t)c_t^h(t) + c_t^h(t + 1) = r(t)\omega_t^h(t) + \omega_t^h(t + 1)$$

$$- b_k^h(t)[r(t)p_k(t) - p_{k-1}^{h,e}(t + 1)]. \tag{5.3}$$

EXERCISE 5.1 Show that the constraints imposed by Equation (5.3) are equivalent to those imposed by Equations (5.1) and (5.2).

Recall that the utility function for each individual is increasing in each of its arguments. This requirement means that an individual would like to choose quantities of private lending and purchases of government k-period bonds to make the right-hand side of Equation (5.3) as large as possible. Making the right-hand side of (5.3) become larger allows the left-hand side to become larger as well. This change increases the consumption that is possible and increases utility.

The part of Equation (5.3) in square brackets, that is,

$$[r(t)p_k(t) - p^{h,e}_{k-1}(t + 1)],$$

can be positive, negative, or 0. We want to determine the quantity of k-period bonds, $b^h_k(t)$, that individual h of generation t chooses for each of those cases. Suppose that the part in square brackets is positive:

$$[r(t)p_k(t) - p^{h,e}_{k-1}(t + 1)] > 0.$$

As a consequence, the return on private bonds—the gross interest rate, $r(t)$—is greater than the gross return on government bonds. In order to make the right-hand side of Equation (5.3) as large as possible, the individual chooses to make $b^h_k(t) = 0$. Because we do not allow individuals to privately issue k-period government bonds, the number of bonds cannot be negative. A purchase of any positive amount of bonds reduces the budget, because that amount of the time t good could have been used to lend on the private lending market, which offers a higher rate of return.

If the part in the brackets is negative,

$$[r(t)p_k(t) - p^{h,e}_{k-1}(t + 1)] < 0,$$

then the gross interest rate in the private lending market is less than the gross return gained by purchasing government bonds, and the individual can make a profit (the spread between the two rates) by borrowing in the private lending market and purchasing k-period government bonds. The more bonds the person can buy, the more the budget line moves out; so the individual would attempt to purchase an infinite number of bonds (borrowing an infinite amount in the private bond market).

If the part in brackets is 0, it does not matter how many government bonds the individual purchases. The gross interest rate on private lending is exactly equal to the gross rate of return on the purchase of government bonds. The individual is indifferent between lending in the private debt market and purchasing government bonds. Any magnitude of holdings of government bonds, $b_k^h(t)$, will do.

We are heading toward the description of a perfect foresight equilibrium. One characteristic of this kind of equilibrium is unanimity of expectations. However, unanimity of expectations is a weaker assumption than perfect foresight. We motivate the introduction of unanimity of expectations by appealing to our upcoming assumption of perfect foresight and then examine economies in which perfect foresight is lacking but everyone at any date t has the same expectations.

The assumption of perfect foresight implies that all individuals will form correct expectations (in the sense that their expectations will be exactly fulfilled). If everyone is correct, then the expectations of all individuals at any date t must be the same. The following proposition gives one of the implications of this unanimity of expectations.

Proposition 5.1 *If there is unanimity, namely,*

$$p_{k-1}^{h,e}(t + 1) = p_{k-1}^e(t + 1),$$

for all individuals h of generation t, and if some k-period bonds exist at time t, then in any equilibrium (in which, in particular, desired bond purchases equal the bonds supplied),

$$r(t)p_k(t) = p_{k-1}^e(t + 1). \tag{5.4}$$

EXERCISE 5.2   Prove the above proposition.

The formula of Equation (5.4) says that the present value (discounted by the gross interest rate on private lending) of the expected price in the next period of the long-term bonds is equal to the current price of these bonds. Another way of saying the same thing is to note that the expected one-period return on the long-term bonds, $p^e_{k-1}(t + 1)/p_k(t)$, is equal to the gross interest rate on one-period private loans, $r(t)$. Individuals are indifferent between private loans and the long-term government bonds. From now on, we assume unanimity of expectations, that is,

$$p^{h,e}_{k-1}(t + 1) = p^e_{k-1}(t + 1).$$

As a result of Proposition 5.1, Equation (5.4) must hold for any equilibrium. In other words, we need only consider pairs of gross interest rates and time t prices for k-period bonds that satisfy that equation. Restricting ourselves to these pairs, the second line of Equation (5.3) is always equal to 0, and the lifetime budget constraint that individuals face is merely

$$r(t)c^h_t(t) + c^h_t(t + 1) = r(t)\omega^h_t(t) + \omega^h_t(t + 1).$$

Dividing through by $r(t)$, we find that this lifetime budget constraint becomes the same lifetime budget constraint that individuals faced in Chapters 2 and 3. Individuals solving their utility maximization problem under this constraint get the same demand functions for consumption when young that we found earlier and, therefore, the same savings functions. The demand function for consumption when young is

$$c^h_t(t) = \chi^h_t(r(t), \omega^h_t(t), \omega^h_t(t + 1)),$$

and the savings function is

$$s^h(r(t)) = \omega^h_t(t) - \chi^h_t(r(t), \omega^h_t(t), \omega^h_t(t + 1)).$$

The savings function gives the desired *net* holdings of assets at each gross interest rate. How this savings is divided between private borrowing and lending and the k-period government bonds is not determined. Any combination of private borrowing and lending and holdings of k-period government bonds that total to $s^h(r(t))$ can be held in equilibrium. It is perfectly acceptable that one individual borrows from others of that generation and purchases all of the government bonds. It is also perfectly acceptable that each individual hold some government bonds, even those who are net borrowers. As in earlier chapters, only the net asset positions of individuals matter. In equilibrium, as we will see below, the aggregate savings of each generation equal the real value of the government bonds. Therefore, not all members of a generation can hold any mix of bonds and private borrowing and lending that they wish. In a generation with $N(t)$ individuals, only $N(t) - 1$ of them, at most, can freely choose their holdings of bonds and private borrowing and lending. The last person must hold the amount of government bonds or borrowing and lending necessary to make the sum of the individual holdings of k-period government bonds equal to the total quantity of k-period government bonds.

Temporary Equilibrium

Before we define a temporary equilibrium, we need to review the physical characteristics of our model. The set of items that we take as given in any period are the utility functions of all individuals who are alive in that period, their lifetime endowments, any taxes and transfers they pay or receive in either period of their lives, and the price that is expected to hold in the next period for the current k-period bonds. This set of items can be expressed as

$$\{u_t^h(\cdot, \cdot), \omega_t^h, t_t^h, p_{k-1}^e(t + 1)\}, \qquad \text{for } h = 1 \text{ to } N(t).$$

The set of utility functions, endowments, and taxes that we need to define a temporary equilibrium are those for all members of the current generation (and only of the current generation). Because everyone has the same expectations of the price of bonds next period, expressing it once covers everyone.

In Chapter 2 we defined a competitive equilibrium as a sequence of prices and quantities by which individuals maximize their utility subject to the constraints they face and for which all markets clear. We wish to look at just one period, where the expectations of the future are given to us exogenously, and to define a notion of an equilibrium for that period alone. This single-period equilibrium we call a *temporary equilibrium*.

Definition   *Given* $\{u_t^h(\cdot, \cdot),\ \omega_t^h,\ t_t^h,\ p_{k-1}^e(t + 1)\}$, *a* time t temporary equilibrium *is a pair of prices* $[r(t),\ p_k(t)]$ *such that the equilibrium conditions*

(i) $r(t)p_k(t) = p_{k-1}^e(t + 1)$ *(present value condition), and*

(ii) $S_t(r(t)) = p_k(t)B_k(t)$ *(utility maximization and market clearing
                                         condition)*

are fulfilled.

To find a temporary equilibrium for an economy with long-term government bonds, we first find the appropriate savings functions for individuals and then for the generation. Finally, we use the market clearing
conditions to find the equilibrium price and quantities.

The derivation of the market clearing condition is identical to the one
done in Chapter 3 and is not repeated for that reason. As was discussed
above, the individual savings functions that make up the aggregate savings function, $S_t(r(t))$, are the same ones we derived earlier. The difficulty we face with the market clearing condition, condition (ii) in the
preceding definition, is that both the gross interest rate, $r(t)$, and the
current price of the k-period bonds are unknowns. We use condition (i)
to get a relationship between these two variables and substitute that into
condition (ii) to solve for a temporary equilibrium of this model.

One way to solve this model is to express condition (i) as the current
price of the bonds in terms of the gross interest rate and the expected
price of the bonds in the next period, that is, to have

$$p_k(t) = \frac{p_{k-1}^e(t + 1)}{r(t)},$$

and to substitute the right-hand side of this equation for $p_k(t)$ in condition (ii). That substitution gives

$$r(t)S_t(r(t)) = p_{k-1}^e(t + 1)B_k(t),$$

which is an equation in only one unknown, $r(t)$. Given a total savings
function, the total number of k-period bonds, and the expected price
of those bonds in time $t + 1$, one can solve for $r(t)$. Then, given $r(t)$,
condition (i) can be used to solve for $p_k(t)$.

At this moment, we only need the information about the endowments
and preferences of generation t, the number of k-period bonds, and the
expected price in time $t + 1$ of those k-period bonds. We do not need

to know anything about any members of any other generation to solve for a temporary equilibrium. The expected price in time $t + 1$ of the k-period bonds carries all the information we need to know about the future generations.

Here is an example that we solve for a temporary equilibrium. Following the example are two exercises that also involve finding temporary equilibria.

Consider an economy where $N(t) = 100$, and all individuals have an endowment of [2, 1], utility functions of

$$u_t^h = c_t^h(t)[c_t^h(t + 1)]^\beta,$$

with $\beta = 1$, and price expectations of

$$p_{k-1}^e(t + 1) = 1.5.$$

There are 100 k-period bonds. The equilibrium condition is that the aggregate savings function is equal to the expected price of the bonds times the number of bonds, all divided by the gross interest rate, or

$$100\left(1 - \frac{1}{2r(t)}\right) = (1.5)\left(\frac{100}{r(t)}\right).$$

This expression can be rearranged to give

$$100r(t) - 50 = 150, \quad \text{or} \quad r(t) = 2.$$

Each person is saving

$$1 - \frac{1}{2(2)} = 0.75,$$

and the current price of the k-period bonds is

$$p_k(t) = \frac{1.5}{2} = 0.75.$$

Each person will have a consumption pair of [1.25, 2.5], where the 2.5 is the planned or expected consumptions at time $t + 1$. This amount will be the actual consumption if the price of the bonds in the next period turns out to be the expected price.

EXERCISE 5.3   In the above economy, describe completely the time t temporary equilibrium if $p_{k-1}^e(t + 1) = 1$.

EXERCISE 5.4   Same as Exercise 5.3, except $p_{k-1}^e(t + 1) = 0.5$.

Notice that in Exercises 5.3 and 5.4 the time t temporary equilibrium depends on the expected price of the bonds. Therefore, what happens at date t depends on what people believe about the future. We can make the relationship between the current price of the bonds and the expected price of the bonds more explicit. Recall that we indicated that one way to solve the above system was to solve for $r(t)$. The other way to solve the system is to replace $r(t)$ in condition (ii) by its equivalent in condition (i). Making that substitution gives

$$S_t\left(\frac{p_{k-1}^e(t + 1)}{p_k(t)}\right) = p_k(t)B_k(t).$$

If savings increase as the gross interest rate increases, then the above equation can be solved for the current price of a k-period bond as a function of the expected price of that bond in the next period. Let $f_t(\cdot)$ be that function, which we call the *price function* for government bonds at time t. Then we can write

$$p_k(t) = f_t(p_{k-1}^e(t + 1)).$$

Using the savings function of the example, above, and assuming that there are 100 k-period bonds, we get

$$100\left(1 - \frac{p_k(t)}{2p_{k-1}^e(t + 1)}\right) = 100\, p_k(t),$$

which gives us the price function $f_t(\cdot)$, or

$$p_k(t) = f_t(p_{k-1}^e(t + 1)) = 2\left(\frac{p_{k-1}^e(t + 1)}{1 + 2p_{k-1}^e(t + 1)}\right).$$

This price function, $f_t(\cdot)$, is graphed in Figure 5.1. Notice that with the specific utility functions, endowments, and quantity of bonds we used, the current price of the k-period bonds will not go above 1. For any positive, finite expected price, the current price of the bonds is below 1. For this economy, 1 is the limit of the current price as the expected price goes to plus infinity.

EXERCISE 5.5   Find $p_k(t)$ as a function of $p^e_{k-1}(t+1)$ for an economy in which $N(t) = 100$, there are 100 k-period bonds, and all individuals have an endowment of [2, 1] and utility functions of

$$u^h_t = [c^h_t(t)]^{1/2} + \beta[c^h_t(t+1)]^{1/2},$$

with $\beta = 1$.

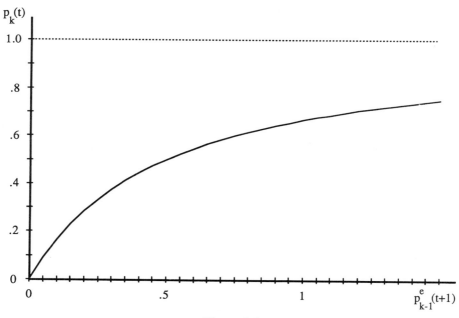

Figure 5.1

Perfect Foresight

Where do the expectations of the time $t + 1$ price of the current k-period bonds come from? How do individuals get information about the future? In the biblical story of Joseph in Egypt and the seven years of plenty and seven years of famine, God provided forecasts for Joseph. Normally, we cannot assume that we will have access to that forecasting technique. We need other mechanisms.

The normal way that forecasts are formed, in economics or in any other science, is by extending the history of the past beyond the current period and into the future. In other words, forecasting is usually done by looking for patterns in historical data and assuming that these patterns will continue into the future. If we are using all of the relevant information, we refer to our forecasts as *rational expectations*. In one view of the universe, if we had access to complete information for making forecasts, then these forecasts would always be correct. (This view is consistent with the theory of a deterministic universe. In theories of stochastic, or random, universes, we could have all current information and still not always be correct. In the stochastic versions, Mother Nature rolls dice.) If we were always correct, then we would claim to have perfect foresight. *Perfect foresight* is the limit of rational expectations as the information set grows to include *all* information. In our model, we assume that individuals have this perfect foresight; they know the future prices of everything. In particular, they know at time t the time $t + 1$ price of the k-period bonds. We are making this assumption not because we really believe that forecasts are perfect, but for the following reasons. First, we believe that individuals have incentives to try to make their forecasts about the future as accurate as possible. Errors in forecasts lower utility. Second, we prefer to consider models where results do not arise because people systematically make errors in their predictions. Assuming that individuals have rational expectations will prevent systematic errors. Perfect foresight, as mentioned above, is the limit case of rational expectations.

We impose perfect foresight by equating expectations at time t of the price at time $t + n$ with the price that occurs in equilibrium at time $t + n$. For the price that is expected at time $t + 1$ for the current k-period bonds, we impose perfect foresight by assuming that

$$p^e_{k-1}(t + 1) = p_{k-1}(t + 1).$$

Given our definition of perfect foresight, we can define a perfect fore-sight competitive equilibrium for an economy with long-term govern-ment bonds. To do this we use our earlier definition of a temporary equilibrium but make each generation's expectations of the future price of the bonds be correct.

Definition *A* perfect foresight competitive equilibrium with long-term government bonds *is a sequence of $p(t)$ and $r(t)$ and other endogenous (depen-dent) variables such that the time t values are a time t temporary equilibrium for* $p_{k-1}^e(t + 1) = p_{k-1}(t + 1)$.

For some sequences of government bond issues, we can easily find the perfect foresight competitive equilibrium. Suppose that at some date t, there are bonds outstanding with k periods until maturity. If during the life of these bonds there are never bonds outstanding with greater time until maturity than these bonds, then we can find the perfect fore-sight competitive equilibrium prices of bonds and interest rates over the life of these bonds in a simple way. Let us see how this determination is made for the particular situation in which the government issues no additional bonds during the life of the k-period bonds.

As we assumed with the one-period bonds, the time $t + k$ price of the time t, k-period bonds will be 1 unit of the good per bond. Given that there are currently $B_k(t)$ k-period bonds, if the government does not issue new bonds that are due in time $t + k$, then there will be in time period $t + k - 1$, the same number of one-period bonds. That is,

$$B_1(t + k - 1) = B_k(t).$$

The one-period bonds are exactly like the bonds we analyzed in the previous chapter. The expected price of the one-period bonds in period $t + 1$ is

$$p_0^e(t + k) = p_0(t + k) = 1.$$

From Equation (5.4) we know, in general, that

$$r(t) = \frac{p_{k-1}^e(t + 1)}{p_k(t)},$$

and, in particular, that

$$r(t + k - 1) = \frac{p_0^e(t + k)}{p_1(t + k - 1)} = \frac{1}{p_1(t + k - 1)}.$$

Using this relationship between the time $t + k - 1$ price of the bonds that come due in time $t + k$ and the current gross interest rate in the aggregate savings equation [condition (ii) of the temporary equilibrium], we get

$$S_t(r(t + k - 1)) = p_1(t + k - 1)B_1(t + k - 1) = \frac{B_1(t + k - 1)}{r(t + k - 1)}.$$

We have one equation in one unknown (with a solution), and we can solve the time $t + k - 1$ temporary equilibrium for $r(t + k - 1)$. From that, we can solve for $p_1(t + k - 1)$, because

$$p_1(t + k - 1) = \frac{1}{r(t + k - 1)}.$$

Working backward through a series of temporary equilibria, we now set the expected price of the one-period bonds in time $t + k - 1$ equal to what they will be under perfect foresight and have

$$p_1^e(t + k - 1) = p_1(t + k - 1).$$

From the point of view of a time $t + k - 2$ temporary equilibrium, we have that the gross interest rate is

$$r(t + k - 2) = \frac{p_1^e(t + k - 1)}{p_2(t + k - 2)}.$$

Substituting in the actual price for the expected price at time $t + k - 1$ and setting that price equal to $1/r(t + k - 1)$, we have that

$$r(t + k - 2) = \frac{1}{p_2(t + k - 2)r(t + k - 1)}.$$

Using condition (ii) for a temporary equilibrium in time $t + k - 2$, we have

$$S_t(r(t + k - 2)) = p_2(t + k - 2)B_2(t + k - 2),$$

which is equal to

$$S_t(r(t + k - 2)) = \frac{B_2(t + k - 2)}{r(t + k - 2)r(t + k - 1)}.$$

When we are two periods from the date at which the long-term bonds are to come due, the aggregate savings are equal to the number of two-period bonds in the economy divided by the current gross interest rate on private loans and the gross interest rate on private loans that will occur in the next period. We can keep solving for temporary equilibria backward in time until we reach time t, using the price we determined from the time $t + s$ temporary equilibrium as a given when solving the time $t + s - 1$ temporary equilibrium. At time t, an equilibrium condition is that the aggregate savings function equals the number of k-period bonds divided by the product of the current and the next $k - 1$ periods' gross interest rates. That is,

$$S_t(r(t)) = \frac{B_k(t)}{\displaystyle\prod_{s=0}^{k-1} r(t + s)}.$$

Because all of the $r(t + s)$ have already been determined for $s = 1$ to $k - 1$ as we calculated the temporary equilibria back from time $t + k$, the only unknown in the above equation is $r(t)$. We can solve for that and obtain the whole sequence $\{r(s)\}$ for $s = t$ to $t + k - 1$. From that sequence of gross interest rates, the whole sequence of prices of the bonds can also be calculated.

Consider the example we used above with $N(t) = 100$, $B_3(t) = 100$, endowments of $[2, 1]$, and individuals' utility functions of $u_t^h = c_t^h(t) \cdot c_t^h(t + 1)$. The government issues 100 bonds that mature in three periods, and it will pay off these bonds by taxing the young of time $t + 3$ so that it can pay 1 unit of the good for each bond. Consequently, the price of these bonds in time $t + 3$ will be equal to 1. Using that information, we can solve for the temporary equilibrium and calculate the gross interest at period $t + 2$. We find $r(t + 2)$ by solving

$$S_t(r(t + 2)) = \frac{100}{r(t + 2)},$$

or $$100\left(1 - \frac{1}{2r(t + 2)}\right) = \frac{100}{r(t + 2)}.$$

Table 5.1 Gross interest rates and prices for three-period government bonds

Period	Price of bonds	Gross interest rate
t	5/8	15/14
$t + 1$	4/7	7/6
$t + 2$	2/3	3/2
$t + 3$	1	—

Solving that equation for $r(t + 2)$, we find that $r(t + 2) = 1.5$. Using this calculation, we can find $r(t + 1)$. The aggregate savings at time $t + 1$ are

$$S_t(r(t + 1)) = \frac{100}{r(t + 1)r(t + 2)},$$

or $\quad 100 - \dfrac{50}{r(t + 1)} = \dfrac{100}{1.5r(t + 1)}.$

Solving that equation for $r(t + 1)$, we find $r(t + 1) = 1.16666$. Using the results for $r(t + 2)$ and $r(t + 1)$, we can calculate $r(t)$. The aggregate savings function is

$$S_t(r(t)) = \frac{100}{r(t)r(t + 1)r(t + 2)}.$$

Substituting in that function the values for $r(t + 1)$ and $r(t + 2)$, we get

$$100 - \frac{50}{r(t)} = \frac{100}{(1.5)(1.1666)r(t)}.$$

That substitution gives us $r(t) = 15/14$. The series of gross interest rates and prices for the three-period government bonds are given in Table 5.1. Notice that the price sequence can also be found from the function $f(\cdot)$ that we illustrated in Figure 5.1. That figure shows the price that occurs as a solution to the temporary equilibrium in time t as a function of the price in time $t + 1$.[2] We know that the price of the bond at time

2. Remember that the curve shown in Figure 5.1 is from exactly the same economy that we used in the above example. Different economies would have different curves.

$t + 3$ will be $p_0(t + 3) = 1$, so we can use Figure 5.1 and find out what the price will be in time $t + 2$. We trace up from 1 on the horizontal axis to the curve and then over to the vertical axis. This line extends to $p_1(t + 2) = 2/3$ on the vertical axis of Figure 5.2. A 45-degree line brings us to the same price, $p_1(t + 2) = 2/3$, on the horizontal axis. From there we trace up and over to find the price for period $t + 1$ that occurs when the time $t + 2$ price is 2/3. The time $t + 1$ price is $p_2(t + 1) = 4/7$ on the vertical axis. There is also a 45-degree line to $p_2(t + 1)$ on the horizontal axis. Tracing up and over gives us the time t price of the bonds, $p_3(t) = 5/8$. The whole set of prices can be read off this curve. If these bonds had been four- or five-period bonds, the up and over process could continue to provide the price of those bonds when there are four or five periods yet to go.

When we write the above discussion using the function $f(\cdot)$, we note a recursive pattern. Given that the price of the k-period bond will be 1 at time $t + k$, we can use the function $f(\cdot)$ to find the time $t + k - 1$ price. That is,

$$p_1(t + k - 1) = f(\mathbf{1}),$$

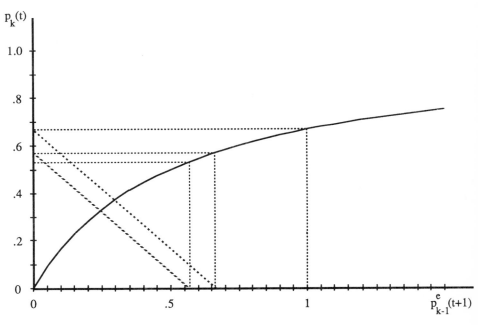

Figure 5.2

where $f(\mathbf{1})$ is the function $f(\cdot)$ applied to the value of 1. The price of the bond at time $t + k - 2$ is found by applying the function $f(\cdot)$ to the price at time $t + k - 1$, or

$$p_2(t + k - 2) = f(p_1(t + k - 1)) = f(f(\mathbf{1})).$$

The price two periods from when the bond comes due is found by applying the function $f(\cdot)$ to the result gotten by applying the function $f(\cdot)$ to 1. The notation $f(f(\mathbf{1}))$ says just that. The price of a three-period bond is found by applying the function $f(\cdot)$ to the result obtained above, so

$$p_3(t + k - 3) = f(p_2(t + k - 2)) = f(f(f(\mathbf{1}))).$$

The time t price of a k-period bond is found by applying the function $f(\cdot)$ k times. This works only if the basic structure of the economy is the same each period. The function $f(\cdot)$ will change with time if the endowments, preferences, population size, number of government bonds, or taxes change. However, if all of these are constant, then the function $f(\cdot)$ is the same for each period.

EXERCISE 5.6 Consider the economy of Exercise 5.3. Suppose the government at time 1 sells 25 bonds, each of which is a title to 1 unit of the time 3 good (these are two-period bonds). The proceeds of the bond sale are distributed equally to the members of generation 0. Members of generation 3 are taxed equally, when young, to pay off the bonds. Describe the competitive equilibrium under the perfect foresight hypothesis.

EXERCISE 5.7 Consider the same economy used in Exercise 5.6. Suppose that the old of period 3 are taxed equally to pay off the bonds. How does this equilibrium differ from the one in Exercise 5.6? What does this result say about Ricardian equivalence?

EXERCISE 5.8 Consider the same economy used in Exercise 5.6, except instead of selling 25 bonds at time 1, the government sells enough bonds to raise 25 units of the time 1 good (which it distributes to the old of generation 0). Describe the competitive equilibrium under the perfect foresight hypothesis.

Term Structure of Interest Rates

At this point, we have two assets of different maturity lengths coexisting in the economy. There are k-period government bonds and one-period private loans. As we demonstrated above, there is a particular relationship between the returns on the one-period loans and the returns on the k-period government bonds.

We define a new bond, one that is somewhat different from the zero coupon bonds that we have been considering up to now. A *k-period coupon bond* offers a stream of payments of $\{x^k(t + i)\}$ for i equals 1 to k. The quantity $x^k(t + i)$ is the *coupon payment* made by the issuer of this bond in the ith period after it is issued.

Definition *The* gross yield *or the* gross internal rate of return on a k-period coupon bond *that offers the stream of payments of* $x^k(t + 1)$, $x^k(t + 2), x^k(t + 3), \ldots, x^k(t + k)$ *and has a price of* $p_k(t)$ *at time t is equal to the value of* $r_k(t)$ *that satisfies*

$$p_k(t) = \sum_{i=1}^{k} \left[\frac{1}{r_k(t)}\right]^i x^k(t + i).$$

Recall that the k-period government bonds that we have been using are zero coupon bonds. For zero coupon bonds, the stream of payment is equal to

$$x^k(t + i) = \begin{cases} 0, & \text{for } i = 1 \text{ to } k - 1, \\ 1, & \text{for } i = k. \end{cases}$$

For the k-period government bonds, it is especially easy to find $r_k(t)$. The gross internal rate of return on a k-period government bond is the one for which

$$p_k(t) = \frac{1}{(r_k(t))^k};$$

or $$r_k(t) = \left(\frac{1}{p_k(t)}\right)^{1/k}. \tag{5.5}$$

EXERCISE 5.9 Consider a pure discount bond that at time t is a promise to 1 unit of the time $t + k$ good. The gross internal rate of return, $r_k(t)$, on this bond is defined above.

a. Under the perfect foresight hypothesis, prove that

$$r_k(t) = (r(t)r(t + 1) \ldots r(t + k - 2)r(t + k - 1))^{1/k}, \tag{5.6}$$

where $r(t + j)$ is the equilibrium one-period gross interest rate at time $t + j, j = 0$ to $k - 1$.

b. Show that the above relationship need not hold if perfect foresight is not assumed.

In a world with perfect foresight the gross internal rate of return on a k-period bond at time t is a geometric average of the one-period interest rates that will exist during the life of the k-period bond.

Suppose that at time t there are bonds that will pay off 1 unit of the good in time $t + 1$, other bonds that will pay off 1 unit of the good in time $t + 2$, and so on, up to bonds that will pay off 1 unit of the good at time $t + k$, for some $k > 2$. At time t, each of these bonds has a price, $p_m(t)$, for the $m = 1$ to k-period bonds that exist. Using Equation (5.5), we can calculate, for each m, the $r_m(t)$ implied by the price $p_m(t)$. The sequence $r_1(t), r_2(t), \ldots$ is called the *term structure of interest rates*.

The hypothesis that the sequence $r_1(t), r_2(t), \ldots$ is determined by Equation (5.6) is called the *expectations hypothesis of the term structure of interest rates*. This hypothesis asserts that the yields at a given time t on bonds with different numbers of periods until maturity are determined by the sequence of one-period interest rates expected to prevail in the future. We can test the perfect foresight version of this hypothesis as follows. From bond prices at time t, the sequence $r_1(t), r_2(t), \ldots$ can be computed by using the definition of the internal rate of return. Then, using Equation (5.6) for $k = 1$, $k = 2$, and so on, we can compute the sequence $r(t), r(t + 1), \ldots$. In particular, Equation (5.6) for $k = 1, 2, 3$, and 4 is as follows:

$$r_1(t) = (r(t))^1, \tag{5.7}$$

$$r_2(t) = (r(t)r(t + 1))^{1/2},$$

$$r_3(t) = (r(t)r(t + 1)r(t + 2))^{1/3},$$

$$r_4(t) = (r(t)r(t + 1)r(t + 2)r(t + 3))^{1/4},$$

and so on. Because we know the $r_m(t)$ sequence, we can calculate the $r(t + j)$ sequence for $j = 0$ to $k - 1$. That is, $r(t)$ is found directly from the first line of the list above. Substituting that value in line 2, the only unknown is $r(t + 1)$, and it is easy to solve for that. Using those two numbers, we can solve for $r(t + 2)$ in line 3.

Our test consists of comparing the sequence of one-period gross interest rates that we determined for the actual one-period interest rates at dates $t + 1$, $t + 2$, and so on. We illustrate this process in the following exercise.

EXERCISE 5.10 The *New York Times* of May 3, 1990, gives the following interest rates on U.S. Treasury bills.

Maturity date	Internal rate of return on May 2, 1990
May 31, 1990	7.42%
June 28, 1990	7.73%

Let t = May 2, 1990; let $r(t) = 7.42$; and let $r_2(t) = 7.73$. Use Equation (5.6) to compute $r(t + 1)$. According to the perfect foresight hypothesis of the term structure of interest rates, your result for $r(t + 1)$ should be the internal rate of return on May 31, 1990 of a Treasury bill that matures on June 28, 1990. According to the *New York Times* of June 1, 1990, the internal rate of return was 7.26. What does this test imply about our perfect foresight version of the expectations hypothesis of the term structure of interest rates?

EXERCISE 5.11 Consider the economy of Exercise 5.8, except the government sells enough one-period bonds at time 1 to get 25 units of the time 1 good. At time 2, the government issues enough bonds to pay off the first issue and then taxes the young at time 3 to pay off these bonds. Describe the perfect foresight equilibrium and compare it to the solution of Exercise 5.8.

EXERCISE 5.12 Based on the results of the above exercise, formulate and prove a general proposition about the irrelevance of the maturity composition of government debt.

One way to approach Exercise 5.12 is to show that corresponding to any perfect foresight equilibrium in which there are long-term bonds is another equilibrium in which the long-term bonds are replaced by a sequence of one-period bonds, but where everything else is the same. Included among the things that are the same in the two equilibria are the consumption allocations, the sequence of one-period interest rates, and taxes and transfers. This equality of equilibria when the length to maturity of the bonds are different is called an *irrelevance of maturity composition*.

Recall the result at the end of Chapter 3 in which we showed that any equilibrium with one-period government borrowing has a corresponding equilibrium with balanced budget taxes and transfers at every date and the same consumption allocations as the equilibrium with government borrowing. This result and the result from Exercise 5.12 imply that an equilibrium with any form of government borrowing can be duplicated by one with balanced budget taxes and transfers. This outcome depends crucially on the assumption that lump-sum taxes and transfers can be levied. Once that assumption is dropped, as it is in public finance analyses of the structure of distorting taxes, then the equivalence between balanced budget tax and transfer policies and government borrowing disappears. The specific result in Exercise 5.12 does not depend on the kind of taxes and transfers in the economies. However, whether irrelevance of maturity composition applies to actual economies is also problematical.

The argument we suggested as a proof for the assertion in Exercise 5.12 assumes the existence of a perfect foresight equilibrium. Tests of whether the term structure of interest rates at a given date has implicit in it correct forecasts of future one-period interest rates will fail. One reason for this failure is the presence of uncertainty in actual economies. Uncertainty can be added to our model by assuming that at each date t there is uncertainty about the aggregate savings functions of future generations, the functions $S_{t+k}(r(t + k))$ for $k \geq 1$. Such uncertainty can come from assuming that people at time t do not know the size of future generations, their endowments, or their preferences. Any such uncertainty would prevent people at time t from correctly forecasting one-period interest rates in the future. It turns out that there is an analogue to the perfect foresight theory of the term structure that covers situations with uncertainty and also implies irrelevance of maturity composition. That theory, however, does not fare much better empirically than the perfect foresight version. For example, despite great effort, such a theory has yet to be reconciled with the observation that the average internal rate of return on Treasury bills with 2 months to maturity exceeds that on Treasury bills with 1 month to maturity most of the time, not just for the single observation reported in Exercise 5.10.

Despite the rather extreme assumptions we have made and despite the fact that we admit those assumptions do not hold exactly (what assumptions ever do), the models we are studying remain important. The body of economic knowledge advances by uncovering observations that are anomalous in significant ways from the point of view of simple models and by attempts to complicate the simple models to account for these anomalies. Part of this process involves learning the simple models.

Reprise

We added long-term government debt to our economy. We did this primarily to introduce into the model a need for people at one date to think about the future. In particular, people at time t who are considering whether to buy government bonds that mature after time $t + 1$ must formulate views about the price at which they will be able to sell those bonds at time $t + 1$. In our economy, they will be sold to members of the next generation. Those sales cannot be arranged at time t because the next generation is not yet present. Hence, the people at time t must think about the future. Everyone in actual economies who holds assets faces similar considerations.

We introduced two notions of equilibrium to deal with such situations. First, we introduced the notion of a temporary equilibrium. In a temporary equilibrium we attributed views about the future to people without considering where those views come from or how they are determined. Second, using the notion of a temporary equilibrium, we introduced the notion of a perfect foresight equilibrium. The perfect foresight hypothesis makes views about the future endogenous; they are determined as part of the equilibrium. The main rationale for assuming perfect foresight is that individuals have incentives to be correct.

The examples we emphasized were ones where a perfect foresight equilibrium was easy to find and, partly because of that, is an obvious and plausible theory. In those examples, we could calculate the sequence of one-period interest rates and the life of the long-term bond. Using that information, we can work backward and find the price of the long-term bond at each date. In subsequent chapters, we apply the perfect foresight assumption to find equilibria in more complicated settings. The main rationale for using this assumption continues to be that people have an incentive to be correct.

CHAPTER **6**

Infinitely Lived Assets

All of the assets we have considered up to now have had a finite maturity date. For intragenerational assets like private borrowing or lending, the life of the asset ended with that of the generation. For government bonds—the only type of outside asset we have yet considered—there was a date at which the asset was paid off. The government, when it issued the bond, named the date at which it would convert the bond into some amount of real goods. The fact that we had a future date at which we knew the real value of the asset, and some other features of the examples we used, allowed us to work back from that future date to find the current (time $t = 1$) price of the asset.

In this chapter and the next we wish to consider assets that do not have a finite maturity date. For these infinitely lived assets, there is no point in the future at which we can fix a particular price on the asset. The techniques we used for pricing bonds will not work for this type of assets. We need a different method for finding an equilibrium with infinitely lived assets.

First, let us consider some of the characteristics we want these assets to have. Suppose that there exists in the economy an additional real object, something different from the objects we have allowed so far. This "stuff" needs to have certain useful properties. We need something that does not rot and cannot be consumed, so that it is around for an infinite number of periods. We want to think about cases where people will want to buy this stuff when young and sell it when old and about the prices that this stuff can have.

Let us give this stuff a comfortable-sounding name. Call it *land*, although things other than what we normally think of as land have these kinds of properties. There is a certain fixed amount of it, denoted **A** (measured in hectares, acres, or whatever is the locally popular unit of measure). The **A** units of land give off a total *crop* of $D(t)$ units of the time t good in each period t. We assume that the crop, $D(t)$, simply appears on the land; there is no need to tend the land in any way. We want to be able to divide the land so that equal amounts give off equal amounts of crop. The simplest way to do this is to have all the land be of the same quality and have the crop be proportional to the amount of land. If that is the case, then each unit of land gives off $D(t)/\mathbf{A}$ units of the good. We use the notation $d(t)$ for the crop per unit of land at time t; that is,

$$d(t) = \frac{D(t)}{\mathbf{A}}.$$

It is not necessary that each physical unit of the land give off the same amount of the crop. We can redefine units of land so that 1 unit of land is the quantity of land that produces $d(t)$ units of output. If the land is of bad quality, then more physical units of land make up one of our crop units; and if the land is of good quality, then fewer physical units of land make up one of our crop units. This description of land captures the ideas that the crop is a very important aspect of the land and that the only economically significant differences in land are in the quantity of the crop it produces. Some of the land might be an arid desert of Nevada (or Patagonia) where thousands of hectares of land are needed to produce the same crop as 100 hectares of Kansas (or Buenos Aires province). However we get to it, 1 unit of the land will generate $d(t)$ units of the good in period t.

We allow ownership of the land, where ownership is defined as the right to all of the crop that comes off the "owned" quantity of land and the right to transfer this claim to someone else. At the beginning of period 1, the old of generation 0 own all of the land in the economy. We do not worry about how they got these claims or what they did to get the claims, only that they have them.

Because ownership gives claims to the crop from the land, we assume that the old collect the crop (without the expenditure of any energy or loss of utility by the exercise) and then can dispose of the land to members of the next generation if they wish to do so. Because the current old will be dead in the next period, there is no incentive for them to hold on to the land. They will therefore attempt to sell the land to the current young (who will be around next period to collect the next harvest). Let $p(t)$ stand for the price of 1 unit of the land at time t. This price is the *ex dividend* price or the price after the time t crop has been collected. The current young will pay $p(t)$ units of the time t good to the old in exchange for the rights to 1 unit of the land. We are interested in how the price, $p(t)$, is determined.[1]

Temporary Equilibrium with Land

We approach the problem of finding the equilibrium for an economy with land in the same way we approached the economy with government bonds. We begin by assuming that the current young have an expectation for the price for the land in the next period and that they use that price for determining what they are willing to pay for the land now, when they are young. In this part of the chapter we do not worry about how that expected price comes about.

The existence of this asset we call land does not change many features of our economy. The individuals in generation t are still interested only in the consumption of as much time t and time $t + 1$ goods as they can get. Their utility functions are the same ones we have been using, functions that depend on the consumptions in both periods of life (except for the old of time 1, who are only interested in their consumption in that period). No one will want land for itself—for nature walks, for camping trips, for places where the deer and the antelope can roam. Land might be completely unproductive sand dunes, or it might be very productive rice paddies. These features affect the price of land, but the basic reason for holding it is still the same; as with any other asset, it is a mechanism for redistributing consumption across one's lifetime.

No one can sell land short. The only sales of land permitted are under

1. We will not consider economies in which the young collude and take the land from the old, as happens in a revolution. An exercise the reader might consider for later (once the method for finding an equilibrium is explained) is to find the price sequence for the land if there will be a revolution at time $t + k$ and all of the land will be "nationalized" without compensation. Assume that after nationalization the land will become collectively owned (by the government, for example) and the output of the land is equally distributed to the old of each period.

the conditions of ownership we mentioned above. This assumption restricts individual holdings of land to be nonnegative.

At every time t, the entire quantity of land is offered for sale by the current old. No tombs exist in this economy, so the old have no use for the land after they are dead and will sell all of it. The quantity of land that is offered for sale each period is the same—given that no new land is generated, as the Dutch did by taking land from the sea, or is lost, as will happen when California falls into the ocean. The total quantity of land sold each period is fixed, that is, the supply is perfectly inelastic; so only the demand in each period for the land determines the price of the land in that period. The time t demand comes from the young of generation t.

Each young person of generation t faces a pair of budget constraints. These constraints must now include the possibility of buying and selling land. We can write the budget constraints for young person h of generation t, who lives in an economy with land, as

$$c_t^h(t) = \omega_t^h(t) - \ell^h(t) - p(t)a^h(t) \tag{6.1}$$

and $\quad c_t^h(t + 1)$

$$= \omega_t^h(t + 1) + r(t)\ell^h(t) + a^h(t)d(t + 1) + a^h(t)p^{h,e}(t + 1), \tag{6.2}$$

where $a^h(t)$ is the quantity of land that individual h of generation t chooses to purchase when young at price $p(t)$ and expects to sell when old at the price that this individual expects will occur in the next period, $p^{h,e}(t + 1)$. Recall that $d(t + 1)$ is the known quantity of crop that will be thrown off by each unit of the land. This individual will get $a^h(t)d(t + 1)$ units of the crop from owning $a^h(t)$ units of the land. Private borrowing and lending is still possible. This assumption is indicated by the inclusion in the budget constraint of $\ell^h(t)$, the amount of private borrowing or lending of person h.

Equation (6.1) says that a young person can choose to lend or borrow in the private market and can choose to buy land at the price $p(t)$. The difference between the young person's endowment and the sum of the expenditures on loans and on land is that individual's consumption when young. Equation (6.2) says that the young person will plan a consumption when old that will be the endowment plus the returns on any private loans, the returns on the sale of the land this person bought when young and the crop that that land threw off at the beginning of period $t + 1$. Recall Chapter 5 where we point out that consumption when old is equal to planned consumption when old only when the expected price is realized. We would be more accurate if we referred to consumption when old as expected consumption when old and, instead of writing the budget constraint when old as we have in Equation (6.2), wrote it as

$$c_t^{h,e}(t + 1)$$

$$= \omega_t^h(t + 1) + r(t)\ell^h(t) + a^h(t)d(t + 1) + a^h(t)p^{h,e}(t + 1). \quad (6.2')$$

This notation emphasizes the expected nature of consumption when old. We have chosen not to do this; but when we write budget constraints with consumption when old, remember that we mean *expected* consumption when old.

EXERCISE 6.1   Suppose that the crop goes to the purchaser (the young) at time t rather than to the seller (the old). Write analogues to Equations (6.1) and (6.2) for this economy.

In the budget constraint given by Equation (6.2), individual h of generation t takes as given

ω_t^h	the endowment pair
$r(t)$	the gross interest rate
$p(t)$	the time t price of the land
$d(t + 1)$	the per unit crop at time $t + 1$
$p^{h,e}(t + 1)$	the expected price of the land at time $t + 1$

Taking the above as given, this individual chooses

c_t^h	the consumption pair
$\ell^h(t)$	the amount of private borrowing or lending
$a^h(t)$	the amount of land to buy

As mentioned earlier, we ignore for the moment the question of how individual h of generation t arrived at the expected price of the land at time $t + 1$.

Recall that we are not allowing short selling of land. Therefore, $a^h(t)$ is constrained to be greater than or equal to 0. The sign of $\ell^h(t)$ is not constrained, so we can solve Equation (6.1) for this private lending and borrowing and substitute that result into Equation (6.2). The result of the substitution can be written (at equality) as

$$r(t)c_t^h(t) + c_t^h(t + 1)$$

$$= r(t)\omega_t^h(t) + \omega_t^h(t + 1) - a^h(t)[r(t)p(t) - d(t + 1) - p^{h,e}(t + 1)]. \tag{6.3}$$

This equation looks very similar to Equations (3.7)—although without taxes—and (5.3), and we will deal with it in the same manner that we dealt with the other lifetime budget constraints.

EXERCISE 6.2 Show that the constraints imposed on consumption by Equation (6.3) are equivalent to the constraints imposed by Equations (6.1) and (6.2).

Given that utility is increasing in both of its arguments, an individual would like to get the left-hand side of Equation (6.3) as large as possible. This goal is achieved by getting the right-hand side of that equation as large as possible. These incentives allow us to draw some conclusions about individual h's demand for land, that is, h's choice of $a^h(t)$.

If the portion of Equation (6.3) in the square brackets is positive—in other words, if

$$r(t) > \frac{d(t + 1) + p^{h,e}(t + 1)}{p(t)},$$

then individual h chooses $a^h(t) = 0$. A choice of any positive $a^h(t)$—the only alternative—would lower the amount of lending that the individual could do in the private lending and borrowing market. Because the private market is offering a higher rate of return than the land, any savings that could have been done in private lending that goes to purchasing land is a net loss for the individual. If the part in square brackets is negative, then the return on land is greater than the cost of borrowing, or

$$r(t) < \frac{d(t + 1) + p^{h,e}(t + 1)}{p(t)}.$$

An individual can make an infinite profit by borrowing at the lower (private market) gross interest rate and use that to buy land. The greater the amount borrowed, the more land individual h can buy and the greater the profit. Neither of these cases can be an equilibrium. If no one wants land and there is a positive amount of it, the only possible price for it is 0; but then the portion of Equation (6.3) in brackets cannot be positive. Alternatively, if everyone wants an unlimited amount of land and wants to borrow an unlimited amount, that option cannot be an equilibrium. Neither the market in land nor the market in private lending and borrowing can clear, and market clearing is one of the conditions for an equilibrium.

The only alternative left is for the portion of Equation (6.3) that is in brackets to equal 0, or for

$$r(t) = \frac{d(t + 1) + p^{h,e}(t + 1)}{p(t)}.$$

If that is the case, then individual h is indifferent between lending in the private borrowing and lending market and buying land. This observation allows us to make the following statement relating the quantity of land that an individual wishes to purchase, $a^h(t)$, to the relationship between the gross interest rate on private borrowing and lending, $r(t)$, and the expected return on purchasing land, $(d(t + 1) + p^{h,e}(t + 1))/p(t)$: Desired land purchases by person h of generation t satisfy

$$a^h(t) = \begin{cases} 0 & \text{if } r(t) > (d(t + 1) + p^{h,e}(t + 1))/p(t), \\ \infty & \text{if } r(t) < (d(t + 1) + p^{h,e}(t + 1))/p(t), \\ ? & \text{if } r(t) = (d(t + 1) + p^{h,e}(t + 1))/p(t). \end{cases}$$

If there is unanimity regarding the expected future price of land, then we get the following proposition.

Proposition 6.1 *If there is unanimity, namely,*

$$p^{h,e}(t + 1) = p^e(t + 1),$$

for all h in generation t, then, in any equilibrium in which desired land purchases equal the land supplied,

$$r(t)p(t) = d(t + 1) + p^e(t + 1). \tag{6.4}$$

EXERCISE 6.3 Prove Proposition 6.1.

The proposition states that the price of land, $p(t)$, the rate of return on private borrowing and lending, $r(t)$, and the expected payoff from the holding of land, $d(t + 1) + p^e(t + 1)$, satisfy a present value formula. If we divide both sides of Equation (6.4) by $r(t)$, then the current price of land can be seen to be the discounted value of the total return that land will yield in time $t + 1$. We are discounting by the gross interest rate on private borrowing and lending. Equivalently, the rate of return on land equals the rate of return on the private borrowing and lending.

From now on we assume unanimity of price expectations. This assumption means that

$$p^{h,e}(t + 1) = p^e(t + 1)$$

for all h of generation t. As we did in Chapter 5 in the economy with long-term government bonds, we can define a time t temporary equilibrium for this economy with land.

Definition *Given $p^e(t + 1)$, a time t temporary equilibrium is a land price, $p(t)$, a gross interest rate, $r(t)$, land purchases, loans granted and received at t, and a pattern of consumption of time t good that*
   (i) maximize utility for all members of generation t subject to their budget constraints, and
   (ii) clear the markets for land, loans, and the consumption good at time t.

To find a temporary equilibrium in an economy with land, we go through a process very similar to the one we went through for the economy with government bonds. We first find the appropriate savings functions for individuals and then for the generation. We then use the market clearing condition to find the equilibrium price and quantities. The particular conditions that will give us the temporary equilibrium for this economy are

$$S_t(r(t)) = p(t)\mathbf{A},$$

and $\quad p(t) = \dfrac{p^e(t+1)}{r(t)}.$

We now explain why these particular conditions determine a temporary equilibrium for an economy with land.

For prices that satisfy Equation (6.4), Equation (6.3) reduces to

$$r(t)c_t^h(t) + c_t^h(t+1) = r(t)\omega_t^h(t) + \omega_t^h(t+1). \tag{6.5}$$

Thus, in a temporary equilibrium, as defined above, the affordable consumption bundles depend only on the gross interest rate, $r(t)$ (and the endowments), exactly as they did in the competitive equilibrium of Chapter 2. In other words, Equation (6.5) is the appropriate budget constraint. Given a particular $r(t)$, an individual who wishes to dissave can do so only by borrowing in the private borrowing and lending market. For this individual, $\ell^h(t)$ is negative. If an individual h wishes to save, there are three options. The individual can lend on the private borrowing and lending market—$\ell^h(t)$ is positive—or can buy land, or do some of both. Because in equilibrium, the rates of return on loans and on land are equal, the individual is interested only in the total amount of savings and is indifferent about the composition of that savings between private lending and land purchases.

Maximization of a utility function subject to the constraint given in Equation (6.5) gives us the same savings functions that we found in Chapter 2, namely, $s_t^h(r(t))$. By summing these functions over all members of generation t, we get the same aggregate savings function for generation t, namely, $S_t(r(t))$.

In an economy in which the only outside asset is land (an economy in which there are no government bonds), the aggregate savings of each generation are equal to the amount it will pay the old for the land. Private lending and borrowing stay inside the generation and do not show up in the aggregate. The payments by generation t to the old of generation $t - 1$ are the total amount of the time t endowment of the young that is not consumed by the young (in aggregate). This difference between endowment and consumption is savings, so aggregate savings of generation t are equal to the price of each unit of land, $p(t)$, times the total units of land, $\mathbf{A}$. This relation is written as

$$S_t(r(t)) = p(t)\mathbf{A}. \tag{6.6}$$

The derivation above can be made explicit. The total time t good available at time t is

$$\sum_{h=1}^{N(t-1)} \omega_{t-1}^h(t) + \sum_{h=1}^{N(t)} \omega_t^h(t) + D(t).$$

Notice that the total amount of the time t good that is available is equal to the sum of endowments and the crop at time t. As a market clearing condition, this total quantity of time t good must equal the total consumption at time t. This condition is

$$\sum_{h=1}^{N(t-1)} c_{t-1}^h(t) + \sum_{h=1}^{N(t)} c_t^h(t) = \sum_{h=1}^{N(t-1)} \omega_{t-1}^h(t) + \sum_{h=1}^{N(t)} \omega_t^h(t) + D(t). \tag{6.7}$$

The total consumption of the old at time t is equal to

$$\sum_{h=1}^{N(t-1)} c_{t-1}^h(t) = \sum_{h=1}^{N(t-1)} \omega_{t-1}^h(t) + D(t) + p(t)\mathbf{A}. \tag{6.8}$$

Subtracting the consumption of the old from the total consumption at time t gives us the total consumption of the young. So subtracting Equation (6.8) from Equation (6.7), we find that

$$\sum_{h=1}^{N(t)} c_t^h(t) = \sum_{h=1}^{N(t)} \omega_t^h(t) - p(t)\mathbf{A};$$

this expression is equivalent to Equation (6.6).

If we sum the budget constraints of the young, we get the same result as above. The budget constraint when young of member h of generation t is

$$c_h^t(t) = \omega_t^h(t) - \ell^h(t) - p(t)a^h(t).$$

Summing over $h = 1$ to $N(t)$, we get

$$\sum_{h=1}^{N(t)} c_t^h(t) = \sum_{h=1}^{N(t)} \omega_t^h(t) - \sum_{h=1}^{N(t)} \ell^h(t) - p(t)\mathbf{A};$$

and, because the sum of private borrowing and lending within a generation equals 0, this result is equal to the expression for total consumption of the young that we derived in the preceding paragraph.

Note that the introduction of the crop, $D(t)$, alters the conditions for feasibility and efficiency of consumption allocations. Efficiency now requires that total consumption be more than the sum of individual endowments and that the entire crop be allocated each period. Equation (6.7) is the efficiency constraint for any period t.

Equation (6.6) contains almost all that is needed to find the temporary equilibrium when $\mathbf{A}$, the utility functions, $N(t)$, $d(t + 1)$, $p^e(t + 1)$, and the endowments are given. We need to find $p(t)$ and $r(t)$ to have the equilibrium completely described. Equation (6.6) says that

$$S_t(r(t)) = p(t)\mathbf{A}. \tag{6.6}$$

Note that both $r(t)$ and $p(t)$ appear in this equation. We have one equation in two unknowns, but we need at least two equations to solve for the two unknowns. As the second equation, we use the constraint that we found from studying the budget constraint, namely, Equation (6.3). That present value result linked the expected price, the current price, and the gross interest rate. The present value result is in Equation (6.4); and, after rearranging, Equation (6.4) shows that the current price equals the discounted value of expected returns, or

$$p(t) = \frac{d(t + 1) + p^e(t + 1)}{r(t)}. \tag{6.4}$$

Substituting this equation into Equation (6.6), we get

$$S_t(r(t)) = \left[\frac{d(t + 1) + p^e(t + 1)}{r(t)}\right]\mathbf{A},$$

which can be rearranged to give

$$r(t)S_t(r(t)) = [d(t + 1) + p^e(t + 1)]\mathbf{A}. \tag{6.9}$$

Everything on the right-hand side of the equation is already given. The left-hand side is a function of $r(t)$ alone. Under mild conditions on $S_t(\cdot)$, there is at least one $r(t)$ that solves this equation. Given any such $r(t)$, Equation (6.4) can then be used to find $p(t)$. That operation completes the determination of the time t temporary equilibrium in an economy with land and unanimous expectations about the price of that land in the next period.

An Example

Consider an economy at date t, where

$$N(t) = 100;$$

$$u_t^h = c_t^h(t)[c_t^h(t + 1)]^\beta, \beta = 1;$$

and $\omega_t^h = [3, 1].$

At time t, the expectation about the time $t + 1$ price of land is $p^e(t + 1) = 2; d(t + 1) = 2;$ and $\mathbf{A} = 100$ units of land.
   The savings function for an individual is

$$s_t^h(r(t)) = \frac{3}{2} - \frac{1}{2r(t)},$$

and the aggregate savings function for the economy is

$$S_t(r(t)) = 150 - \frac{50}{r(t)}.$$

The condition for a temporary equilibrium is Equation (6.9). Therefore, substituting into Equation (6.9) the specific savings function, quantity of land, crop size, and expected price gives us

$$r(t)S_t(r(t)) = [d(t + 1) + p^e(t + 1)]\mathbf{A}, \tag{6.9}$$

or $r(t)\left[150 - \dfrac{50}{r(t)} \right] = 100[2 + 2]$.

That result can be rearranged to yield $150r(t) = 450$, or $r(t) = 3$.

The current price of the land, $p(t)$, is found from Equation (6.4). Substituting the values we have in this example into that equation gives $p(t) = \frac{4}{3}$. Individuals are each saving

$$s_t^h(t) = \frac{3}{2} - \frac{1}{2r(t)} = \frac{3}{2} - \frac{1}{6} = \frac{4}{3}.$$

A time t temporary equilibrium demands that we know, at time t, the expected time $t + 1$ price of the land. To be able to study the evolution of these economies over time, we need to be able to construct sequences of equilibria based on sequences of expected one-period-ahead prices on the land. We use the term *sequence of temporary equilibria* to refer to a sequence comprising a time t temporary equilibrium at each $t \geq 1$. Notice that for some of the exercises below, the expected time $t + 1$ price of land will not be the price that occurs at time $t + 1$.

EXERCISE 6.4 Describe completely the sequence of temporary equilibria for each of the following economies.

a. $N(t) = 100$, $u_t^h = c_t^h(t)c_t^h(t + 1)$, $\omega_t^h = [2, 1]$, for all h and $t \geq 1$. $\mathbf{A} = 100$, $d(t + 1) = 1$, and $p^e(t + 1) = 1$ for all $t \geq 1$.

b. The same as a except that $p^e(t + 1) = \frac{1}{2}$ for all $t \geq 1$.

c. The same as a except that

$$d(t) = \begin{cases} \frac{1}{2} & \text{if } t \text{ is odd,} \\ \frac{3}{2} & \text{if } t \text{ is even.} \end{cases}$$

d. The same as a except that for all $t \geq 1$,

$$\omega_t^h = \begin{cases} [2, 1], & \text{for } h = 1, 2, \ldots, 50, \\ [1, 1], & \text{for } h = 51, 52, \ldots, 100. \end{cases}$$

e. The same as a except that for all h,

$$\omega_t^h = \begin{cases} [2, 1], & \text{for } t \text{ odd}, \\ [1, 1], & \text{for } t \text{ even}. \end{cases}$$

A Price Function

Equation (6.6) can be solved another way. We can rearrange Equation (6.4) as

$$r(t) = \frac{d(t + 1) + p^e(t + 1)}{p(t)}$$

and substitute the right-hand side into (6.6). That substitution gives

$$S_t\left[\frac{d(t + 1) + p^e(t + 1)}{p(t)}\right] = p(t)\mathbf{A}. \tag{6.10}$$

Under some conditions on the savings functions,[2] Equation (6.10) can be solved for $p(t)$ as a function of the expected price, $p^e(t + 1)$. We call such a function the *price function*. This price function, which we write as

$$p(t) = f_t(p^e(t + 1)),$$

is similar to the price function for government bonds defined in Chapter 5. The function would be logically identical to the one in Chapter 5 if we wrote it as

$$p(t) = f_t(p^e(t + 1) + d(t + 1)).$$

We choose to write it without $d(t + 1)$ as an explicit parameter to emphasize the relationship between expected time $t + 1$ and time t prices. For the economy in Exercise 6.3a, Equation (6.10) becomes [we will

---

2. A sufficient condition for solution is that the aggregate savings function is increasing in terms of $r(t)$; that is, at higher gross interest rates, individuals will save more.

leave both $p^e(t + 1)$ and $d(t + 1)$ as variables]

$$100 - \frac{50p(t)}{d(t + 1) + p^e(t + 1)} = 100p(t).$$

After a little algebraic manipulation, we get the function

$$p(t) = f_t(p^e(t + 1))$$
$$= \frac{2d(t + 1) + 2p^e(t + 1)}{2d(t + 1) + 2p^e(t + 1) + 1}. \tag{6.11}$$

This function is graphed in Figure 6.1 for the cases where $d(t + 1) = 0$ (the solid line), $d(t + 1) = .5$ (the dashed line), and $d(t + 1) = 1$ (the dotted line). For a given $d(t + 1)$, the time t price for the land can be found for each expected price for time $t + 1$. The solid line on this graph is the same as the one in Figure 5.1. The graph in Figure 5.1 shows the time t price for a k-period government bond as a function of the price expected for that bond in time $t + 1$.

Figure 6.1 is different from Figure 5.1 in one very important way. The existence of a positive quantity of the crop, $d(t + 1)$, that is thrown off by the land changes the relationship between current price and expected future price. Consider two economies that differ only by the long-term asset that is available to the citizens. Economy 1 has land;

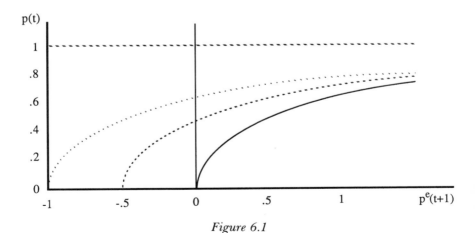

Figure 6.1

economy 2 has k-period government bonds. Assume there are the same number of k-period bonds as units of land and that there is no crop thrown off by the land. Otherwise the economies are identical—in preferences, population, and endowments. If the expected price of 1 unit of land in time $t + 1$ in economy 1 were the same as the expected price of one $k - 1$-period bond in time $t + 1$ in economy 2, then the current prices of land and bonds would be the same and the gross interest rate on private borrowing and lending would be the same in each of these economies. In both cases the relationship between the expected price and the current price is given by Figure 5.1. In both of these economies, if the expected price of the asset in time $t + 1$ is 0, then the current price of the asset is 0.

When there is a positive crop, that is, when $d(t + 1) > 0$, the function between expected price in time $t + 1$ and the time t price changes. The most interesting place to note this change is when the expected price of land equals 0. In Figure 6.1, when the expected price of the land is 0, the current price is not 0 for the cases where $d(t + 1)$ equals .5 and 1. The rights to the crop that the land will throw off have value, and the current young will be willing to pay something for those rights even though they know that the sale price of the land in the next period will be 0. (Of course, if the land is going to continue to throw off a crop, then the land *will* have a positive price in the equilibrium that occurs at time $t + 1$. We are, however, speaking about arbitrarily formed expectations and are not yet considering how they are formed.)

Set the expected time $t + 1$ price of the land in Equation (6.11) equal to 0. The equation is then

$$p(t) = \frac{2d(t + 1)}{2d(t + 1) + 1}. \tag{6.12}$$

This equation shows that the time t price of the land rises with the amount of the crop, with an upper limit of $p(t) = 1$. The smaller the crop, the closer the price is to 0, with the price being exactly 0 when the crop is also 0. The three curves in Figure 6.1 confirm this observation. The solid line is the case where $d(t + 1)$ equals 0, and the price at time t is 0 when the expected time $t + 1$ is 0. The dashed and dotted lines are the cases where $d(t + 1)$ is greater than 0 (.5 and 1, respectively), and the greater the crop, the higher the price when the expected time $t + 1$ price is 0. The $p(t)$ that we find from Equation (6.12) is the intercept on the vertical axis of the price equation (6.11). Notice that, in this example, the current price, $p(t)$, will never be greater than 1 and will asymptotically approach 1 as $p^e(t + 1)$ goes to infinity. Because Equation (6.12) gives the lower bound of the current price of land and 1 is the upper bound, the larger the crop, the smaller the set of possible current prices of land.

For this example economy, the greater the crop, the higher the time t price of the land for every expected time $t + 1$ price. The dotted and dashed lines of Figure 6.1 are above the solid line $[d(t + 1) = 0]$ for all expected time $t + 1$ prices. Similarly, the dotted line $[d(t + 1) = 1]$ is above the dashed line $[d(t + 1) = .5]$ for all illustrated expected time $t + 1$ prices.

Up to now, we have not worried about where the price $p^e(t + 1)$ comes from. It is generated by the beliefs of the young; but these beliefs must be based on something. We need to consider where these beliefs come from.

We have shown how similar the modeling of land is to the modeling of government long-term bonds. There is, however, one very important difference. The long-term bonds finally reached maturity and were paid off (if not rolled over) by taxing the young of some generation to get the revenues. The promise of the government helps to generate a final, time $t + k$ price for the bond. Recall that we worked backward from the price of the bonds at that date (1 unit of the good per bond) to find the price of the k-period bond at any earlier date. With land, there is no date at which a particular price is fixed by the government (or anyone else), so finding an equilibrium requires a different approach.

Perfect Foresight Competitive Equilibria

We have already defined the time t temporary equilibrium as the time t gross interest rate and price pair, $[r(t), p(t)]$, that results in land purchases, private borrowing and lending, and a consumption pattern that maximizes utility (given the budget constraints) and clears all markets for the given expected price of land, $p^e(t + 1)$. We want to point out that the particular temporary equilibrium we are in depends on the price of land that is expected to hold in the next period.

Definition *A perfect foresight competitive equilibrium for an economy with land is a sequence of $p(t)$'s and $r(t)$'s and the other endogenous (dependent)* *variables such that the time t values are a time t temporary equilibrium for an economy with land where $p^e(t + 1) = p(t + 1)$.*

In a perfect foresight competitive equilibrium, the price of land that is expected to hold in the next period is always the price that does hold. We are now interested in infinite sequences of prices and gross interest rates. The time t temporary equilibrium is an equilibrium for only one period. But we want the equilibrium price of time $t + 1$ to be the price that is expected at time t to hold at time $t + 1$, for all $t \geq 1$. A perfect foresight competitive equilibrium is a sequence of values for the endogenous variables with the property that the tth term of the sequence is a time t temporary equilibrium given that beliefs about prices in the future are given by the subsequent terms in the sequence.

From now on, we use the term *equilibrium* to refer to a perfect foresight competitive equilibrium.

As mentioned earlier, we studied perfect foresight equilibria in the chapter on long-term government bonds (Chapter 5). There, however, the problem was somewhat simpler than the one we have here. The government, which issued the k-period bonds at time t, promised to pay them off at time $t + k$ at a rate of 1 unit of the time $t + k$ good per bond. This promise by the government (which we assumed was always kept) fixed a value that these bonds would have at some future date. Because this price of bonds (1 unit of the time $t + k$ good per bond) was known to all in the perfect foresight equilibrium, it was possible, under some other conditions, to work successively backward from time $t + k$ and find the perfect foresight equilibrium. The price of the bonds at time $t + k - 1$ was found by applying the (now) standard one-period bond analysis. Once the price at time $t + k - 1$ was found, the same method was used to find the price at time $t + k - 2$, and so on until the price at time t was reached. The whole sequence of prices depended on the knowledge of the time $t + k$ price of the bonds.

For a time t temporary equilibrium to hold, the present value condition must hold for the current price of land, or,

$$r(t)p(t) = d(t + 1) + p^e(t + 1), \tag{6.4}$$

and the markets must clear while the citizens are maximizing utility subject to their budget constraints, or

$$S_t(r(t)) = p(t)\mathbf{A}. \tag{6.6}$$

Replacing the price expected at time $t + 1$ with the price that actually occurs in the equilibrium sequence, we rewrite Equation (6.4) as

$$r(t)p(t) = d(t + 1) + p(t + 1). \tag{6.13}$$

Substituting a rearrangement of this expression into Equation (6.6), for $r(t)$, we get

$$S_t\left(\frac{d(t + 1) + p(t + 1)}{p(t)}\right) = p(t)\mathbf{A}. \tag{6.14}$$

If we can find a nonnegative[3] $p(t)$ sequence that satisfies Equation (6.14) for all $t \geq 1$, then we will have found an equilibrium. Once this $p(t)$ sequence is found, it is quite straightforward to find the $r(t)$ sequence from Equation (6.13). The two sequences, $\{p(t)\}$ and $\{r(t)\}$, can be shown to satisfy the definition of a perfect foresight competitive equilibrium.

We use two methods for finding equilibria for these perfect foresight economies. One we call guess and verify. There are two versions of the guess and verify method. In one we choose prices for time t and see whether the sequence of $p(t + n)$'s that result from that $p(t)$ obey some equilibrium conditions. This method, although sometimes ungainly, will find equilibria if they exist. The second version of the guess and verify method applies to stationary economies, that is, economies in which the environment is always the same. We hypothesize that there exists a stationary price sequence and solve for that single price. If there are nonstationary equilibrium prices, this method does not find them. This second guess and verify technique will usually allow us to find *some* of the equilibria fairly easily.

The second method is a graphical analysis of the models. We use the price functions we found above and consider, graphically, the price sequences that can fulfill those price functions. The graphical method has the advantage of allowing us to find *all* of the equilibria for an economy. In the following sections we use these solution techniques on some example economies.

---

3. Recall that we are allowing only nonnegative prices, so free disposal of the land is allowed.

Three Example Economies

We consider three example economies and refer to them by number. Economy 1 is similar to an economy we have used a lot already. In it, everyone is identical, population is constant, and a fixed quantity of land throws off a fixed quantity of crop. Economy 2 is the same as economy 1 except that we have rich and poor, and the rich are relatively richer only in the first period of their life. Economy 3 is similar to economy 1 except that there is a 10 percent growth of population each period. Economy 3 will be used, mostly, in exercises. These economies are defined below.

Economy 1 $N(t) = 100$, $\mathbf{A} = 100$, $d(t) = 1$, $\omega_t^h = [2, 1]$, $u_t^h = c_t^h(t) \cdot c_t^h(t + 1)$, *for all h and all t.*

Economy 2   *Same as economy 1 except*

$$\omega_t^h = \begin{cases} [2, 1], & \text{for } h \text{ odd,} \\ [1, 1], & \text{for } h \text{ even.} \end{cases}$$

Economy 3   *Same as economy 1 except* $N(t) = (1.1)N(t - 1)$ *and* $N(1) = 100$.

EXERCISE 6.5   Write out the explicit form of Equation (6.14) for each of the three economies.

Notice that explicitly writing out Equation (6.14) for economy 3 requires that the savings function be time dependent. We already have been writing a general form of the savings equation that is time dependent, and we have denoted that time t savings function by $S_t(r(t))$. When the aggregate savings function is autonomous, when it is independent of time, we drop the t subscript and indicate that the savings *function* is the same at all time periods by writing it as $S(r(t))$.

Equation (6.14) for time $t = 1$ is written as

$$S_1\left(\frac{d(2) + p(2)}{p(1)}\right) = p(1)\mathbf{A}.$$

The functional form of the savings function, $d(2)$, and **A** are all known. The above equation has two unknowns, $p(1)$ and $p(2)$. We may be able to solve the equation to give us one of the prices as a function of the other. However, we still do not know what that other price is. We can gain another equation by moving one step into the future. At that date, time $t = 2$, there is another version of Equation (6.14) that must hold for an equilibrium. This equation is

$$S_2\left(\frac{d(3) + p(3)}{p(2)}\right) = p(2)\mathbf{A}.$$

Again, the functional form of the savings function, $d(3)$, and **A** are given. The equation can be solved for $p(2)$ as a function of $p(3)$, and we can substitute that functional form into the time 1 version and find $p(1)$ as a function of $p(3)$. Unfortunately, $p(3)$ remains unknown. We can move on to time period $t = 3$ and solve Equation (6.14) for that date and find $p(3)$ as a function of $p(4)$. This function can be substituted into the equation above to find $p(2)$ as a function of $p(4)$ and substituting once again, we can find $p(1)$ as a function of $p(4)$.

The problem we encounter with the above analysis is that we are always one equation short. We always have some $p(T)$ that needs to be determined in order to find the values for the whole sequence of $p(t)$'s. In the case of k-period government bonds issued at time t, $p(t + k)$ equaled 1 and the whole sequence could be found on the basis of that knowledge. But looking at the pricing of land from this perspective, we cannot find enough equations to match the number of unknowns. We always come up one short. Does this one extra unknown mean that there are an infinite number of equilibria that can solve these economies?

Often when there are fewer equations than unknowns, there are an infinite number of solutions. Consider the pairs of (x, y)'s that solve the equation

$$y = 10 + 2x.$$

In this example there are infinite pairs of solutions. For any x, there is a corresponding y that solves the equation. If we had another linear equation that expressed x as a function of z, for example,

$$x = 13 - 7z,$$

it would still not help us. Substituting into the above equation, we find y as a function of z, but there is still an infinite set of pairs (now of y and z) that solve

$$y = 36 - 14z.$$

With linear equations, it seems, there is no way out of our lack of one equation.

Our equations are somewhat more complicated than linear equations. We also have restrictions about permissible values for the $r(t)$'s and $p(t)$'s that are in our sequence. For example, we do not permit any of the $r(t)$'s or any of the $p(t)$'s to be less than 0. There may also be upper bounds on the prices of land at time t that can be equilibrium prices. Recall that when we graphed the price function for

$$p(t) = f_t(p(t + 1)),$$

in Figure (6.1), the set of $p(t)$'s were limited by an upper bound. If we begin with a $p(t)$ that results in a $p(t + 1)$ larger than the upper bound for $p(t + 1)$ in the function

$$p(t + 1) = f_{t+1}(p(t + 2)),$$

then we cannot find a $p(t + 2)$ to satisfy the sequence. Such a sequence would violate the upper bound restriction and could not be an equilibrium sequence. We may be able to use these two types of restrictions to reduce to a finite number the infinite number of sequences that can fulfill our equations.

To consider whether it is necessarily the case that we have an infinite number of solutions, we proceed as follows with a technique we might call an uninformed guess and verify. We can arbitrarily choose a positive value for $p(1)$ and use the explicit form of Equation (6.14) for time 1 to find $p(2)$ (or possibly more than one). Then we can use that value (those values, if nonunique) for $p(2)$ and the explicit form of Equation (6.14) for time 2 to find $p(3)$ (or possibly more than one). We throw out any negative $p(t)$ or any that exceed the upper bound if we have multiples. If, for *any* starting $p(t)$, the process always generates a nonnegative sequence that does not violate the upper bound constraint, then our situation is analogous to having one linear equation in two unknowns. If, on

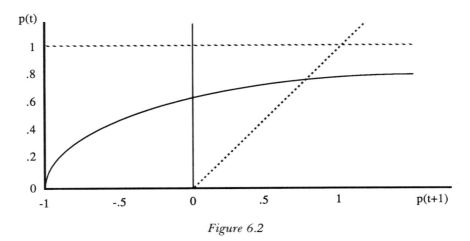

Figure 6.2

the other hand, we encounter a unique negative $p(t)$ for any t [or the case where all of the multiple $p(t)$'s are negative for some t] or one that violates the upper bound, then that sequence cannot be an equilibrium. It might be possible to eliminate all but one or a few sequences of $p(t)$'s. If it is, then we can escape the indeterminacy that is threatened by fewer equations than unknowns.

For economy 1, we can write out explicitly Equation (6.14) and then solve for $p(t + 1)$ as a function of $p(t)$. The explicit form of (6.14) is

$$100\left(1 - \frac{p(t)}{2(p(t + 1) + d(t + 1))}\right) = 100p(t),$$

and solving that equation to get $p(t + 1)$ as a function of $p(t)$, we have

$$p(t + 1) = .5\left(\frac{p(t)}{1 - p(t)} - 2d(t + 1)\right). \tag{6.15}$$

Equation (6.15) is graphed[4] in Figure 6.2, but with $p(t + 1)$ on the horizontal axis (in keeping with our presentation of these graphs in the

---

4. The function that is actually graphed is $p(t)$ as a function of $p(t + 1)$. For example economy 1, that function is

$$p(t) = \frac{2d(t + 1) + 2p(t + 1)}{2d(t + 1) + 2p(t + 1) + 1}.$$

earlier chapters). To find the $p(t + 1)$ [in this case, there is only one $p(t + 1)$ for each $p(t)$], trace over from the chosen $p(t)$ to the curve and then read down to find the value for $p(t + 1)$ that is generated by that $p(t)$. Because economy 1 has the same savings function in every period, the function giving $p(t + 1)$ as a function of $p(t)$ is the same for every period. Note that this constancy is not true for economy 3.

EXERCISE 6.6 Write out the explicit version of Equation (6.15) for economies 2 and 3.

Using Equation (6.15), we can check several values of $p(1)$ to see whether they could be equilibria. Table 6.1 gives the numerical sequences that arise from some choices of $p(1)$. To demonstrate how the numbers in Table 6.1 were determined, we present one of the calculations. A choice of $p(1) = .75$ gives us

$$p(2) = .5\left(\frac{.75}{.25} - 2\right) = .5$$

and $p(3) = .5\left(\frac{.5}{.5} - 2\right) = -.5.$

Because $p(3)$ is negative, $p(1) = .75$ cannot be an equilibrium for this economy. Figure 6.3 illustrates how the graph of the function (6.15) can

Table 6.1 Sequences of $p(t)$'s arising from various guesses for $p(1)$

$p(1)$	$p(2)$	$p(3)$	$p(4)$
2/3	0.0	−1.0	—
0.7	1/6	−0.9	—
0.75	0.5	−0.5	—
0.77	0.673	0.033	−0.983
0.78[a]	0.78[a]	0.78[a]	0.78[a]
0.8	1.0	—[b]	—

a. 0.78 = 0.780776.
b. Price violates the upper bound.

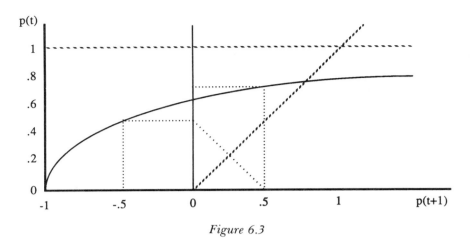

Figure 6.3

be used to determine the potential equilibria. The dotted line traces out
the calculations for a choice of $p(1) = .75$. We trace over from .75 to
the function and down to .5. The 45-degree line from .5 on the horizontal axis to .5 on the vertical axis indicates that we are moving one
step into the future and we now look at the results we get for $p(3)$ when
$p(2)$ is .5. From .5 on the vertical axis, we trace over to the function (in
the negative direction) and find a value of $-.5$ for $p(3)$.

The horizontal, dashed line at $p(t) = 1$ in Figure 6.3 is the upper
limit of the function that gives us $p(t)$ from $p(t + 1)$ for economy 1.
Also notice that the curve for the function crosses the vertical axis
$[p(t + 1) = 0]$ at $p(t) = \frac{2}{3}$. The only potential $p(1)$'s that make any sense
to investigate are those between $\frac{2}{3}$ and 1. Any $p(1)$ below $\frac{2}{3}$ will give a
negative $p(2)$. Any $p(1)$ above 1 violates the upper bound. The range of
allowable values for $p(1)$ can be reduced quite quickly. A $p(2)$ greater
than 1 also violates the upper bound, and $p(1) = .8$ gives a $p(2)$ of 1. So
$p(1)$ must be between .666 and .8.

The unique equilibrium to economy 1 is the point at which the
45-degree line out of the origin crosses the function in Figure 6.3. At
$p(1) = .780776, p(1) = p(2) = p(3) = \ldots$. For economy 1, all other values for $p(1)$ either generate some $p(t) < 0$ or some $p(t)$ that is undeter-
mined because $p(t - 1)$ was greater than 1.

In the equilibrium we found for example economy 1, the consumptions of each generation are the same as the consumptions of every
other generation. We will call this kind of equilibrium, where the con-

sumptions are the same in every period, a *stationary equilibrium.* In economies in which the environmental variables (the preferences, the endowments, the population, and in this case, the quantity of land) are the same in every period, a stationary equilibrium implies that the rates of returns on all valued assets are the same in each period.

Definition *Given an economy with a stationary environment, in the sense that the environmental variables are the same in each period, a* stationary equilibrium *is a perfect foresight competitive equilibrium in which the consumptions are the same for every generation.*

In an economy with a stationary environment, there is a "smart" guess and verify method. Because the physical environment is the same in every period, one can guess that there might be an equilibrium in which the price of land is the same in every period (there might be other equilibria as well). Using the price function for the stationary economy, we find the price, $p(t)$, such that

$$p(t) = f(p(t + 1)) = f(p(t)),$$

because we are guessing that there exists an equilibrium in which $p(t) = p(t + 1)$. The price function does not have a time subscript because, in a stationary environment, it is the same for every period. The stationary equilibrium—the one where the price is the same in every period—can be found by solving this equation. It can also be found from the aggregate savings function, where

$$S\left(\frac{d(t + 1) + p(t + 1)}{p(t)}\right) = p(t)\mathbf{A}.$$

Setting $p(t + 1)$ equal to $p(t)$, the above equation has only one unknown, $p(t)$, and can be solved for a stationary equilibrium. If such a solution to this equation exists, it is an equilibrium for the economy. The equilibrium gross interest rate can be calculated from

$$r(t) = \frac{p(t) + d(t + 1)}{p(t)}.$$

EXERCISE 6.7 Find an equilibrium for economy 2.

EXERCISE 6.8 Find an equilibrium for economy 1, except that $d(t) = 0.5$ for all t.

EXERCISE 6.9 Show that $p(t) = p$, for some constant p, and $p(t + 1) = 1.1p(t)$ are not equilibria for economy 3.

EXERCISE 6.10 Consider economy 1 but with $d(t) = d > 0$ for all t. Show that, for each $d(t)$, the only equilibrium land price sequence is one with a constant price of land and that the price, p, depends on the value of d. What happens to the land price, p, as we look at different economies where d goes to 0?

The Price of Land and the Crop

Consider an economy like economy 1, except that it has different $d(t)$'s. Figure 6.4 shows $p(t)$ as a function of $p(t + 1)$ for three of these economies. The solid curve is for the economy where $d(t) = 1$ for all t. The dashed line is for the economy where $d(t) = .5$ for all t. The dotted line is for the economy where $d(t) = 0$ for all t. Note that for the savings functions we are using here, the point where the curve crosses the hori-

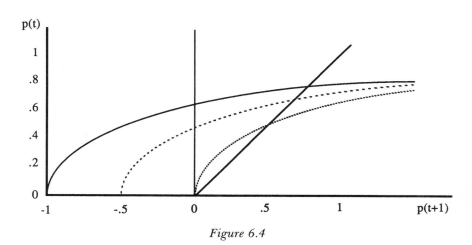

Figure 6.4

zontal axis is $-d(t)$. The 45-degree line [the line from the origin to point (1, 1), which is the set of points where $p(t) = p(t + 1)$] crosses each of the three curves at the stationary equilibrium price of land for economy 1 with the appropriate size crop.

The shapes of the three curves illustrated (and curves for economy 1 with any positive crop) are exactly the same. The only differences are the points of contact with the horizontal axis. Each of these curves is monotonic in $p(t)$ and in the limit goes to $p(t) = 1$. In other words, the $d(t) = .5$ curve will always be above the $d(t) = 0$ curve. Given that some crop d^1 is greater than some crop d^2, the curve for d^1 will always be above the curve for d^2.

We find the stationary equilibrium for these particular variations of economy 1 at the point where they cross a 45-degree line out of the origin [a $p(t) = p(t + 1)$ line]. The higher lines (that go with the larger crop) intersect the 45-degree line at higher prices. For these economies, as the crop goes to 0, the price of land goes toward $\frac{1}{2}$. Note that for the case where $d(t) = 0$, there is a second stationary equilibrium. The 45-degree line "crosses" that curve at the point where both $p(t)$ and $p(t + 1)$ equal 0. There are two possible stationary equilibria for the case where there is no crop. Using the economy 1 with $d(t) = 0$, the reader should demonstrate that, for $p(1)$ less than $\frac{1}{2}$ (but positive), the sequence of prices, $\{p(t)\}$, $t = 2$ to ∞, does not go to negative prices but converges to 0. The demonstration can be done using Figure 6.4 and tracing the time path for some $p(t)$'s less than $\frac{1}{2}$. There are an infinite number of these paths for the economy with $d(t)$ equal to 0, one for each $p(1)$ strictly between $\frac{1}{2}$ and 0.

Figure 6.5 shows the equilibrium price for constant crop sizes between 0 and 4 units of the good. The curve is found by solving Equation 6.15 for stationary equilibria, where $p(t)$ equals $p(t + 1)$. One then gets the price as a function of the crop. The curve in Figure 6.5 confirms the results of the preceding paragraph in which we illustrated how larger crops would generate higher equilibrium prices for land.

Figure 6.6 shows a version of economy 1 where $d(t)$ is less than 0. In this economy, owning land generates a cost that is proportional to the quantity of land that one owns. It could be that the land requires maintenance or that the physical crop is 0 but the government imposes a tax on land that is proportional to the amount of land owned. There are an infinite number of equilibria for this economy, two of them stationary and the rest converging to the lower of the two stationary equilibria.

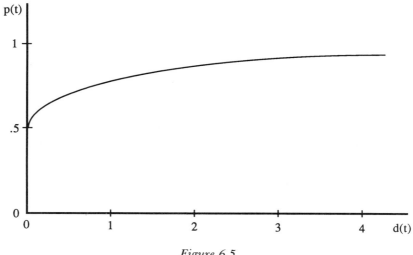

Figure 6.5

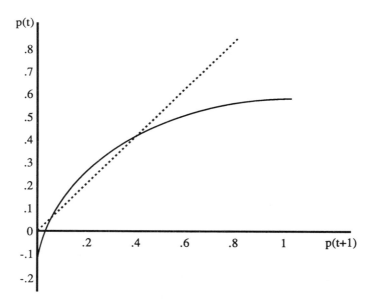

Figure 6.6

For $p(1)$ positive but below the lower point where the curve crosses the 45-degree line, $p(t)$ for $t > 1$ is increasing and converges to the lower intersection of the curve and the 45-degree line. For cases where $p(1)$ is between the two points where the curve crosses the 45-degree line, $p(t)$ is decreasing and approaches the same lower intersection as above. In the terminology of chaos theory, the lower of the two stationary equilibria is called an *attractor* in the sense that a price sequence that begins with a price near it will converge over time to that equilibrium price. The upper stationary equilibrium is called a *repeller* in the sense that a price sequence that begins near it (but not exactly at the stationary equilibrium price) will start a path that moves away from that stationary equilibrium. Prices above the upper stationary equilibrium price cannot be equilibria. Prices below the upper stationary equilibrium follow equilibrium paths toward the lower stationary equilibrium.

---

*EXERCISE 6.11 (Consumption versus income taxes) For economies with land, formulate and prove an equivalence result between consumption and income taxes along the lines of the one in Exercise 3.2.

EXERCISE 6.12 Read a little about Henry George, a nineteenth-century American who advocated a single tax, a tax on land rents (which the reader can interpret as the crop). How would one use the model of this section to analyze the effects of the kind of tax system that George favored?

International Capital Movements

Many countries become concerned about foreign ownership of their assets. Newspapers and politicians in the United States (and other countries) decry the selling of the country to foreign interests. Farmland, factories, office buildings, and residential structures have been sold to foreign owners. For each of the years in the mid-1980s, foreign citizens have purchased more than $100 billion worth of U.S. assets.

The sale to foreign nationals of a nation's assets is directly related to the net trade flows of that nation. Is it good or bad for a country (in Pareto superiority terms) to have net imports or net exports? Why might a country choose to export more than it imports? The difference between the value of exports and the value of imports is made up with asset flows. If a country exports more than it imports, then it will be investing the difference in assets of some foreign country. The issue of foreign ownership of assets and of unbalanced trade flows can be addressed by using our model with land.

Consider a world with two countries. Call one country V and the other country W. We might suppose, for simplicity, that everyone has the same preferences, independent of which country they live in. We might also suppose that everyone has the same endowment and that both countries have the same population size (which does not change over time). These countries are different in the quantities of land that they have. (This is, after all, a chapter on land.) Suppose that country V is the land-poor country and that country W is the land-rich country. Country V has $\mathbf{A}^V$ units of land and country W has $\mathbf{A}^W$ units of land, and $\mathbf{A}^V < \mathbf{A}^W$. Each unit of land, independent of which country it is in, generates a crop of $d(t + 1)$ units of the time $t + 1$ good, for all $t \geq 1$. If the crop sizes were different in the two countries, all we would need to do is change the size of a unit of land in one of the countries until the crop from each unit of land is the same. We allow goods to be transported between the two countries without cost. Assume that neither people nor land can move between countries. (We outlaw migration and conquest.)

There are certain restrictions that the governments of the countries can choose to impose on the ownership of land in their country. We limit ourselves to three regimes (sets of restrictions): (1) laissez-faire (LF), (2) portfolio autarky (PA), and (3) international borrowing (IB). Informally, a LF regime is one in which anyone can own assets from any country. As a result, a LF regime behaves as if there were only one world economy. A PA regime is one in which people can own only the assets of their own country. Individuals are only allowed to purchase goods and not assets from the rest of the world. In an IB regime, only citizens can own the land inside a country, but everyone is free to make private borrowing and lending agreements with any citizen of any country. These regimes can change over time, so the world might be in portfolio autarky up to time t and in laissez-faire for all time thereafter.

Definition   *In a* laissez-faire *regime at time t, any member of generation t can buy land located anywhere. There can also be private borrowing and lending between members of different countries.*

Definition   *In a* portfolio autarky regime at time *t*, *a member of generation t in country i can buy land located only in country i and can lend to and borrow from only the other citizens of country i.*

Definition   *In an* international borrowing regime at time *t*, *a member of generation t in country i can buy and sell land located only in country i but can lend to and borrow from citizens of any country.*

EXERCISE 6.13   The preferences and endowments are those given in economy 1. Country V has a population of 100, $N^V(t) = 100$ for all $t \geq 0$, and 100 units of land, $\mathbf{A}^V = 100$. Country W has $N^W(t) = 100$ for all $t \geq 0$ and $\mathbf{A}^W = 200$. The crop from 1 unit of land in any country is $d^i(t + 1) = 1$, for $i = $ V or W. Describe and compare equilibria under PA for all $t \geq 1$ and under LF for all $t \geq 1$. Describe who is better off under which policy.

Consider the economy of Exercise 6.13, except the amount of land in country V is 30 units and the amount of land in country W is 60 units. The savings function of person *h* of country *i* and generation *t* is

$$s^{hi}(r(t)) = 1 - \frac{1}{2r(t)}.$$

In the portfolio autarky regime, the equilibrium in each country is found, ignoring the other country. The two countries are completely independent. For country V, we solve

$$100\left(1 - \frac{1}{2r^V(t)}\right) = 30p^V(t)$$

and $$r^V(t) = \frac{p^V(t + 1) + d(t + 1)}{p^V(t)},$$

for a stationary price path $p^V(t) = p^V$. In the PA equilibrium, $p^V = 2.1893$ and $r^V = 1.4568$.

For country W, we solve

$$100\left(1 - \frac{1}{2r^W(t)}\right) = 60p^W(t)$$

and $\quad r^W(t) = \dfrac{p^W(t + 1) + d(t + 1)}{p^W(t)},$

for a constant price path, $p^W(t) = p^W$ for all t. The only difference in the savings equation for country W is the number of units of land, which is 60 instead of the 30 in country V. In the PA equilibrium, $p^W = 1.2103$ and $r^W = 1.8262$. The consumptions and utility levels achieved by the citizens of countries V and W are

$$c_t^{hV} = [1.3432, 1.9568] \qquad u_t^{hV} = 2.6284$$

$$c_t^{hW} = [1.2738, 2.3262] \qquad u_t^{hW} = 2.9631.$$

Recall that the old of period 1, the members of generation 0, are interested only in their consumption when old. In this equilibrium, they will consume the same as every other generation does when it is old. So the old of country V consume 1.9568 units of the time 1 good and the old of country W consume 2.3262 units of the time 1 good.

For the laissez-faire regime, we solve the model as if there were only one country with 200 members of every generation and 90 units of land. To find the equilibrium, we solve

$$200\left(1 - \frac{1}{2r(t)}\right) = 90p(t),$$

and $\quad r(t) = \dfrac{p(t + 1) + d(t + 1)}{p(t)}$

for a stationary price path, $p(t) = p$. We can drop the country superscripts because the prices and gross interest rates are the same in both countries. In the LF equilibrium, $p(t) = 1.5473$ and $r(t) = 1.6463$. The consumption and utility for citizens of both countries are

$$c_t^h = [1.3037, 2.1463] \qquad u_t^h = 2.7981.$$

The consumption of the old at date 1 depends on their initial holdings of land. If, for the above example, the old of each country at date 1 owned all of their own country's land, then (1) the old of each country would get to consume all of the crop produced by the land in their country, (2) the old of country V could sell all of their land to the young of country V, and (3) the old of country W would sell land to the young of both countries. Since the old at date 1 own different quantities of land, their consumptions are different. At time 1, 15 units of land get sold by the old of country W to the young of country V. The old in country W at time 1 do very well in the LF regime. Note that there is a net inflow of goods into country W at time t of 1.5473 units of the good for each unit of land times the 15 units of land sold to the young of country V. The total inflow is 23.21 units of the good. In every period after that, 15 units of the good flow from country W to country V. That amount of goods is equal to the amount of crop that is thrown off by the land in country W that is owned by the citizens of country V.

Consider the above economy in an international borrowing regime. By the rules of that regime, the 30 units of land in country V are owned by the citizens of country V and the 60 units of land in country W are owned by the citizens of country W. This regime is different from the portfolio autarky regime in that citizens of country V can borrow from or lend to citizens of country W. This world market in private borrowing and lending has the effect of making the gross interest rates in both countries the same. Under this regime,

$$r^V(t) = r^W(t),$$

for all t for which this regime holds. To see why these gross interest rates must be equal, suppose that they were not. There are two options (which are symmetric): (1) that $r^V(t) < r^W(t)$ or (2) that $r^V(t) > r^W(t)$. Because these are symmetric (we merely switch countries), assume that case 1 holds and that $r^V(t) < r^W(t)$. At time t, a person h of country W can go to country V and borrow **X** units of goods to be paid back at time $t + 1$ with $r^V(t)$**X** units of the time $t + 1$ good. This person h can lend these **X** units of the time t good in country W at the interest rate $r^W(t)$ and get back $r^W(t)$**X** units of the time $t + 1$ good. Person h has used none of her own goods to make these transactions (because the amount borrowed equals the amount loaned) and will make a profit of **X**$(r^W(t) - r^V(t))$ in time $t + 1$. Actions of this type are called *arbitrage* in the lending market. This being the case, everyone in the economy at time t will want to borrow as much as possible (will *want* to borrow an infinite amount) in country V and lend that amount in country W. Because there is only a finite amount of goods available in each country in each time period, it is impossible for an infinite amount to be borrowed, so this set of interest rates cannot be an equilibrium. Because the case where $r^V(t) > r^W(t)$ is symmetric, that set of interest rates cannot be an equilibrium. With international private borrowing and lending allowed, the interest rates in the two countries must be the same.

If we restrict our consideration to stationary equilibria, then the present value conditions become, in country V,

$$r^V(t) = \frac{p^V(t) + d(t + 1)}{p^V(t)},$$

and, in country W,

$$r^W(t) = \frac{p^W(t) + d(t + 1)}{p^W(t)}.$$

Because we have just shown that arbitrage will force $r^V(t)$ to be equal to $r^W(t)$ for every t in which the international borrowing regime holds, then the present value conditions mean that the price of land in both the countries will be equal; that is, $p^V(t) = p^W(t)$ for each of those periods as well. We call the world interest rate $r(t)$ and the world price of land $p(t)$.

The budget constraints of citizens of country i under this regime are

$$c_t^{hi}(t) = \omega_t^{hi}(t) - \ell^{hi}(t) - p(t)a^{hi}(t)$$

and $c_t^{hi}(t + 1) = \omega_t^{hi}(t + 1) + r(t)\ell^{hi}(t) + p(t + 1)a^{hi}(t),$

where $a^{hi}(t)$ is restricted to be country i land only. Rewriting the budget constraint when young in terms of savings gives us the equation

$$s^{hi}(r(t)) = \ell^{hi}(t) + p(t)a^{hi}(t).$$

Summing over all citizens of country i of generation t, the aggregate savings function is

$$S^i(r(t)) = \mathcal{L}^i(t) + p(t)\mathbf{A}^i,$$

where

$$\mathcal{L}^i(t) = \sum_{h=1}^{N^i(t)} \ell^{hi}(t)$$

is the net international lending (or borrowing, if negative) at time t of the citizens of country i. To require international market clearing conditions in a world with only two countries means that

$$\mathcal{L}^V(t) = -\mathcal{L}^W(t),$$

or that net international lending is equal to 0.

Substituting the aggregate savings condition for each of the countries into the international market clearing condition, we have

$$S^V(r(t)) - p(t)\mathbf{A}^V = \mathcal{L}^V(t) = -\mathcal{L}^W(t) = -S^W(r(t)) + p(t)\mathbf{A}^W,$$

or, rearranging, that

$$S^V(r(t)) + S^W(r(t)) = p(t)\mathbf{A}^V + p(t)\mathbf{A}^W.$$

This last expression is exactly the same condition we had in the laissez-faire regime. So the equilibrium in a regime in which foreign land cannot be owned but international private borrowing and lending is allowed is the same as the laissez-faire equilibrium. Private borrowing and lending allow the barrier on ownership of foreign land to be neutralized.

If none of the land in any of the countries gave off a crop, then it would benefit the old at time t of the country with the larger amount of land to open the sale of their land to both countries. When there is no crop, the rates of return under portfolio autarky are the same in both countries (and are the same as the rate of return in the laissez-faire regime). However, with populations of equal size, under the PA regime the price of land in the country with more of it is lower than in the other country. If some generation (say, t) gets (as a complete surprise to everyone) the world changed from PA to LF, then the old of that generation in the country with more land (country W) will get a higher price for their land than they paid for it and make a return on their holdings of land. The old of the other country get a lower return on their land. If it were known that the LF regime were to begin at time t, then the young at time $t - 1$ would know this and know they would be getting a higher return on their land. This knowledge would drive up the price of land at time $t - 1$. The young of time $t - 2$ would know that the price of land will be driven up at time $t - 1$ and that knowledge would drive up the price of land at time $t - 2$. This price change would keep working backward in time. In the other country, knowledge of the fall in the price of land would have a similar but opposite effect on the time path of the price of land. This discussion highlights some of the differences on the current price of land that are generated by foreseen or unforeseen future events.

EXERCISE 6.14 Describe the equilibria for the economy in Exercise 6.13, except assume that the world is in portfolio autarky in time $t = 1$ and is in laissez-faire for time $t = 2$ to ∞. Assume that it is known at time $t = 1$ that the world will go to the LF regime in period 2. (Hint: Solve this by solving for the LF equilibrium first and then use the results for time $t = 2$ to solve for the equilibria under PA at time $t = 1$.)

Exercise 6.14 suggests something about the importance of future government policies. What happens in the economy today depends not only on the policy in effect today but also on the policies that are expected to be in effect in the future. It matters today whether the world will have a LF or a PA regime in period 27. For this reason, it is important to think in terms of the whole time path of government policy and not just the policy that should be in effect today.

Reprise

Infinitely lived assets can exist and have value (positive prices) if they have particular useful properties. We choose to call our asset land and to let it give forth a crop at each time period t.

We assume that all members of generation t have the same expectations (which are point expectations), and we use the temporary equilibrium concept to describe what happens in these economies. One result of this assumption is that the time t price of land is equal to the present value of the returns that the land generates, both from the crop and the sale of the land in the next period. If land gives off a positive quantity of the crop, the time t price of land is positive even if the time $t + 1$ price of the land is 0. In our examples, the greater the crop, the greater the time t price for any given expected time $t + 1$ price.

We use the hypothesis of perfect foresight to find equilibria for our economies with land. In the guess and verify solution method, a $p(1)$ is chosen and the $p(t)$ for $t \geq 2$ are calculated. In the cases we looked at in this chapter, a nonequilibrium choice for $p(1)$ would quite quickly lead to a $p(t)$ that is either negative or above the upper bound. Because neither of these conditions is appropriate for an equilibrium path of prices, a $p(1)$ that generates the path that eventually becomes negative or goes above the upper bound cannot be an equilibrium $p(1)$.

In stationary environments, it is possible to find stationary price paths for the economy. The construction of a curve that gives the time t price that results from any possible time $t + 1$ prices allows us to find, at least visually, a fixed point in the price sequences [a fixed point is a point where $p(t) = p(t + 1)$]. That fixed point is an equilibrium price for the economy.

International capital flows can be considered in this model by the separation of the economy into two countries, each with its own quantity of land. Two regimes, one that allows the ownership of foreign assets (called the laissez-faire regime) and another that forbids such ownership (called the portfolio autarky regime) were considered. A regime that restricts the ownership of land in other countries but allows international private borrowing and lending has an equilibrium identical to the laissez-faire regime's equilibrium.

CHAPTER 7

Equilibrium Fluctuations

Economies undergo fluctuations. We observe fairly regular oscillations in economic activity, prices, wages, investment, and consumption. Economists denote different types of fluctuations by the length of the cycles. Cycles of 1 year or less are called *seasonals*, because these are particular economic events that follow the cycle of the seasons (the Christmas buying binge in the United States and the August holiday in France are two examples). The phenomenon called *the business cycle* is a fluctuation that has a cycle of between 2 and 10 years. Two special characteristics of the business cycle are the irregularity of its length and the difficulty we have in predicting its peaks and troughs. *Long-wave cycles* range from 20 years (studied in depth by Simon Kuznets) to 60 years (studied by the Russian economist N. D. Kondratieff).

In this chapter we explore several ways of generating equilibrium fluctuations in economies where the future is known (where the agents have perfect foresight). These economies are in equilibrium in the sense that given the price paths, all the individuals will be maximizing their utility subject to their budget constraints and all markets will clear. Furthermore, the assets in the economy will obey the present value criteria, so all of the conditions we required for an equilibrium are met. Because fluctuations are events that happen over time, we are particularly interested in the cycles that occur in the paths of prices, gross interest rates, and consumption. The cycles we generate are very long, because each life takes up only two periods; and we must be careful when we interpret our cycles as good models of the 2- to 8-year-long business cycles that are observed by the National Bureau of Economic Research.

We use two methods to analyze business cycles. These two methods mirror (darkly) two main directions that current economic research is following in its attempts to explain business cycles. The first method we can call the *real business cycle* approach, because the real environment of the economy is changing in some regular pattern. These real cycles can come from changes in preferences, in endowments, or in the crop that gets thrown off by each acre of land. In stochastic (random) models of economic fluctuations, the changes in these variables are shocks that cannot be predicted. In addition, one of the most interesting aspects of the real business cycle research is the attempt to explain the mechanisms by which these shocks persist in the economy and generate fairly regularly shaped waves.

The second method of research on business cycles goes under the (humorous, to an economist) title of *sunspot theories*. Modern sunspot theories, like the real business cycle theories, are based on economies with stochastic shocks. In these economies there are some variables that people *think* are important in determining the path of the economy and are variables that people can get good data about. Individuals use these variables to determine their behavior, and this behavior sets off cycles of the appropriate length. The variables that people believe cause business cycles do cause business cycles because people respond to them, so the resulting economies have cycles of the same lengths as the variables that are the basis for the predictions. The name *sunspot* comes from a theory of business cycles that was popular in the nineteenth century. As they were (mis)measured at the time, business cycles and sunspot cycles were observed to be of the same length; and many believed that the sunspot cycles *caused* the business cycles, even though a direct theoretical connection is not easy to make. The current sunspot theory suggests that sunspots could cause business cycles if people believed they did, even if there were no direct link.

In the deterministic setting we are using in this book, we have to modify and simplify these theories. We do not have random shocks occurring in our economies. We do not have propagation mechanisms that will cause a shock (that we do not have) to persist. However, for our approximation to the real business cycles, we allow cycles in some of the fundamental variables in our economies (in the preferences, endowments, and crops) and we experiment with ways of finding the equilibrium cycles in prices and consumption that result from these cycles in the environment. Our proxies for the sunspot models are economies where the environment is the same every period, but the dynamic structure of the economy is such that cycles can arise. The mathematics for solving these kinds of models is fairly new and has been in the popular press a lot under the name of chaos theory. We discover that some utility functions give rise to economies that can have chaotic dynamical structures.

Real Cycles

Let us define another example economy. Call this one economy 4. It includes one of the methods mentioned above for getting real cycles.

Economy 4   *The same as example economy 1 of Chapter 6 except that*

$$d(t) = \begin{cases} \frac{1}{2} & \text{when } t \text{ is odd,} \\ \frac{3}{2} & \text{when } t \text{ is even.} \end{cases}$$

In this economy the crop has a two-period cycle. In even-numbered periods it is three times larger than it is in the odd-numbered periods. This oscillation in the crop means that the kind of function (and curve[1]) we found giving us $p(t + 1)$ as a function of $p(t)$ is not immediately applicable. We were able to use the $p(t) = p(t + 1)$ line in economies 1 and 2 to find a stationary price sequence that fulfilled the equilibrium conditions. There, the relationship between $p(t)$ and $p(t + 1)$ was the same for every period. That relationship is not the same for every period in this model. In odd-numbered periods, the crop is smaller than in the even-numbered periods. The size of the crop was one of the exogenous (predetermined) variables of the equation of $p(t + 1)$ as a function of $p(t)$. Because this exogenous variable is now changing its value in a two-period cycle, the single function will no longer work.

Consider the problem for the young of even-numbered generations. They have the same preferences, population, and endowments as every-

---

1. Recall that the function that we actually graphed gave us $p(t)$ as a function of $p(t + 1)$. In finding the equilibrium $p(1)$, we started on the vertical axis and traced down to the horizontal axis. This function is merely the inverse of the one discussed in the text above. When we draw the function in the figures, we will continue to follow the convention we began in Chapter 5 of putting $p(t + 1)$ on the horizontal axis.

one else. They also know that when they get old and can collect the crop from the land they have bought (if they bought some land), the crop, $d(\text{odd})$, will be $\frac{1}{2}$. The young of even-numbered generations will be old in odd-numbered periods and will collect the crop that is thrown off in odd-numbered periods. We can write the equilibrium conditions that must hold during the lives of members of the even-numbered generations as

$$S_{\text{even}}(r(t)) = p(t)\mathbf{A}$$

and $r(t)p(t) = p(t + 1) + d(\text{odd}).$

These conditions hold for $t = 2, 4, 6, 8, \ldots$. If we knew the time $t + 1$ price (for $t + 1 = $ odd), then we could find the solution to the time t temporary equilibrium when t is even. Combining the above results, we can write out the function for the time t price (when t is even) as a function of the time $t + 1$ price. That function can be written as

$$p(t) = f^{\text{e}}(p(t + 1)),$$

where the $f^{\text{e}}(\cdot)$ is the function that holds for the even-numbered generations.

   Likewise, we can write out the time t temporary equilibrium conditions for periods when t is odd. The members of the odd generations will be able to collect the large ($\frac{3}{2}$) crop that is thrown off by every unit of land. If we restrict ourselves to the time t temporary equilibrium conditions that must hold for members of the odd generations, then those are

$$S_{\text{odd}}(r(t)) = p(t)\mathbf{A}$$

and $r(t)p(t) = p(t + 1) + d(\text{even}),$

and they hold for $t = 1, 3, 5, 7, \ldots$. Combining the above equations, we can write out the function for the time t price (when t is odd) as a function of the time $t + 1$ price, namely,

$$p(t) = f^{\text{o}}(p(t + 1)),$$

where the $f^o(\cdot)$ is the function that holds for the odd-numbered generations.

To find an equilibrium for this economy, we need to find a price path
that obeys

$$p(t) = \begin{cases} f^o(p(t+1)) & \text{when } t \text{ is odd,} \\ f^e(p(t+1)) & \text{when } t \text{ is even.} \end{cases} \tag{7.1}$$

EXERCISE 7.1   Find the explicit forms of $f^o(p(t+1))$ and
$f^e(p(t+1))$ for economy 4.

The functions $f^o(\cdot)$ (solid line) and $f^e(\cdot)$ (dashed line) for economy
4 are graphed in Figure 7.1. Notice that Equation (7.1) says that
$p(1) = f^o(p(2))$, $p(2) = f^e(p(3))$, $p(3) = f^o(p(4))$, $p(4) = f^e(p(5))$, and so
on. If we substitute the expression $f^e(p(3))$ for $p(2)$ in the equation
$p(1) = f^o(p(2))$, we get

$$p(1) = f^o(f^e(p(3))).$$

Likewise, if we substitute $f^e(p(5))$ for $p(4)$ in $p(3) = f^o(p(4))$, we get

$$p(3) = f^o(f^e(p(5))).$$

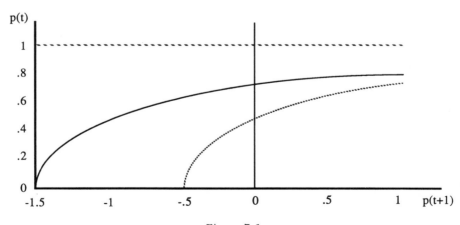

Figure 7.1

We can find the price in any odd period by knowing the price of the following odd period. This equation for the price in any odd period will be called $g^o(\cdot)$ and is

$$p(t) = f^o(f^e(p(t + 2))) \equiv g^o(p(t + 2)), \qquad \text{if } t \text{ is odd.} \qquad (7.2)$$

EXERCISE 7.2   Write out the explicit form of $g^o(\cdot)$ for economy 4.

Equation (7.2) is useful because it says that the odd-dated terms of an equilibrium $p(t)$ sequence satisfy $p(t) = g^o(p(t + 2))$, where $g^o(\cdot)$ is a function that does not depend on time. We can use this equation just as we used the representation of $p(t)$ as a function of $p(t + 1)$ to find an equilibrium. We found for the case where every period was like the next that a constant price $p(t) = p$ was the equilibrium. Suppose that we think of the above problem as one in which all of the periods were the same and the economy is such that the function that gives us $p(t)$ as a function of $p(t + 1)$ is the same, mathematically, as the function $g^o(\cdot)$. That economy would have an equilibrium with a constant price path and could be found by graphing the function $g^o(\cdot)$ and finding the point where $p(t + 2)$ equals $p(t)$. We could also solve it by choosing $p(1)$'s and using the inverse of Equation (7.2) to find the $p(3)$'s that would give those $p(1)$'s. Repeating this procedure and finding the $p(t)$'s for larger t's, we can see which ones do not violate the restrictions that have been imposed on prices (that they are nonnegative and determined).

Suppose that we do solve Equation (7.2) and find a price $p(1)$, such that $p(1) = g^o(p(1))$. We can then use the $f^e(\cdot)$ portion of Equation (7.1) and solve for $p(2)$. Because $p(3)$ equals $p(1)$ in this price sequence, we would use $f^e(\cdot)$ to find $p(2)$. We can set $p(5)$ equal to $p(1)$ and find $p(4) = f^e(p(5))$. This $p(4)$ will be exactly equal to $p(2)$. Remember that $g^o(\cdot)$ is a composite function constructed to ensure that the $p(1)$ we get from solving $f^o(p(2))$, using the $p(2)$ found just above, is equal to the equilibrium $p(1)$. Figure 7.2 shows the equation $g^o(\cdot)$ and the $p(t + 2) = p(t)$ line that gives us the equilibrium price.

In Figure 7.3 (in which the curves are duplicates of those in Figure 7.1), we trace (with the dotted line) the price $p(1)$ over to the f^o curve (solid line) and down to find $p(2)$. The 45-degree line takes that $p(2)$ to

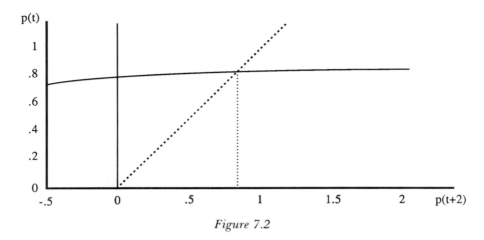

Figure 7.2

the vertical axis and we trace that over to the f^e curve (dashed line) and trace down to $p(3)$ and then trace $p(3)$ up the 45-degree line back to the vertical line. This last price matches up perfectly with the $p(1)$ we found in Figure 7.2. The cycle of $p(1)$, $p(2)$ will repeat itself indefinitely.

The price sequence for economy 4 oscillates between $p(t) = .8165$ for t odd and $p(t) = .7247$ for t even. The gross interest rates oscillate and are

$$r(t) = \begin{cases} (.7247 + 1.5)/.8165 = 2.7247 & \text{for } t \text{ odd,} \\ (.8165 + .5)/.7247 = 1.8167 & \text{for } t \text{ even.} \end{cases}$$

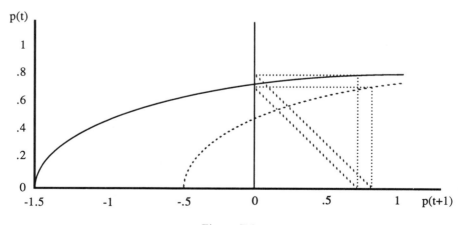

Figure 7.3

The consumption and utility of the odd-numbered and even-numbered generations are

$$c^h_{\text{odd}} = [1.1835, 3.2247] \qquad u^h_{\text{odd}} = 3.8164,$$

$$c^h_{\text{even}} = [1.2753, 2.3165] \qquad u^h_{\text{even}} = 2.9542.$$

Interestingly, the price of land is low when the crop is large and is high when the crop is small. This relation occurs because of the oscillating nature of the crop. In periods when the crop is large, it is known that the crop will be small the next period. The future crop is the one that is important in determining the price of the land.

Real business cycles can have almost any periodicity if some real variable of the economy has a cycle of the required length. An economy in which the crop has a four-period cycle, for example:

$$d(t) = \begin{cases} 1 & \text{for } t = 1, 5, 9, 13, 17, \ldots \\ {}^3\!/_2 & \text{for } t = 2, 6, 10, 14, 18, \ldots \\ 1 & \text{for } t = 3, 7, 11, 15, 19, \ldots \\ {}^1\!/_2 & \text{for } t = 4, 8, 12, 16, 20, \ldots \end{cases}$$

will have a four-period cycle in the prices, gross interest rates, consumption, and utility. In this economy, the members of generations 2 and 4 will face different prices and gross interest rates even though the crop will be the same for those two generations when they are old. Generation 4 will get a better price for the land that it sells than will generation 2 and hence will have higher utility.

Economy 1 with a real cycle in endowments, for example,

$$\omega^h_t = \begin{cases} [2, 1], & \text{for } t \text{ even,} \\ [1, 1], & \text{for } t \text{ odd,} \end{cases}$$

will result in a two-period cycle. Likewise, a version of economy 1 with periodic changes in the utility functions, for example, $\beta = 1$ for generations t even and $\beta = {}^1\!/_2$ for generations t odd, will exhibit cycles. Each of these methods will generate cycles. None of them will result in cycles in prices, gross interest rates, consumption or utility of any length different from the cycle in the environmental variable.

Here are three exercises. The first asks you to calculate an equilibrium path for an economy in which the endowments cycle, and the other two point out important problems in attempting to predict the equilibria of other economies based on one sample economy.

EXERCISE 7.3   Consider example economy 1 from Chapter 6, except that the endowments are $\omega_t^h = [2, 1]$ for t even and $\omega_t^h = [1, 1]$ for t odd. Find an equilibrium for this economy.

*EXERCISE 7.4 (Time-series versus cross-section observations) Suppose that you have time-series data for economy 4, data that consist of observations on the pairs $[d(t), p(t)]$ for different dates. Plot these pairs on a chart with $d(t)$ on the horizontal axis and $p(t)$ on the vertical axis. Now consider the following questions: What are the equilibrium prices of land in two other economies that are identical to economy 4 except that in one $d(t)$ is always $\frac{1}{2}$ and in the other $d(t)$ is always $\frac{3}{2}$? Is there a simple way to use the time-series observations for economy 4 to answer these questions? Why?

*EXERCISE 7.5 (An "estimation" problem)   You are an economist living in economy 4. You are asked what the equilibrium land price would be in economies that are identical except that they have different time patterns of crops—for example, crops that do not vary over time. Here is what you know. You have data on **A** and on $[d(t), p(t)]$ for your economy. You also know that the aggregate savings function for every generation has the form:

$$S(r(t)) = a_0 - \frac{a_1}{r(t)}.$$

You do not start out knowing the pair of parameters $[a_0, a_1]$. Outline in detail a procedure for answering the question.

Exercises 7.4 and 7.5 illustrate important aspects of macroeconomic modeling and forecasting. Data from one equilibrium price path do not give us direct information about other equilibria. Exercise 7.4 points out this difficulty. Exercise 7.5 is a very similar problem, except that we have information about the *structure* of the savings function, even if we do not initially know the parameters of the function. Use of this additional information helps us form a model that allows predictions of out-of-sample events (things that have not occurred yet).

Multiple Nonstationary Equilibria

As mentioned in the introduction, the term *sunspot equilibria* is best left for economies in which there are stochastic elements. In a deterministic setting, such as we have been using here, a close equivalent to the sunspot equilibria are economies with multiple, nonstationary equilibria. We consider such economies in this section.

Economies 1 through 4 generate unique equilibria when $d(t)$ is greater than 0. Those same economies with $d(t)$ equal to 0 have multiple equilibria: two are stationary, one has a positive equilibrium price and one has an equilibrium price of 0. There are also other equilibria where the price of land monotonically goes to 0. We are now going to look at another class of economies, with different preferences, that have cyclic equilibria. In these economies, however, the cycles are not generated by changes in the physical environment. We study this class of economies by finding the equilibria for a particular example economy that is a member of this class. Initially we set $d(t)$ equal to 0, but later allow it to be positive.

Economy 5 $N(t) = 100$; $\mathbf{A} = 100$; $d(t) = 0$ *(initially); the endowments are* [2, 1]; *and the utility functions are*

$$u_t^h = -(c_t^h(t) - b^y)^2 - \beta(c_t^h(t + 1) - b^o)^2, \tag{7.3}$$

where $\beta = 4$ *and* $b = [b^y, b^o] = [2, 2]$.

Economy 5 is one in which there is no crop—although we add a small crop in the next section. Otherwise, it is very much like economy 1. The utility function is new. Individuals with this utility function have a *bliss point* at a consumption point [2, 2]. This point is the optimal consumption point, and more or less of either good diminishes utility as a quadratic function of the distance from the bliss point. One can think of the bliss point as a point of satiation. At consumption points below and to the left of the bliss point, the usual rule of "more is better than less" holds. At consumption points with more of both goods than the bliss points, utility is reduced and a smaller amount of the goods will make one better off. It is possible to eat and drink too much at some holiday feast and go beyond the point of (at least long-term) maximum utility. The minus signs in the utility function say that the further one is from the bliss point [that is, the larger are $(c^i - b^i)$ for $i = y$ and o], the lower the level of utility. Notice that 0 is the highest value for this utility function. Several of the indifference curves that come from this utility function are illustrated in Figure 7.4. The larger ellipses are indifference curves of lower utility.

The results we get in this section do not require the exact utility function shown in Figure 7.4. This particular utility function and the chosen endowments give us especially simple equations with which to work. The resulting equations are the classic equations of the mathematics of chaos theory. The main feature of the indifference curves that is important in generating the cyclical behavior is the strong inelasticity of demand for consumption with respect to $r(t)$ in the second period of

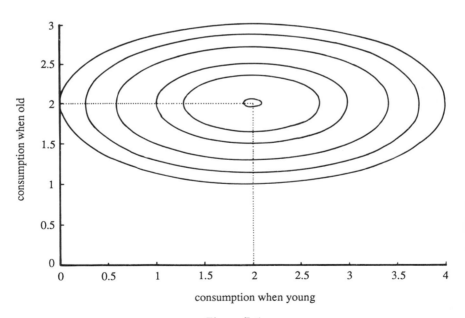

Figure 7.4

life. Any utility function and endowment that display this property should also work, but the details will be different.

Consider the utility maximization problem that an individual faces when that individual has the utility function shown in Figure 7.4. In the problems we are considering, the endowment is below the bliss point, with more consumption preferred in the second period than the endowment allows. At positive prices (which are the only ones we allow), individuals will be willing to trade away from the endowment and consume more second-period good. If one looks at only the lower left-hand quarter of the ellipses in Figure 7.4, this portion of the curves looks a lot like regular indifference curves. Beginning with the endowment we have in the example and restricting ourselves to positive prices, all chosen consumption points will be on this quarter of the indifference ellipses.

The savings function is found in the normal manner. The budget constraints

$$c_t^h(t) = \omega_t^h(t) - \ell^h(t) - p(t)a^h(t),$$

and $$c_t^h(t + 1) = \omega_t^h(t + 1) + r(t)\ell^h(t) + (p(t + 1) + d(t + 1))a^h(t),$$

which we used in the other economies with land, still hold. Recall that $a^h(t)$ is the quantity of land that individual h of generation t chooses to purchase and that $\ell^h(t)$ is the amount of private borrowing or lending that this individual does. Combining these budget constraints yields the single budget constraint of

$$c_t^h(t) + \frac{c_t^h(t + 1)}{r(t)} = \omega_t^h(t) + \frac{\omega_t^h(t + 1)}{r(t)}$$
$$- a^h(t)\left[p(t) - \frac{p(t + 1) + d(t + 1)}{r(t)} \right].$$

The usual present value conditions imply that the portion of the above equation in square brackets equals 0. Therefore, utility is maximized with respect to

$$c_t^h(t) + \frac{c_t^h(t + 1)}{r(t)} = \omega_t^h(t) + \frac{\omega_t^h(t + 1)}{r(t)}.$$

Maximizing the utility function in Equation (7.3) with respect to this budget constraint gives a savings function of

$$s_t^h(t) = \frac{(\omega_t^h(t) - b^y) - \beta r(t)(\omega_t^h(t+1) - b^o)}{1 + \beta[r(t)]^2}, \qquad (7.4)$$

where $\beta = 4$. The equilibrium conditions that we need are utility maximization and market clearing in the markets for land, private borrowing, and the consumption good. The aggregate savings function incorporates the utility-maximizing condition for all members of a given generation. As before, the market clearing conditions imply that the aggregate savings function is equal to the value of the land in every period, so

$$S_t(r(t)) = N(t)s^h(t) = p(t)\mathbf{A}, \qquad \text{for all } t. \qquad (7.5)$$

The other equilibrium condition that we need is the present value constraint we found from the budget constraints, which says that

$$r(t) = \frac{p(t+1) + d(t+1)}{p(t)}. \qquad (7.6)$$

We can solve for $p(t)$ as a function of $p(t+1)$. Substituting into Equation (7.4) the values for the endowments and the bliss point in the individual savings functions we get

$$s_t^h(t) = \frac{\beta r(t)}{1 + \beta[r(t)]^2}.$$

We substitute this individual savings function into Equation (7.5) and then replace the gross interest rate by the present value condition of Equation (7.6). The function $f_t(\cdot)$, for which $p(t) = f_t(p(t+1))$, is

$$p(t) = [\beta(p(t+1) + d(t+1)) - \beta(p(t+1) + d(t+1))^2]^{1/2}. \quad (7.7)$$

For economy 5 we set β equal to 4 and $d(t+1)$ equal to 0. The specific $f_t(\cdot)$ for this economy is

$$p(t) = [4p(t+1) - 4(p(t+1))^2]^{1/2}. \qquad (7.8)$$

Equation (7.8) is graphed in Figure 7.5. The main difference between this function and the ones we found for economy 1 is the fact that this curve has a bell shape and turns down. This shape means that there are two values of $p(t + 1)$ that will give the same value of $p(t)$—except for the point $p(t + 1) = .5$, which is the only time $t + 1$ price that results in a time t price of 1. We can find two stationary equilibrium price sequences, where $p(t) = p(t + 1)$. These are found at the points where the 45-degree line crosses the $p(t) = f_t(p(t + 1))$ curve. The two stationary equilibria are at $p(t + 1) = 0$ and $p(t + 1) = .8$.

The utility functions, endowments, crops, population, and quantity of land are the same for every period in this model. None of the environmental parameters are changing. Therefore, the individual savings functions and all the other variables except $p(t)$ and $p(t + 1)$ [which determine $r(t)$] are not changing through time. This fact means that the function we found should be time independent, and observation of Equation (7.8) confirms this result. Because the function is the same in

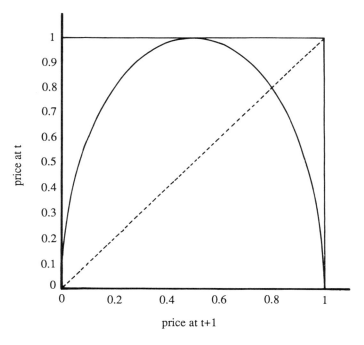

Figure 7.5

every period, the subscript t in the expression $f_t(\cdot)$ is not necessary and
the function will be written as simply $f(\cdot)$.

On the basis of our analysis above in the real business cycle model,
we can look for two-period cycles by looking for equilibria where
$p(t) = p(t + 2)$ but where $p(t) \neq p(t + 1)$. We find these cycles by first
using the function $f(\cdot)$ to find the $p(t + 1)$ that equals $f(p(t + 2))$ and
then find the $p(t)$ that equals $f(p(t + 1))$. This composite function is
written

$$p(t) = f(f(p(t + 2))) = g^2(p(t + 2)).$$

This composite function, $g^2(\cdot)$ [where the superscript 2 indicates that
it represents the composite function made from using $f(\cdot)$ twice], is illustrated in Figure 7.6a. Notice that there are two prices where
$p(t + 2) = p(t)$ on the function $g^2(\cdot)$ and where $p(t) \neq 0$ or $.8$ (the
stationary equilibria we found earlier). These prices are $p(t) =$

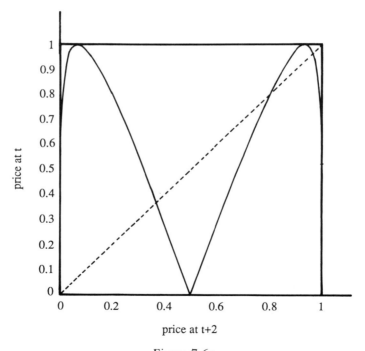

Figure 7.6a

$p(t + 2) = .3686$ and $.9648$. If the economy were to start on one of these prices (for example, $.3686$), then an equilibrium time path of prices would be

$p(1)$	$p(2)$	$p(3)$	$p(4)$	$p(5)$	$p(6)$	
.3686	.9648	.3686	.9648	.3686	.9648	etc.

Figure 7.6b shows how the two-period cycle is generated from the function $f(\cdot)$. These price paths are formed by following the same method that we used for finding an equilibrium in Chapter 6. Choose a $p(1)$, see what $p(2)$ is consistent with that $p(1)$, see what $p(3)$ is consistent with that $p(2)$, and so on. In Figure 7.6b, we can see that there are two $p(2)$'s consistent with $p(1) = .3686$. One of these is the price that will cause the two-period cycle to occur [$p(2) = .9648$]; the other [$p(2) = .0352$; shown as a dotted line] leads to a price path that is difficult to predict. A $p(1)$ of $.9648$ [or a $p(2)$ of the same value] could result in a $p(2)$ [or a $p(3)$] equal to $.3686$, in which case the two-period cycle occurs, or a $p(2)$ equal to $.6314$ (shown as a dotted line), in which case

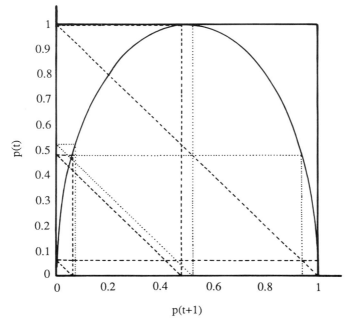

Figure 7.6b

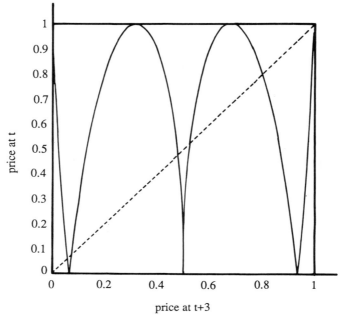

Figure 7.7a

the price path is difficult to predict. If the citizens of this economy expect[2] the price path to have this particular two-period cycle, then it will.

Figure 7.7a shows the curve that results when $f(\cdot)$ is applied three times. We call the resulting function $g^3(\cdot)$, and it is equal to

$$p(t) = g^3(p(t + 3)) \equiv f(f(f(p(t + 3)))).$$

In Figure 7.7a we find those points for which $p(t) = p(t + 3)$ by drawing in the 45-degree line. Notice that there are six points where $p(t) = p(t + 3)$ that are not the stationary equilibria at 0 and .8—although the 45-degree line also crosses the $g^3(\cdot)$ curve at those two points. One of the intersections is very difficult (read impossible) to see. The line going up from $p(t + 3) = .93$ to what looks like the upper right-hand corner of the box really comes down the right-hand side

2. The use of the word *expect* in this context is somewhat inexact. This world is one with perfect foresight. In the current economy, we mean that there exists a viable equilibrium in which people can act on the forecast of a two-period cycle and be correct.

again to the lower corner at $p(t + 3) = 1$. This line is so close to the side of the box that it cannot be separated from the edge. However, it is there. There are two intersections between the 45-degree line and $g^3(t + 3)$ in the upper right-hand corner of the graph. One of the three-period cycles is shown on the $f(\cdot)$ curve in Figure 7.7b. The dashed lines mark out the three-period cycle that goes from .4784 to .9991 to .0611 before returning to .4784. (Note that .4784 was arbitrarily chosen from among these three values as the starting point for the cycle. Either of the other two numbers could have been chosen.) A second three-period cycle exists. That cycle uses the other three intersections in Figure 7.7a.

EXERCISE 7.6 For economy 5, with the two- and three-period cycles given above, calculate the interest rate path, the consumption paths, and the path of utility. Compare the consumption and utility paths to the stationary equilibrium with $p(t) = .8$.

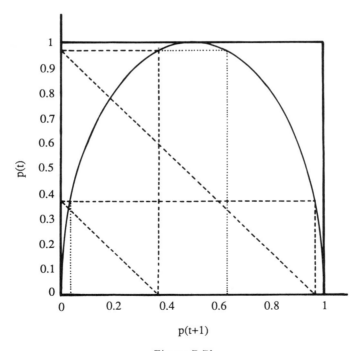

Figure 7.7b

The fact that we can find a three-period cycle has surprising importance. The kind of analysis we are doing is known in the mathematics literature as chaos theory. One of the most interesting theorems that has been generated from that theory concerns the number of different-length cycles that a system can have. Three is the magic number. If a system has a three-period cycle, it contains some starting value that will give a cycle of any chosen periodicity. Once we have shown that a three-period cycle exists, cycles of 157, 26, or 91,645 periods—or of *any* other periodicity—also exist in that system. This theorem is a corollary to a theorem known as Sarkovskii's theorem and is very simple in its statement. Let f be a mapping from the real numbers to the real numbers.

Sarkovskii's Corollary   *Let $f : \mathbb{R} \to \mathbb{R}$ be continuous. Suppose f has a periodic point of period three. Then f has periodic points of all other periods.*[3]

This corollary means that it is possible for our simple economy to have business cycles of any periodicity if that is what people know (expect) it will have. That result is very exciting for two reasons. One is that our economy, which is exactly the same in every period in terms of the physical environment (preferences, endowments, taxes, crops, population, and land), can follow a price path that oscillates. The second is that we have no way of knowing a priori which of the infinite number of possible periodicities the economy will be on. In fact, if the period of the cycle is long enough—several billion time periods, for example—it might not be realized by (or matter to) any agent that the economy is following a cycle. The price path might look random.

EXERCISE 7.7   Find the $f(\cdot)$ function for economy 5, except with $\beta = 5$. Do two-period cycles exist in this economy? Do three-period cycles exist? How is this economy different from the one where $\beta = 4$?

Equilibria with the Crop > 0

In the economies studied in Chapter 6, the addition of any positive crop changed the set of possible equilibria. When the crop was 0, there were

---

3. For a proof, see Devaney (1986), pp. 60–62.

multiple price paths for land that could occur. There were the two stationary price paths: one at $p(t) = 0$ for all t and the other at some positive value that depended on the parameters of the environment. There also existed an infinite number of equilibrium paths for which the price converged monotonically to 0. The addition of even the smallest amount of crop to the economy removed the zero-price stationary equilibrium and the entire set of price paths that converged to 0. With the utility functions of Chapter 6, any small amount of crop guaranteed the uniqueness of the equilibrium at the positive stationary price path.

The inclusion of a nonzero crop in the current model has important implications as well, but these implications are not so stark. In particular, a very small crop does not have the effect of eliminating the multiplicity of equilibria, although a large enough crop will. We pass through stages where the number of possible equilibria are reduced as the quantity of the crop increases. There are two crop sizes at which the nature of the equilibria change abruptly.

Consider economy 5, except with the crop now strictly positive. The derivation of all of the equations of the model follow the same form as above, except that wherever $p(t + 1)$ appears, one needs to use $[p(t + 1) + d(t + 1)]$. The main result is that the function $f(\cdot)$, which gives the time t price as a function of the time $t + 1$ price, is

$$p(t) = [\beta(p(t + 1) + d(t + 1)) - \beta(p(t + 1) + d(t + 1))^2]^{1/2}, \quad (7.7)$$

where the $d(t + 1)$ are no longer 0. The effect of the inclusion of the crop in this function is to cause a shift in the $f(\cdot)$ function to the left by the amount of the crop. Figure 7.8 shows the graph of Equation (7.7) for $d(t + 1)$ equal to .05 (solid), .1 (dashed), .2 (dotted), and .3 (dot-dash). Notice that a crop greater than 1 will cause difficulties in this model. A crop greater than 1 would shift the $f(\cdot)$ function so that the domain consists only of negative numbers. We are not allowing negative prices and so cannot deal with a crop that is too big. The crop is too big because, if the old harvest it and consume it all, then their consumption (when old) is greater than their bliss point. Free disposal of excess crop results in a price of land that is equal to 0 and has everyone consuming at the [2, 2] bliss point.

Small amounts of the crop do not change the basic nature of the cycles that can arise in this model. Large crops (as suggested by the example of a crop greater than 1) do change the nature of the equilibria in important ways. As we will see, for economy 5, the important crop sizes

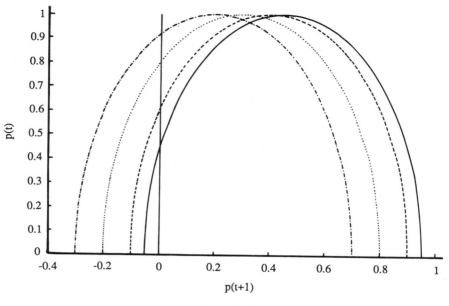

Figure 7.8

are $d(t) = .106922$ and $d(t) = .2$. These are two points where the nature of the cycles that can occur in the economy change drastically. We will look at these two crop sizes presently. First, however, we want to show that very small positive crops do not change the basic nature of the equilibria.

Figures 7.9a to d show the $f(\cdot)$, $g^2(\cdot)$, $g^3(\cdot)$, and $f(\cdot)$ with the three-cycle path drawn in, respectively, for economy 5 with a crop of $d(t) = .05$. The $f(\cdot)$ curve in Figure 7.9a is the bell curve shifted .05 to the left. Notice that the stationary equilibrium at $p(t) = 0$ that existed when $d(t)$ equaled 0 is no longer an equilibrium. There is only one stationary equilibrium path, at $p(t) = .77$. The addition of a positive crop into this model has reduced the number of stationary equilibrium paths from 2 to 1.

Figure 7.9b has an interesting feature. The missing center section of the $g^2(\cdot)$ curve occurs because, if price $p(t + 2)$ were somewhere between .3 and .6 (approximately), $p(t + 1)$ would be over .95 and would not map into any $p(t)$. Therefore, prices between .3 and .6 cannot be members of an equilibrium price path. Also, the right-hand section of the

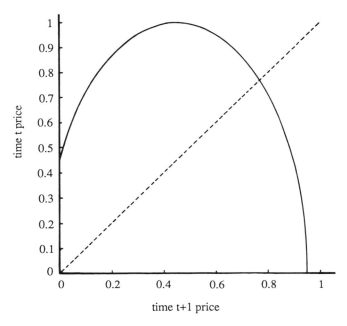

Figure 7.9a

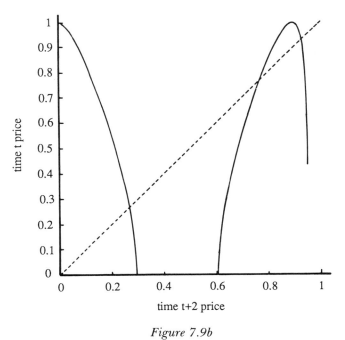

Figure 7.9b

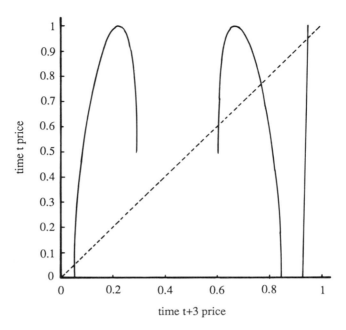

Figure 7.9c

curve in Figure 7.9b ends at $p(t + 2)$ = .95 and $p(t)$ = .43. In Figure 7.9a one can see that a $p(t + 2)$ = .95 gives a $p(t + 1)$ of 0; and using the curve in Figure 7.9a again, we see that $p(t + 1)$ = 0 gives a $p(t)$ = .43, the point where $f(\cdot)$ crosses the y-axis.

There are three intersections in Figure 7.9b between $g^2(\cdot)$ and the 45-degree line. One of these is at the stationary equilibrium where $p(t)$ = .77 for all t. The other two are at .27 and .93. This path is an equilibrium price path with a two-period cycle oscillating between .27 and .93.

Figure 7.9c shows $g^3(\cdot)$ for economy 5 with $d(t)$ = .05. This curve has three segments, and the points between these segments represent prices that cannot be equilibrium paths.[4] The stationary equilibrium price path is shown at $p(t)$ = .77. Three other intersections exist between $g^3(\cdot)$ and the 45-degree line. The cycle that results is shown in Figure 7.9d. Sar-

---

4. Mathematical note: As one calculates g^i's for larger i's, more and more prices are removed from the set of possible members of equilibrium price paths. As i goes to infinity, the set of possible members of equilibrium price paths goes to the Cantor set.

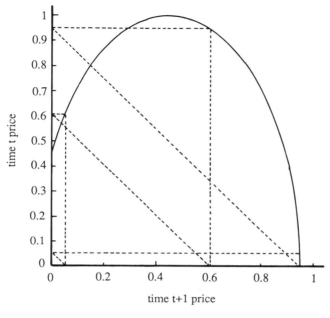

Figure 7.9d

kovskii's corollary tells us that, because there is a cycle of periodicity three, there also exists prices for cycles of any length periodicity. In terms of the potential dynamic paths that it can follow, economy 5 with a crop of .05 is very similar to the same economy with no crop. The major change that came about by the addition of a small crop is that a lot of potential price paths are no longer possible.

EXERCISE 7.8   Using Figure 7.9a, show that there are many price paths that converge to the stationary price path at $p(t) = .77$. For each $p(1)$ for which you find a path that converges to $p(t) = .77$, describe a price path for that same $p(1)$ that does not converge to .77.

As $d(t)$ gets larger, the curves in Figure 7.9a–c move to the left. We are interested in finding the lowest $d(t)$ for which there is a three-cycle equilibrium for economy 5. Notice in Figure 7.9c that one of the points of the cycle of periodicity three moves toward 0 as the curve moves to the left [as $d(t)$ increases]. The last time there is a point in a three-period cycle is when one of these points is exactly equal to 0. For any larger $d(t)$, the lower intersection of $g^3(\cdot)$ and the 45-degree line is a negative price and a three-period cycle does not exist. To find the largest crop for which there is a three-period cycle, we find the crop size for which 0 is one of the cycling points. For the economy we have here, that crop size is $d(t) = .106922$ and the three-period cycle is at 0, .6180, and .8931. For any crop larger than this, the economy does not have a three-period cycle and may not have equilibria with many other periodicities. For an interval of crop sizes bigger than $d(t) = .106922$, the economy does have an equilibrium with a two-period cycle.

A crop that is the slightest bit larger than .2 is large enough to guarantee that there are no cycles at all and that the only permissible equilibria are the stationary price path equilibrium or price paths that converge over time to the stationary price path. Figure 7.10 shows the $f(\cdot)$ function for the economy where $d(t) = .2$. Notice that the value of the function

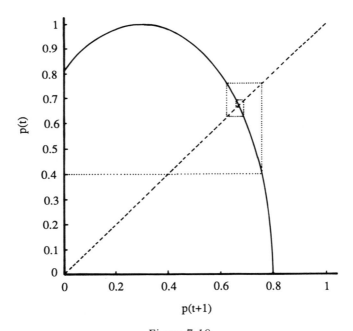

Figure 7.10

at $p(t + 1) = 0$ is .8. The value .8 is also the highest price that can occur at time $t + 1$. No equilibrium price path can have any price other than its initial price above .8. Because no $p(t)$ for $t > 1$ can be above .8, the "hump" portion of the $f(\cdot)$ curve is not involved in determining equilibrium price sequences. Except for $p(t + 1) = 0$, only the monotone portion of that curve, the part with $p(t)$ between .8 and 0, determines the equilibrium sequence. With a monotone (effective) $f(\cdot)$ function, no continuing cycles can occur.

A crop of .2 is the limit for which a two-period cycle can occur. That is why we said in the paragraph above that no cycles occur for crops *greater* than .2. In economy 5 with a crop of .2, there is a two-period cycle possible. In that cycle, prices oscillate between 0 and .8. As with the three-period cycle, the limit is found when 0 becomes one of the prices in the oscillating path.

The dotted line in Figure 7.10 follows an equilibrium price path for the case where $p(1)$ equals .4. The dotted lines are drawn up (or down) to the 45-degree line and then left (or right) to the $f(\cdot)$ curve, and they give the $p(t + 1)$ that must occur in order to have the $p(t)$ price be in the equilibrium. As t increases, the price sequence forms a cobweb that converges to the stationary equilibrium price path.

One other corollary of Sarkovskii's theorem says that if there is no cycle of two periods, then there are no cycles with any periodicity. Two-period cycles are the easiest to get; so if we show that no two-period cycles exist, then no cycles exist. In economy 5, when $d(t)$ is greater than .2, no cycles exist.

EXERCISE 7.9 Consider economy 5, except with $\beta = 5$. What is the largest $d(t)$ that will permit an equilibrium with a two-period cycle?

Reprise

Business cycles are periodic oscillations in important economic variables. We have looked at factors that can lead to cycles in the price of the private asset—land—and in consumption and utility. The sources that we have studied are real and psychological (in a certain sense). The real business cycles are generated by cyclical movements in some of the environmental parameters of the economy. The equilibrium time paths of prices, gross interest rates, and consumption respond to these environmental changes in a very direct way and generate cycles of the same length as the cycles in the environment.

More sophisticated economic models attempt to build persistence into the cycles. In these models, series of small shocks combine with the structure of economic decision making to cause cycles of longer duration than those of the small shocks. Some of the models that have been built to do this include features such as time to build restrictions (capital equipment requires several periods of investment before it can become productive) or economies of scale (so that firms prefer to shut down periodically rather than maintain a low level of production). Work is still very much in progress in this area.

Economies can have equilibria with cycles even if the environmental variables are constant throughout time. Depending on the form of the utility function, economies can have multiple (infinite) equilibria, some of which have fixed cycles. In an important way, these models are indeterminate. They do not tell us which of the infinite possible equilibria will actually occur. The current price of the land depends on the expected future path of the price of land. Neither of these is tied down by anything in the model. In sunspot equilibria, individuals use some other variable (sunspots, for example) to predict what periodicity the economy is going to have, and the economy can follow an equilibrium path that copies the cycle of the predicting variable. Unfortunately, if a different variable were chosen, with a different periodicity, the equilibrium would be different. We do not know how the predictive variable is chosen.

CHAPTER 8

A Storage Technology

The economies we have considered up to now have had no intertemporal production, no physical way to convert resources at one date into resources at another date. The only way for an individual to transfer resources from one period to another has been through the purchase of some kind of asset. The assets we have considered have been land, government bonds, and private borrowing and lending. Although we have had equilibria in which individuals could transfer resources across time, society as a whole has had no way to transfer resources across time. In this chapter we introduce and study a technology that allows this transfer to occur.

The technology we study is a simple linear storage technology. Individuals are able to keep some of the good they have when they are young and store it until they are old, when they can consume it. Perhaps the technology is such that individuals get back less than they stored. This case can be thought of as storage with depreciation. Or perhaps individuals get back more than was originally stored. We can view this case as an example of an economy with a simple, one-factor production technology. In this last case the stored good can be thought of as investment and the quantity of the good that results from storage can be thought of as production.

Feasible Allocations

The storage technology is a linear, constant returns to scale, intertemporal technology: for every unit of the good that is put into storage, λ

units of the good are returned the next period. This λ can be any nonnegative number, but it does not vary with the amount of the good that is stored. If k units of the time t good are stored by an individual, where k is any nonnegative number, then λk units of the time $t + 1$ good are the result of this simple storage technology.

Let $K(t + 1)$ be the total amount of time t good that is stored until time $t + 1$.[1] We can think of it as the amount of time t good that is put into the storage technology just described. Therefore, $K(t + 1)$ units of the good stored at time t results in $\lambda K(t + 1)$ units of the good in time $t + 1$. The fact that we can move goods across time means that our old definition of feasible consumption allocations is no longer valid. We need to redefine feasible consumption allocations for economies that permit storage. Until now, a feasible allocation was simply one for which $C(t)$, the total consumption at time t, is not greater than $Y(t)$, the total amount of the nonstorable good that existed at that time t. Now that goods can be transferred (stored) across time, the period by period definition is no longer sufficient.

Definition   *A path of total consumption,* $C(1), C(2), C(3), \ldots, C(t),$ *is* feasible *for an economy with storage if, given* $K(1),$ *there exists a nonnegative* $K(t)$ *sequence for* $t > 1$ *that satisfies*

$$C(t) + K(t + 1) \le Y(t) + \lambda K(t), \qquad \text{for all } t \ge 1. \tag{8.1}$$

Note that $K(1)$ is the quantity of the time 0 good that those who are old at time 1 chose to store at time 0. For economies that begin at time 1, $K(1)$ is already determined (is exogenous).

The right side of Equation (8.1) equals the total amount of time t good that is available to the economy at date t. This amount is the sum of the total new endowment, $Y(t)$, which includes the crop from land, and the production from the good that was invested at time $t - 1$, $\lambda K(t)$. The left side of the equation gives the total usage of that good. The good can be used either for consumption, $C(t)$, or for investment, $K(t + 1)$. Thus, the definition of feasibility says that the total use of the time t good cannot exceed the total amount of that good that is available.

1. This notation might seem a bit odd. A similar notation is used in the next chapter, where it is more natural. Think of $K(t + 1)$ as the quantity of the time t good being stored for use as capital in time $t + 1$. This $K(t + 1)$ units of capital produces $\lambda K(t + 1)$ units of the time $t + 1$ good.

EXERCISE 8.1   Suppose $N(t) = 1$, $Y(t) = 1$ for all $t \geq 0$, $\lambda = 2$, $K(1) = 0$, and the utility function is $u_t^h = c_t^h(t)c_t^h(t + 1)$, for all h and $t \geq 1$. Show that the following consumption allocation is feasible but not Pareto optimal:

$$c_t^h = [\text{½}, \text{½}] \quad \text{for all } h \text{ and } t \geq 1, \quad \text{and} \quad c_0^h(1) = \text{½}.$$

EXERCISE 8.2   Prove the following. A feasible consumption allocation satisfying

$$\frac{u_{t1}^h(c_t^h(t), c_t^h(t + 1))}{u_{t2}^h(c_t^h(t), c_t^h(t + 1))} < \lambda$$

for some h and some $t \geq 1$ is not Pareto optimal. (Note that the expression on the left is the marginal rate of substitution of some person h of some generation $t \geq 1$.)

Competitive Equilibrium

In this chapter individuals have an additional way to get goods when old. Not only can they engage in private borrowing and lending and in the purchase of land, but they also have the additional option of storing some of the good until the next period. Given this additional option, the budget constraints faced by individual h of generation t are

$$c_t^h(t) = \omega_t^h(t) - \ell^h(t) - p(t)a^h(t) - k^h(t + 1) \tag{8.2}$$

and $c_t^h(t + 1) = \omega_t^h(t + 1) + r(t)\ell^h(t)$

$$+ a^h(t)[d(t + 1) + p^e(t + 1)] + \lambda k^h(t + 1), \tag{8.3}$$

where $k^h(t + 1)$, the only new symbol, is the amount of time t good that is invested (stored) by this individual at date t.

As we did in earlier examples with budget constraints for each period of life, we use this pair of constraints to obtain a single constraint that is equivalent with regard to consumptions. By eliminating ℓ^h, we obtain the single budget constraint:

$$c_t^h(t) + \frac{c_t^h(t+1)}{r(t)} = \omega_t^h(t) + \frac{\omega_t^h(t+1)}{r(t)}$$

$$- a^h(t)\left[p(t) - \frac{d(t+1) + p^e(t+1)}{r(t)} \right]$$

$$- k^h(t+1)\left[1 - \frac{\lambda}{r(t)} \right]. \qquad (8.4)$$

EXERCISE 8.3   Prove that in any competitive equilibrium, perfect foresight or not, $r(t) \geq \lambda$ for all t.

The result from the Exercise 8.3 is important for this model. The interest rate on private borrowing and lending, $r(t)$, must be equal to or greater than the return on storage, λ. It is possible that the return on storage is low enough (or the loss from storage is high enough) that no one wants to use this method for transferring consumption from youth to old age, given the other alternatives. In that case, $k^h(t+1)$ equals 0 for all h. The equilibrium condition on storage has two characteristics. Both

$$r(t) \geq \lambda,$$

and $$k^h(t+1)\left[1 - \frac{\lambda}{r(t)} \right] = 0$$

must hold in equilibrium. To see why the second equation always equals 0 in equilibrium, consider the two possible cases. If $r(t) > \lambda$, then the return on private borrowing and lending is greater than the return on storage and $k^h(t+1)$ equals 0. If $r(t) = \lambda$, then individuals are indifferent between storage and holding other assets, so $k^h(t+1)$ can be greater than 0 but the portion of the second equation in square brackets is equal to 0. The second equation embodies this pair of constraints. We also see from Equation (8.4) that this version of the world also has the following equilibrium condition: the expected return on land must equal the interest rate on private borrowing and lending, namely,

$$p(t) = \frac{p^e(t + 1) + d(t + 1)}{r(t)}.$$

For $r(t)$ and $p(t)$ sequences that are possible equilibrium sequences, we can find the savings functions for individuals by the usual method. If the interest rate on private borrowing and lending, $r(t)$, is greater than the return from storage, λ, then $r(t)$ is the determinant of savings. No one will want to use storage with its lower rate of return. If $r(t)$ is equal to the return on storage, then individuals will be indifferent to the use of private borrowing or lending and storage, but the return on storage will determine the interest rate. In either case the last two lines of Equation (8.4) will both equal 0 in equilibrium, and the budget constraint that individuals face in equilibrium is the first line of Equation (8.4), that is

$$c_t^h(t) + \frac{c_t^h(t + 1)}{r(t)} = \omega_t^h(t) + \frac{\omega_t^h(t + 1)}{r(t)}.$$

This expression is exactly the same budget constraint we have used in our earlier derivations of the savings function; therefore, our old savings functions continue to be applicable in this economy.

The market clearing equilibrium condition imposes three restrictions on this economy. First, the sum of the holdings of land of generation $t - 1$ equals the total amount of land, $\mathbf{A}$. Second, the total amount of private borrowing and lending of generation $t - 1$ is equal to 0 and can be dropped from the above equation. Third, the feasibility condition holds with equality. Recall that the feasibility condition is

$$C(t) + K(t + 1) = Y(t) + \lambda K(t).$$

Expressed in terms of disaggregated variables, the above equation is

$$\sum_{h=1}^{N(t)} c_t^h(t) + \sum_{h=1}^{N(t-1)} c_{t-1}^h(t) + \sum_{h=1}^{N(t)} k^h(t + 1)$$

$$= \sum_{h=1}^{N(t)} \omega_t^h(t) + \sum_{h=1}^{N(t-1)} \omega_{t-1}^h(t) + d(t)\mathbf{A} + \sum_{h=1}^{N(t-1)} \lambda k^h(t).$$

The old at time t consume whatever they get. This fact means that total consumption of the old at time t is

$$\sum_{h=1}^{N(t-1)} c_{t-1}^h(t) = \sum_{h=1}^{N(t-1)} \omega_{t-1}^h(t) + r(t-1) \sum_{h=1}^{N(t-1)} \ell^h(t-1)$$

$$+ (d(t) + p(t)) \sum_{h=1}^{N(t-1)} a^h(t-1) + \sum_{h=1}^{N(t-1)} \lambda k^h(t-1).$$

The $\ell^h(t-1)$ sum to zero and drop out. Subtracting the consumption of the old from the feasibility condition gives

$$\sum_{h=1}^{N(t)} c_t^h(t) = \sum_{h=1}^{N(t)} \omega_t^h(t) - p(t)\mathbf{A} - \sum_{h=1}^{N(t)} k^h(t+1).$$

Savings for individual h of generation t equal

$$s_t^h(r(t)) = \omega_t^h(t) - c_t^h(t),$$

and aggregate savings at time t, $S_t(r(t))$, are

$$S_t(r(t)) = \sum_{h=1}^{N(t)} s_t^h(r(t)) = \sum_{h=1}^{N(t)} \omega_t^h(t) - \sum_{h=1}^{N(t)} c_t^h(t).$$

Substituting the right side of this expression into the above constraint on the young gives the market clearing equilibrium condition,

$$S_t(r(t)) = p(t)\mathbf{A} + K(t+1),$$

where $K(t+1)$ is the total amount of storage by the members of generation t.

Notice that if we sum the budget constraints when young of the members of generation t, we get

$$\sum_{h=1}^{N(t)} [\omega_t^h(t) - c_t^h(t) - \ell^h(t) - p(t)a^h(t) - k^h(t+1)] = 0.$$

Because $\ell^h(t)$ sum to 0, we can rearrange this equation to get the same market clearing condition,

$$S_t(r(t)) = p(t)\mathbf{A} + K(t + 1),$$

that we found above.

Assembling the above equilibrium conditions, we can write the following definition.

Definition   *A perfect foresight competitive equilibrium for an economy with storage and land is a nonnegative sequence of land prices and interest rates and of total storage amounts, $K(t + 1)$, that for all $t \geq 1$ satisfy*
  (i) $S_t(r(t)) = p(t)\mathbf{A} + K(t + 1),$
  (ii) $p(t) = (p(t + 1) + d(t + 1))/r(t),$
  (iii) $r(t) \geq \lambda,$ *and*
  (iv) $K(t + 1)[1 - \lambda/r(t)] = 0.$

Given this definition of a competitive equilibrium, we consider two methods of solving for one.

Finding a Competitive Equilibrium

As before, we use both the guess and verify method and graphical analysis to find equilibria. Recall that the guess and verify method can give us *some* of the equilibria quite easily, whereas the graphical method can lead us to *all* equilibrium sequences. We do the guess and verify method first.

Suppose that we are in a stationary environment, so the environmental variables are the same for all periods. Two of the more useful implications of this assumption are that in each period $S_t(r(t))$ is the same function, $S(r(t))$, and the crop, $d(t + 1)$, has the same value, d. Given that the environment is stationary, we can guess that there is a stationary equilibrium, where $p(t) = p$, $r(t) = r$, and $K(t) = K$ for all $t \geq 1$. We check to see whether there exists a $\{p, r, K\}$ triplet that fulfills the equilibrium conditions. In particular, condition (iv) in the definition of the competitive equilibrium indicates that there are two types of relevant guesses. One guess is that $K = 0$ and only land is held as an asset (no storage occurs). The other is that $r = \lambda$.

If $K = 0$, then the equilibrium for this economy is identical to our earlier equilibria in an economy with land. So it seems reasonable first to check and see whether $K = 0$ can be one of the characteristics of the equilibrium triplet. To make this check, we use conditions (i) and (ii), with $p(t + 1) = p(t) = p$, and see whether there exists a p that satisfies

$$S\left(\frac{p + d}{p}\right) = p\mathbf{A}.$$

If we can solve this equation for a nonnegative p, then we can calculate the accompanying gross interest rate from

$$r = \frac{p + d}{p}.$$

If such a p, r, and K triplet exists, they are, by construction, nonnegative and they already fulfill conditions (i), (ii), and (iv) of a competitive equilibrium. We only need to determine whether condition (iii) is also fulfilled. If the gross interest rate, r, that we found above is greater than or equal to λ, then we have found a stationary equilibrium for our economy.

If, on the other hand, the gross interest rate we found above is one where $r < \lambda$, then our initial assumption, that $K = 0$, must be revised. The only viable alternative is $K > 0$. If condition (iv) is to hold, it must be that $\lambda = r$. Setting r equal to λ, we find the price from condition (ii):

$$\frac{p + d}{p} = r,$$

or $$p = \frac{d}{r - 1}.$$

If such a nonnegative price exists, then we use this price and condition (i) to find K, where

$$K = S(\lambda) - p\mathbf{A}.$$

If all of the p, r, and K that we have found are nonnegative, then they constitute a competitive equilibrium for our economy. If not, then no stationary equilibrium exists for this economy.

Before going on to graphical analysis of competitive equilibrium, do the following two exercises. Note that you are asked to find equilibria in economies in which there is no land; so, for these exercises, $\mathbf{A} = 0$. The only alternative asset to storage is private borrowing and lending.

EXERCISE 8.4 Describe an economy without land with a stationary equilibrium that satisfies $r > \lambda$.

EXERCISE 8.5 Describe an economy without land with a stationary equilibrium that satisfies $r = \lambda$.

For our graphical analysis of the competitive equilibrium, we continue with the assumption of a stationary environment but discard the assumption we made above that the equilibrium price, interest rate, and storage sequences need to be stationary.

Because $K(t + 1)$ is nonnegative, then a variant of condition (i) is

$$S(r(t)) \geq p(t)\,\mathbf{A},$$

with equality holding when $K(t + 1) = 0$. Given the present value condition (condition ii), we can rewrite this inequality as

$$S\left(\frac{p(t + 1) + d}{p(t)}\right) \geq p(t)\,\mathbf{A}.$$

With appropriate conditions on the aggregate savings function, we can, as we have done before, write a price function,

$$p(t) \leq f(p(t + 1)), \tag{8.5}$$

where the function, $f(\cdot)$ is the same price function we found in earlier chapters. Equation (8.5) holds with equality when $K(t + 1)$ equals 0. Because the savings that do not go into land go into storage when positive storage occurs, the above savings inequality is

$$S(r(t)) > p(t)\,\mathbf{A}.$$

The curved (solid) line in Figure 8.1 is the price function for an economy with $N(t) = 100$, $\omega_t^h = [2, 1]$, $\mathbf{A} = 100$, $d = 1$, and a utility func-

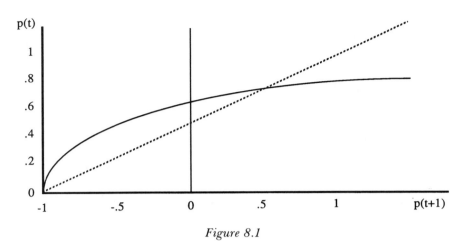

Figure 8.1

tion of $u_t^h = c_t^h(t)c_t^h(t + 1)$. It is one of the price functions you saw earlier in Figure 6.1. The inequality in Equation (8.5) bounds time t prices,
$p(t)$'s, to be on or below this curved line.

We next combine conditions (ii) and (iii) to write

$$\lambda \leq r(t) = \frac{p(t + 1) + d}{p(t)},$$

which can be rearranged as

$$p(t) \leq \frac{p(t + 1)}{\lambda} + \frac{d}{\lambda}. \tag{8.6}$$

Equation (8.6) holds with equality when $r(t)$ equals λ. The straight
(dashed) line in Figure 8.1 shows Equation (8.6) at equality for an economy with $d = 1$ and $\lambda = 2$. Equation (8.6) restricts equilibrium $p(t)$'s to
be on or below this line.

Equilibrium condition (iv) indicates that either Equation (8.5) or
Equation (8.6) or both hold in an equilibrium. The relationship between
$p(t + 1)$ and $p(t)$ that holds in equilibrium must satisfy both of these
inequalities, with one of them holding with equality when the other does
not. The solid line in Figure 8.2 gives the relationship between $p(t + 1)$
and $p(t)$ that must hold in an equilibrium. At $p(t + 1)$'s where the line
for Equation (8.5) is below the line for Equation (8.6), then Equation

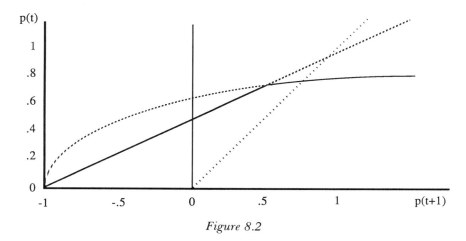

Figure 8.2

(8.5) holds with equality and we are on its graph. At those $p(t + 1)$'s where the line for Equation (8.6) is below the line for Equation (8.5), then Equation (8.6) holds with equality and we are on its graph. The kinked curve (solid line) giving the relationship between $p(t + 1)$ and $p(t)$ can be written as

$$p(t) = \min\left\{ f(p(t + 1)), \frac{p(t + 1)}{\lambda} + \frac{d}{\lambda} \right\}, \qquad (8.7)$$

where $\min\{\cdot, \cdot\}$ indicates the minimum of the two functions at each value of $p(t + 1)$.

The dotted (45-degree) line in Figure 8.2 represents possible stationary equilibria. The points where the 45-degree line crosses the solid line are stationary equilibrium prices, the same stationary equilibrium prices we would have found with the guess and verify method. Notice that in Figure 8.2, the equilibrium is one where no storage takes place. The return on land is higher than the return on storage. This relation is indicated by the fact that the 45-degree line crosses the kinked solid line on its curved portion, where Equation (8.5) holds with equality.

In Figure 8.3, the stationary equilibrium is one where some storage does take place. The economy shown in Figure 8.3 is identical to the one shown in Figure 8.2 except for the return on storage. The return on storage in the economy shown in Figure 8.3 is $\lambda = 2.5$. In this version of the economy where the return on storage is high enough ($\lambda = 2.5$)

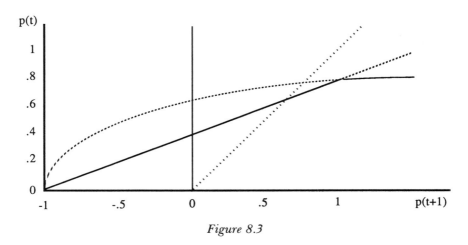

Figure 8.3

to allow storage to occur, the stationary equilibrium price of land is lower than in the version ($\lambda = 2$) where no storage occurs.

For the economies illustrated in Figures 8.2 and 8.3, the stationary equilibria that occur where the 45-degree line crosses the function given in Equation (8.7) are unique. This uniqueness can be illustrated by the same method we used in Chapter 6. Choose some price, $p(1)$, different from the stationary equilibrium price. Then trace out the price sequence $\{p(t)\}$ for $t = 1$ to ∞. If the price sequence violates one of our restrictions (becomes negative or exceeds the upper bound), then we reject that price path. Figure 8.4 shows this price path worked out for the economy

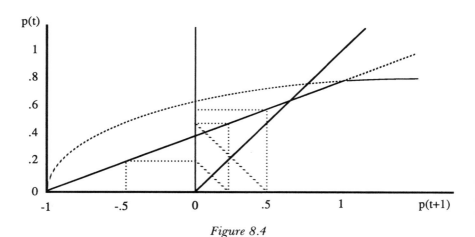

Figure 8.4

of Figure 8.2 beginning at $p(1)$ equals .6. The dotted line traces out the time path of the $p(t)$'s. By time $t = 3$, the price has become negative, so $p(1)$ equals .6 is rejected. By a similar method, all $p(1)$'s except the stationary equilibrium value can be rejected.

All economies with storage do not necessarily have a unique equilibrium. In Chapter 6 we found that economies with land that has no crop could have two stationary equilibria and an infinite number of nonstationary ones. We get a similar result when we have storage with a λ less than 1. Figure 8.5 illustrates Equation (8.7) for an economy where the crop, d, is equal to 0 and λ equals .8. There are two stationary equilibria for this example economy, one when $p(t) = 0$ and one when $p(t) = .5$, for all $t \geq 1$. For any $p(1)$ less than .5, there is a price sequence that converges to 0 and is an equilibrium price path. The dotted line in Figure 8.5 traces out the path of prices for $p(1) = .4$. Notice that the path of the dotted line converges toward 0. A similar price path would occur for any $p(1)$ strictly between .5 and 0.

In our example economy with no crop and a λ greater than 1, there is only one—stationary—equilibrium at $p(t) = 0$. The storage technology offers a greater rate of return than land, and no one will wish to hold land. That being the case, the equilibrium price of land is 0.

EXERCISE 8.6 Describe an economy with land and with an equilibrium with $r(t) > λ$ for all $t \geq 1$.

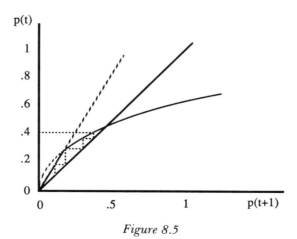

Figure 8.5

EXERCISE 8.7 Describe an economy with land and with an equilibrium with $r(t) = \lambda$ for all $t \geq 1$.

EXERCISE 8.8 In an economy with storage, how is a tax on land rents (crops) different from a tax on endowment?

EXERCISE 8.9 Consider an economy without land in which the equilibrium is one where storage occurs at every date and where $\lambda > 1$. Show that consumption and income taxes are not in general equivalent in the sense of the Exercise 3.2. Assume that the income tax is levied on the endowment, on gross interest, and on the gross return from storage. Show that in general, an equilibrium with $z_y > 0$ is not Pareto optimal. Is the same true if $z_c > 0$? Explain.

Budget constraints for the consumption and income taxes described in Exercise 8.9 are

$$c_t^h(t) = (1 - z_y)\omega_t^h(t) - \ell^h(t) - k^h(t + 1) - z_c c_t^h(t),$$

when young, and

$$c_t^h(t + 1)$$
$$= (1 - z_y)[\omega_t^h(t + 1) + r(t)\ell^h(t) + \lambda k^h(t + 1)] - z_c c_t^h(t + 1),$$

when old. As usual, we combine these two constraints to form a single constraint by solving the constraint when young for $\ell^h(t)$ to get

$$\ell^h(t) = (1 - z_y)\omega_t^h(t) - k^h(t + 1) - (1 + z_c)c_t^h(t).$$

We substitute the right side of this equation into the budget constraint when old. After some rearranging, we get the single constraint,

$$\frac{(1 + z_c)}{(1 - z_y)}\left[c_t^h(t) + \frac{c_t^h(t + 1)}{(1 - z_y)r(t)}\right] = \omega_t^h(t) + \frac{\omega_t^h(t + 1)}{(1 - z_y)r(t)}$$
$$- \frac{k^h(t + 1)}{(1 - z_y)}\left[1 - \frac{\lambda}{r(t)}\right]. \qquad (8.8)$$

The assumption of the exercise is that we are choosing income and consumption taxes, z_y and z_c, so that

$$q = \frac{(1 + z_c)}{(1 - z_y)}$$

for some constant $0 < q < 1$.

The first time we saw this consumption and income tax problem—in Exercise 3.2—the second line of Equation (8.8) was equal to 0. The combined budget constraint was

$$q \left[c_t^h(t) + \frac{c_t^h(t + 1)}{(1 - z_y)r(t)} \right] = \omega_t^h(t) + \frac{\omega_t^h(t + 1)}{(1 - z_y)r(t)}, \tag{8.8'}$$

where q is the constant defined above. Once q is fixed, the only variable that matters for an equilibrium (where the aggregate supply function equals 0) is the gross interest rate times 1 plus the tax rate on income. Assume we have an initial equilibrium $r^1(t)$ for some income tax rate z_y^1 and some constant q. We can find the equilibrium gross interest rate that goes with another income tax rate, $z_y^2 \neq z_y^1$, and a consumption tax rate that leaves q unchanged. The above budget constraint (Equation 8.8') holds for the same consumption pattern that held in the first equilibrium if $r^2(t)$ is such that

$$(1 - z_y^2)r^2(t) = (1 - z_y^1)r^1(t).$$

The relevant gross interest rate for an equilibrium was $(1 - z_y)r(t)$. As z_y changed (keeping q constant), $r(t)$ changed so that the resulting $(1 - z_y)r(t)$ was constant. Changes in income and consumption taxes that left q constant did not change the equilibrium pattern of consumption.

In the economy in Exercise 8.9 with storage and with $\lambda > 1$, the arbitrage condition generated from the second line of Equation (8.8) requires that $r(t) = \lambda$ (we are assuming in the exercise that storage occurs). This restriction means that $r(t)$ is fixed and cannot adjust as the income tax changes and therefore cannot compensate for the tax changes. Because the second line in Equation (8.8) equals 0—from the arbitrage condition—the relevant budget constraint is Equation (8.8') but with $r(t)$

replaced by λ. This constraint is

$$\mathscr{q}\left[c_t^h(t) + \frac{c_t^h(t + 1)}{(1 - z_y)\lambda}\right] = \omega_t^h(t) + \frac{\omega_t^h(t + 1)}{(1 - z_y)\lambda}.$$

Now, changes in the tax rate on income change the discount on second-period consumption and endowment. An increase in the tax rate on income (with a corresponding change in the consumption tax rate so as to leave $\mathscr{q}$ unchanged) reduces storage and reduces the amount of good that is available in the second period of life.

To answer the part of the exercise about the Pareto inferiority of the income tax, compare this tax to a lump-sum tax. Compare the total amount of good that is available each period t in an economy with an income tax and an economy with a lump-sum tax that raises the same amount of government revenue.

Reprise

The introduction of a storage technology changes the definition of feasibility because goods can now be directly transferred from period to period. Competitive equilibria with storage require two conditions beyond the market clearing and utility maximization conditions. The usual arbitrage condition still holds, but it is now paired with a condition on a lower bound for the gross interest rate: the gross interest rate (on private borrowing and lending or on land) cannot be less than the return on storage. It is possible that the return on land is higher than that of storage, but if storage occurs, then in economies where land produces a crop, the return on storage and land must be the same.

We looked at two ways of solving for competitive equilibria for this model with storage. In an economy in which the environment is stationary, the guess and verify technique will find a stationary equilibrium if one exists. Graphical analysis of the model allows us to consider nonstationary equilibria in economies with stationary environments. In the graphical analysis, we can draw in both of the constraints on the price path; then our price function is the lower bound of these two constraints.

CHAPTER 9

The Neoclassical Growth Model

All of the economies we have discussed so far have been endowment economies: individuals begin each period of their life with some given quantity of goods. We have not worried about how these goods were generated or how the individual came into possession of them. The only kind of economic growth possible has been growth in the population or some exogenously assumed growth in the endowments.

Even the most casual observations of life point out that, except possibly for the very young and the very rich, ours is not an endowment economy. Many individuals provide their labor to firms in return for wages. Individuals accumulate assets that aid in the production of additional quantities of goods. It is widely believed that the accumulation of this type of assets is important in determining the growth rate of an economy beyond that generated by population growth. Expressing endowments in terms of labor and making savings go into investment are two of the additions we wish to make to our basic model.

In this chapter we present a version of a well-known model that is the starting point for most studies of economic growth and development. The basic production side of the model was first set out in its clearest form by Robert Solow (1956, 1970). The version we use has two-period overlapping generations and was first described by Peter Diamond (1965). For this model, the savings decisions of individuals and the time path of the capital stock are fairly simple to analyze. We use this model to study how growth of output and consumption is affected by growth in population and the labor force, by exogenous technical changes, and by the preference patterns that determine the rate at which people save.

The Physical Environment and the Feasible Allocations

The environment here is like those of earlier chapters except in two respects. First, people in generations t, $t > 0$, are endowed with labor rather than with goods. Second, time t good is produced with a *technology* that uses as inputs time t labor and time $t - 1$ good, which was stored from time $t - 1$ to time t and which we call time t capital. This technology is represented by a *production function*,

$$\gamma(t)F(L(t), K(t)),$$

where the first argument of $F(\cdot, \cdot)$ is the time t labor input and the second argument is the time t capital input. We assume that the function $F(\cdot, \cdot)$ is the same at all dates, whereas the parameter $\gamma(t)$ represents the level of technology at time t. As in the storage economy, we assume that members of generation 0 start out with some time 1 capital, some time 0 good that they stored and carried over to time 1. Individuals care only about their own consumption. In particular, they do not care about leisure, so they supply all of their labor into the labor market.

We make a number of simplifying assumptions throughout this chapter. In the economies we consider here, there is no land, no storage, and no government bonds, although all of these could be added as extra assets. We wish to concentrate on economies in which labor is used with some capital to produce output. Both capital and labor are required to get output. Individuals are paid wages for their labor inputs and rentals for the use of their capital. In general, individuals can be endowed with labor in both periods of their life. The *lifetime labor endowments*, Δ_t^h, of member h of generation t is

$$\Delta_t^h = [\Delta_t^h(t), \Delta_t^h(t + 1)],$$

where $\Delta_t^h(s)$ is the labor endowment of young person h of generation t at date $s = t$ and $t + 1$. When young, individuals can choose to save some of their wages. In equilibrium, because we have assumed away all other methods of savings, the aggregate savings of the young will be the next period's *capital stock*. We will assume that all capital carried over from date t depreciates (is completely used up) during period $t + 1$. Given some initial capital stock carried over from period 0, we are interested in the equilibrium paths of the capital stock and output for time $t = 1$ to ∞.

If each individual in the economy has the same labor endowment, the total amount of labor at date t is

$$L(t) = N(t)\Delta_t^h(t) + N(t - 1)\Delta_{t-1}^h(t).$$

The gross growth rate of the population is n, so $N(t) = nN(t - 1)$ for all t.

The total capital stock at date t is given, in equilibrium, by the total savings, when young, of the current old. Let $k^h(t)$ be the capital owned at date t by member h of generation $t - 1$. The total capital stock of the economy is equal to

$$K(t) = \sum_{h=1}^{N(t-1)} k^h(t).$$

The time t output is produced by the capital and labor available at date t. All capital and all labor are employed. We are assuming that the economy comprises many small competitive firms, each of which is using the same technology in production. The production function, which is a function of labor and capital used by the firm, displays constant returns to scale (is homogeneous of degree one), has positive first derivatives, and negative own second derivatives (positive but diminishing marginal products). We assume that the first derivative with respect to each argument goes to ∞ as the ratio of that argument to the other argument goes to 0. Because the economy is competitive and the production functions display constant returns to scale, all firms are using labor and capital in the same ratio and every firm is a larger or smaller version of every other one. Consider some firm using $\Delta(t)$ units of labor and $k(t)$ units of capital. Output for that firm can be written as

$$v(t) = \gamma(t)F(\Delta(t), k(t)).$$

The *constant returns to scale* condition means that if the amount of labor and capital were increased by the same proportion, then output would increase by that proportion as well. If the above firm were to use $a\Delta(t)$ units of labor and $ak(t)$ units of capital, then it would produce $av(t)$ units of output for any positive a. Doubling the inputs, for example, doubles the output. Because each firm is a (possibly) different sized version of every other and production displays constant returns to scale, we can write total output for the economy as a function of the total amount of labor and the total amount of capital. Total output at date t is

$$Y(t) = \gamma(t)F(L(t), K(t)).$$

For our examples in this chapter, we use a particular, constant returns to scale production function. The production function we use is called a *Cobb-Douglas production function* and has the form

$$Y(t) = \gamma(t)L(t)^{1-a}K(t)^a, \tag{9.1}$$

where a is some parameter strictly between 0 and 1. The term $\gamma(t)$ is a parameter of the production function and represents the level of technology at time t. Increases in $\gamma(t)$ mean that the economy can produce more output with the same amount of labor and capital; such an increase is called an *improvement in technology*. We assume that $\gamma(t)$ grows at a rate $1 + g$, so

$$\gamma(t + 1) = (1 + g)\gamma(t).$$

As we assumed above, these production functions display positive but diminishing marginal products for each of the factors of production (the labor and capital) separately. If we keep the amount of capital constant and increase labor 60 percent, for example, output will go up less than 60 percent and the increased output from adding the last worker hired will be less than the increased output gained by hiring the first of those additional workers. The same will hold true if we fix labor and increase capital. As the quantity of one factor used in production diminishes, the marginal product of that factor increases. We assume that the marginal product of each factor goes to ∞ as the quantity of that factor goes to 0. The Cobb-Douglas production function has this characteristic.

Figure 9.1 (upper graph) shows the output that is generated using different amounts of capital and a fixed amount of labor with a production function like the one in Equation (9.1). In the figure, we used $a = \frac{1}{2}$, $\gamma(t) = 5$, and $L(t) = 1$. The *marginal product of capital* is the slope of the production curve shown in Figure 9.1. Notice that the slope of the curve diminishes as the quantity of capital increases. The lower graph in Figure 9.1 shows the marginal product of capital as a function of the capital used in the production function illustrated in the upper

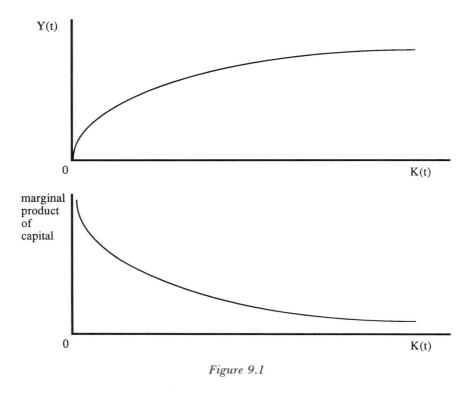

Figure 9.1

graph. The shape of both the production function and the marginal product of capital curve in this figure are characteristic of production functions with diminishing marginal product of capital.

EXERCISE 9.1   Consider an economy with the Cobb-Douglas production function given in Equation (9.1), where $\gamma(t) = 6$, $L(t) = 9$, $K(t) = 15$, and $a = .4$. What is the output in this economy? Suppose that both capital and labor increase by one third, to $L(t) = 12$ and $K(t) = 20$. What is the new level of output? What is the percentage increase of this level of output over the initial level of output?

Goods produced in one period can only be carried over to the next period as capital. This assumption means that the feasibility condition for this economy (for a general F function) is

$$C(t) + K(t + 1) \leq \gamma(t)F(L(t), K(t)),$$

or $\quad \displaystyle\sum_{h=1}^{N(t)} c_t^h(t) + \sum_{h=1}^{N(t-1)} c_{t-1}^h(t) + \sum_{h=1}^{N(t)} k^h(t + 1) \leq \gamma(t)F(L(t), K(t)).$

Total production in each period t is divided between consumption at date t and storage at date t, the second of which becomes the capital stock at time $t + 1$.

Equilibrium Outputs, Inputs, and Factor Rentals at Each Date

Before giving a complete definition of an equilibrium for this economy, it is convenient to describe certain features of the equilibrium at any date that depend only on the capital stock at that date, $K(t)$; the technology at that date, $\gamma(t)$; and the economy's labor endowment at that date, $L(t)$. Recall that part of the production function, $F(\cdot, \cdot)$, is the same at every date.

As suggested above, we assume that production occurs in firms that hire labor and capital competitively and produce time t good using a technology represented by the production function, $\gamma(t)F(\cdot, \cdot)$. The marginal product of labor is equal to the first derivative of the production function with respect to labor. In a competitive economy, the marginal product of labor is equal to the wage rate. By assumption, all of the labor in the economy at date t is supplied to the firms. Because the supply of labor is fixed each period, the demand for labor determines the wage. Our single production function represents the actions of many small competing firms. These small firms will hire workers until the wage equals the marginal product of labor. Therefore, the wage rate in this economy is equal to

$$\text{wage}(t) = (1 - a)\gamma(t)L(t)^{-a}K(t)^a. \tag{9.2}$$

In a competitive economy the rental rate on capital is equal to the marginal product of capital, which equals the first derivative of the production function with respect to capital. The rental rate on capital is equal to

$$\text{rental}(t) = a\gamma(t)L(t)^{1-a}K(t)^{a-1}. \tag{9.3}$$

Both the wage rate and the rental rate depend only on the relative amounts of labor and capital and not on the absolute amounts. This relation is a characteristic of all constant returns to scale production functions, but we illustrate it using only Cobb-Douglas production functions. Look at the powers to which the quantity of labor and the quantity of capital are raised in the wage and rental equations. In each of these equations the power of one is the negative of the power of the other. In the wage equation, for example, we have

$$L(t)^{-a}K(t)^a = \left[\frac{K(t)}{L(t)}\right]^a;$$

and in the rental equation, we have

$$L(t)^{1-a}K(t)^{a-1} = \left[\frac{L(t)}{K(t)}\right]^{1-a}.$$

If both labor and capital were doubled, nothing would happen to the marginal product of either labor or capital and nothing would happen to the wage or the rental rate.

If there is only one wage rate determined by a competitive market for labor, then the preceding discussion implies that each firm will be using labor and capital at the same ratios. Firms with more capital will hire more labor than firms with less capital, but the ratios of labor to capital will be the same. The rentals on each unit of capital will also be the same in large and small firms.

Summarizing, the wage in this economy at time t is the marginal product of labor. With homogeneous-of-degree-one production functions (constant returns to scale), the marginal product of labor is determined by the ratio of labor to capital in each firm. This ratio is the same in every firm and is equal to the ratio for the economy. The wage rate in this economy at time t is

$$\text{wage}(t) = (1 - a)\gamma(t)\left[\frac{K(t)}{L(t)}\right]^a, \tag{9.4}$$

and the rental rate is

$$\text{rental}(t) = a\gamma(t)\left[\frac{K(t)}{L(t)}\right]^{a-1}. \tag{9.5}$$

The total wage bill equals the wage times the amount of labor hired. Because, by assumption, all $L(t)$ units of labor are hired, the wage bill is equal to

$$\text{wage}(t)L(t) = (1 - a)\gamma(t)\left[\frac{K(t)}{L(t)}\right]^{a}L(t)$$

$$= (1 - a)Y(t).$$

The total wage bill is $1 - a$ of total output.

The total bill for rental of capital equals the rental times $K(t)$, or

$$\text{rental}(t)K(t) = a\gamma(t)\left[\frac{K(t)}{L(t)}\right]^{a-1}K(t)$$

$$= aY(t).$$

The total payment to capital is a of total output.

Notice that the firms gain no profits from producing goods. All of the output of the firms goes to pay the wage and the rental bills. The wage bill is $(1 - a)Y(t)$ and the rental bill is $aY(t)$; adding these together totals $Y(t)$.

EXERCISE 9.2   For the economy in Exercise 9.1, what are the wage and rental rates before and after the increase in labor and capital? What are the total wage bills and total return on capital both before and after the increase in capital and labor?

The Individual Choice Decision under Perfect Foresight

Individual h of generation t wishes to maximize utility subject to the budget constraints. The budget constraint that this individual faces when young is

$$c_t^h(t) = \text{wage}(t)\Delta_t^h(t) - \ell^h(t) - k^h(t + 1),$$

where $\Delta_t^h(t)$ is the fixed amount of labor that this individual supplies to the labor market and $k^h(t + 1)$ is the amount of capital this person chooses to hold to period $t + 1$. As usual, $\ell^h(t)$ is the amount of private borrowing or lending that individual h chooses to make. All individuals take the wage rate at time t as given and not affected by their labor supply.

The budget constraint that individual h faces when old is

$$c_t^h(t + 1) = \text{wage}(t + 1)\Delta_t^h(t + 1) + r(t)\ell^h(t)$$

$$+ \text{rental}(t + 1)k^h(t + 1),$$

where $\Delta_t^h(t + 1)$ is the amount of labor that individual h of generation t supplies to the labor market in time $t + 1$. As before, $r(t)$ is the gross interest rate on private borrowing and lending. All individuals take the wage rate at time $t + 1$ and the rental rate at time $t + 1$ as given and unaffected by their personal decision to supply labor or invest in capital. Although it is not necessary at this point, we assume perfect foresight (because soon we will be studying perfect foresight equilibria), so the wages and rentals that are expected for time period $t + 1$ are the ones that occur in that date. We made a similar assumption for our earlier economies.

We can combine the two budget constraints into a single lifetime budget constraint by solving the budget constraint when old for $\ell^h(t)$ and substituting that into the budget constraint when young. This substitution gives the lifetime budget constraint

$$c_t^h(t) + \frac{c_t^h(t + 1)}{r(t)} = \text{wage}(t)\Delta_t^h(t) + \frac{\text{wage}(t + 1)\Delta_t^h(t + 1)}{r(t)}$$

$$- k^h(t + 1)\left[1 - \frac{\text{rental}(t + 1)}{r(t)}\right].$$

As usual, we wish to show that the portion of the lifetime budget constraint in brackets must equal 0 in an equilibrium and, therefore, that

$$\text{rental}(t + 1) = r(t).$$

Given wages and supplies of labor, the present value of lifetime consumption is maximized by making

$$- k^h(t + 1)\left[1 - \frac{\text{rental}(t + 1)}{r(t)}\right]$$

as large as possible. If rental$(t + 1) > r(t)$, then the portion in the square brackets is negative and everyone wants to borrow as much as possible at time t and purchase capital. Everyone wants $k^h(t + 1)$ equal to infinity. This case cannot be an equilibrium, first, because there are no lenders and, second, because it is not possible in an economy with finite output to make an infinite amount of investment.

If rental$(t + 1) < r(t)$, then the portion of the lifetime budget constraint in square brackets is positive, and maximizing the present value of lifetime consumption is achieved by having $k^h(t + 1)$ equal to 0 for all h. We are restricting individual holdings of capital to be nonnegative, so 0 is as small as $k^h(t + 1)$ can get. Because every member of generation t chooses zero holdings of capital, $K(t + 1)$ also equals 0. But with no capital in period $t + 1$, the marginal product of capital would be infinite; and because the marginal product of any factor equals its wage (or rental), the rental on capital would also be infinite. The initial assumption that rental$(t + 1)$ is less than $r(t)$ leads to a contradiction. This case cannot be an equilibrium.

Equality between rental$(t + 1)$ and $r(t)$ is the only possibility remaining. In this case, each individual is indifferent between private borrowing and lending and holding capital. The portion of the lifetime budget constraint in brackets equals 0, and the lifetime budget constraint is the same one we had when we first introduced a savings function (Equation 2.3), except that wages replace the goods endowment in each period of life. This lifetime budget constraint is

$$c_t^h(t) + \frac{c_t^h(t + 1)}{r(t)} = \text{wage}(t)\,\Delta_t^h(t) + \frac{\text{wage}(t + 1)\,\Delta_t^h(t + 1)}{r(t)}.$$

Individuals maximize utility subject to this lifetime constraint. They take the wage rates as given and always supply all of their labor endowment. In this economy, savings for person h of generation t is equal to

$$s_t^h(r(t)) = \text{wage}(t)\,\Delta_t^h(t) - c_t^h(t).$$

Substituting this definition into the lifetime budget constraint gives

$$c_t^h(t + 1) = \text{wage}(t + 1)\Delta_t^h(t + 1) + r(t)s_t^h(r(t)).$$

These two consumption expressions are substituted into the utility function to get utility as a function of the savings decision. The equation we get is identical to the one with goods endowment, except that wages times labor supply at each date replaces the goods endowment. The example utility function we have been using, that is,

$$u_t^h = c_t^h(t)[c_t^h(t + 1)]^\beta,$$

becomes

$$u_t^h = [\text{wage}(t)\Delta_t^h(t) - s_t^h(r(t))]$$
$$\cdot [\text{wage}(t + 1)\Delta_t^h(t + 1) + r(t)s_t^h(r(t))]^\beta.$$

Taking the derivative with respect to $s_t^h(r(t))$, setting it equal to 0 and then solving for $s_t^h(r(t))$ gives a savings function for individual h of generation t of

$$s_t^h(r(t)) = \frac{\beta\,\text{wage}(t)\Delta_t^h(t)}{1 + \beta} - \frac{\text{wage}(t + 1)\Delta_t^h(t + 1)}{(1 + \beta)r(t)}.$$

If β equals 1, as it has for most of the examples we have used, then the individual savings function is

$$s_t^h(r(t)) = \frac{\text{wage}(t)\Delta_t^h(t)}{2} - \frac{\text{wage}(t + 1)\Delta_t^h(t + 1)}{2r(t)}.$$

Notice the similarity between the individual savings function we have found here and the individual savings function we had in earlier chapters for economies with this same utility function. Where, in the earlier version, we had the goods endowment when young, we now have the wages earned from supplying all of the labor when young. Where we had the goods endowment when old, we now have the wages earned from supplying all of the labor endowment when old. Otherwise, the savings functions are identical in form.

Aggregate savings, $S_t(r(t))$, are found by summing the individual savings functions. Let $L_t(t)$ be the total labor supplied by the young at time t, and let $L_t(t + 1)$ be the labor supplied by the old (of generation t) at time $t + 1$. If all members of generation t have the same utility function, then aggregate savings can be written as

$$S_t(r(t)) = \frac{\text{wage}(t)L_t(t)}{2} - \frac{\text{wage}(t + 1)L_t(t + 1)}{2r(t)}.$$

This aggregate savings function is written as a function of the gross interest rate alone. It would be more accurate to represent it as a function of the gross interest rate, the wages at dates t and $t + 1$ and the supply of labor that generation t has over its lifetime. We will continue to express aggregate savings as a function of the gross interest rate alone but will sometimes replace wages at dates t and $t + 1$ with their equilibrium values. Make this substitution in Exercise 9.3.

EXERCISE 9.3   Find the savings function for member h of generation t of an economy with the production function given in Equation 9.1, with $\gamma(t) = \gamma(t + 1) = 6$, $N(t) = 100$, $K(t) = 150$, $L(t) = L(t + 1) = 1200$, $\Delta_t^h(t) = 9$, $\Delta_t^h(t + 1) = 3$, $a = .4$, and a utility function of

$$u_t^h = c_t^h(t)[c_t^h(t + 1)]^{1/2}.$$

You may not need to use all of the information about this economy in this exercise, but you might in future discussions of this economy.

A Definition of Equilibrium

Equilibrium conditions for this economy can be found in the usual way. Recall that all capital from period $t - 1$ is used up in the production at date t. In each period, the total output is divided between consumption and investment. Recall that the feasibility condition (at equality) for this economy is

$$C(t) + K(t + 1) = \gamma(t)F(L(t), K(t))$$

or $\displaystyle\sum_{h=1}^{N(t)} c_t^h(t) + \sum_{h=1}^{N(t-1)} c_{t-1}^h(t) + \sum_{h=1}^{N(t)} k^h(t+1) = \gamma(t)F(L(t), K(t))$.

Aggregate consumption of the old at time t is equal to

$$\sum_{h=1}^{N(t-1)} c_{t-1}^h(t) = \text{wage}(t)L_{t-1}(t) + \text{rental}(t)K(t) + r(t)\sum_{h=1}^{N(t-1)} \ell^h(t).$$

Total private borrowing and lending of generation $t - 1$ equals 0, so the last term of this equation drops out. The zero profit condition (which we found above from the constant returns to scale characteristics of our production function) is

$$\gamma(t)F(L(t), K(t)) = \text{wage}(t)[L_t(t) + L_{t-1}(t)] + \text{rental}(t)K(t),$$

where $L(t) = L_t(t) + L_{t-1}(t)$.

Substituting the zero profit condition into the feasibility constraint and then subtracting the consumption of the old at time t gives

$$\sum_{h=1}^{N(t)} c_t^h(t) = \text{wage}(t)L_t(t) - \sum_{h=1}^{N(t)} k^h(t+1).$$

This condition is the same as the condition we would get by summing the budget constraints of the young at date t. Using the definition of individual savings and summing over the members of generation t to get aggregate savings, we get the equilibrium condition of

$$S_t(r(t)) = K(t+1).$$

One of our conditions for an equilibrium is that all aggregate savings go to capital accumulation.

Given the arbitrage condition on the gross interest rate on private borrowing and lending and the rental on capital, individuals are indifferent between holding capital or engaging in private lending. The capital holdings of $N(t) - 1$ members of generation t are individually indeterminate [but cannot sum to more than $K(t + 1)$]. However, as an equilibrium condition, the capital holdings of all the members of generation t must sum to $K(t + 1)$, so the holdings of the $N(t)$th member must be equal to

$$k^{N(t)}(t + 1) = K(t + 1) - \sum_{h=1}^{N(t)-1} k^h(t + 1).$$

A competitive equilibrium for our economy with production requires the usual general conditions. Individuals maximize utility subject to their budget constraints and all markets clear. In this case there is a market for goods, for labor, for capital, and for private borrowing and lending at each date t. We define equilibrium conditions for this economy with production.

Definition   *A perfect foresight competitive equilibrium for an economy with labor endowments and a production function of $\gamma(t)F(L(t), K(t))$ is a sequence of $K(t)$, $r(t)$, wage(t), and rental(t) for $t \geq 1$ such that, given an initial $K(1) > 0$,*

$$S_t(r(t)) = K(t + 1),$$

$$r(t) = \text{rental}(t + 1),$$

$$\text{wage}(t) = \frac{\partial[\gamma(t)F(L(t), K(t))]}{\partial L(t)},$$

and $$\text{rental}(t) = \frac{\partial[\gamma(t)F(L(t), K(t))]}{\partial K(t)},$$

hold for all $t \geq 1$.

The first equation is the market clearing condition in the goods market and has utility maximization satisfied in the savings function. The second is the present value condition that is the result of arbitrage in the loan market. The third and fourth are the demand equations that give the wage and rental for clearing the labor and capital markets.

We wish to find the time path for $K(t)$ given any $K(1) > 0$. We show how to find this path for an economy with a Cobb-Douglas production function and with individual utility functions of

$$u_t^h = c_t^h(t)[c_t^h(t + 1)]^\beta,$$

for $\beta = 1$. We already have the savings function for this economy; we derived it earlier. Aggregate savings at time t are

$$S_t(r(t)) = \frac{\text{wage}(t)L_t(t)}{2} - \frac{\text{wage}(t + 1)L_t(t + 1)}{2r(t)},$$

and equal $K(t + 1)$ in equilibrium. The arbitrage condition is that $r(t)$ equals rental$(t + 1)$. We make this substitution. For the Cobb-Douglas production function (Equation 9.1),

$$Y(t) = \gamma(t)L(t)^{1-a}K(t)^a,$$

the wages at time t are (Equation 9.4)

$$\text{wage}(t) = (1 - a)\gamma(t)\left[\frac{K(t)}{L(t)}\right]^a,$$

and the rentals at time t are (Equation 9.5)

$$\text{rental}(t) = a\gamma(t)\left[\frac{K(t)}{L(t)}\right]^{a-1}.$$

Substituting the wages and rentals into the aggregate savings function at equilibrium, we get

$$K(t + 1) = (1 - a)\gamma(t)\left[\frac{K(t)}{L(t)}\right]^a L_t(t)(2)^{-1}$$

$$- (1 - a)\gamma(t + 1)\left[\frac{K(t + 1)}{L(t + 1)}\right]^a L_t(t + 1)$$

$$\cdot \left(2a\gamma(t + 1)\left[\frac{K(t + 1)}{L(t + 1)}\right]^{a-1}\right)^{-1}.$$

Solving for $K(t + 1)$, we get

$$K(t + 1) = \frac{(1 - a)\gamma(t)\left[\dfrac{1}{L(t)}\right]^a \dfrac{L_t(t)}{2}}{1 + \dfrac{1 - a}{2a}\left[\dfrac{L_t(t + 1)}{L(t + 1)}\right]}K(t)^a. \tag{9.6}$$

If the environmental variables, including technology, are the same in every time period, then the time path for capital is very simple. Let κ be

$$\kappa = \frac{(1 - a)\gamma(t)\left[\dfrac{1}{L(t)}\right]^a \dfrac{L_t(t)}{2}}{1 + \dfrac{1 - a}{2a}\left[\dfrac{L_t(t + 1)}{L(t + 1)}\right]}.$$

If there is no technological growth, then $g = 0$ and $\gamma(t + 1) = \gamma(t)$. If the population is constant and has constant labor endowments, then $L(t) = L(t + 1)$, and the labor supplied by the young, $L_t(t)$, and by the old, $L_t(t + 1)$, are the same for every period. Substituting κ into Equation (9.6), to remind us that this portion of the equation is not changing over time, we have

$$K(t + 1) = \kappa K(t)^a, \tag{9.7}$$

or, taking natural logs (ln) of Equation (9.6),

$$\ln(K(t + 1)) = \ln(\kappa) + a\ln(K(t)).$$

The current capital stock is a simple function of the capital stock of the previous period. It is linear when plotted as a logarithmic function. This function describes the equilibrium path for our example economy when the environmental variables are the same in each period. The function given in Equation (9.7) is shown in Figure 9.2. As before, there are two ways of finding equilibria: guess and verify and graphical analysis. We consider the guess and verify approach first.

We guess that there are stationary equilibria for this economy: equilibria in which $K(t) = K(t + 1) = K$. Substituting this guess into Equation (9.7), we get

$$K(t) = \kappa K(t)^a,$$

or $$\mathbf{K} = \kappa^{1/(1-a)} = \left[\frac{(1 - a)\gamma(t)\left[\dfrac{1}{L(t)}\right]^a \dfrac{L_t(t)}{2}}{1 + \dfrac{1 - a}{2a}\left[\dfrac{L_t(t + 1)}{L(t + 1)}\right]}\right]^{1/(1-a)}.$$

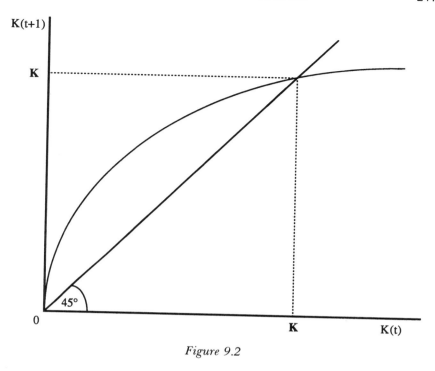

Figure 9.2

This **K** is the unique positive stationary equilibrium quantity of capital. Notice that Equation (9.7) can also be solved for $K(t + 1) = K(t) = 0$. In other words, in a second stationary equilibrium there is no capital, no production, and no consumption.

We can use a graphical method to find these same stationary equilibria. The 45-degree line that is drawn in Figure 9.2 crosses the function of $K(t + 1)$ in terms of $K(t)$ at the values of the capital stock that are stationary state equilibria. Notice that the graph shows both the equilibria we found: the one with a positive value for the capital stock, **K**, and the one with a zero capital stock. If the economy begins with no capital, then it cannot produce anything and never leaves that equilibrium. The equilibrium with a positive quantity of capital is stationary for a different reason. If the economy begins with a capital stock equal to **K**, then it will continue to choose to have that capital stock for all future periods.

This graphical method for finding the stationary state capital stock seems very similar to the method we used for finding stationary state equilibrium prices in economies with land. There is one very important difference, however. In the economies with land, we found a function that gave us current prices for land based on expected (or perfectly foreseen) *future* prices for land. The price function for land used expectations about the future to find the prices for the present. The function we are using here works in the other temporal direction. We are using the *past* quantities of capital to determine what the capital stock will be in the future (although we need to know the future labor supply, which is an environmental variable).[1] The similarity is that we look for fixed points to describe the stationary state equilibrium.

Stationary states are only one of many possible equilibrium paths. A stationary state path occurs when $K(1)$ is 0 or has the value given in the above equation. Any other value for $K(1)$ will generate an equilibrium path that is not stationary. In general, we would not expect an economy to begin with a stationary state quantity of capital. But we can show that for some economies with a constant environment the capital stock converges to that (positive) stationary state value for any (positive) initial capital stock.

EXERCISE 9.4   For the economy in Exercise 9.3, find the stationary state capital stock, output, and consumption allocations.

In the rest of this chapter, we analyze the equilibrium paths that this production economy follows under four different conditions. In the preceding discussion of a stationary state equilibrium, the environment was the same for every period. Neither the population nor the technology changed. In the next section, we analyze the general equilibrium paths for this economy. Next we allow population to change by setting the population growth parameter, n, to be greater than 1. Then we consider technological growth, by setting g to be greater than 0. Finally, we consider economies with different savings rates, generated by different β's in the utility functions.

---

1. We do assume here that individuals have perfect foresight about the wages and rentals they will receive in the next period. Because the quantity of labor is an environmental variable, this assumption means that they will know the aggregate equilibrium amount of capital their generation will decide to hold. In this sense they are using knowledge about both the past and the future to determine their equilibrium behavior.

Equilibrium Paths when $n = 1$ and $g = 0$

Suppose that the economy begins with something other than the stationary state quantity of capital. In terms of the way we set up the problem, $K(1)$ is given exogenously to us. We want to know what the time paths of capital and output will look like given any possible $K(1)$. We also want to know whether the initial capital stock of an economy matters much in the long run.

The function given in the equation

$$K(t + 1) = \frac{(1 - a)\gamma(t)\left[\dfrac{1}{L(t)}\right]^a \dfrac{L_t(t)}{2}}{1 + \dfrac{1 - a}{2a}\left[\dfrac{L_t(t + 1)}{L(t + 1)}\right]} K(t)^a \tag{9.6}$$

completely describes the time path of output for these economies. This first-order difference equation tells us the time t quantity of capital for any time $t - 1$ quantity of capital. Equation (9.6) gives us the time path of capital when the economy has the particular production function and the particular utility function that we assumed. Other production functions and other utility functions result in different behavior and different time paths for capital. If we let time $t = 1$, then the exogenous time 1 capital stock, $K(1)$, starts off the economy. We calculate the time 2 capital stock from Equation (9.6) and use the value we get from that calculation to find the time 3 capital stock. By repeating this process, we can completely describe the time path of the capital stock. Equation (9.6) (or its equivalent when there are other utility or production functions) and an initial $K(1)$ are all we need to know the entire future of an economy.

Merely looking at Equation (9.6) may not be enough to give us a good idea of where this economy is heading. We can use the graph of $K(t + 1)$ as a function of $K(t)$ that is expressed in that equation (much as we did earlier with the price equations) to follow the time path of the capital stock. Because, in these examples, the quantity of labor supplied by each generation is constant each period, the output each period is calculated by using the previous period's savings, $K(t)$, in the economy-wide version of the production function in Equation (9.1).

Figure 9.3 is a copy of Figure 9.2. Suppose that the economy begins

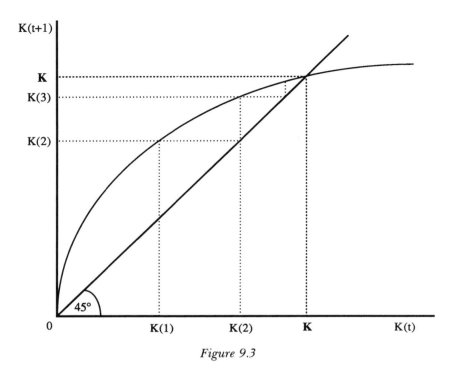

Figure 9.3

with $K(1)$ units of capital, where $K(1)$ is less than the stationary equilibrium quantity of capital, **K**. Using the curve in Figure 9.3 that represents
Equation (9.6), we trace up at the value $K(1)$ and then over to find the
$K(2)$ that will occur in the next period. That $K(2)$ is also given on the
horizontal axis, so we can trace up from that value to the curve and find
$K(3)$. This procedure can be repeated to find the entire sequence of the
capital stock. Notice that this sequence is converging toward the stationary equilibrium quantity of capital, **K**.

Figure 9.4 is the same as Figure 9.3, except we follow the path of the
capital stock for an economy where the initial capital stock, $K(1)$, is
greater than the stationary equilibrium quantity, **K**. The sequence of
capital stocks, $K(2)$ and $K(3)$, indicate that the capital stock is converging
to the stationary equilibrium quantity of capital from above.

Notice that it does not matter in the long run what the initial capital
stock of the economy is—except in the case where the initial capital
stock is 0, then it will remain 0 forever. The economy goes to the same
level of capital, of output, and of rental rates, independent of the initial

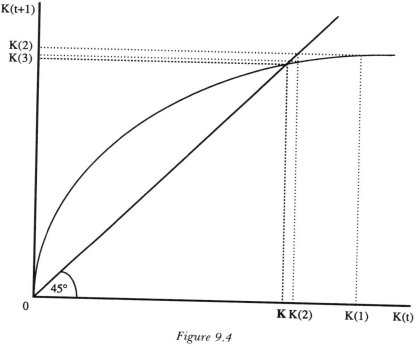

Figure 9.4

capital stock. The early generations have different consumption patterns and different utility levels, but in the long run all of these are the
same for any starting $K(1)$ that is greater than 0.

EXERCISE 9.5 For the economy of Exercise 9.4, find the time
path of the capital stock and of output for an initial capital stock
equal to one half of the stationary state level. What is the time
path for these variables if the initial capital stock is twice the
stationary state level?

Equilibrium Paths when $n > 1$ and $g = 0$

Consider an economy with population growth, so let n be greater than
1. With this assumption, $N(t + 1)$ equals $nN(t) > N(t)$. We begin with

some given population at date 0, $N(0)$, and the population at any date t can be found by

$$N(t) = n^t N(0).$$

Assume that all individuals of all generations are identical in terms of the amount of labor endowment that they have in each period of their life. As before, the labor endowment pair of any individual is

$$\Delta_t^h = [\Delta_t^h(t), \Delta_t^h(t + 1)] = [\Delta_0^h(0), \Delta_0^h(1)],$$

where the last pair gives the labor endowment of a member of generation 0. The total time t labor supply of the young at date t is

$$L_t(t) = N(t)\Delta_t^h(t) = n^t N(0)\Delta_0^h(0) = n^t L_0(0),$$

where $L_0(0)$ is the total labor supply of the young at time 0. The total time t labor supply of the old at date t is

$$L_{t-1}(t) = N(t - 1)\Delta_{t-1}^h(t) = n^{t-1}N(0)\Delta_0^h(1) = n^{t-1}L_0(1),$$

where $L_0(1)$ is the total labor supply of the old at date 1. The total labor supply at date t is the sum of the total time t labor endowment of the young and of the old. It is

$$L(t) = n^t L_0(0) + n^{t-1}L_0(1).$$

The savings functions for individuals are the same as before, that is,

$$s_t^h(t) = \frac{\text{wage}(t)\Delta_t^h(t)}{2} - \frac{\text{wage}(t + 1)\Delta_t^h(t + 1)}{2r(t)}.$$

With a growing population, the number of individuals each period is increasing, and aggregate savings equals

$$S_t(r(t)) = N(t)s_t^h(t) = n^t N(0)s_t^h(t)$$

or, for the example economy,

$$S_t(r(t)) = \frac{\text{wage}(t)n^t L_0(0)}{2} - \frac{\text{wage}(t + 1)n^t L_0(1)}{2r(t)}.$$

For the example economy, the wage at date t is

$$\text{wage}(t) = (1 - a)\gamma(t)\left[\frac{K(t)}{n^t L(0)}\right]^a,$$

(9.4')

and the rental at date $t + 1$ [which equals $r(t)$ in equilibrium] is

$$\text{rental}(t + 1) = a\gamma(t)\left[\frac{K(t + 1)}{n^{t+1} L(0)}\right]^{a-1}.$$

(9.5')

From the equilibrium conditions that $S_t(r(t)) = K(t + 1)$ and that wages and rentals at each date equal the functions given in Equations (9.4') and (9.5'), we get that

$$K(t + 1) = \tilde{\kappa} n^{(1-a)t} K(t)^a,$$

(9.7')

where $\tilde{\kappa} = \dfrac{(1 - a)\gamma(t)\left[\dfrac{1}{L(0)}\right]^a \dfrac{L_0(0)}{2}}{1 + \dfrac{1 - a}{2a}\left[\dfrac{L_0(1)}{nL(0)}\right]}.$

Taking the natural log of Equation (9.7'), we get

$$\ln(K(t + 1)) = \ln(\tilde{\kappa}) + (1 - a)t \ln(n) + a \ln(K(t)).$$

We wish to know the limit value of the growth rate of the capital stock, $k(t) = K(t + 1)/K(t)$, as t goes to ∞ when we begin with some $K(1)$ greater than 0. From the standard properties of logs, we know that $\ln(k(t)) = \ln(K(t + 1)/K(t)) = \ln(K(t + 1)) - \ln(K(t))$. Rewriting the above equation for the natural log of the capital stock at time t, we get

$$\ln(K(t)) = \ln(\tilde{\kappa}) + (1 - a)(t - 1)\ln(n) + a \ln(K(t - 1)).$$

We subtract this equation from the one above it to get

$$\ln(K(t + 1)) - \ln(K(t))$$
$$= (1 - a)\ln(n) + a[\ln(K(t)) - \ln(K(t - 1))],$$

or $\quad \ln(k(t)) = (1 - a)\ln(n) + a \ln(k(t - 1)).$

(9.8)

Note that some terms have dropped out. To find the limit value of the growth rate of the capital stock, we take the limit of this equation as t goes to ∞. Because

$$\lim_{t \to \infty}[\ln(k(t))] = \lim_{t \to \infty}[\ln(k(t-1))],$$

if such a limit exists (and we assume it does), we can rearrange Equation (9.8) to get

$$\lim_{t \to \infty}[\ln(k(t))] = \ln(n),$$

or $\lim_{t \to \infty}(k(t)) = \lim_{t \to \infty}\left(\dfrac{K(t+1)}{K(t)}\right) = n.$

In the limit, the growth rate of the capital stock equals the growth rate of the population.

Equilibrium Paths when $n = 1$ and $g > 0$

Up to now the parameter in the production function that indicates the level of technology has been kept constant: $\gamma(t)$ has equaled γ, for all t. It is not too difficult to imagine a world in which there is exogenous technological growth. In this kind of a world, there is continuous improvement in the level of technology. This improvement in technology shows up as increases in the output that comes from the same quantities of labor and capital inputs.

An increase in $\gamma(t)$ as t increases is called *neutral* technological growth. The neutrality occurs because the parameter $\gamma(t)$ has equal effects on both the returns to capital and the returns to labor in the production function

$$Y(t) = \gamma(t)L(t)^{1-a}K(t)^a.$$

Technological improvements that favor labor (called *labor augmenting*) can be described by a production function of the form

$$Y(t) = \{\gamma^L(t)L(t)\}^{1-a}K(t)^a, \tag{9.9}$$

where $\{\gamma^L(t)L(t)\}$ is the quantity of technology-augmented labor. Technological improvements that favor capital (called *capital augmenting*) can be described by a production function of the form

$$Y(t) = L(t)^{1-a}\{\gamma^K(t)K(t)\}^a, \tag{9.10}$$

where $\{\gamma^K(t)K(t)\}$ is the quantity of technology-augmented capital. In Equation (9.9), an increase in $\gamma^L(t)$ is called labor augmenting because it has the same effect on output as an identical proportional increase in the quantity of labor. If $\gamma^L(t)$ were to increase by 50 percent, this increase would result in the same change in output as a 50 percent increase in the quantity of labor would. In a similar fashion, an increase in $\gamma^K(t)$ has the same effect on output as an identical proportional increase in the quantity of capital.

Assume that the neutral technology is growing at a rate g and that at time 0 there is a technology level given by $\gamma(0)$. The level of technology at time 1 is $\gamma(1) = \gamma(0)(1 + g)$. At time 2, it is equal to $\gamma(2) = \gamma(1)(1 + g) = \gamma(0)(1 + g)^2$. The pattern that emerges is that, for any time t, the level of technology is

$$\gamma(t) = \gamma(0)(1 + g)^t.$$

To describe the time path of the capital stock and output for an economy with technological growth, we need merely substitute the new description of the technology parameter into Equation (9.6). That substitution gives us

$$K(t + 1) = \frac{(1 - a)\gamma(0)(1 + g)^t\left[\dfrac{1}{L(t)}\right]^a\dfrac{L_t(t)}{2}}{1 + \dfrac{1 - a}{2a}\left[\dfrac{L_t(t + 1)}{L(t + 1)}\right]}K(t)^a, \tag{9.11}$$

or $\qquad K(t + 1) = (1 + g)^t\kappa K(t)^a, \tag{9.12}$

where now

$$\kappa = \frac{(1 - a)\gamma(0)\left[\dfrac{1}{L(t)}\right]^a\dfrac{L_t(t)}{2}}{1 + \dfrac{1 - a}{2a}\left[\dfrac{L_t(t + 1)}{L(t + 1)}\right]}.$$

This equation gives the capital stock in any period starting with some initial $K(1)$. The output level in each time period can be found by using the production function with the time t and time $t + 1$ labor supplies, the time t capital stock, and the time t level of technology. Aggregate output at time t is

$$Y(t) = Y(t) = \gamma(0)(1 + g)^t L(t)^{1-a} K(t)^a.$$

An interesting characteristic of this economy is that the limit of the rate of growth of the capital stock is greater than the rate of growth of technology. We can calculate the limit of the growth rate in a manner similar to the one we used at the end of the preceding section. Writing Equation (9.12) in natural logs, we get

$$\ln(K(t + 1)) = t \ln(1 + g) + \ln(\kappa) + a \ln(K(t)).$$

Using this equation, we subtract $\ln(K(t))$ from $\ln(K(t + 1))$ to get

$$\ln(K(t + 1)) - \ln(K(t))$$
$$= \ln(1 + g) + a[\ln(K(t)) - \ln(K(t - 1))],$$

or $\ln(k(t)) = \ln(1 + g) + a \ln(k(t - 1)),$

where $k(t) = K(t + 1)/K(t)$ is the growth rate of the capital stock at date t. Note that some terms drop out. Take the limit of both sides of this equation as t goes to ∞ and, because

$$\lim_{t \to \infty}[\ln(k(t))] = \lim_{t \to \infty}[\ln(k(t - 1))],$$

rearrange to get

$$(1 - a)\lim_{t \to \infty}[\ln(k(t))] = \ln(1 + g),$$

or $\lim_{t \to \infty}(k(t)) = \lim_{t \to \infty}\left(\dfrac{K(t + 1)}{K(t)}\right) = (1 + g)^{1/(1-a)}.$

For an economy where the rate of growth of technology, g, equals .05 and $a = .5$, the limit of the growth rate of the capital stock equals

$(1 + .05)^2$ or 1.1025. The rate of growth of the capital stock is greater than the rate of growth of technology. Notice that the rate of growth of output is equal to the rate of growth of the capital stock (and not of technology). The ratio $Y(t + 1)/Y(t)$ is

$$\frac{Y(t + 1)}{Y(t)} = \frac{\gamma(0)(1 + g)^{t+1}L(t + 1)^{1-a}K(t + 1)^a}{\gamma(0)(1 + g)^tL(t)^{1-a}K(t)^a}$$

$$= (1 + g)\left[\frac{K(t + 1)}{K(t)}\right]^a,$$

and the limit of that ratio is

$$\lim_{t \to \infty}\left[\frac{Y(t + 1)}{Y(t)}\right] = (1 + g)\lim_{t \to \infty}\left[\frac{K(t + 1)}{K(t)}\right]^a = (1 + g)^{1/(1-a)}.$$

The limit of the growth rate of output is the same as the limit of the growth rate of capital.

In an economy with technological growth, the initial capital stock, $K(1)$, does not matter in determining the long-run rate of growth of the economy. The economies with the larger initial capital stock will always have a larger capital stock and a larger output than economies with smaller initial capital stocks, but the differences become smaller over time and converge to the same time path of capital stock and output. Figure 9.5 shows the time paths for three economies, each with the same rate of growth of technology. The solid line shows the time path of output for an economy where $K_1(1)$ is on the long-run growth path and the initial output is Y_1. The dotted line shows the time path of output for an economy where $K_2(1)$ is less than $K_1(1)$ and the initial output is Y_2. The dashed line is the time path for an economy where $K_3(1)$ is greater than $K_1(1)$ and the initial output equals Y_3. Notice that all of these economies converge to the same time path of output (not merely the same growth rate of output).

EXERCISE 9.6   For the economy of Exercise 9.5 with the same initial capital stock as in that exercise, find the time path of the capital stock and output when the growth rate of technology is $g = .05$.

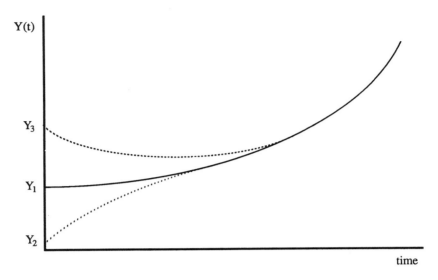

Figure 9.5

Differential Savings Rates

We often read in the popular press that some countries are growing faster than others because the citizens of the faster-growing countries have a savings rate that is higher than those of other countries. The countries that are most often used in this context are Japan and Korea, where the savings rate is over 25 percent of income. In the United States, the private savings rate is on the order of 7 to 8 percent of gross national output. This differential is used to explain how Japan and Korea can grow so much faster than the United States. We can use the neoclassical growth model that we have developed here to look at the effects on growth rates and output levels of different rates of savings.

We have been working with the utility function

$$u_t^h = c_t^h(t)[c_t^h(t + 1)]^\beta,$$

where we have been setting $\beta = 1$. The parameter β determines the relative weight that the second-period consumption has in the utility function. The greater the weight of second-period consumption (the larger β is), the more an individual will want to save to facilitate that consumption. Changing β changes the desire to save. To see what effects differential savings rates have on the time path of these economies, we compare the output and capital stock paths for economies with β = 1 (which we have been doing so far) and β = 3.

In equilibrium the capital, $K(t + 1)$, that generation t chooses to carry over from time t to time $t + 1$ is that generation's savings. The aggregate savings function with β included is

$$S(r(t)) = \frac{\beta \, \text{wage}(t)L_t(t)}{1 + \beta} - \frac{\text{wage}(t + 1)L_t(t + 1)}{(1 + \beta)r(t)}.$$

As we did before, we set aggregate savings equal to the capital stock and solve for $K(t + 1)$ in terms of $K(t)$. This equation, with the β's and the rate of growth of technology included, is

$$K(t + 1) = (1 + g)^t \frac{\beta(1 - a)\gamma(t)\left[\dfrac{1}{L(t)}\right]^a \dfrac{L_t(t)}{1 + \beta}}{1 + \dfrac{1 - a}{(1 + \beta)a}\left[\dfrac{L_t(t + 1)}{L(t + 1)}\right]} K(t)^a. \tag{9.6'}$$

When β = 1, this equation is equal to Equation (9.6) and gives all of the results that we have obtained so far, including the time paths of the capital stock shown in Figures 9.3 and 9.4.

First, we use Equation (9.6') to find the stationary state capital stock when there is no growth in technology, recalling that this stock is the quantity of capital that the economy goes to in the limit if it begins with a positive quantity of capital. Setting $g = 0$ and $\gamma(t) = \gamma$, the stationary state capital stock is given by

$$K = \left[\frac{\beta(1 - a)\gamma\left[\dfrac{1}{L(t)}\right]^a \dfrac{L_t(t)}{1 + \beta}}{1 + \dfrac{1 - a}{(1 + \beta)a}\left[\dfrac{L_t(t + 1)}{L(t + 1)}\right]}\right]^{1/(1-a)}.$$

This equation is different from our initial equation for the stationary state capital stock only by the inclusion of the β parameter (which was 1 in the first version). Suppose that we have two economies that are identical except for β. In one $\beta = 1$ and in the other $\beta = 3$. To further simplify the analysis, set $\Delta_t^h(t + 1)$ equal to 0 for all h; so individuals have labor endowments only when they are young. This assumption means that $L_t(t + 1)$ equals 0 and $L(t) = L_t(t)$. The equation for the stationary state capital stock (the limit value for the capital stock) becomes

$$K = \left[\frac{\beta}{(1 + \beta)} \right]^{1/(1-a)} [(1 - a)\gamma L(t)^{1-a}]^{1/(1-a)}.$$

The variables in the second set of brackets are the same for both economies. The ratio of the capital stock in the economy with $\beta = 1$ and the capital stock in the economy with $\beta = 3$ is given by

$$\frac{\left[\dfrac{1}{1 + 1} \right]^{1/(1-a)}}{\left[\dfrac{3}{1 + 3} \right]^{1/(1-a)}}.$$

In an example economy where $a = .5$, the ratio of the stationary state capital stocks is $4/9$. The economy with $\beta = 3$ has a capital stock that is 2.25 times larger than the otherwise identical economy with $\beta = 1$. Output for the economy with $\beta = 3$ is 1.50 times greater than that for the economy with $\beta = 1$. The output ratio is smaller than the capital stock ratio because the two economies are using the same quantity of labor and there is a diminishing marginal product of capital.

Now consider an economy where the growth rate of technology is not equal to 0. Equation (9.6') can be written in the same form as Equation (9.12) that we used in the earlier section on finding the limit growth rate of an economy. For the two economies—one with $\beta = 1$ and the other with $\beta = 3$—we have two versions of Equation (9.12), namely,

$$K(t + 1) = (1 + g)^t \kappa_1 K(t)^a \tag{9.12'}$$

and $\quad K(t + 1) = (1 + g)^t \kappa_3 K(t)^a. \tag{9.12''}$

The only difference between these equations is the value of the constants, the κ's, which are functions of the value of β. Notice, however, that the limit of the rate of growth of the capital stock that we found in the above section,

$$\lim_{t \to \infty} \left[\frac{K(t + 1)}{K(t)} \right] = (1 + g)^{1/(1-a)},$$

does not depend on the value of κ, but only on the values of a and g. Therefore, the limiting rate of growth of the capital stock, and of output, is not determined by the rate of savings in an economy.

The rates of growth of the capital stock for both economies and the rates of growth of output for both economies converge to the same value over time. If these two economies begin with the same quantity of capital, then the economy in which $\beta = 3$ has higher initial growth rates of capital and output than does the economy with $\beta = 1$. The levels of capital and output in the economy with $\beta = 3$ are greater than those in the economy with $\beta = 1$ in all time periods but the first. Because the stationary state capital stock and output for the economy with $\beta = 3$ was greater than those for the identical economy with $\beta = 1$, it should be no great surprise that the time path for the economy with $\beta = 3$, when there is growth, has consistently higher capital stocks and output.

Reprise

In a neoclassical growth model where individuals have a labor endowment instead of a goods endowment, the savings decisions of members of generation t determine the quantity of the good that will be available and the wage in time $t + 1$. Because the wage of the young of any generation is crucial in determining the amount of savings they will make, it is important in determining the next period's output. In an economy without technological growth, the economy settles rather quickly to a limit quantity of capital.

If there is technological growth, the eventual rate of growth of output and the capital stock depend on the parameters of the production function and not on the parameters of the utility function. The savings decisions do determine the level of output the economy will have at each point on the growth path (countries that save more will have a higher level of output at each date) but not the rate of growth.

Paul Romer (1986) has extended the neoclassical growth model to include the accumulation of human capital (of knowledge). In these models the rate of accumulation of knowledge for each individual depends on the aggregate level of knowledge already in the economy. Economies that begin with different levels of knowledge can have different rates of growth.

As we noted above, the model studied here is the starting point of studies of economic growth and development. As we have seen, it implies that limiting growth rates do not depend on the savings rate and are influenced by policy only to the extent that policy affects the growth of the labor force or technological change. Stimulated in part by empirical studies of the growth rates of different countries, there was considerable interest in the 1980s in the development of models in which growth rates are endogenous and dependent on the rate of savings and other factors that can be influenced by economic policy—for example, tax policy. For a discussion of such models and the motivation for them, see Lucas (1988).

PART TWO

MONETARY ECONOMIES

In Chapters 10–12 we introduce into our models some "stuff" we call money and consider the welfare effects of a number of government policies involving this money stuff. Some of the topics we cover are inflation and real government revenues from inflation, open market operations in which a government exchanges money for government bonds, and the effects of legal restrictions on the holding of money.

An adequate theory of money has to be consistent with at least two observations. First, the theory must explain why individuals hold on to some intrinsically useless stuff that the government has issued and calls money. The kind of money we are talking about is called *fiat* money, because the government has made this stuff money by fiat (has declared that certain pieces of paper of a particular design and color will be money).

Second, the model must also explain why this money is used and held even when there coexist assets in the economy that give higher real rates of return than money does. For example, people use and hold money even in the presence of government-issued bonds that offer a higher rate of return than money does.

It is fairly easy to get a model to display these properties if money is "forced" into it. Among the devices used to get these results are the assumptions that money is an argument of the utility functions, that it is an argument of the production function, and that making transactions using other things is expensive relative to making transactions using money. The weakness of these assumptions is that they do not make explicit the difficulties involved in making transactions that the use of money helps to overcome. Exactly what those difficulties are has implications, and those implications are missed if the above assumptions are used.

Up to now, no one has formulated a model of transaction difficulties that has won wide assent. We have no widely accepted model of monetary exchange. In the three chapters that follow, we use models of money in a way that many economists regard as unsatisfactory. Although the model we use makes the nature of the difficulties in transactions quite clear and leads to individuals choosing to hold the intrinsically worthless stuff we call money, it does not immediately allow the coexistence of another asset that gives higher rates of return. We can get that feature by imposing a variety of legal restrictions that include the prevention of individuals from creating assets that compete with fiat money. The weakness with our initial approach is that it does not lead to the kind of economizing on money holdings that we think we observe. The weakness to the second set of models is that they probably ascribe too much to laws and regulations that inhibit private financial intermediation.

There is a third critique of these models. Some economists claim that the kinds of difficulties in transactions that we have in our model are not the difficulty that fiat money is usually used to solve. These individuals point to the once in a lifetime transaction that we have in our models and compare that to the frequency with which money changes hands in, for example, the U.S. economy. These economists claim that this model is better for describing other assets—government bonds and land, which might be held for many years—than for describing fiat money, which is exchanged an average of seven times a year (using M1 as a definition of money).

Despite these weaknesses, some useful insights can be gained from using an overlapping generations model for fiat money. Moreover, there is currently no other way to model a monetary economy that is clearly superior.

CHAPTER **10**

Money and Inflation

We are already very close to having equilibria with money in our model. To show this, let us first make clear what money does. The thing we designate as money needs several properties. It needs to be storable, so that it can be held from one time period to another. We want it to be intrinsically worthless, so it must not appear in the utility function. We want equilibria in which individuals will be willing to trade this stuff for goods that do show up in their utility function.

In the chapters about economies with land (Chapters 6 and 7), considerable attention was given to the case where the crop, $d(t + 1)$, was equal to 0. We are now at the point where the attention we gave to those economies pays off. Land on which there is no crop may fulfill all of the properties we wish money to have. Land does not appear in the utility function but in some equilibria trades for positive quantities of goods at each date t.

Land without a crop is different from land with a crop in one very important way. To appreciate this fact, recall that the gross rate of return on land with a crop, $d(t)$, is

$$\frac{p^e(t + 1) + d(t + 1)}{p(t)}.$$

This expression is equal to

$$\frac{p^e(t + 1)}{p(t)} + \frac{d(t + 1)}{p(t)},$$

and, given the restriction that prices are nonnegative,

$$\frac{p^e(t + 1)}{p(t)} + \frac{d(t + 1)}{p(t)} \geq \frac{d(t + 1)}{p(t)}.$$

For any constant positive crop, $d(t + 1)$, we know that

$$\frac{d(t + 1)}{p(t)} \to \infty,$$

as $p(t)$ goes to 0. For an economy with $d(t + 1) > 0$ for all t, the above discussion suggests that equilibrium $p(t)$'s are greater than 0 for all t. The rate of return on land can become as large as necessary to get people to pay some positive price for land at each date t.

For economies with $d(t + 1) = 0$ for all t, the situation is somewhat different. First, there always exists an equilibrium in which the price of land at date t, $p(t)$, exactly equals 0 if the expected price of land at time $t + 1$, $p^e(t + 1)$, also equals 0. If $p^e(t + 1) = 0$, then, with no crop, no one will wish to purchase land at time t and $p(t) = 0$.

There may exist additional equilibria in which the price of land is strictly greater than 0 for all t. Note, however, that such equilibria may not exist. Whether or not a nonzero equilibrium price exists depends on the environment of the economy—in particular, on the endowment pattern and alternative assets. In this section we wish to concentrate on those economies in which $d(t)$ equals 0 for all t and that have equilibria with $p(t) > 0$ for all t. In these economies we concentrate on the equilibria with strictly positive prices and on stationary equilibria, if they exist.

Exercise 10.1 is included to remind the reader of some of the different types of equilibria that can arise in economies with a zero crop.

EXERCISE 10.1 Describe example economies of your choice (you may need different economies for different parts of the question) with a crop, $d(t + 1) = 0$ for all t that have an equilibrium where
  a. the price of land is the same positive number each period.
  b. the price of land is 0 in every period.
  c. the price of land is decreasing to 0 over time.

d. the price of land converges to some positive limit over time.

e. the price of land oscillates between two prices over time.
(Hint: You may need to refer to the chapter on economic fluctuations to get some of these results.)

Equilibria with Fixed Money Supply

Consider an economy without any land. (What do the people stand on? is not a valid question.) There are **G** units (pounds, for example) of a yellow rock that exist in this economy. The yellow rock does not deteriorate from one period to the next and does not directly provide any utility for individuals. Interestingly enough, these yellow rocks just happen to come in the form of small, uniformly sized disks. (If we wish to add some historical verisimilitude, we can put scratches on these disks that show where they can be cut to form wedges exactly equal to one eighth of a disk. We could choose to call the resulting pieces, when cut, pieces of eight.) Each yellow disk is identical to every other yellow disk.

If a young person of generation t happens to gain ownership of one of these yellow disks, this individual can hold on to the disk and end up with 1 yellow disk when old. The useful physical property of these disks is that they transfer at exactly a one-for-one rate from time t to time $t + 1$, for all t.

Economy 1 *Example economy 1 has a population of $N(t) = 100$; each of the 100 individuals in this economy has a utility function and an endowment of $u_t^h = c_t^h(t) c_t^h(t + 1)$, and $\omega_t^h = [2, 1]$. This economy also has $G(t) = \mathbf{G} = 200$ identical yellow disks. At time 0, these yellow disks are distributed equally among the time 1 old. The holdings of yellow disks by member h of generation 0, $g^h(0)$, equals 2.*

Note how simple this example economy is. There are no taxes, no government bonds, and no land, and the only outside asset is the yellow disks. For a complete description of this type of economy, we needed to describe the distribution of the holdings of the yellow disks by the old at time 0 to begin the economy. Different distributions of the yellow disks can result in different utilities for different members of generation 0 but will not affect the utilities of the members of other generations.

Economy 1 is already quite familiar, and we already know that the aggregate savings function for generation t of economy 1 is

$$S(r(t)) = 100\left[1 - \frac{1}{2r(t)}\right] = 100 - \frac{50}{r(t)}.$$

Because there is nothing else around in this economy, aggregate savings must go into the yellow disks if it is to go anywhere; so, letting the price of these yellow disks at time t be $p(t)$, we have an equilibrium condition,

$$S(r(t)) = p(t)G(t).$$

In economy 1, the equilibrium condition is

$$100 - \frac{50}{r(t)} = 200p(t).$$

From the budget constraints, we get an arbitrage condition between the gross interest rate on private borrowing and lending and the time t and $t + 1$ prices of the yellow disks, namely,

$$r(t) = \frac{p(t + 1)}{p(t)}.$$

Substituting this relation into the equilibrium condition gives

$$100 - \frac{50p(t)}{p(t + 1)} = 200p(t)$$

or $\qquad p(t) = \dfrac{100p(t + 1)}{200p(t + 1) + 50}.$ $\qquad\qquad$ (10.1)

Equation (10.1) gives $p(t)$ as a function of $p(t + 1)$. We used this type of price function—$p(t) = f(p(t + 1))$—in earlier chapters. Graphing this price function gives the curve shown in Figure 10.1.

Figure 10.1 includes a 45-degree line from the origin. The prices at which the 45-degree line cross the price function (Equation 10.1) are the prices of the yellow disks for which a stationary perfect foresight equilibrium exists. Notice that the 45-degree line crosses this price func-

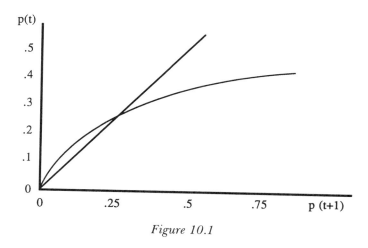

Figure 10.1

tion at $p(t + 1) = .25$ and 0. Notice, as before for the economy with land and no crop, that if $p(t)$ is between .25 and 0 for any t, then the perfect foresight equilibrium that is consistent with that $p(t)$ is a series of prices for the yellow disks that converge to a price of 0.

The above example has two stationary and multiple nonstationary equilibria. We want to differentiate between the two stationary equilibria. The one where the price of the yellow disks is always 0 we call a nonmonetary equilibrium, because the disks do not fulfill any of the properties of money that we wish to model. The other stationary equilibrium and the nonstationary equilibria with positive prices for the yellow disks in every period we call monetary equilibria.

Definition *A monetary perfect foresight equilibrium is one for which the price of money is never 0.*

Definition *A nonmonetary perfect foresight equilibrium for an economy in which something called money exists is one in which the price of that money is always 0.*

Currently, we do not use yellow disks as money. We use (in the United States, green) pieces of paper that the government has chosen to call money. These pieces of paper are called *fiat money* because the government has made them money by fiat. Fiat money has three important characteristics.

Definition   *Fiat money is (a) intrinsically useless; (b) unbacked; and (c) costless for the government to produce.*

Characteristics (a) and (c) seem self-evident, although characteristic (c) is not literally true. The pieces of paper a government uses as fiat money cost very little relative to their value in exchange. "Costless" is the limit case that we use to simplify the analysis. Characteristic (b) may not be true and is what differentiates bonds, at least as we have been defining them, from fiat money. A *backed money* is one for which some agent in the economy promises to exchange that money at some future date for a specific quantity of some good. Recall that with government bonds, the government promised to pay at time $t + 1$ 1 unit of the time $t + 1$ good for each of the bonds that it sold at time t. The bond is backed by this promise of the government to convert it into something real. Governments have issued backed paper money. These governments have promised that at any time individuals can go to some designated location and convert their paper money into a fixed quantity of some prespecified good. Robert Hall has recommended that the United States have a backed money and that the backing be of a specific mix of heavily used commodities that would include plywood and fertilizer. With fiat money, no one in the economy is guaranteeing a fixed rate of exchange for the paper money and goods. This situation does not mean there may not be equilibria in which the price of goods in terms of fiat money is constant; it means merely that no one is guaranteeing this rate of exchange.

One of the important roles of the government in declaring some particular form of paper (or other stuff) as money is that it promises to control the quantity of that stuff in the economy. Let $M(t)$ be the number at the end of period t of these pieces of paper that the government has declared money. Let $m^h(t)$ be the number of units of fiat money held by member h of generation t.

Economy 2   *Economy 2 is the same as economy 1, except there are no yellow disks, $\mathbf{G} = 0$, and there are $M(t) = \mathbf{M} = 200$ pieces of green pieces of paper that the government has declared to be fiat money. At time 1, these pieces of paper are distributed, so $m^h(0) = 2$ for all h of generation 0.*

EXERCISE 10.2   Find the stationary monetary equilibrium for economy 2. Find the stationary nonmonetary equilibrium. Include in the description the consumption allocations of a sample generation. Describe a simple nonstationary monetary equilibrium.

Fiat Money and Other Assets

In the introduction to Part Two we mentioned some of the ways an overlapping generations (OLG) model falters as a model of money. One of the most important of these weaknesses, in a perfect foresight OLG model, resides in its inability to allow different rates of return on money and on other assets. An important empirical observation we can make, even with only casual evidence, is that fiat money does not give the same rate of return (gross interest rate) that other assets in the economy do. Even the government issues assets—government bonds—that offer a higher gross interest rate *in terms of money* than money does.

To show this weakness explicitly, we introduce a second asset—an asset in addition to fiat money—into the model. We use economy 2, which is described in the preceding section, as the basic model. Several options are available for generating the second asset. We could reintroduce government bonds: one-period bonds that are paid off each period or that are rolled over are possible. In Chapters 8 and 9 we introduced a storage technology; that is an easy way to add the second asset. However, because we have developed the idea of money as land without a crop, we choose to illustrate the equality-of-returns result by using land with a strictly positive crop as the second asset.

Assume that we have an economy 2 containing land that generates a strictly positive crop each period. In this economy there are **M** units of fiat money and **A** units of land. Each unit of land produces $d(t) > 0$ units of the time t good in each period t. For individual h of generation t, the budget constraints are

$$c_t^h(t) = \omega_t^h(t) - \ell^h(t) - p^m(t)m^h(t) - p^l(t)a^h(t),$$

and
$$c_t^h(t + 1) = \omega_t^h(t + 1) + r(t)\ell^h(t) + p^m(t + 1)m^h(t)$$
$$+ a^h(t)(p^l(t + 1) + d(t + 1)).$$

Because we have two assets, we need prices for both of them: $p^m(t)$ is the time t price of fiat money and $p^l(t)$ is the time t price of land. As we have done in earlier chapters, we combine these two constraints into one by eliminating the quantity of private borrowing and lending, $\ell^h(t)$. This operation gives us the single budget constraint of

$$c_t^h(t) + \frac{c_t^h(t + 1)}{r(t)} = \omega_t^h(t) + \frac{\omega_t^h(t + 1)}{r(t)}$$

$$- m^h(t)\left[p^m(t) - \frac{p^m(t + 1)}{r(t)}\right]$$

$$- a^h(t)\left[p^l(t) - \frac{p^l(t + 1) + d(t + 1)}{r(t)}\right].$$

The usual arbitrage conditions must hold; so, if both money and land are held—which means that both $m^h(t)$ and $a^h(t)$ must be strictly greater than 0—then the two parts of the above equation that are inside the square brackets must each be equal to 0. If they are not equal to 0, then arbitrage is possible between the two assets and each individual can drive consumption to ∞. Because that case cannot be an equilibrium (there is only a finite amount of the time t good in each period t), the parts in brackets must equal 0. In equilibrium, the gross interest rate on private borrowing and lending must be equal to

$$r(t) = \frac{p^m(t + 1)}{p^m(t)}$$

from the arbitrage condition on money and must also be equal to

$$r(t) = \frac{p^l(t + 1) + d(t + 1)}{p^l(t)}$$

from the arbitrage condition on land.

The result we desired is immediate. Both money and land must offer the same gross interest rate as private borrowing and lending do.

EXERCISE 10.3 Show that in economy 2, with the addition of land that generates a positive crop as the second asset, a constant price for money cannot be an equilibrium.

EXERCISE 10.4 Consider economy 2 with the addition of a storage technology as the second asset. (See Chapter 8 if you need a refresher on storage technologies.) Any of the time t good that is put into storage gives back $\lambda > 1$ units of the time $t + 1$ good. Show that if both fiat money and the storage technology are used, they must give the same rate of return. Show that no monetary equilibrium exists. Does this last result hold if $\lambda < 1$?

EXERCISE 10.5 Consider an economy like that in Exercise 10.4, except that the population grows at a rate n [so $N(t + 1) = nN(t)$], $n > \lambda$. Is there a monetary equilibrium?

Inflation

The price of money that we have been using, $p^m(t)$, is not what we normally think of as prices. This price tells us how many goods are given up to purchase 1 unit of money. Normally, prices are denominated in units of money, a certain number of which must be given up to purchase 1 unit of a good. Our normal concept of a price for the time t good is equal to $1/p^m(t)$.

Inflation, as we usually think of it, is an increase in the number of units of money that are needed to purchase goods in general. In our model economies there is only one good, so inflation occurs when there is an increase in the number of units of fiat money needed to purchase that one good. In economies with many goods, we need to differentiate between relative price changes, where the price of one good goes up relative to other goods, and inflation, where the prices of goods in terms of money generally rise. Determining inflation rates (the rate at which prices in terms of money increase in general) in an economy with many goods is a fairly tricky indexing problem. We need to know how to weight the different rates of change in the different prices to get a general price level change. With our one-good economy, we can ignore that problem, but in real economies the rate of inflation that is reported depends on the goods that are included in the basket used for calculating the price index.

If inflation occurs when the price of goods in terms of money rises, then in our model it occurs when the price of money in terms of goods declines, because the price of money in terms of goods is merely the reciprocal of the price of goods in terms of money. So equilibria in which $p^m(t)$ declines through time are equilibria with inflation. The nonstationary equilibrium that you described in Exercise 10.2 is an example of an economy with inflation. The price of money goes to 0 in all of the nonstationary equilibria for that economy.

EXERCISE 10.6 Consider economy 2, with fiat money as the only asset. Show that the stationary equilibrium with valued money [where $p^m(t)$ is strictly greater than 0] is Pareto superior to any nonstationary equilibrium.

EXERCISE 10.7 Consider economy 2, except half the members of each generation have an endowment of [2, 1] and half have an endowment of [1, 1]. Are stationary monetary equilibria Pareto superior to nonmonetary equilibria in this economy?

Refer to Exercise 10.1. All of the time paths for economies with land without a crop in that exercise are also potential equilibrium time paths for economies with fiat money. The earlier development of economic fluctuations of the sunspot variety are equally valid for economies with fiat money and the appropriate type of utility functions.

There is an aspect of the theory of fluctuations developed in Chapter 7 that suggests that almost any time path for money is possible if individuals believe that that time path will occur. For the rest of the chapter, we will restrict our discussion to the stationary equilibrium in which fiat money has value. Stationary equilibria, in this case, are those for which all generations have the same consumptions and the same utility. We are studying inflation, so it makes no sense to speak of stationary states as equilibria with constant prices.

Money Creation and Inflation

A government that declares some particular object to be fiat money usually maintains a monopoly on the right to produce that object and to issue additional amounts of it. In terms of welfare, it matters a lot how new assets or new quantities of old assets are introduced into the economy. In this section, we look at two transfer schemes in which the government chooses to give some new fiat money to the old of each time period. In the next section, the government chooses to use newly issued fiat money to purchase some time t good for its own use in every period t.

Let $M(t)$ stand for the quantity of money in the economy *after* the time t transfer or government purchases have taken place. This quantity of money, $M(t)$, is the amount that generation t can carry over into period $t + 1$. Because only the young at date t will be purchasing money, $M(t)$ is the total amount they can purchase.

Consider economy 2 except that $M(t)$ is no longer a constant. The government chooses to increase the money supply by some growth rate $\mu > 1$, so $M(t + 1) = \mu M(t)$ for all t. If, for example, μ equals 1.15, then the time $t + 1$ money supply is 15 percent ($\mu - 1$, or $1.15 - 1 = 0.15$) larger than the time t money supply. The government divides the new fiat money that it issues at time $t + 1$,

$$M(t + 1) - M(t) = (\mu - 1)M(t),$$

equally among the time $t + 1$ old. The beliefs of the members of each generation on what determines this allocation of new money matters in their consumption choices and in the resulting utility.

We consider two allocation methods. Perfect foresight is assumed in both cases. In the first, each individual h of generation t receives $(\mu - 1)m^h(t)$ units of new fiat money when old. The allocation of the new fiat money that person h of generation t receives at date $t + 1$ in this method depends on the amount of fiat money that person h of generation t is already holding. Recall that $m^h(t)$ is the notation we used for fiat money holdings in the budget constraints.

The second method is to allocate at date $t + 1$ to all members of generation t an amount of fiat money equal to $(\mu - 1)M(t)/N(t)$, independent of the amount of money that the individual is already holding. The population of generation t is $N(t)$, so the above equation says that the new money is divided equally among all members of generation t when they are old. Notice that if all members of each generation are identical, the amount of new money that the old will receive in each period will be exactly the same in each of these allocation methods. What is different is the way the allocation method affects the incentives of individuals.

First, we consider the allocation based on the holdings one already has of money—we call this allocation method *policy 1*. For an individual living in a world with this government policy, the budget constraints are

$$c_t^h(t) = \omega_t^h(t) - \ell^h(t) - p^m(t)m^h(t),$$

and $\quad c_t^h(t + 1) = \omega_t^h(t + 1) + r(t)\ell^h(t) + p^m(t + 1)\mu m^h(t).$

The amount of fiat money this individual has when old is equal to the $m^h(t)$ units purchased when young and the $(\mu - 1)m^h(t)$ units that were given to this individual, based on money holdings, by the government. These amounts total $\mu m^h(t)$. Eliminating $\ell^h(t)$, we get the single budget constraint,

$$c_t^h(t) + \frac{c_t^h(t + 1)}{r(t)} = \omega_t^h(t) + \frac{\omega_t^h(t + 1)}{r(t)}$$

$$- m^h(t)\left[p^m(t) - \frac{\mu p^m(t + 1)}{r(t)} \right].$$

The arbitrage condition for this budget constraint is

$$r(t) = \frac{\mu p^m(t + 1)}{p^m(t)}.$$

Therefore, only the top line of the budget constraint matters in determining savings. This result is the same as the one we got when we first found the savings function, so savings for individual h of generation t of economy 2 is

$$s^h(r(t)) = \frac{\omega_t^h(t)}{2} - \frac{\omega_t^h(t + 1)}{2r(t)} = 1 - \frac{1}{2r(t)}.$$

Equilibrium for this economy occurs when aggregate savings equal the value of money, which is the only outside asset. This condition is true in each period. If we are looking for a stationary equilibrium, we want the consumption to be the same for every generation. For that to be the case in economy 2, the savings must be the same for every generation. For generation t, savings (at equilibrium) are

$$S(r(t)) = p^m(t)M(t).$$

For generation $t + 1$, the equilibrium condition on savings is

$$S(r(t + 1)) = p^m(t + 1)M(t + 1).$$

Because savings in periods t and $t + 1$ must be equal in a stationary state, we have

$$S(r(t)) = S(r(t + 1)),$$

or $p^m(t)M(t) = p^m(t + 1)M(t + 1),$

which means that

$$p^m(t)M(t) = p^m(t + 1)\mu M(t)$$

given that μ is the growth rate of money. A simple algebraic manipulation shows that $p^m(t)$ equals $\mu p^m(t + 1)$. Substituting that relation into the arbitrage condition gives

$$r(t) = \frac{\mu p^m(t + 1)}{p^m(t)} = \frac{p^m(t)}{p^m(t)} = 1$$

no matter what value we have for μ. Individuals receive exactly the amount of additional fiat money (based on their holdings of fiat money) that will compensate them for the inflation. They know that this compensation will occur, and they take it into account when they calculate their return on holding fiat money. Even though the quantity of fiat money is changing, the stationary monetary equilibrium is identical to the one where the quantity of money is constant.

Using $r(t) = 1$ in the savings function for our example economy gives individual savings of

$$s^h(r(t)) = s^h(1) = 1 - \frac{1}{(2)(1)} = \frac{1}{2}$$

and a consumption allocation of [1.5, 1.5]. Notice that this consumption allocation is the same as the one you found in the stationary monetary equilibrium in Exercise 10.2.

The preceding example is a special case of the following proposition, which we will not prove.

Proposition 10.1 *Consider an economy in which new money allocations are proportional to money holdings. Given that there exists a monetary equilibrium for* $\mu = 1$, *then the consumption allocations of that equilibrium are an equilibrium consumption allocation for any* $\mu > 0$.

The second policy we consider—which we call *policy 2*—is one where each old person receives the same quantity of fiat money, an allocation independent of the quantity of money that individual is holding. For policy 2, the budget constraint is somewhat different from that for policy 1. The policy 2 budget constraint for individual h of generation t is

$$c_t^h(t) = \omega_t^h(t) - \ell^h(t) - p^m(t)m^h(t),$$

and $\quad c_t^h(t + 1) = \omega_t^h(t + 1) + r(t)\ell^h(t) + p^m(t + 1)m^h(t)$

$$+ \frac{p^m(t + 1)(\mu - 1)M(t)}{N(t)},$$

where $N(t)$ is the population of generation t. Converting these two constraints into one by eliminating $\ell^h(t)$ gives

$$c_t^h(t) + \frac{c_t^h(t + 1)}{r(t)} = \omega_t^h(t) + \frac{\omega_t^h(t + 1)}{r(t)}$$

$$- m^h(t)\left[p^m(t) - \frac{p^m(t + 1)}{r(t)}\right]$$

$$+ \frac{p^m(t + 1)(\mu - 1)M(t)}{N(t)r(t)}.$$

The arbitrage condition from this budget constraint is that the part of this equation in square brackets equals 0, or that

$$r(t) = \frac{p^m(t + 1)}{p^m(t)}.$$

This condition differs from the arbitrage condition under policy 1 by not including the rate of growth of the money supply, μ. Because the additional money is given to the old each period independent of their savings behavior, it does not enter the decision making process in the same way. The value of the new money the old receive is viewed by them as an addition to their endowment when old and affects their decision to save the same as would any lump-sum transfer. The effects on individual savings functions are the same as the lump-sum taxes and transfers of Chapter 3, where the after-tax endowments were used in the savings functions.

Because the second line of the lifetime budget constraint equals 0, individuals maximize their utility subject to the constraint

$$c_t^h(t) + \frac{c_t^h(t + 1)}{r(t)}$$

$$= \omega_t^h(t) + \left[\omega_t^h(t + 1) + \frac{p^m(t + 1)(\mu - 1)M(t)}{N(t)} \right] \left[\frac{1}{r(t)} \right].$$

A savings function can be found from the utility function and this lifetime budget constraint in the usual way.

For the economy 2 utility functions, the individual's savings function that results from utility maximization subject to the above budget constraint is

$$s^h(r(t)) = \frac{\omega_t^h(t)}{2} - \left[\omega_t^h(t + 1) + \frac{p^m(t + 1)(\mu - 1)M(t)}{N(t)} \right] \left[\frac{1}{2r(t)} \right].$$

Notice that the second part of the savings function (the part after the minus sign) is equal to endowment when old plus the real value of the money transfer. Otherwise, this savings function is identical to earlier ones.

EXERCISE 10.8 Derive the above savings function from the example economy utility function and endowments and the appropriate budget constraints.

Again, because we are looking for a stationary monetary equilibrium, we know that the aggregate savings are the same in every period. When we use the same reasoning as above, this observation implies that

$$r(t) = \frac{p^m(t + 1)}{p^m(t)} = \frac{M(t)}{M(t + 1)} = \frac{M(t)}{\mu M(t)} = \frac{1}{\mu}.$$

The gross interest rate is equal to $1/\mu$ under policy 2. We do not have quite enough information to determine the savings of an individual. We know the gross interest rate, and that information has usually been enough to get a specific result for savings. The savings function we have here includes the price of money and the total quantity of money as arguments. We need to find either $p^m(t + 1)M(t)$ or $p^m(t)M(t)/\mu$— which are equivalent expressions—to determine savings. We use the equilibrium condition for aggregate savings to find the latter expression. The equilibrium condition for aggregate savings is

$$S(r(t)) = N(t)s^h(r(t)) = p^m(t)M(t).$$

Substituting the individual savings function for the example economy that we found above into this equation and using an endowment of [2, 1], we get

$$N(t)\left\{1 - \left[1 + \frac{p^m(t + 1)(\mu - 1)M(t)}{N(t)}\right]\left[\frac{1}{2r(t)}\right]\right\} = p^m(t)M(t).$$

Substituting $1/\mu$ for $r(t)$ and $p^m(t)/\mu$ for $p^m(t + 1)$ gives

$$1 - \frac{\mu}{2} - \left[(\mu - 1)p^m(t)M(t)\right]\left[\frac{1}{2N(t)}\right] = \frac{p^m(t)M(t)}{N(t)}.$$

Multiplying through by 2 and bringing the $p^m(t)M(t)/N(t)$ components together, we find that

$$\frac{p^m(t)M(t)}{N(t)} = \frac{2 - \mu}{1 + \mu}.$$

This expression gives the equilibrium quantity of savings for an individual as a function of the growth rate of the money supply.

The above example involves a specific economy. We can use a graphical analysis of Figure 10.2 to illustrate how the equilibrium consumption point is found for a general utility function. We can then use the same graph to illustrate that, for policy 2, the consumption allocation occurring in equilibrium with a μ greater than 1 is not, in general, Pareto optimal.

The 45-degree line in Figure 10.2 is the budget line for an individual in a stationary monetary equilibrium where the money supply is constant. It also represents the set of symmetric, feasible, and efficient consumption pairs. Given a set of preferences indicated by the indifference curves in the figure and a gross interest rate of 1 on money, the consumption allocation indicated by c_2 is chosen by members of generations $t \geq 1$. Point c_2 is also the consumption point for members of generations $t \geq 1$ in the stationary equilibrium when the government allocates the fiat money transfers as a percentage of each individual's money holdings.

Consider policy 2, according to which the government is increasing the money supply at a rate μ by lump-sum gifts of money to the old. Three conditions must hold for a stationary equilibrium. The inflation rate must equal μ, the rate of growth of the money supply. This condition means that the gross interest rate individuals face when holding money is $1/\mu$; and, with our normal marginal rate of substitution conditions, consumption will occur at a point on an indifference curve with

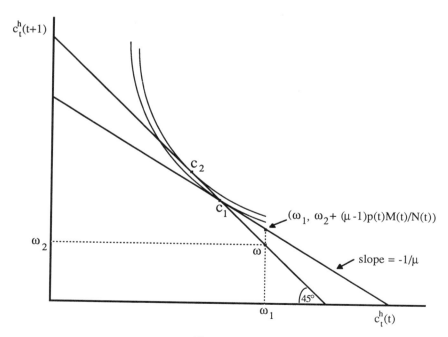

Figure 10.2

a slope of $-1/\mu$. Second, the consumption pair is feasible, efficient, and symmetric, so it occurs on the 45-degree line in Figure 10.2. Third, there is a real transfer caused by the gift of money an individual receives when old, and that lump-sum transfer changes the effective endowment point.

The above set of conditions indicates how one can find, graphically, the equilibrium in an economy with a stationary environment of identical individuals. The equilibrium consumption allocation occurs on the 45-degree line, where

$$c_t^h(t) + c_t^h(t + 1) = \omega_t^h(t) + \omega_t^h(t + 1),$$

at a point where the slope of an indifference curve has a slope equal to -1 over the rate of growth of the money supply, $-1/\mu$. First, we find the point—call it c_1—on the 45-degree line where it is tangent to an indifference curve. Given some μ, we draw the budget line with a slope of $-1/\mu$ through c_1. The vertical distance from the endowment point, ω_1, to the point on this budget line directly above it is the value of the money transfer to each of the old; namely, $(\mu - 1)p(t + 1)M(t)/N(t)$. Because μ is known, the equilibrium $p(t + 1)$ can be found for any $M(t)$ and $N(t)$. A condition for equilibrium is that savings are positive (because everyone is identical and individuals cannot be net sellers of fiat money), so an equilibrium exists if savings, which equal $\omega_1 - c_t^h(t)$, are positive.

We can also use Figure 10.2 to illustrate that under policy 2, any positive growth rate of the money supply ($\mu > 1$) results in a consumption allocation that is Pareto inferior to the consumption allocation that results when μ equals 1.

Because the physical constraint on symmetric allocations, which is also the no-inflation budget line, is tangent to the highest indifference curve at point c_2, any movement away from that point results in a reduction of utility for members of generations $t \geq 1$. Because the increased inflation, caused by the gifts of money, moves the chosen consumption points back toward the endowment, both the old of time 0 and everyone else in the economy suffer a reduction in utility. The old from generation 0 receive absolutely less of the time 1 good than they would with no inflation and all other generations are on a lower indifference curve. The stationary monetary equilibrium that results from this gift of fiat money, which generates the inflation, is Pareto inferior to the stationary monetary equilibrium that results from a fixed money supply.

Seignorage

So far, money creation has been used exclusively to make transfers. Governments often use their ability to issue new money to purchase real resources from the rest of the economy. This purchase results in a transfer of real resources from the rest of the economy to the government. Normally, transfers from the private economy to the government occur through taxes—the payments that the government forces individuals to make to the government. Because some methods of money creation result in transfers from the private economy to the government, we can also think of these methods of money creation as a form of taxation. The special name we give to taxation by money creation is *seignorage*. Originally, seignorage referred to all of the rights of the king, or the *señor* (meaning "lord" in Spanish); but in modern times the meaning has contracted to refer only to the king's or the government's right to tax by money creation.

Consider an economy in which the government increases the money supply by a rate μ each period, so $M(t + 1) = \mu M(t)$. The government sells the newly issued money to the young at the same time the old are selling their money to the young. If the young at time t are purchasing $M(t)$ units of money, then $M(t - 1)$ of that is purchased from the old and $(\mu - 1)M(t - 1)$ of that is purchased from the government.

There are no transfers of money to the old, so individuals, when old, own and can sell only the money that they purchased when they were young. With that assumption in mind, we write the budget constraints faced by member h of generation t as

$$c_t^h(t) = \omega_t^h(t) - \ell^h(t) - p^m(t)m^h(t),$$

and $c_t^h(t + 1) = \omega_t^h(t + 1) + r(t)\ell^h(t) + p^m(t + 1)m^h(t).$

Combining these two constraints by eliminating $\ell^h(t)$, we find as the single lifetime budget constraint,

$$c_t^h(t) + \frac{c_t^h(t + 1)}{r(t)} = \omega_t^h(t) + \frac{\omega_t^h(t + 1)}{r(t)}$$

$$- m^h(t)\left[p^m(t) - \frac{p^m(t + 1)}{r(t)}\right].$$

This constraint gives us an arbitrage condition of $r(t) = p^m(t + 1)/p^m(t)$. Only the top line of the lifetime budget constraint matters for individual utility maximization. This expression is the same lifetime budget constraint we have seen many times and yields the same individual savings function. The other equilibrium condition—the market clearing condition—for any time $t \geq 1$ is found the usual way and is

$$S(r(t)) = p^m(t)M(t).$$

In a stationary monetary equilibrium (for an economy without growth), the savings of one generation are the same as those for any other generation. Therefore, the quantity of the time t good that is spent on purchasing money (the only asset in the current framework) is the same as the quantity of the time $t + 1$ good that is spent on purchasing money. Not only must the gross interest rates be the same in time t and $t + 1$ for this to hold, but the real value of money must be constant, so

$$p^m(t)M(t) = p^m(t + 1)M(t + 1),$$

for all $t \geq 1$. Because the money supply is increasing at the rate μ, we substitute in $\mu M(t)$ for $M(t + 1)$ in the above equation and recall the arbitrage condition to get

$$r(t) = \frac{p^m(t + 1)}{p^m(t)} = \frac{M(t)}{M(t + 1)} = \frac{M(t)}{\mu M(t)} = \frac{1}{\mu}.$$

The gross interest rate is equal to 1 over the rate of increase of the money supply, $1/\mu$, and is constant in a stationary monetary equilibrium. We drop the time notation on gross interest rates in the following discussion. Recall that the prices we are using here are the price of money in terms of goods and that "normal" prices of goods in terms of money are given by $1/p^m(t)$. Inflation is the rate of change of the price of goods in terms of money and is given by

$$\frac{\dfrac{1}{p^m(t + 1)} - \dfrac{1}{p^m(t)}}{\dfrac{1}{p^m(t)}},$$

which equals

$$\frac{p^m(t)}{p^m(t + 1)} - 1 = \mu - 1.$$

The equilibrium inflation rate is equal to the gross rate of increase of the money supply minus 1, or $\mu - 1$.

In a stationary monetary equilibrium, it is fairly simple to calculate the amount of seignorage for each rate of increase in the money supply. The following proposition presents the formula for making this calculation.

Proposition 10.2 *Let $\mu > 1$ be the gross rate of increase of the money supply. If aggregate savings, $S(1/\mu) > 0$, then there exists a stationary monetary equilibrium with $r(t) = 1/\mu$ for all t and seignorage of*

$$[1 - r(t)]S(r(t)) = \left(1 - \frac{1}{\mu}\right)S\left(\frac{1}{\mu}\right).$$

Let us consider how one finds this formula. Keep in mind that we are concentrating on stationary monetary equilibria in this discussion.

Government revenues (we use **g** to denote government revenues) from the money creation (calculated at time $t + 1$) are equal to

$$\mathbf{g} = p^m(t + 1)[M(t + 1) - M(t)].$$

Substituting in $\mu M(t)$ for $M(t + 1)$, we get

$$\mathbf{g} = p^m(t + 1)(\mu - 1)M(t).$$

Our arbitrage (present value) condition is that $r(t) = p^m(t + 1)/p^m(t) = 1/\mu$, so $p^m(t + 1) = p^m(t)/\mu$. Making this substitution and rearranging, we find that the government revenues from a growth rate of the money supply of μ are

$$\mathbf{g} = \left(\frac{\mu - 1}{\mu}\right)p^m(t)M(t) = \left(1 - \frac{1}{\mu}\right)p^m(t)M(t).$$

The equilibrium condition for this economy is that savings at time t equals the amount spent on money, so $p^m(t)M(t)$ equals $S(r)$. We showed above that r equals $1/\mu$. Substituting both of these expressions into the above equation gives government revenues from money creation (seignorage) equal to

$$\mathbf{g} = \left(1 - \frac{1}{\mu}\right) p^m(t) M(t) = \left(1 - \frac{1}{\mu}\right) S\left(\frac{1}{\mu}\right) = (1 - r)S(r).$$

We can graph real government revenues against the gross rate of growth of the money supply (which is 1 plus the rate of inflation in a stationary monetary equilibrium). For economy 2, real seignorage is equal to

$$\mathbf{g} = (1 - r)\left(100 - \frac{50}{r}\right).$$

Figure 10.3 shows the graph of real seignorage against the gross rate of growth of the money supply for economy 2. This curve is fairly

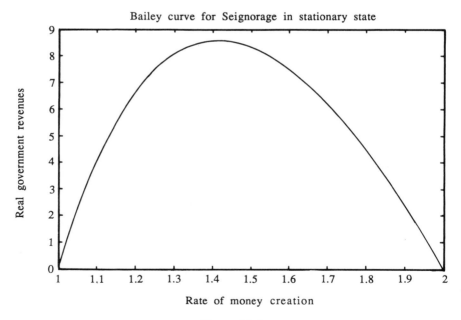

Bailey curve for Seignorage in stationary state

Rate of money creation

Figure 10.3

standard and has recently become well known for other types of taxes under the name of a Laffer curve. With respect to real government revenues as a function of money creation, this type of curve was shown in work by Martin Bailey (1956). In honor of Bailey, we call this graph a *Bailey curve*.

Note that as the rate of growth of the money supply increases from 0, the real government revenues first increase, but that as the rate of growth of the money supply continues to increase, the revenues begin to decline. With some utility functions and endowment patterns, this decline in revenues does not occur and the curve approaches an upper limit. However, these seem to be special cases and a Bailey curve "usually" turns down.

Figure 10.4 shows how individuals allocate their lifetime consumption in response to positive inflation. In a stationary monetary equilibrium with a fixed money supply, consumption is at point c_1. For some rate of money creation $\mu > 1$, the relevant budget line swings and consumption

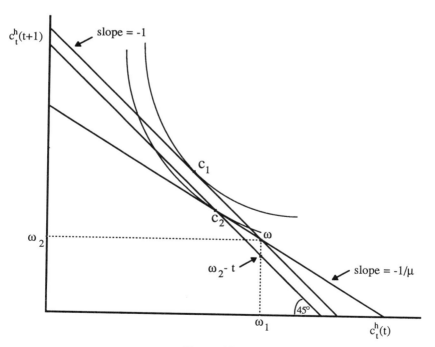

Figure 10.4

occurs at point c_2. The amount of tax that the government extracts from this individual can be found by drawing a 45-degree line through point c_2. Directly above the point ω_1 on the abscissa, the vertical distance between the endowment point and the intersection of the new 45-degree line gives the amount of tax taken from this individual measured in terms of the time $t + 1$ good.

In the Bailey curve, all but one (the maximum) of the feasible levels of government revenues could be raised by two different rates of growth of the money supply. Figure 10.5 shows the other inflation rate that raises the same amount of revenue as growth rate μ. Point c_3 is on the same 45-degree line as c_2 and is at the tangency of the budget line through ω at inflation rate μ_2 and the indifference curve set. Notice that at the higher inflation rate the government collects the same revenue, but this member of the economy has a lower utility level.

The heavy line in Figure 10.6 is the locus of the consumption points that this individual chooses when faced with different inflation rates. This curve is similar to the Bailey curve in several ways. The distance

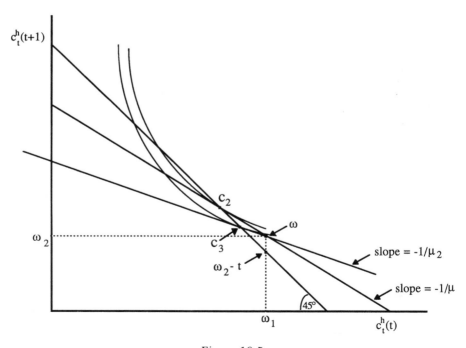

Figure 10.5

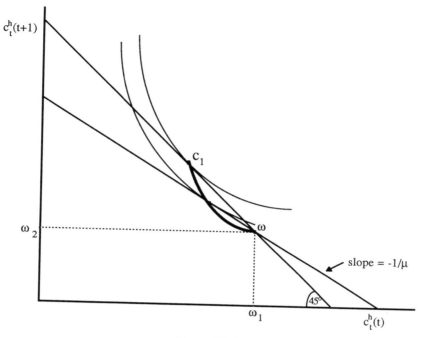

Figure 10.6

between a point on this curve and the 45-degree line through point ω measures the amount of government revenues. At point c_1 and ω, the government collects no revenues. As the inflation rate increases (as the budget line swings from the 45-degree line downward), the amount of government revenues increases and then decreases. Figure 10.6 illustrates the individual behavior that generates the Bailey curve.

EXERCISE 10.9 Consider an economy with a downward-turning Bailey curve. Each level of seignorage (except one) can be achieved with two rates of money creation. For an economy with identical individuals, show that achieving any level of seignorage by using the smaller rate of money creation (smaller rate of growth of the money supply) is Pareto superior to using the large rate. Is this statement true if there is diversity—for example, if half the population at any date has one endowment and the other half a different endowment?

It is important to remember that the Bailey curve represents the revenues for economies that are in stationary monetary equilibria at the particular inflation rate. In economies that are in a nonstationary equilibrium, we cannot determine from Figure 10.3 the current revenues from the current rate of money creation.

Some people denote as *hyperinflation* an inflation in which the inflation rate is continually increasing. Others use the term to refer to an inflation rate above some specific—high—level. Phillip Cagan, for example, has fixed on a monthly inflation rate of 50 percent to mark the beginnings of hyperinflation. Under this criterion, the recent inflations in Bolivia (1985), Argentina (1989), and Nicaragua (1989) would qualify as hyperinflations. Argentina (1985), Brazil (1985 and 1989), and Peru (1989) might also qualify for hyperinflations if the cutoff were a bit lower. Whatever number we choose to designate a hyperinflation, we note one consistent characteristic of the above examples, namely, that the government generated government revenues in excess of 5 percent (and as high as 12 percent in some cases) of total national output by money creation.

It might well be the case that these hyperinflations occur when the government attempts to raise real revenues by money creation that are in excess of the highest real government revenues on the Bailey curve for their particular country. The amount of revenues that the government is attempting to raise in this case cannot be achieved by a stationary inflation rate but may be obtainable by an ever-increasing inflation rate. We have not explicitly modeled the nonstationary equilibria that we are suggesting are best suited for hyperinflations, so this last discussion should be interpreted as hypothesis and not proof.

EXERCISE 10.10   Find the Bailey curve for an economy identical to economy 2, except that the utility function for all members of all generations is

$$u_t^h = [c_t^h(t)]^{1/2} + [c_t^h(t + 1)]^{1/2}.$$

EXERCISE 10.11   Find the Bailey curve for an economy identical to economy 2 except that the endowment pattern for all members of all generations is [1, 2]. (Recall that the economy 2 endowment pattern is [2, 1].)

EXERCISE 10.12 In economy 2, the government will follow this policy: in period 1 it will increase the money supply to generate as much revenue as it can. For periods 2 through ∞, it will keep the money supply constant. How much revenue can the government raise in period 1? (Hint: Begin by finding the equilibrium for periods 2 and onward. Then find the period 1 revenue-maximizing inflation rate. You cannot simply use the seignorage equation given above.) How is the burden of the inflation tax shared between the young and old of period 1?

In Exercise 10.12 we assumed that the government keeps the money supply constant from period 2 onward. In period 1 the rate of inflation that maximizes seignorage revenues is not the Bailey curve maximum. The Bailey curve maximum is for stationary equilibria. The one-period revenue-maximizing rate of inflation is very large (equal to ∞ in the limit). If such a high inflation rate generates the maximum amount of government revenue from seignorage in period 1 (as it does), why would the same rate of inflation not maximize revenues in period 2, *once the economy is in period 2?* In other words, it might be a revenue-maximizing strategy, in period 1, for the government to promise to keep the money supply constant for all future periods and issue a lot of money in period 1. Once the economy has moved to period 2, what policy should the government follow then? If the government's objective is to maximize revenues in period 2, then once period 2 has been reached the best strategy for the government to follow may not be to honor its promise of no money creation. It would seem that the revenue-maximizing strategy would be to promise not to increase the money supply in the future (period 3 and onward) and to issue money in period 2.

The fact that the promised policy is not the best strategy for the government to follow once the future has been reached raises an important question about the credibility of the government when it makes promises about future policy. If the optimal policy today is for the government to promise to do something in the future that is not the optimal thing to do once the future has been reached, we say that the initial policy is *time inconsistent.* A revenue-maximizing policy might be to promise to keep the future money supply constant and to keep breaking this promise. Once the government starts breaking its promises, are the private agents in the economy going to keep believing the promises of the government? Might they not learn that the government's promises are not going to be kept and change their behavior in response to the expectation that the promises will be broken? Although our perfect foresight models (in which the future is known) do not allow us to carefully analyze these issues, the ability and willingness of a government to commit itself to a policy and to fulfill that commitment are important in determining the effects of economic policies in the real world. How many U.S. presidents have promised to balance the federal budget by the end of their first term in office?

Nonoptimality of Seignorage

Seignorage is an expensive way, in terms of utility, to raise government revenues. For any amount of government revenues that can be raised in a stationary monetary equilibrium using money creation, the same revenues can be raised by lump-sum taxes and leave everyone in the economy better off. This idea is what we wish to show. Keep in mind during the following discussion that, although we do not always mention it, whenever we work with an economy with money creation, we are always analyzing it in a stationary monetary equilibrium.

Consider an economy in which the government wishes to raise a quantity of revenues, **g**, each period. Assume that **g** is below the maximum amount that can be raised by seignorage as indicated on a Bailey curve for the economy, so it is feasible to use a stationary inflation rate to raise this amount of revenues. The same amount of revenues could also be raised by a pair of lump-sum taxes

$$t_t^h = [t_t^h(t), t_t^h(t + 1)]$$

on each individual h of generation t. Recall that lump-sum taxes appear in our models by changing the effective endowment of individuals. We wish to impose an amount of lump-sum taxes on individuals sufficient to raise **g** units of tax revenue. In a stationary perfect foresight equilibrium with lump-sum taxes [and with a constant population of $N(t) = N$ for generation t], the total government revenues at time $t \geq 0$ are equal to

$$\mathbf{g} = \sum_{h=1}^{N(t)} t_t^h(t) + \sum_{h=1}^{N(t-1)} t_{t-1}^h(t). \tag{10.2}$$

The total government revenues are equal to the sum of the lump-sum taxes on the young and the old.

The following three propositions hold for stationary monetary equilibria. Note carefully how each proposition is more specific than the one before it. You will be asked to prove the first two propositions yourself, and we will illustrate how to prove the third. In the exercises, do not use the results of Proposition 10.5 to prove the other two.

Proposition 10.3 *Any stationary equilibrium in which the government raises positive revenue through seignorage is not Pareto optimal.*

This proposition says that we can find a consumption allocation that raises the same revenue for the government and is Pareto superior to the consumption allocation achieved in the stationary equilibrium with seignorage. Nothing is implied about how the Pareto superior consumption allocation is reached. In particular, we do not require that it be a competitive equilibrium.

Proposition 10.4 *There is a stationary equilibrium with lump-sum taxes and transfers that raises the same amount of government revenue and is Pareto superior to any stationary equilibrium in which the government raises positive revenue through seignorage.*

Note that the equilibrium with taxes and transfers need not be a monetary equilibrium. In fact, it is possible to find nonmonetary equilibria with lump-sum taxes and transfers that are Pareto superior to any monetary equilibrium with positive revenue raised by seignorage.

EXERCISE 10.13 Prove Proposition 10.3.

EXERCISE 10.14 Prove Proposition 10.4.

Proposition 10.5 *There is a stationary monetary equilibrium with lump-sum taxes and transfers and $\mu = 1$ that is Pareto superior to any stationary equilibrium in which the government raises positive revenues through seignorage.*

This proposition states that we can find a stationary *monetary* equilibrium with no inflation but with lump-sum taxes and transfers that is Pareto superior to any stationary equilibrium with positive seignorage.

We use Figures 10.7 and 10.8 to illustrate that everyone can be better off in the monetary equilibrium with $\mu = 1$ and some set of lump-sum taxes and transfers. The individual whose behavior we illustrate in Figure 10.7 is a net borrower in the initial, stationary equilibrium with seignorage. Figure 10.8 illustrates the behavior of a net lender. This pair of figures covers all the possibilities.

In the inflationary equilibrium, with $\mu > 1$, individual h with an endowment of ω^h is consuming at point c^h in Figure 10.7. Notice that point c^h is to the right and below point ω^h. Individual h is consuming more than his endowment when young and less when old and, to do so, must be a net borrower. Point c^h is at a tangency of his indifference curve set and the budget line with slope $-1/\mu$ that goes through the endowment point, ω^h.

In the initial equilibrium, individual j with endowment ω^j chooses to consume at point c^j in Figure 10.8. Individual j is a net lender and, facing the inflation rate $\mu - 1$, is choosing to consume less when young

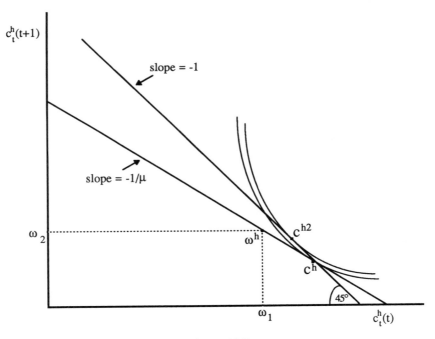

Figure 10.7

and more when old than her endowment point. Notice that her consumption point is on a budget line with slope $-1/\mu$ that runs through her endowment point, ω^j.

Consider an alternative stationary monetary equilibrium with a lump-sum tax and transfer scheme such that each individual k of generation t faces a tax and transfer pair of

$$t_t^k = \omega_t^k - c_t^k = [\omega_t^k(t) - c_t^k(t), \omega_t^k(t+1) - c_t^k(t+1)]. \qquad (10.3)$$

After the taxes and transfers, individuals h and j are at the consumption point they chose to be at in the equilibrium with positive seignorage. Notice that, in a stationary environment, this lump-sum tax and transfer scheme raises exactly the same amount of revenue *from each individual* as did seignorage. Because, in the equilibrium with seignorage, the revenues to the government each period are exactly equal to the aggregate amount of the endowment that was not consumed by those individuals

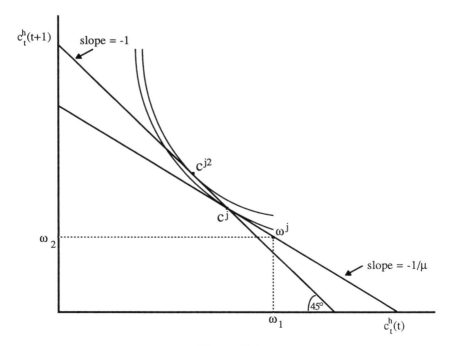

Figure 10.8

alive in that period, we can write

$$\mathbf{g} = \sum_{h=1}^{N(t)} (\omega_t^h(t) - c_t^h(t)) + \sum_{h=1}^{N(t-1)} (\omega_{t-1}^h(t) - c_{t-1}^h(t)).$$

At each date t, the lump-sum tax and transfer scheme that we have proposed raises exactly the same amount of revenue. To see this, use Equation (10.2) and substitute in the tax-transfer scheme described in Equation (10.3). This substitution results in the equation for government revenues given above.

In the alternative monetary equilibrium, the government is gaining $\mathbf{g}$ units of revenue by taxes and is not raising any seignorage. The rate of growth of the money supply, μ, equals 1, so there exists a monetary equilibrium in which the gross interest rate is equal to 1. Each individual can trade from the after-tax and transfer endowment point to a preferred consumption point along the budget lines with a slope of -1 illustrated in Figures 10.7 and 10.8. In each of these figures the individual chooses to consume at point c^{h2} and c^{j2}. These consumption points are on higher indifference curves than are the points c^h or c^j, respectively. We can get to higher indifference curves because the initial consumption points were at points on an indifference curve tangent to the budget line with a slope of $-1/\mu$, with $\mu > 1$. Moving to the left from these points along a line with a slope of -1 yields higher utility. The new consumption points, c^{h2} for borrowers and c^{j2} for lenders, are on indifference curves tangent to the budget line with the slope of -1. All members of all generations $t \geq 1$ have higher utility in the economy with lump-sum taxes.

The old at date 1 (the members of generation 0) have increased consumption. The tax-transfer scheme leaves them at the consumption point they would have had under the seignorage, yet they are holding fiat money with a positive real value. Trading this fiat money for goods increases their consumption and, therefore, their utility. The welfare of all members of the economy is increased in the stationary monetary equilibrium under the tax-transfer scheme. The proposed tax-transfer scheme is Pareto superior to seignorage.

Because seignorage is Pareto inferior to lump-sum taxes, why do so many countries use it to raise revenues? First, very few countries collect revenues with anything that is like a lump-sum tax. Almost all taxes that are in use have effects on allocation decisions. In a world in which lump-sum taxes cannot be imposed, an optimal mix of distorting taxes may very well include a positive amount of seignorage. Second, collecting normal kinds of taxes (income, value-added, and excise, for example) requires certain levels of accounting expertise among the government agents and the population. Many countries do not have a very high level of that expertise. Collecting taxes by inflation (and import duties) are technically easy ways of raising revenues. Third, many countries have large sectors of the economy that are informal or underground. Members of these sectors (the producers of illegal goods or the producers of legal goods who are avoiding taxes or avoiding the long delays that come from dealing with unhelpful government bureaucracy) do not pay other kinds of taxes, and seignorage can be used to capture some revenue from them.

Reprise

A constant money supply monetary equilibrium is very much like an equilibrium in an economy with land where the crop size is 0. The major difference with fiat money is that the government has a monopoly on the production of the money stuff and can use this monopoly to extract tax revenues through seignorage. If a lump-sum tax is available, then extracting the same amount of revenue through these lump-sum taxes is Pareto superior to using seignorage. If lump-sum taxes are not available, then some seignorage may be part of an optimal tax mix. The relationship between the rate of increase of the money supply and the amount of real revenues that the government gains from seignorage follows a Bailey curve. There are usually two rates of increase of the money supply (and in stationary states, constant rates of inflation) that give each level of feasible real revenues. In economies in which all members of each generation are alike, the higher rate of inflation generates an equilibrium that is Pareto inferior to the one generated by the lower rate of inflation that gives the same revenues. This Pareto inferiority need not hold when there is diversity.

CHAPTER **11**

Multiple Currencies and Exchange Rates

There are many fiat monies in the world. We note, as examples, the Costa Rican colon, the Gambian dalasi, the United States dollar, the French franc, the Romanian leu, the German mark, the Qatar riyal, and the Japanese yen. Most, although not all, countries have chosen to produce their own fiat monies. There are some regional monies that are used in several countries, for example, the CFA franc is used by 12 central African countries. Some smaller countries have chosen to use the currency of a larger neighbor. Many of these different monies can be exchanged one for another, but some governments (especially in centrally planned economies) prohibit the export and foreign sale of their fiat monies. The price at which one money is traded for another is called an *exchange rate*. In this chapter we explore the determination of exchange rates.

Frequently, the discussion of the determination of exchange rates proceeds on the assumption that currency flows between nations are in balance. The discussion proceeds as follows. There are individuals in country A who demand the currency of country B so that they might purchase the goods or assets of country B. There are individuals in country B who demand the currency of country A so that they might purchase the goods and assets of country A. The discussion almost always involves pairs of countries, so those who are demanding country A's currency are supplying that of country B. At each relative price between the two currencies (at each exchange rate), individuals in country A will supply a particular amount of their local currency for a particular amount of the currency of country B, and vice versa. Expressed in units of country A's currency per unit of country B's, there is a demand for that currency from the citizens of country B and a supply (generated by the reciprocal demand) of that currency from the citizens of country A. The point at which these supply and demand curves intersect determines the market clearing exchange rate between the two currencies.

Notice that in the above discussion there is an implicit assumption that country A's currency is needed to purchase goods or assets from citizens of country A. The same is assumed for country B. One way that this assumption could be made explicit is to invoke a law that requires purchases of goods or assets from the citizens of any country to be made in the currency of that country. It is precisely this type of law that we *do not* wish to invoke. We wish, first, to find out what determines the exchange rate in a system in which neither legal restrictions nor other governmental controls are determining the price of one currency against another. We can then add some government controls and observe how that changes equilibrium exchange rates.

The results we get challenge some long-held notions of economists. For example, Milton Friedman has written:

> The basic fact is that a unified currency and a system of freely floating exchange rates are members of the same species even though superficially they appear very different. Both are free market mechanisms for interregional or international payments. Both permit exchange rates to move freely. Both exclude any administrative or political intermediary in payments between residents of different areas. Either is consistent with free trade between areas, or with lessening of trade restrictions (1968, p. 7).

Exchange rates do not behave as other prices do. Rather than finding that a freely floating exchange rate system is well behaved, we find that the exchange rate between two currencies is indeterminate in the sense that if there are two fiat currencies without any legal constraints on the holdings of one currency or the other, any exchange rate can be an equilibrium exchange rate. Which exchange rate actually occurs will matter to the old of time 0 but will not matter to any member of any other generation.

Before we show the accuracy of these findings, however, we need to make clear what we mean by a freely floating exchange rate system. We need to make clear the rules under which members of different countries can make exchanges. In Chapter 6 we defined laissez-faire and portfolio autarky regimes for economies with private assets. We use similar definitions for regimes in economies with multiple fiat monies.

Definition   *In a* laissez-faire *regime at time t, any member of generation t can purchase or sell the fiat money of any country to any other member of generation t and can borrow and lend to anyone.*

Definition   *In a* portfolio autarky *regime at time t, a member of generation t who is a citizen of country i can only hold from time t to time t + 1 the fiat money of country i. Also, private borrowing and lending can only take place among members of the same country.*

We explore the effects of these two regimes in economies with stationary environments with no storage or production. As further simplifications, we assume that there are only two countries and that the good can be transported costlessly between them. We limit ourselves to economies in which there is only one good in each period, so situations of balanced trade mean that no net trade in goods takes place. Situations with no trade in goods serve as a proxy for cases where each country is exporting different goods and the value of exports from each country are equal. In cases where the trade is not balanced, some net amount of an asset is being traded between the two countries to make up the difference in the goods trade.

We get an additional arbitrage condition from the assumption of costless transportation of goods between countries. We require that the prices of the two goods and the exchange rate be such that no one can make profits by purchasing the good in country 1 (for example) for X units of money, sending the good to the other country and selling it for Y units of that country's money, and then exchanging the currency back into the original currency for a quantity different from X units of country 1's money. If this were possible, each individual would attempt to do so, and this behavior would result in the export of all of the country's good in each period in which this tactic occurred. Because it is only the good that matters in utility functions, this case cannot be an equilibrium. This arbitrage condition is called *purchasing power parity*. It means that a given quantity of one country's fiat money will be able to purchase the same amount of good in either the home country or, exchanged for the other currency, in the foreign country.

Indeterminacy with Laissez-Faire Floating Rates

We showed in Chapter 10 that, in a monetary equilibrium, fiat money must give the same rate of return as other assets. The same logic tells us that if there are two fiat monies, in an equilibrium in which they both have value, they must each give the same rate of return. We get this result from the arbitrage conditions.

In a time t laissez-faire regime, the budget constraints for member h of generation t are

$$c_t^h(t) = \omega_t^h(t) - \ell^h(t) - p^A(t)m^{Ah}(t) - p^B(t)m^{Bh}(t),$$

and $c_t^h(t + 1) = \omega_t^h(t + 1) + r(t)\ell^h(t)$

$$+ p^A(t + 1)m^{Ah}(t) + p^B(t + 1)m^{Bh}(t),$$

where $p^i(t)$ is the time t price of country i's fiat money and $m^{ih}(t)$ is the amount of country i's money purchased by member h of generation t, for $i = A$ and B. This budget constraint is the same for citizens of country A or country B because, in a laissez-faire regime, anyone can purchase either of the two fiat monies.

These two budget constraints can be combined by eliminating $\ell^h(t)$ to get

$$c_t^h(t) + \frac{c_t^h(t + 1)}{r(t)} = \omega_t^h(t) + \frac{\omega_t^h(t + 1)}{r(t)}$$

$$- m^{Ah}(t)\left[p^A(t) - \frac{p^A(t + 1)}{r(t)}\right]$$

$$- m^{Bh}(t)\left[p^B(t) - \frac{p^B(t + 1)}{r(t)}\right].$$

Following the usual arguments about arbitrage and assuming that both currencies have positive prices, we get the present value conditions,

$$r(t) = \frac{p^i(t + 1)}{p^i(t)}, \tag{11.1}$$

for i equals A and B. The rate of return (the rate of change of prices) of the two moneys must be the same if both the monies are to have value.

Let $E(t)$ be the exchange rate at time t. We define this exchange rate as the number of units of country A's money that is needed to purchase 1 unit of country B's money. This definition is somewhat arbitrary; we might just as well have defined the exchange rate to be in terms of the number of units of country B's money needed to purchase 1 unit of country A's money. Because $p^i(t)$ is the price of country i's money in terms of the time t good, arbitrage in the goods market (that is, purchasing power parity) means that the exchange rate, $E(t)$, and the price of the goods must satisfy

$$E(t) = \frac{p^B(t)}{p^A(t)}.$$

Suppose that the above equation does not hold, for example, that

$$\bar{E}(t) > \frac{p^B(t)}{p^A(t)}.$$

With this exchange rate, a citizen of country B can take 1 unit of good and convert it into $1/p^B(t)$ units of country B's currency. Exchanging this for country A's currency at the exchange rate, $\bar{E}(t)$, generates $\bar{E}(t)/p^B(t)$ units of country A's currency. But if the above inequality holds, this amount of country A's currency can be used to purchase more than 1 unit of the time t good in country A. If the inequality continues to hold, there is an infinite one-way flow of currency from country B to country A. Such a flow cannot occur in equilibrium, because only a finite amount of each currency exists.

The following two propositions are very strong. The first tells us what the time path of exchange rates must be in a perfect foresight, laissez-faire world: exchange rates must be constant over time. Because we do not observe constant exchange rates, we must use care in applying this first proposition. The second proposition is equally disturbing. It says that one exchange rate is as good as any other in a perfect foresight, laissez-faire world.

Proposition 11.1 *In a perfect foresight, laissez-faire, monetary equilibrium, the exchange rates will be constant over time.*

Let $E(1)$ be the exchange rate between the money of country A and the money of country B at time period 1. The arbitrage condition (Equation 11.1) says, when considering period 1, that

$$r(1) = \frac{p^A(2)}{p^A(1)} = \frac{p^B(2)}{p^B(1)}.$$

Rearranging the two right-hand parts of this equation and using the goods arbitrage condition at time 1 and 2 give

$$E(1) = \frac{p^B(1)}{p^A(1)} = \frac{p^B(2)}{p^A(2)} = E(2).$$

The exchange rate at time 1 is the same as the exchange at time 2. Because the arbitrage conditions hold in all periods, the above result generalizes to

$$E(t) = \frac{p^B(t)}{p^A(t)} = \frac{p^B(t+1)}{p^A(t+1)} = E(t+1).$$

Reapplying this result sequentially means that $E(t) = E(1)$ for all t. The exchange rate is constant through time. The next proposition involves the determination of that constant exchange rate.

Proposition 11.2 *In an economy with fixed supplies of two, country-specific monies, if there exists a perfect foresight, laissez-faire, monetary equilibrium with constant money supplies at some exchange rate, then there exists a perfect foresight, laissez-faire, monetary equilibrium at any exchange rate.*

Consider a monetary equilibrium in which the constant exchange rate is E^1, and the prices of the two monies in terms of the time t good are sequences $\{p^{A1}(t)\}$ and $\{p^{B1}(t)\}$ for $t = 1$ to ∞. To show that any other exchange rate can be a monetary equilibrium, we need only find the prices that would go along with that exchange rate and give exactly the same consumption allocation and holdings of each money as those given by the original exchange rate and prices. Recall that an equilibrium is a series of prices that clear all markets and in which individuals are maximizing their welfare subject to their budget constraints. If a new price sequence leaves the budget constraints unchanged, then the same consumption allocation will be an equilibrium if the market for money clears. The budget constraints faced by individual h of generation t (it does not matter which country this individual is from) are

$$c_t^h(t) = \omega_t^h(t) - \ell^h(t) - p^{A1}(t)m^{Ah}(t) - p^{B1}(t)m^{Bh}(t),$$

and $\quad c_t^h(t+1) = \omega_t^h(t+1) + r(t)\ell^h(t)$
$$+ p^{A1}(t+1)m^{Ah}(t) + p^{B1}(t+1)m^{Bh}(t).$$

Substituting in the exchange rate, the budget constraints become

$$c_t^h(t) = \omega_t^h(t) - \ell^h(t) - p^{A1}(t)[m^{Ah}(t) + E^1 m^{Bh}(t)],$$

and $\quad c_t^h(t+1) = \omega_t^h(t+1) + r(t)\ell^h(t) + p^{A1}(t+1)[m^{Ah}(t) + E^1 m^{Bh}(t)].$

The market clearing condition for money in a laissez-faire regime is

$$S^A(r(t)) + S^B(r(t)) = p^{A1}(t)[\mathbf{M}^A + E^1 \mathbf{M}^B]. \tag{11.2}$$

$S^i(r(t))$ is the aggregate savings function for country i, and $\mathbf{M}^i$ is the (fixed) money supply for country i, $i = $ A and B.

Consider some second constant exchange rate, E^2. The aggregate money supply in terms of the money of country A is now $\mathbf{M}^A + E^2\mathbf{M}^B$. Consider the price sequence $p^{A2}(t)$ and $p^{B2}(t)$ defined by

$$p^{A2}(t) = \frac{p^{A1}(t)[\mathbf{M}^A + E^1\mathbf{M}^B]}{\mathbf{M}^A + E^2\mathbf{M}^B} \tag{11.3}$$

and $\quad p^{B2}(t) = E^2 p^{A2}(t).$

At every period, t, these price sequences give exactly the same gross interest rate, $r(t)$, as did the price sequence $p^{A1}(t)$ and $p^{B1}(t)$. Because the gross interest rates under these price sequences are the same as those under the original price sequences, the aggregate savings (and each person's own savings) in each country at each time period t are the same as those in the original price sequence. Solving the first equation of (11.3) for $p^{A1}(t)$ and substituting that expression into Equation (11.2) gives the required market clearing condition,

$$S^A(r(t)) + S^B(r(t)) = p^{A2}(t)[\mathbf{M}^A + E^2\mathbf{M}^B].$$

Notice that the two equilibria may not be exactly alike. If the old at time 1 (the members of generation 0) hold only their own country's money, then changes in the exchange rate will change the percentage of the goods that are spent on money that go to each old person. The two equilibria are identical for all members of all other generations.

Definition   *Economy 3 contains two countries: A and B. All citizens of both countries have the same utility functions and the same endowments as the members of economy 2 have. Country A has a population $N^A(t) = 100$, and country B has one of $N^B(t) = 50$ for all $t \geq 0$. The money supply of country A is $\mathbf{M}^A(t) = 200$ and of country B is $\mathbf{M}^B(t) = 100$, for $t \geq 0$. Each member of generation 0 from country i owns 2 units of country i's money, i = A and B.*

EXERCISE 11.1   Consider economy 3. Describe the laissez-faire, monetary equilibrium with an exchange rate equal to 2. Describe the laissez-faire, monetary equilibrium for this economy with an exchange rate equal to 4.

When there are no restrictions on the holding of currencies, we have seen that the exchange rate is constant through time. The resulting economy behaves as if it were one economy with one, albeit mixed, currency. The world money supply (in terms of the fiat money of country A) is $\mathbf{M}^A + E\mathbf{M}^B$. The world's aggregate savings equal the price of country A's fiat money times the world money supply. In different monetary equilibria with different exchange rates, the world money supply as measured in terms of country A's fiat money is different. With constant supplies of both money A and money B, the gross interest rates are the same in the two equilibria, and so are aggregate savings. Only the price levels are different—and sufficiently different to make the value of the world money supplies, in terms of time t goods, the same in each of the equilibria.

Seignorage in a Multiple Money World

In any laissez-faire, monetary equilibrium with two or more valued currencies, the exchange rate between any two of those currencies is con-

stant over time. (See Proposition 11.1.) This condition holds whether
the money supplies are constant or changing over time. The proof of
that proposition did not require the time paths of the money supplies
to be constant. If the two monies are being held, they must offer the
same rates of return. Identical rates of return between the monies require a constant exchange rate.

Given that the exchange rates are fixed, we can consider a multiple
currency world as one in which only one global currency exists. That
money can be expressed in terms of any country's currency. If we have
three currencies (of countries A, B, and C), then the world money supply at time t, in terms of country A's money, is

$$\mathbf{M}^{\mathrm{W}}(t) = \mathbf{M}^{\mathrm{A}}(t) + E^{\mathrm{B/A}}\mathbf{M}^{\mathrm{B}}(t) + E^{\mathrm{C/A}}\mathbf{M}^{\mathrm{C}}(t).$$

$E^{i/\mathrm{A}}$ is the exchange rate for country i's currency in terms of country
A's currency. There is no time parameter in the exchange rates because
they are constant through time. The world money supply is a linear
function of the individual countries' money supplies. The exchange
rates are the weighting parameters in that linear function.

Because everyone is willing and able (because of laissez-faire) to hold
any currency and currency is the only outside asset, world aggregate
savings sum to the value of the world money supply. In the three-
country example used above, world savings are

$$S^{\mathrm{W}}(r(t)) = S^{\mathrm{A}}(r(t)) + S^{\mathrm{B}}(r(t)) + S^{\mathrm{C}}(r(t)),$$

and, for equilibrium,

$$S^{\mathrm{W}}(r(t)) = p^{\mathrm{A}}(t)\mathbf{M}^{\mathrm{W}}(t) = p^{\mathrm{A}}(t)[\mathbf{M}^{\mathrm{A}}(t) + E^{\mathrm{B/A}}\mathbf{M}^{\mathrm{B}}(t) + E^{\mathrm{C/A}}\mathbf{M}^{\mathrm{C}}(t)].$$

For a moment, imagine that there is a world government that can
increase the world money supply and collect seignorage from that
money issue. We can find stationary monetary equilibria for this economy just as we found stationary monetary equilibria for the single-
country case above. The real revenues that this imaginary world government can raise from seignorage, $\mathbf{g}^{\mathrm{W}}$, are equal to

$$\mathbf{g}^{\mathrm{W}} = (1 - r)S^{\mathrm{W}}(r),$$

where r is the (constant) gross interest rate for the stationary, monetary
equilibrium. The gross interest rate, r, is equal to $1/\mu^{\mathrm{W}}$, where μ^{W} is the

gross rate of increase of the world money supply. Given the gross rate of increase in the world money supply, μ^W, the world money supply at time $t + 1$ is

$$\mathbf{M}^W(t + 1) = \mu^W \mathbf{M}^W(t).$$

Plotting the real revenues from seignorage against the gross rate of increase in the world money supply gives a world Bailey curve just like the one in Figure 10.3. There is a maximum amount of seignorage that the imaginary world government can raise; call it max $\mathbf{g}^W$.

We do not have a world government that is attempting to generate seignorage. Instead, we have a number of individual countries, each of whom is attempting to generate real revenues from seignorage. We restrict our discussion to cases where the sum of the seignorage that the countries of the world are attempting to raise is less than max $\mathbf{g}^W$. This restriction keeps us in equilibria in which the desired levels of seignorage can be obtained in stationary monetary equilibria. In our three-country case we restrict the discussion to cases where

$$\mathbf{g}^A + \mathbf{g}^B + \mathbf{g}^C \leq \text{max } \mathbf{g}^W.$$

The following proposition is stated as a two-country case, but it extends in the obvious way to an economy with any finite number of countries, each with their own fiat money.

Proposition 11.3 *Given* $\mathbf{g}^A > 0$ *and* $\mathbf{g}^B > 0$, *if there exists an* $r > 0$, *such that*

$$(1 - r)[S^A(r) + S^B(r)] = \mathbf{g}^A + \mathbf{g}^B,$$

and $S^A(r) + S^B(r) > 0,$

then, for any constant exchange rate, $0 < E < \infty$, *there exists an equilibrium with time paths of the rates of growth of each country's money supply,* $\{\mu^A(t)\}$ *and* $\{\mu^B(t)\}$, *that will raise* $\mathbf{g}^A$ *for the government of country A and* $\mathbf{g}^B$ *for the government of country B.*

We prove this proposition by guessing at a solution and then verifying that solution. We choose the r from the statement of the proposition to be an equilibrium gross interest rate and then verify that a stationary

monetary equilibrium exists that has that gross interest rate and generates the required government revenues. To get an equilibrium, we need
to find the time path of the growth rate of the money supply for each
country, $\{\mu^A(t)\}$ and $\{\mu^B(t)\}$, of $r(t)$, and of $p(t)$ for any feasible set of real
government revenues, $\mathbf{g}^A$ and $\mathbf{g}^B$, and for any exchange rate, E. Let the
r of the statement of the proposition be the gross interest rate where

$$(1 - r)[S^A(r) + S^B(r)] = \mathbf{g}^A + \mathbf{g}^B,$$

for some feasible $\mathbf{g}^A$ and $\mathbf{g}^B$. Choose any E between 0 and ∞. At time 1,
there are money supplies $\mathbf{M}^A(0)$ and $\mathbf{M}^B(0)$ held by the old of generation
0 (the distribution does not matter for this proof, although it matters in
terms of the utility of individual old).

In a stationary, monetary equilibrium at time t, one of the equilibrium
conditions that holds at each date t is

$$S^A(r) + S^B(r) = p^A(t)[\mathbf{M}^A(t) + E\mathbf{M}^B(t)].$$

Because $\mathbf{M}^A(t) = \mu^A(t)\mathbf{M}^A(t - 1)$ and $\mathbf{M}^B(t) = \mu^B(t)\mathbf{M}^B(t - 1)$, that equation can be written as

$$S^A(r) + S^B(r) = p^A(t)[\mu^A(t)\mathbf{M}^A(t - 1) + \mu^B(t)E\mathbf{M}^B(t - 1)].$$
$$(11.4)$$

There are three unknowns in this equation: the price of country A's
money at time 1 and the growth rates of both country A's money supply
and country B's money supply—$p^A(t)$, $\mu^A(t)$, and $\mu^B(t)$, respectively. We
know from the way seignorage works that the real revenues from seignorage for each country are

$$\mathbf{g}^A = p^A(t)[\mu^A(t) - 1]\mathbf{M}^A(t - 1),$$

for country A, and

$$\mathbf{g}^B = p^A(t)[\mu^B(t) - 1]E\mathbf{M}^B(t - 1),$$

for country B. There are two unknowns in each of these equations, the
price of country A's money and the growth rate of country i's money

supply at time t, i = A and B. Each of these equations can be solved for the growth rate of the money supply. These are

$$\mu^A(t) = \frac{\mathbf{g}^A + p^A(t)\,\mathbf{M}^A(t-1)}{p^A(t)\,\mathbf{M}^A(t-1)},$$ (11.5)

and $$\mu^B(t) = \frac{\mathbf{g}^B + p^A(t)\,E\mathbf{M}^B(t-1)}{p^A(t)\,E\mathbf{M}^B(t-1)}.$$ (11.6)

Substituting these growth rates into Equation (11.4) and simplifying gives

$$S^A(r) + S^B(r) = \mathbf{g}^A + \mathbf{g}^B + p^A(t)[\mathbf{M}^A(t-1) + E\mathbf{M}^B(t-1)].$$
(11.7)

From this expression, we get $p^A(t)$. The hypotheses of the proposition imply that $p^A(t) > 0$.

We have one thing left to show—that $p^A(t+1)/p^A(t) = r$. The growth rates for the two monies that we found above must yield a growth rate for the world money supply equal to $1/r$ in order to be consistent with the interest rate that is being used in the aggregate savings functions. This rate of growth of the world money gives the desired rate of change of prices. From the seignorage condition that we used to begin this proof and Equation (11.7), we have that

$$S^A(r) + S^B(r) = \frac{\mathbf{g}^A + \mathbf{g}^B}{(1-r)}$$

$$= \mathbf{g}^A + \mathbf{g}^B + p^A(t)[\mathbf{M}^A(t-1) + E\mathbf{M}^B(t-1)].$$

The two right-most parts of this equation can be rearranged to give

$$\frac{\mathbf{g}^A + \mathbf{g}^B}{1-r} = \frac{p^A(t)[\mathbf{M}^A(t-1) + E\mathbf{M}^B(t-1)]}{r}.$$

Because the left side of this equation equals aggregate savings, and all aggregate savings at time t go into money, we get

$$r p^A(t)[\mathbf{M}^A(t) + E\mathbf{M}^B(t)] = p^A(t)[\mathbf{M}^A(t-1) + E\mathbf{M}^B(t-1)].$$

When we divide both sides of this equation by $p^A(t)$, we see that the world money supply is growing at a rate equal to $1/r$.

EXERCISE 11.2   Consider economy 3, except that we only know that $\mathbf{M}^A(0) = 200$ and $\mathbf{M}^B(0) = 100$. The money supply at other dates is yet to be determined. The two governments wish to raise, in every period $t \geq 1$, revenue by seignorage of $\mathbf{g}^A = 4$ and $\mathbf{g}^B = 3$. What are the first five elements of the time paths of the two monies if the exchange rate at time 1 is $E = 3$?

EXERCISE 11.3   In the economy of Exercise 11.2, what are the first five elements of the time paths of the two monies if the exchange rate at time 1 is $E = 1$?

As an example, consider an economy with two countries, A and B; all of the members of the economy have the endowments and preferences of economy 2 from Chapter 10. The populations are constant at $N^A(t) = 100$ and $N^B(t) = 100$. At time 0, the money supply of country A is $\mathbf{M}^A(0) = 300$ and the money supply of country B is $\mathbf{M}^B(0) = 300$ as well. Country A collects 6 units of the time t good and country B collects 4 units of the time t good from seignorage, $t \leq 1$. The exchange rate at time 1 is 2. We want to find the money growth rates for this economy for the first several periods.

We want to find first the gross interest rate that will generate a total seignorage of 10 (6 + 4) units of the time t good. We use the equation

$$(1 - r)[S^A(r) + S^B(r)] = \mathbf{g}^A + \mathbf{g}^B,$$

and substitute in the appropriate aggregate savings functions to get

$$(1 - r)\left[\left(100 - \frac{50}{r}\right) + \left(100 - \frac{50}{r}\right)\right] = 6 + 4 = 10.$$

There are two r's that solve that equation, $r = 0.885$ and 0.565. That there should be two inflation rates giving this amount of total seignorage should be no surprise. From what we have seen about the Bailey curve, we should expect two inflation rates to achieve the desired seignorage (except for the maximum seignorage level, for which there is a unique rate of inflation). The larger of these interest rates gives an equilibrium that is Pareto superior to the smaller (Why is that?), and that is the one we will use. Using this gross interest rate in the aggregate savings function, we find that aggregate savings for the world are 87 units of the good in each period.

Because we know the growth rate of the world money supply ($\mu^W = 1/r = 1.13$), we can find the price at time 1 of country A's money. At time 0, there were

$$\mathbf{M}^A(0) + E\mathbf{M}^B(0) = 300 + (2)(300) = 900 = \mathbf{M}^W(0).$$

A growth rate of the world money supply of 1.13 means that the world money supply at time 1 is $(900)(1.13) = 1017$. Because world aggregate savings are 87 units of the time t good, we have

$$87 = p^A(1)(1017),$$

or $p^A(1) = .0855.$

Now we use Equations (11.5) and (11.6) to find the growth rates for the two currencies. From Equation (11.5), we find that the growth rate for the fiat money of country A that will give 6 units of the time t good as seignorage is

$$\mu^A(1) = \frac{6 + (.0855)(300)}{(.0855)(300)} = 1.234.$$

$\mathbf{M}^A(1)$ equals $(300)(1.234)$ equals 370.2. For country B, the growth rate that will give 4 units of the time t good as seignorage is

$$\mu^B(1) = \frac{4 + (.0855)(600)}{(.0855)(600)} = 1.078.$$

$\mathbf{M}^B(1)$ equals $(300)(1.078)$ equals 323.4 units of country B's fiat money.

Notice that the time 1 old in country A are consuming (300) $(.0855) = 25.65$ units of the time 1 good. The old in country B are consuming $2(300)(.0855) = 51.3$ units of the time 1 good (within a rounding error). The government of country A consumes 6 units of the time 1 good, and the government of country B consumes 4 units of the time 1 good. Because the young of each country are saving 43.5 units of the time 1 good, there is a net trade deficit for country A of 11.85 $(43.5 - 6 - 25.65)$ units of the time 1 good.

Each young person at time 1 is holding 5.085 units of money measured in terms of country A's fiat money. It is impossible to tell how much of each of the two monies each person is holding, and it does not matter. The exchange rate will remain constant, so one money is as good as the other.

In period 2 the world money supply will grow again by 1.13, so the 1017 units of money from time 1 becomes $\mathbf{M}^W(2) = (1.13) \cdot (1017) = 1149.2$. The price of country A's money at time 2 is

$$87 = p^A(2)(1149.2),$$

or $p^A(2) = .0757.$

The growth rate of country A's money supply that gives 6 units of seignorage is

$$\mu^A(2) = \frac{6 + (.0757)(370.2)}{(.0757)(370.2)} = 1.2141,$$

and $\mathbf{M}^A(2)$ is $(1.2141)(370.2) = 449.46$. For country B, the growth rate is

$$\mu^B(2) = \frac{4 + (.0757)(2)(323.4)}{(.0757)(2)(323.4)} = 1.0817,$$

and $\mathbf{M}^B(2) = (1.0817)(323.4) = 349.8$. Notice that in period 2, country 1 had a net trade deficit of only 1 unit of the time 2 good. The large trade deficit in period 1 was caused by the equalization of the money holdings around the world. What would have been the net trade flow if the exchange rate had been $E = 1$?

In the above example, the growth rate of country A's money is getting smaller as time passes, and the growth rate of country B's money is getting larger as time passes. The ratio of the two money stocks, as measured in terms of country A's money, was

$$\frac{\mathbf{M}^A(0)}{E\mathbf{M}^B(0)} = \frac{300}{(2)(300)} = .5.$$

The ratio of the amount of seignorage the countries are raising is

$$\frac{\mathbf{g}^A}{\mathbf{g}^B} = \frac{6}{4} = 1.5.$$

To gain these seignorage levels, country A increases its money supply faster than country B: $\mu^A(1) = 1.234$ and $\mu^B(1) = 1.078$. By the end of the first period, the ratio of the two monies is

$$\frac{\mathbf{M}^A(1)}{E\mathbf{M}^B(1)} = \frac{370.2}{(2)(323.4)} = .5724.$$

During period 2, country A is still increasing its money supply at a faster rate than country B is, but at a slower rate than in period 1. The growth rates are $\mu^A(2) = 1.2141$ and $\mu^B(2) = 1.0817$. Note that the growth rate of country B's money has increased.

The growth rates of the two monies are approaching each other and, in the limit, will become the same. The ratios of money supplies are also approaching a limit. Measured in terms of either one of the monies, the ratio of the money supplies, $\mathbf{M}^A(t)/[E\mathbf{M}^B(t)]$, are approaching the ratio of the amount of seignorage, $\mathbf{g}^A/\mathbf{g}^B$. We formalize these observations in the following proposition.

Proposition 11.4 *Consider a two-country economy where each country is raising a fixed amount of government revenues by seignorage. In the limit, the growth rate of each money becomes $1/r$, and the ratio of the two monies becomes $\mathbf{M}^A(t)/[E\mathbf{M}^B(t)] = \mathbf{g}^A/\mathbf{g}^B$, as t goes to ∞.*

To prove Proposition 11.4, we show that whenever $\mathbf{M}^A(t)/[E\mathbf{M}^B(t)] < \mathbf{g}^A/\mathbf{g}^B$—that is, whenever $\mathbf{M}^A(t)$ is "too small"—then $\mu^A(t) > \mu^B(t)$. Also, whenever $\mathbf{M}^A(t)/[E\mathbf{M}^B(t)] > \mathbf{g}^A/\mathbf{g}^B$—whenever $\mathbf{M}^A(t)$ is "too big"—then $\mu^A(t) < \mu^B(t)$.

We use Equations (11.5) and (11.6) written for any time t to find the growth rates of the two money supplies. These equations are

$$\mu^A(t) = \frac{\mathbf{g}^A + p^A(t)\mathbf{M}^A(t-1)}{p^A(t)\mathbf{M}^A(t-1)},$$

and $\quad \mu^B(t) = \dfrac{\mathbf{g}^B + p^A(t)E\mathbf{M}^B(t-1)}{p^A(t)E\mathbf{M}^B(t-1)}.$

We find the ratio of the growth rates, $\mu^A(t)/\mu^B(t)$, by dividing the first of the above equations by the second and dividing out the $p^A(t)$ that is in the denominator of both of them. Some rearranging yields

$$\frac{\mu^A(t)}{\mu^B(t)} = \frac{\dfrac{\mathbf{g}^A}{\mathbf{M}^A(t-1)} + p^A(t)}{\dfrac{\mathbf{g}^B}{E\mathbf{M}^B(t-1)} + p^A(t)}.$$

If $\mathbf{M}^A(t-1)/[E\mathbf{M}^B(t-1)] < \mathbf{g}^A/\mathbf{g}^B$, then

$$\frac{\mathbf{g}^A}{\mathbf{M}^A(t-1)} > \frac{\mathbf{g}^B}{E\mathbf{M}^B(t-1)},$$

and $\mu^A(t)$ is greater than $\mu^B(t)$. If $\mathbf{M}^A(t-1)/[E\mathbf{M}^B(t-1)] > \mathbf{g}^A/\mathbf{g}^B$, then

$$\frac{\mathbf{g}^A}{\mathbf{M}^A(t-1)} < \frac{\mathbf{g}^B}{E\mathbf{M}^B(t-1)},$$

and $\mu^B(t)$ is greater than $\mu^A(t)$. If $\mathbf{M}^A(t)/[E\mathbf{M}^B(t)] = \mathbf{g}^A/\mathbf{g}^B$, then the growth rates of the two monies are the same; and, because the growth rate of the world money supply is $1/r$, each of them must equal $1/r$. The dynamics drive the money supplies toward a ratio equal to the ratio of the real revenues from seignorage.

Portfolio Autarky Regimes

In a portfolio autarky regime, each country is completely independent from other countries. The price level in each country is determined as if that country were the only country in the world. The rates of change of the price levels and the amount of seignorage that a government can raise is determined by a one-economy model for each of the countries.

Individual h of country k (k = A or B) of generation t faces the budget constraints

$$c_t^{kh}(t) = \omega_t^{kh}(t) - \ell^{kh}(t) - p^k(t)m^{kh}(t)$$

and $$c_t^{kh}(t + 1) = \omega_t^{kh}(t + 1) + r^k(t)\ell^{kh}(t) + p^k(t + 1)m^{kh}(t),$$

because the portfolio autarky rules limit this individual to holding only own country's assets between periods. Combining these two budget constraints by eliminating $\ell^{kh}(t)$, we get the single budget constraint

$$c_t^{kh}(t) + \frac{c_t^{kh}(t + 1)}{r(t)} = \omega_t^{kh}(t) + \frac{\omega_t^{kh}(t + 1)}{r(t)}$$

$$- m^{kh}(t)\left[p^k(t) - \frac{p^k(t + 1)}{r^k(t)}\right].$$

The usual arbitrage condition implies that

$$r^k(t) = \frac{p^k(t + 1)}{p^k(t)},$$

and that the second line of the single budget constraint equals 0. Summing the single budget constraint over $N^k(t)$, we get

$$\sum_{h=1}^{N^k(t)} c_t^{kh}(t) + \frac{\displaystyle\sum_{h=1}^{N^k(t)} c_t^{kh}(t + 1)}{r(t)} = \sum_{h=1}^{N^k(t)} \omega_t^{kh}(t) + \frac{\displaystyle\sum_{h=1}^{N^k(t)} \omega_t^{kh}(t + 1)}{r(t)}.$$

We sum the budget constraints of the old at date $t + 1$ (the members of generation t) and subtract that from the above equation to get

$$\sum_{h=1}^{N^k(t)} \omega_t^{kh}(t) - \sum_{h=1}^{N^k(t)} c_t^{kh}(t) = \sum_{h=1}^{N^k(t)} \ell^{kh}(t) + p^k(t) \sum_{h=1}^{N^k(t)} m^{kh}(t). \tag{11.8}$$

Because portfolio autarky requires that private borrowing and lending only take place between citizens of the same country,

$$\sum_{h=1}^{N^k(t)} \ell^{kh}(t) = 0.$$

The left side of Equation (11.8) equals aggregate savings, $S^k(r^k(t))$, so Equation (11.8) becomes

$$S^k(r^k(t)) = p^k(t)\,\mathbf{M}^k(t).$$

The equilibrium conditions in each country k = A and B are

$$S^k(r^k(t)) = p^k(t)\,\mathbf{M}^k(t)$$

and $$r^k(t) = \frac{p^k(t+1)}{p^k(t)}.$$

The arbitrage condition in the international goods market (purchasing power parity) implies that the exchange rate is determined by

$$E(t) = \frac{p^B(t)}{p^A(t)}.$$

The time path of the exchange rate is determined by the (separate) time paths of the price of money in terms of goods in each of the two countries. In a portfolio autarky regime, we first solve for the equilibrium paths of prices in each country and then use the above equation to find the equilibrium time path of exchange rates.

EXERCISE 11.4 Consider the economy of Exercise 11.2, except the exchange rate at time 1 is not given. What is that exchange rate at time 1 if the world is in a portfolio autarky regime? Describe the path of the exchange rate for three more periods.

Reprise

Fiat monies are not like other goods, and one should not expect markets to determine the relative prices of fiat monies in a laissez-faire regime. The constancy through time and the indeterminacy result on exchange rates between fiat monies is based on the assumption that there is no government intervention in the foreign exchange markets or on the absence of legal restrictions on asset holdings. This theory suggests that we look to such intervention and restrictions to explain the observed behavior of foreign exchange markets. This conclusion is especially true if we wish to explain the observed differences in rates of return that have occurred in Latin American countries in much of the 1980s. In these countries, both the local currency and the U.S. dollar were held as assets although the gross real rate of return on the local currency was very small (as low as 0.5 percent a year) and the gross real rate of return on the U.S. dollar was close to 1.

The observation that the exchange rate under the portfolio autarky is determined by the purchasing power parity (goods arbitrage) condition makes some people say that purchasing power parity is a theory of exchange rate determination. However, purchasing power parity held under each of the regimes, and there were very different implications under the two regimes as to how the exchange rate would be determined. Given these differences, purchasing power parity is not a complete theory of exchange rates.

CHAPTER 12

Legal Restrictions and Monetary Policy

Every government imposes some legal restrictions on the asset holdings of its citizens. These restrictions come in many forms. The portfolio autarky regime we discussed in the last chapter is an example of just such a legal restriction. There, citizens were legally permitted to use only their own country's fiat money. But there are many other restrictions that governments impose on their citizens. The rationale for these restrictions is to increase the use of the domestic fiat money or to increase the seignorage that can be raised.

Banking regulations, rules for stock markets, and mandated interest rates are also examples of legal restrictions. In most countries, banks operate under a wide range of rules. They often face limits on the interest rates they can pay on demand deposits. They are required to hold reserves or to purchase government bonds or to do both. They are often prohibited from having accounts in foreign fiat monies. They face restrictions on the type of loans they can make and on the interest rates they can charge. Although it may not often be the case that all of these examples occur in any one country, all countries impose at least some of these restrictions. Because a large percentage of individuals' assets are held in banks, restrictions on the operations of banks impose restrictions on the asset portfolios that individuals can hold.

Legal tender laws are one of the milder forms of legal restrictions. Generally speaking, a legal tender law says that the court system of the country will enforce contracts that are written in terms of the national currency. In particular, tax obligations of the citizens to the state can always be paid in the national currency. In his *Travels*, Marco Polo reports that in China under Genghis Khan, failure to accept the government's fiat money was punishable by death. This rule is an example of an unusually harsh legal tender law.

In economies in which the government is attempting to generate revenues via seignorage, legal restrictions on the use of other countries' currencies or on the writing of contracts denominated in other countries' currencies are common. These restrictions are intended to force the use of the local currency. The higher the inflation, the more the citizens attempt to economize on the use of the local currency. Various legal restrictions are imposed to prevent the substitution of other assets for money.

In this chapter we examine the effects of three kinds of legal restrictions on the asset choices that people can make. The first is a simple credit control that places a maximum on the amount that each person can borrow. The second is a restriction on the form that positive savings can take: a fraction of any such savings must be in the form of fiat money. This restriction is an attempt to mimic reserve requirements. The third restriction is one that prevents individual savers from sharing large denomination bonds issued by the government. This restriction is meant to mimic restrictions on private intermediation.

In all three cases the restrictions affect the government's ability to get command over resources through seignorage. The second and third restrictions also can give rise to equilibria in which the return on fiat money is less than the return on other assets. In particular, government bonds and fiat money have different returns. These different returns, in turn, give rise to a financing or portfolio choice for the government. It matters what portion of a given deficit is financed by additions to the stock of fiat money and what portion is financed by additional government borrowing. Choices concerning the stock of fiat money and the stock of government bonds can be thought of as choices of monetary policy, so the second and third restrictions lead us to discussions of monetary policy.

We restrict the discussion in this chapter to economies where the available assets are private borrowing or lending, fiat money, and, in some cases, government bonds. There is neither storage nor land. We also restrict our analysis to economies in which the environment is stationary, although we allow within-generation differences in endowments for the discussion of the first two restrictions. We focus exclusively on stationary monetary equilibria.

Consumption Choice under Credit Controls

In this section we allow the government to impose credit controls on the members of the economy. These *credit controls* place an upper bound on the amount of real borrowing that any member of the economy may undertake. For some members of the economy, these controls will not be directly binding (on those who wish to lend or on those who wish to borrow less than the borrowing ceiling, for example). On others, these restrictions may be binding. Those who might wish to borrow more than the limit when they face certain gross interest rates will find the credit controls binding. We call the upper bound on private borrowing imposed on individual h of generation t $x^h(t)$.

We restrict our discussion to economies with private borrowing and lending and fiat money. Individuals in an economy with credit controls of the type mentioned above face the budget constraints

$$c_t^h(t) = \omega_t^h(t) - \ell^h(t) - p(t) m^h(t),$$

when young, and

$$c_t^h(t + 1) = \omega_t^h(t + 1) + r(t) \ell^h(t) + p(t + 1) m^h(t),$$

when old. The credit controls show up as the restriction

$$c_t^h(t) - \omega_t^h(t) \le x^h(t),$$

that is, consumption when young cannot exceed endowment by more than the upper bound on net private borrowing. A budget line incorporating these three constraints is shown in Figure 12.1. The dashed line in the figure indicates the portion of our normal budget constraint that is eliminated by the borrowing restriction. The shaded area is the budget set. The distance $x^h(t)$ is the maximum amount of borrowing that this individual is allowed to undertake.

Combining the two budget constraints by eliminating $\ell^h(t)$, we get the single constraint

$$c_t^h(t) + \frac{c_t^h(t + 1)}{r(t)} = \omega_t^h(t) + \frac{\omega_t^h(t + 1)}{r(t)}$$

$$- m^h(t) \left[p(t) - \frac{p(t + 1)}{r(t)} \right].$$

The second line of this budget constraint gives us the arbitrage (present value) condition

$$r(t) = \frac{p(t + 1)}{p(t)}.$$

As usual, we define savings as

$$s_t^h(t) = \omega_t^h(t) - c_t^h(t),$$

and, given a utility function for each individual, we get a savings function

$$s_t^h(t) = s_t^h(r(t)).$$

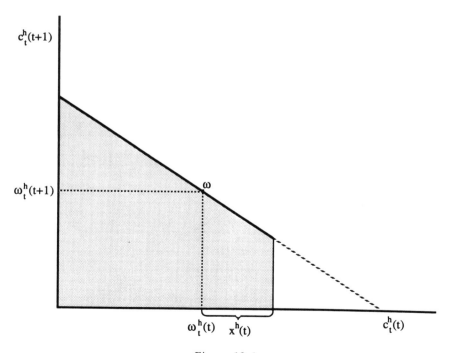

Figure 12.1

The credit controls impose the restriction

$$s_t^h(t) \geq -x^h(t),$$

so we can indicate this restriction by a *constrained individual savings function* of

$$\bar{s}_t^h(r(t), x^h(t)) = \max\,[s_t^h(r(t)), \, -x^h(t)],$$

where $\max[\cdot, \cdot]$ chooses the larger of $s_t^h(r(t))$ or $-x^h(t)$ for each $r(t)$. The constrained individual savings function has as variables both the gross interest rate and the credit bound. Changes in either of these variables could change the amount of borrowing an individual is able to undertake.

Figure 12.2 illustrates a case where the credit controls are binding,

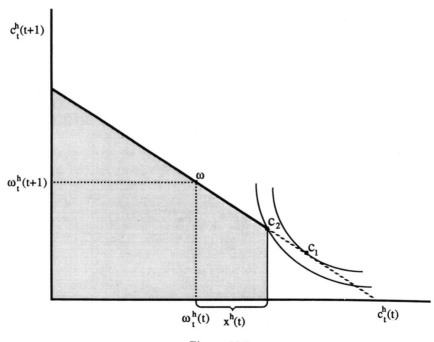

Figure 12.2

and Figure 12.3 illustrates a case where they are not. An individual whose preferences are those given in Figure 12.2 and who faced no credit restrictions would choose to consume at point c_1 when facing gross interest rate $r(t)$. To reach this consumption point requires time t borrowing of $c_1(t) - \omega_t^h(t)$, which is greater than allowed by the credit controls. Given the credit controls, the highest indifference curve is reached at point c_2, where time t borrowing exactly equals the credit limit. Notice that the indifference curve at point c_2 is not tangent to the $r(t)$ budget line but just touches the constrained (shaded) budget set. Given the gross interest rate, $r(t)$, and the credit controls, $x^h(t)$, and the preferences illustrated in Figure 12.3, this individual is not restricted by these credit controls. The individual illustrated in the figure is borrowing but does not wish to borrow so much that he encounters the credit constraint. With a smaller borrowing constraint, this individual could also find the credit controls binding.

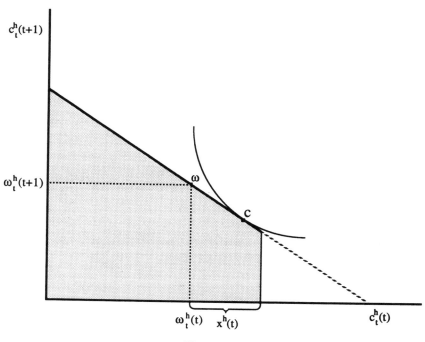

Figure 12.3

EXERCISE 12.1   For $r(t)$ equals 2, 1, and ½, find the savings of an individual with an endowment of $[1, 2]$ and a utility function of

$$u_t^h = c_t^h(t) c_t^h(t + 1),$$

but who faces credit controls of $x^h(t) = .4$. What happens to the savings function if the credit controls are changed to $x^h(t) = .2$? For the same three interest rates, find the savings of an individual with the same utility function and the same credit controls as above but with an endowment of $[2, 1]$.

The graphical description of the borrowing constraint in Figure 12.2 and the results of Exercise 12.1 demonstrate an important characteristic of the function $\bar{s}_t^h(r(t), x^h(t))$. This function is nonincreasing in $x^h(t)$ and can be decreasing in that variable. If, for some $r(t)$, the credit controls are constraining borrowing, then a decrease in $x^h(t)$ will decrease borrowing (which is an increase in savings). In this case $\bar{s}_t^h(r(t), x^h(t))$ increases as $x^h(t)$ decreases. When the constraint is not binding, it is possible that decreases in the constraint will eventually make it binding (as in the situation illustrated in Figure 12.3). If an individual is a lender at some $r(t)$, then changes in the credit controls impose no direct constraint on this individual's behavior because they only restrict the borrowers. However, the change in the credit controls may change the equilibrium gross interest rate that this individual faces by changing the behavior of some of the borrowers in the economy.

At any fixed $r(t)$, individual savings will either be unchanged by a decrease in the $x^h(t)$ or will increase as the credit controls limit the amount of borrowing the individual can undertake.

Equilibrium Conditions under Credit Controls

Consider an economy in which each generation is identical but individuals within each generation may differ. The constant population equals N. We impose the same credit controls on all members of each generation t, so $x^h(t) = x(t)$. We find the equilibrium conditions for this economy in the usual way. Taking the feasibility constraints at date t and subtracting the budget constraint of the old at that date leaves us with

$$\sum_{h=1}^{N} \omega_t^h(t) - \sum_{h=1}^{N} c_t^h(t) = p(t)M(t).$$

We can also get this result by summing the budget constraints of the young at each date t. Given the definition of savings, we can write this sum as

$$\sum_{h=1}^{N} \bar{s}_t^h(r(t), x(t)) = p(t)M(t).$$

Define a *constrained aggregate savings function* at date t as the sum of all the constrained individual savings functions at that date. Because all the members of that generation face the same credit bound, we can write that constrained aggregate savings function as

$$\bar{S}(r(t), x(t)) = \sum_{h=1}^{N} \bar{s}_t^h(r(t), x(t)).$$

All of the individual constrained savings functions, $\bar{s}_t^h(r(t), x(t))$, are non-increasing in $x(t)$, so the aggregate constrained savings function is also nonincreasing in $x(t)$. In those cases where $x(t)$ is binding for some individuals, a reduction in $x(t)$ increases the constrained savings of those individuals—because reduced borrowing is increased savings—and subsequently increases aggregate constrained savings.

From above, we have the equilibrium condition

$$\bar{S}(r(t), x(t)) = p(t)M(t).$$

Recall that another equilibrium condition is the present value constraint, so, under perfect foresight,

$$p(t) = \frac{p(t + 1)}{r(t)}.$$

Our third equilibrium condition is the government's budget constraint; and for an economy with no taxes except seignorage and with government expenditures of **g**, this constraint is

$$\mathbf{g} = p(t)[M(t) - M(t - 1)],$$

or $$\mathbf{g} = \left(1 - \frac{1}{\mu}\right) p(t) M(t).$$

To study stationary equilibria, we set $x(t) = x$, for all t. In a stationary monetary equilibrium (from Proposition 10.2), we know that seignorage equals

$$\mathbf{g} = \left(1 - \frac{1}{\mu}\right) \bar{S}\left(\frac{1}{\mu}, x\right).$$

We wish to study different stationary equilibria where x has different values and to compare the seignorage that is raised by a given inflation rate. As mentioned above, the aggregate constrained savings function is nonincreasing in x and is decreasing in x—decreases as x increases—when the credit controls are strictly binding for some individuals. At any rate of increase of the money supply, μ, a reduction in x either leaves aggregate savings unchanged or increases it. If aggregate savings increase, then the seignorage that the government will gain from increasing the money supply at rate μ will also increase.

EXERCISE 12.2 Consider an economy with $N(t) = 30$. All members of this economy have the utility function of Exercise 12.1. Twenty of each generation have endowments of $[2, 1]$ and 10 have endowments of $[1, 2]$. The money supply is initially distributed so that $m^h(0) = 10$ for all members of generation 0 and $\mu = 1$ for all t. Find the price of money in a stationary monetary equilibrium when there are no credit controls. Find the price of money in a stationary equilibrium when $x = .4$. Compare the utilities of the lenders, the borrowers, and the old at time 1 in these two equilibria.

EXERCISE 12.3 Consider the economy of Exercise 12.2. Let $\mu = 1.25$ for all t. How much seignorage does the government raise with and without credit controls? Compare the utilities of the lenders, the borrowers, and the old at time 1 in these two equilibria.

Credit Controls in an Example Economy

Consider an economy with $N(t) = 100$. The utility function for all individuals is

$$u_t^h = c_t^h(t) c_t^h(t + 1),$$

and endowments are

$$\omega_t^h = \begin{cases} [3, 1], & \text{for } h \text{ even,} \\ [1, 2], & \text{for } h \text{ odd.} \end{cases}$$

The members of generation 0 begin with 10 units of fiat money each at date 1. We will consider only stationary equilibria in this economy with a stationary environment, so we can leave out time subscripts from the savings functions.

The unconstrained savings functions for these individuals are

$$s^{even} = \frac{3}{2} - \frac{1}{2r(t)}$$

and

$$s^{odd} = \frac{1}{2} - \frac{1}{r(t)}.$$

The solid lines in Figure 12.4 show the graphs of these savings functions. The upper savings function is for the even-named individuals and the lower one is for the odd-named individuals. For the range of gross interest rates illustrated in the figure, the odd are borrowers. Below the dashed line is the portion of the savings function of the odd-named individuals that is out of bounds when credit controls of $x(t) = .6$ are imposed. At gross interest rates above .90909, the credit controls do not restrict the borrowing decisions of the odd. At gross interest rates below that, the odd would wish to borrow more than the credit controls and are constrained by them. Notice that these credit controls do not restrict the even until the interest rate is very low. Below the dotted line is the portion of the savings function of the odd that is out of bounds when credit controls of $x(t) = .3$ are imposed. The largest gross interest rate where these credit controls bind the odd is $r(t) = 1.25$. Again, for the even, the restriction is not binding until the interest rate is very small.

The aggregate unconstrained savings function is

$$S(r(t)) = 100 - \frac{75}{r(t)}.$$

Using Proposition 10.2, we find that the function for seignorage is

$$g = \left(1 - \frac{1}{\mu}\right)[100 - 75\mu],$$

and the unconstrained Bailey curve for this economy is shown as the solid line in Figure 12.5.

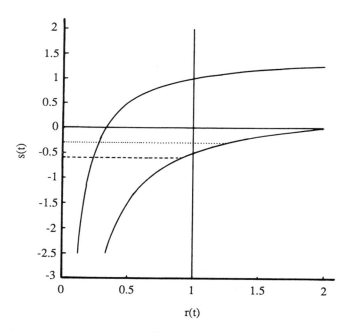

Figure 12.4

If the government imposes credit controls of $x(t) = .6$, we can see from Figure 12.4 that these controls will not be binding until the gross interest rate is .90909, or the rate of growth of the money supply, μ, equals 1.1, because $r(t) = .90909 = 1/\mu = 1/1.1$. For μ between 1 and 1.1, the Bailey curve is the same as the unconstrained curve because the aggregate savings function is the same as that in the unconstrained case. For μ greater than 1.1, the credit controls are binding for the odd, and the aggregate savings function is

$$\overline{S}(r(t), .6) = 50\left[1 - \frac{1}{2r(t)}\right] + 50[-.6],$$

and the seignorage equation is

$$\mathbf{g}_{x(t) = .6} = \left(1 - \frac{1}{\mu}\right)\left\{50\left[1 - \frac{\mu}{2}\right] - 30\right\}.$$

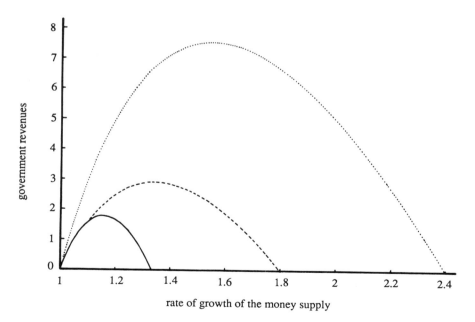

Figure 12.5

The Bailey curve for the economy under a credit control of $x(t) = .6$ is shown in Figure 12.5 as the dashed line. It diverges from the no-credit-controls Bailey curve where the constraint begins to bind on the odd borrowers.

When the credit controls are reduced to .3, they are binding for the odd even when there is not inflation. The price of money with these credit controls is higher than without when $\mu = 1$. For $\mu \geq 1$, the aggregate savings function is

$$\overline{S}(r(t), .3) = 50\left[1 - \frac{1}{2r(t)}\right] + 50[-.3],$$

and the seignorage equation is

$$g_{x(t) = .3} = \left(1 - \frac{1}{\mu}\right)\left\{50\left[1 - \frac{\mu}{2}\right] - 15\right\}.$$

The Bailey curve for the economy under a credit control of $x(t) = .3$ is the dotted line in Figure 12.5. Because the credit controls hold at $\mu = 1$, the Bailey curve under aggregate savings is higher at any positive rate of inflation than it is without the controls; and, accordingly, seignorage is also higher.

It should not be surprising to find that when governments decide to use seignorage to raise revenues, they also tend to impose controls on credit. During the high inflation periods of the 1980s, the Argentine government intervened in the banking system and placed controls on the amount of loans that the system could make. The Central Bank of Argentina was issuing regulations to the private banking system so fast that the larger banks had a staff of two or three economists whose job it was solely to read and interpret the regulations that were issued each day.

EXERCISE 12.4   For the economy in Exercise 12.2, construct the Bailey curve with (a) no credit controls; (b) $x(t) = .4$; and (c) $x(t) = .2$.

Monetary Policy

Central banks direct monetary policy. Sometimes this monetary policy involves changing the rules under which banks operate. In many other cases these monetary policies take the form of changes in the mix of fiat money and government bonds in the economy. The government bonds that the central banks buy and sell in open market operations are promises to pay a fixed quantity of the government's own fiat money at some specified time in the future. These bonds are different from the government bonds we discussed in earlier chapters. Our earlier government bonds promised to pay a fixed quantity of the time $t + n$ good once period $t + n$ arrived. Now we want to consider only government bonds that promise to pay in fiat money at some time period $t + n$.

In the model we have been using, it is far from clear why changes in the mix of fiat money and bonds (pieces of paper that promise to pay a fixed quantity of this same fiat money in the future) should have any effects on the economy at all. In the previous chapter, with economies where we had no restrictions on which assets and how much of any asset an individual could hold, we saw that fiat money must give the same rate of return as any other asset if all assets are to have strictly positive prices. If fiat money and bonds give the same rate of return, how are they different and how can changing one for the other have any real effects (on savings or consumption, for example)? When the rates of return are the same, the aggregate amount of bonds and of fiat money determine the price level. Changes in the mix of bonds and fiat money do not matter if the aggregate amount is kept unchanged. The rates of return on fiat money and bonds must be different for changes in the mix to have real effects.

The equality of the rates of returns on all assets in economies without restrictions suggests that some kind of restrictions must be in effect in order to get the differences in rates of returns between fiat money and government bonds that we observe in real economies. We look to actual economies for hints of the relative importance of various restrictions. First we observe that fiat money issue is a monopoly of the central government in most economies. Most governments use considerable real resources while attempting to maintain this monopoly by discovering and punishing counterfeiting. A second important restriction is in the denominations the governments choose for fiat money and bonds. Generally, bonds come in large denominations (in the United States the smallest transferable government bond has a face value of $10,000). When smaller denomination government bonds are issued, these bonds usually carry restrictions on the right to transfer them to other individuals.

In the United States two perfectly secure assets that give rates of return that are higher than that given by fiat money are U.S. savings bonds, which are available in small denominations, and U.S. Treasury bills, which are large-denomination, short-term government bonds. These assets do not completely dominate fiat money. They contain important characteristics (restrictions) that make them different from fiat money.

United States savings bonds come in fairly small denominations. In some series they have been as small as $20. However, savings bonds come with a restriction on negotiability. They cannot be traded among individuals. If one wished to exchange a savings bond for fiat money before its maturity date (the date it promises to pay off), one can only exchange it with the U.S. government and pay a substantial penalty for doing so. An individual is legally restricted from transferring a savings bond to another individual.

Treasury bills or other negotiable U.S. government bonds come in denominations of $10,000 or larger. Until September 1, 1977, U.S. Treasury bills were bearer securities. A *bearer security* is one that is owned by whoever has actual possession of the paper on which the security is written. Now the U.S. government keeps records of who owns its Treasury bills, but they are transferable by merely notifying the appropriate authorities. Treasury bills can be transferred from one individual to another quite easily, although not quite as easily as fiat money. However, the large denominations of Treasury bills make them substantially different from fiat money because individuals infrequently make such large transfers. In other words, Treasury bills are too big for most day-to-day transactions.

The government's monopoly on the production of fiat money prevents *private intermediation* of other, larger denomination government assets. Suppose that Treasury bills pay a positive interest rate and fiat money does not. If individuals or organizations of individuals (like a bank) could purchase U.S. Treasury bills and issue their own currency for the face value of the Treasury bill, this private currency would dominate the government's fiat money. The private groups could offer an interest rate on their currency larger than the interest rate on the government's fiat money and still profit by the even higher interest rate they are paid on the Treasury bills. Such private intermediation would drive down the interest rate on Treasury bills until the interest differential between the government's fiat money and Treasury bills was equal to the real cost that the banks (or individuals) face in doing the intermediation. This behavior is a result of the arbitrage opportunities that exist across the two assets. Checking accounts (*demand deposits*) in banks can work like private fiat money. The bank can take in deposits, use them to purchase U.S. Treasury bills (for example), and use the interest paid on the bonds to offer positive nominal interest rates on these deposits.

We proceed in this section to get differential rates of return on money and other assets by adding some restrictions on the holdings of those other assets. The first restriction we incorporate into the model is a requirement that, whenever an individual chooses to hold government bonds or to engage in private lending, this individual must also hold a proportional quantity of fiat money. This reserve requirement can generate a positive nominal interest rate on bonds. With this model, monetary policy can have different effects on the welfare of borrowers and lenders. In the second case, we introduce indivisible government bonds that are so large that the amount of fiat money that an individual chooses to hold is not enough to purchase one bond. Intermediation (dividing up the bonds between several individuals) is prohibited, and the resulting equilibria can have differential interest rates on bonds and fiat money.

The Government

For the rest of this chapter, we assume that the government has two options for raising revenue. It can issue fiat money or it can borrow. The time path of government expenditures is given exogenously by the sequence $\{g(t)\}$. This time path is independent of the way the government chooses to finance the expenditures. For that to be the case, expenditures cannot include the interest payments that the government makes if it has chosen to borrow in some period, because borrowing is a financing method. Because we have restricted the financing of government expenditures to money creation or borrowing, it is better to think of the sequence $\{g(t)\}$ as the sequence of government deficits, that is, the difference between total government expenditures and the amount of taxes the government has raised.

Given that the government uses money creation or borrowing to finance its deficit, the government budget constraint in each period is

$$g(t) = p(t)[M(t) - M(t - 1)] + p(t)[P(t)B(t + 1) - B(t)],$$

where $M(t)$ is the amount of money in the economy at the end of period t, $B(t)$ is the number of nominally denominated government bonds that come due at time t, and $P(t)$ is the time t price of bonds in terms of fiat money. As we mentioned above, these bonds are different from the government bonds that we used earlier. In Chapter 3, the bonds, $B(t)$, were bonds that were offered at date $t - 1$ and promised to pay 1 unit of the time t good when they came due. The bonds in this government budget constraint are promises to pay 1 unit of fiat money at time t. Because $P(t)$ is the price of these bonds in terms of fiat money, $p(t + 1)/p(t)P(t)$ is the gross interest rate on holding bonds from period t to period $t + 1$. As before, $p(t + 1)/p(t)$ is the gross interest rate on holding fiat money.

The government budget constraint says that, at time t, the government can cover its deficit, $g(t)$, by issuing new fiat money or by issuing additional one-period government bonds. For a given sequence of government deficits, $\{g(t)\}$, there can exist many choices of sequences of $M(t)$ and $B(t)$ that can satisfy the government's budget constraint. We call the choice of one sequence—$\{M(t), B(t)\}$—out of that set of possible sequences a choice of *monetary policy*.

Discussing choices of monetary policy would not make much sense unless (1) both fiat money and government bonds are held in equilibrium and (2) money and bonds offer different rates of returns; in particular, that $P(t) < 1$. If $P(t)$ equals 1, then bonds and money are identical and different paths have no effects on the economy. We are interested in determining the effects of different choices of monetary policy on individual utility, so we need money and bonds to be different, to offer different rates of return. The models we use in the rest of this chapter can generate different rates of return for money and bonds and result in monetary policy choices that can matter.

Individual Choice with Reserve Requirements

We now define the reserve requirement. Generally, reserve requirements in real economies are imposed only on financial intermediaries (such as banks). Private lending, such as the purchase of private bonds, does not normally require reserves. However, a considerable portion of private lending goes through banks. In this model, we impose reserve requirements on all private lending, both to capture the importance of banks (which we do not explicitly model) and to simplify the exposition.

Individuals have available to them private borrowing and lending, government bonds, and fiat money. They also face a reserve requirement. Individuals wishing to lend to either private individuals or to the government are required to hold a quantity of fiat money equal, in real terms, to some fraction of their lending. We are interested in the total lending of individuals, so we denote the total lending of individual h of generation t as $L^h(t)$, and this amount equals the sum of an individual's private lending and lending to the government:

$$L^h(t) = \ell^h(t) + p(t)P(t)b^h(t + 1),$$

where $b^h(t + 1)$ denotes the number of nominal one-period government bonds held by individual h.

Definition   As a reserve requirement, *we require all lenders to hold a quantity of money with a real value equal to $\Lambda = \lambda/(1 - \lambda)$ times the real value of their lending, whether to private individuals or to the government. We call λ the reserve requirement.*

Under this definition of a reserve requirement, borrowers do not need to hold any reserves and lenders hold money reserves on lending of any type. A general way of writing the reserve requirement is

$$p(t)m^h(t) \geq \Lambda[\max(0, \ell^h(t) + p(t)P(t)b^h(t + 1))]$$
$$\geq \Lambda[\max(0, L^h(t))].$$

The real value of money holdings is Λ times the maximum of $L^h(t)$ or 0. This notation indicates that whenever desired borrowing is positive [when $L^h(t) < 0$], 0 is the maximum of this pair and the individual does not need to hold any money. Given this definition of a reserve requirement, individual h of generation t faces the three budget constraints:

$$c_t^h(t) = \omega_t^h(t) - p(t)m^h(t) - \ell^h(t) - p(t)P(t)b^h(t + 1), \qquad (12.1)$$

$$c_t^h(t + 1) = \omega_t^h(t + 1) + r^m(t)p(t)m^h(t) + r^L(t)\ell^h(t)$$
$$+ r^m(t)p(t)b^h(t + 1), \tag{12.2}$$

and $\quad p(t)m^h(t) \geq \Lambda[\max(0, L^h(t))],$ \hfill (12.3)

where $\Lambda = \lambda/(1 - \lambda)$, $r^m(t) = p(t + 1)/p(t)$ is the gross interest rate on money, and $r^L(t)$ is the gross interest rate on lending. Equations (12.1) and (12.2) are the usual budget constraints, except that the gross interest rates on money and lending can be different. Equation (12.3) is the reserve requirement. The real value of money holdings must be greater than or equal to Λ times the lending, when lending is positive.

We combine the first two budget constraints by eliminating $\ell^h(t)$ and get

$$c_t^h(t) + \frac{c_t^h(t + 1)}{r^L(t)} = \omega_t^h(t) + \frac{\omega_t^h(t + 1)}{r^L(t)}$$

$$- p(t)m^h(t)\left[1 - \frac{r^m(t)}{r^L(t)}\right]$$

$$- p(t)P(t)b^h(t + 1)\left[1 - \frac{r^m(t)}{P(t)r^L(t)}\right]. \tag{12.4}$$

The portion of this equation in the square brackets on the third line must equal 0. The reserve requirements on the holding of bonds or of private borrowing and lending are identical; by our usual arbitrage arguments, we get the usual present value condition on bonds. Private lending and government bonds must pay the same real interest rate. This arbitrage (present value) condition is

$$P(t) = \frac{r^m(t)}{r^L(t)},$$

or, substituting in the definition of $r^m(t)$,

$$r^L(t) = \frac{p(t + 1)}{p(t)P(t)}.$$

The interest rate on private borrowing and lending, $r^L(t)$, equals the real rate of return on government bonds, $p(t + 1)/(p(t)P(t))$.

We now consider the value of the portion of this equation in the square brackets on the second line of Equation (12.4). There are three possibilities: $r^m(t)$ might be greater than, equal to, or less than $r^L(t)$. The first of these three possibilities cannot hold in an equilibrium. If $r^m(t) > r^L(t)$, then everyone would want to borrow an infinite amount at the lower private market interest rate and spend an infinite amount on fiat money. The reserve requirement (Equation 12.3) is not binding and the demands of members of the economy cannot be fulfilled, so this case cannot be an equilibrium.

Consider the case where $r^m(t) = r^L(t)$. Then individuals are indifferent between lending and holding fiat money—both offer the same rate of return. In this case people are willing to hold enough fiat money, so the reserve requirement is not binding. The second line of Equation (12.4) equals 0, and we have our usual linear constraint on consumption. In this case the nominal price of government bonds, $P(t)$, equals 1.

The remaining possibility is for $r^m(t) < r^L(t)$. When this occurs, all individuals want to minimize their holdings of fiat money, but the reserve requirement causes borrowers and lenders to behave differently. Let us consider borrowers and lenders separately. Borrowers, those who choose $c_t^h(t) > \omega_t^h(t)$, are only in the market for private borrowing and lending. Because the interest rate they pay on borrowing is greater than the return they would get if they held fiat money, they would make pure losses if they borrowed and purchased fiat money. These borrowers have $\ell^h(t) < 0$ and, from Equation (12.3), are not required to hold any fiat money. Anyone borrowing is to the right of their endowment point in Figure 12.6 and faces the gross interest rate, $r^L(t)$. The budget line to the right of the endowment point in the figure illustrates the borrower's possibilities.

Lenders get a higher rate of return on private lending and government bonds than on holding fiat money; and, if they could, they would choose to hold no fiat money. For lenders, $L^h(t) = \ell^h(t) + p(t)P(t)b^h(t + 1) > 0$. However, the reserve requirement (Equation 12.3) requires them to also hold some fiat money. Given that the return on fiat money is less than that on lending, the lenders will hold the minimum amount of fiat money that they can. The reserve requirement equation holds at equality for lenders.

Given that an individual lends $L^h(t)$, then the reserve requirement demands that this individual also hold a real value of money equal to $p(t)m^h(t) = \Lambda L^h(t)$. For each $L^h(t)$ of lending that generates a return of

$r^L(t)$, the individuals must also hold $\Lambda L^h(t)$ units of fiat money that generate a rate of return of $r^m(t)$. The budget constraint when young (Equation 12.1) implies that

$$\omega_t^h(t) - c_t^h(t) = \Lambda L^h(t) + L^h(t) = (1 + \Lambda)L^h(t),$$

or $\quad p(t)m^h(t) = \omega_t^h(t) - c_t^h(t) - \dfrac{\omega_t^h(t) - c_t^h(t)}{1 + \Lambda}$

$$= \left[\frac{\Lambda}{1 + \Lambda}\right][\omega_t^h(t) - c_t^h(t)].$$

Recalling that $\Lambda/(1 + \Lambda) = \lambda$ and substituting the last line of the above
expression into the single budget constraint (Equation 12.4), we get

$$c_t^h(t) + \frac{c_t^h(t + 1)}{r^a(t)} = \omega_t^h(t) + \frac{\omega_t^h(t + 1)}{r^a(t)},$$

where $r^a(t) = \lambda r^m(t) + (1 - \lambda)r^L(t)$ is the average interest rate on lending. In Figure 12.6 the budget line to the left of the endowment point

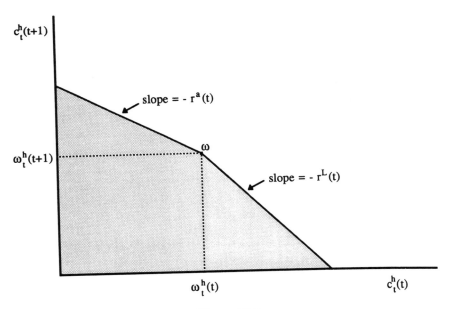

Figure 12.6

(the budget line of the savers) has a slope of $-r^a(t)$, because the relevant interest rate is the average rate of return received by savers.

The kinked budget line in Figure 12.6 with a slope of $-r^L(t)$ to the right of the endowment point and a slope of $-r^a(t)$ to the left of the endowment point describes the constraints that are faced by any individual in this economy. Notice that this concept of a budget line still works when $r^L(t)$ equals $r^m(t)$; in that case, however, it is a straight line, without the kink.

Let $s^h(r^a(t), r^L(t))$ be the savings function for an individual facing the budget constraints of the type described in Figure 12.6. Depending on the preferences of the individual and the location of the endowment point, an individual will be either a lender or a borrower for a given pair of interest rates, $r^a(t)$ and $r^L(t)$. Summing up the individual savings functions for all members of generation t, we get an aggregate savings function,

$$S(r^a(t), r^L(t)) = \sum_{h=1}^{N(t)} s^h(r^a(t), r^L(t)).$$

The kinked budget line is important for illustrating our claim that different choices of monetary policy can have different effects on borrowers and lenders. If, for a given sequence of government deficits, different choices of monetary policy result in different sets of interest rates for borrowers and lenders, then choices of monetary policies can make some individuals better off and others worse off.

Equilibrium with Reserve Requirements and No Government Bonds

Given the government budget constraints and the behavior of individuals that we found above, we can define a competitive equilibrium the usual way. The most important difference from earlier definitions of equilibrium is the addition of the reserve requirement.

Definition *Given* λ, $M(0) > 0$, $B(0)$, *and sequences for* $g(t)$, *an equilibrium consists of sequences of* $p(t)$, $r^m(t)$, $r^L(t)$, $r^a(t)$, $M(t)$, *and* $B(t)$ *that for all* $t \geq 1$ *satisfy*

$$g(t) = p(t)(M(t) - M(t - 1)) + p(t)(P(t)B(t + 1) - B(t)), \quad (12.5)$$

$$S(r^{a}(t), r^{L}(t)) = p(t)M(t) + p(t)P(t)B(t + 1), \tag{12.6}$$

$$r^{a}(t) = \lambda r^{m}(t) + (1 - \lambda)r^{L}(t), \tag{12.7}$$

$$r^{m}(t) = \frac{p(t + 1)}{p(t)}, \tag{12.8}$$

$$r^{L}(t) \geq r^{m}(t), \tag{12.9}$$

$$p(t)M(t) \geq \lambda \sum_{h=1}^{N(t)} \max[0, s^{h}(r^{a}(t), r^{L}(t))], \tag{12.10}$$

with at least one of Equations (12.9) and (12.10) holding with equality.

Equation (12.5) is the cash-flow constraint of the government, which we discussed earlier. Equation (12.6) equates aggregate savings to the assets supplied by the government (in this case, fiat money and government bonds). Equation (12.7) defines the average interest rate, $r^{a}(t)$. Equation (12.8) defines the return on money in an economy with perfect foresight. Equation (12.9) is the condition on interest rates on loans we derived earlier, and Equation (12.10) is the reserve requirement. The proviso that at least one of Equations (12.9) and (12.10) holds with equality can be explained as follows. If the value of the money supply is strictly greater than the amount required for reserves, individuals are choosing to hold additional fiat money as savings. Individuals will only choose to do this when the gross interest rate on fiat money is the same as the gross interest rate on lending. If the gross interest rate on lending is higher than the gross interest rate on fiat money, then any, nonrequired, money holdings is not utility maximizing (because it would be strictly inside the budget constraint). When Equation (12.9) is a strict inequality, Equation (12.10) holds at equality.

We now restrict our attention to stationary equilibria. A stationary equilibrium requires that the government run the same deficit each period; so we set $g(t) = \mathbf{g} \geq 0$. As usual, a stationary equilibrium also requires that the gross interest rates be the same for all time $t \geq 1$. To indicate that we are dealing only with stationary equilibria, we drop the time notation from the three gross interest rates, r^{m}, r^{L}, and r^{a}.

We wish to distinguish between those equilibria in which the reserve requirement is binding and those in which it is not. The word *binding* is used to refer to situations in which the entire money supply is being held in order to fulfill the reserve requirement. This case is so named because it leads people to do something different from what they would do in its absence. In any binding equilibrium, Equation (12.10) holds at equality, so the real value of fiat money exactly equals the amount required for reserves. In a nonbinding equilibrium, fiat money is held as an asset beyond the amount required for reserves.

Definition   A binding (stationary) equilibrium *is a stationary equilibrium in which $r^L > r^m$.*

Definition   A nonbinding (stationary) equilibrium *is a stationary equilibrium in which $r^L = r^m$.*

Given the definitions of binding and nonbinding stationary equilibria, we wish to define the conditions required for a stationary equilibrium.

Definition   *Given* λ, $M(0) > 0$, $B(0)$, *and* **g**, *a* stationary equilibrium *consists of values for* r^m, r^L, r^a, v, w, *and the sequence* $\{p(t)\}$ *that satisfy*

$$g = (1 - r^m)v + (1 - r^L)w, \tag{12.11}$$

$$S(r^a, r^L) = v + w, \tag{12.12}$$

$$r^a = \lambda r^m + (1 - \lambda)r^L, \tag{12.13}$$

$$r^m = \frac{p(t + 1)}{p(t)}, \tag{12.14}$$

$$r^L \geq r^m, \tag{12.15}$$

$$v \geq \lambda \sum_{h=1}^{N(t)} \max[0, s^h(r^a, r^L)], \tag{12.16}$$

$$g = S(r^a, r^L) - p(1)(M(0) + B(1)), \tag{12.17}$$

where either (12.15) or (12.16) must hold with equality, where v *denotes a constant real value of the fiat money,* $p(t)M(t)$*; and* w *denotes a constant real value of government bonds,* $p(t)P(t)B(t + 1)$*.*

Each of the above equations is a direct, stationary-state version of the matching equation in the general definition of a competitive equilibrium, except for Equation (12.17). This last equation determines the initial price level, $p(1)$, from the initial stocks of money and government bonds. This equation is solved after the solution to the rest of the stationary equilibrium is found.

In general, monetary policy is a choice of a time path for both fiat money and government bonds. In a stationary equilibrium, to specify a monetary policy, we only need to specify a ratio between money and bonds, which we will call m. So

$$m = M(t)/B(t + 1).$$

In a stationary binding equilibrium the ratio of bonds to money must be a constant, because the ratios of w and v and r^m and r^L must be constant. The ratio v/w equals

$$\frac{p(t)M(t)}{p(t)P(t)B(t + 1)} = \frac{M(t)}{P(t)B(t + 1)},$$

and the ratio r^m/r^L equals

$$\frac{\dfrac{p(t + 1)}{p(t)}}{\dfrac{p(t + 1)}{p(t)P(t)}} = P(t).$$

But $P(t)$ is a constant, so m must equal $M(t)/B(t + 1)$. In a nonbinding equilibrium, the ratio of money to bonds does not need to be a constant, but nothing is lost by making it so.

An Example of a Binding Stationary Equilibrium

Consider an economy in which all individuals are identical. As we have seen before, this assumption implies that no one can be a borrower. We want to consider equilibria in which both money and government bonds are held and have positive prices. Holding both money and bonds implies that

$$s^h(r^a, r^L) > 0,$$

for all $h = 1$ to N, at the equilibrium r^a and r^L. Given this assumption about savings, Equation (12.16)—from the definition of a stationary equilibrium—becomes

$$v \geq \lambda N s^h(r^a, r^L) = \lambda S(r^a, r^L). \tag{12.18}$$

Because we are interested in an equilibrium in which the reserve requirement is binding, Equation (12.18) holds with equality. Using Equations (12.12) and (12.18) at equality, we get

$$v = \lambda(v + w).$$

Notice that this equation implies that

$$(1 - \lambda)v = \lambda w,$$

or $\quad v = \left(\dfrac{\lambda}{1 - \lambda}\right)w = \Lambda w,$

or $\quad \dfrac{v}{w} = \Lambda. \tag{12.19}$

The ratio of the real value of the money holdings and the real value of government bonds equals Λ when the reserve requirement is binding. Recall that $v = p(t)M(t)$ and $w = p(t)P(t)B(t + 1)$, so the above ratio becomes

$$\frac{v}{w} = \frac{p(t)M(t)}{p(t)P(t)B(t + 1)} = \frac{M(t)}{P(t)B(t + 1)}. \tag{12.20}$$

As an example, suppose that Λ equals $\frac{1}{2}$; so, for every unit of time t good that is lent, .5 unit of time t good must be put into fiat money. Suppose also, that the government chooses a ratio of nominal stocks of money and bonds, $m = M(t)/B(t + 1)$, equal to $\frac{1}{3}$. The nominal money supply equals only ⅓ of the nominal value of the bonds. Using Equations (12.19) and (12.20), we see that

$$\Lambda = \frac{M(t)}{P(t)B(t + 1)}.$$

Substituting into this equation the values the government has chosen for the reserve requirement and for the ratio of money to bonds, we find that the nominal price of bonds is

$$P(t) = \frac{m}{\Lambda} = \frac{1/3}{1/2} = \frac{2}{3}.$$

Because the gross interest rate on money is

$$r^m = \frac{p(t + 1)}{p(t)},$$

and the gross interest on bonds is

$$r^L = \frac{p(t + 1)}{p(t)P(t)},$$

the gross interest rate on bonds can be written as

$$r^L = \frac{r^m}{P(t)},$$

which for this example is

$$r^L = \frac{r^m}{2/3} = 1.5r^m.$$

Bonds offer a nominal interest rate of 50 percent.

We can describe the preceding analysis as follows. The government sets a reserve requirement on bonds that is higher than the ratio of money to bonds that it supplies to the economy. This practice makes money scarce relative to bonds and drives up the price of money (or equivalently, drives down the price of bonds). The price of bonds, in terms of money, drops until the real value of the new bonds at date t is small enough to enable the value of the money to be sufficient to cover the reserve requirement. Because 1 bond pays 1 unit of fiat money in the next period, a lower nominal price for the bonds means a higher gross interest rate on bonds than on money.

EXERCISE 12.5   Find the stationary monetary equilibrium for an economy with 100 identical individuals in each generation, all of whom have an endowment of [2, 1], and utility function of $c_t^h(t)c_t^h(t + 1)$. The reserve requirement $\Lambda = \frac{1}{2}$, and the government chooses a ratio of money to bonds of $m = \frac{1}{3}$. Each member of generation 0 enters time 1 with 1 unit of fiat money and 3 bonds. Government deficit, **g**, equals 0.

EXERCISE 12.6   Find the stationary monetary equilibrium for the economy in Exercise 12.5, except the ratio of money to bonds is $m = \frac{1}{4}$. Each member of generation 0 enters time 1 with 1 unit of fiat money and 4 bonds.

EXERCISE 12.7   Consider an economy with the population, government deficit, money, and bond holdings of the old at time t, and the utility functions of Exercise 12.5, except the even-named individuals have an endowment of [3, 1] and the odd-named individuals have an endowment of [1, 2]. The government imposes a reserve requirement of $\frac{1}{2}$, and the ratio of money to bonds is $m = \frac{1}{2}$. Find the stationary monetary equilibrium for this economy. Compare this equilibrium, in terms of individual utilities, to an economy with no reserve requirement.

A Two-Group Example of a Binding Equilibrium

In the preceding section, all individuals were identical and the only borrower was the government. An economy of identical individuals does not let us examine the claim that monetary policy can have different effects on borrowers and lenders. To examine this claim, we need an economy with equilibria in which some of the members of each generation will wish to borrow and others to lend. Exercise 12.7 illustrated an economy with two groups, borrowers and lenders; but the government deficit was fixed at 0. Another aspect of a reserve requirement we wish to consider in this section is the effect it has on seignorage. We look at two economies, one where money is held in a stationary nonbinding equilibrium with fixed money supply and another where it is not held. In the second case, the return on private borrowing and lending dominates the return on money, and the government cannot collect seignorage. The reserve requirement allows seignorage.

We use the basic economy of Exercise 12.7. The members of each generation with an endowment of [3, 1] are the lenders and those with an endowment of [1, 2] are the borrowers. In our initial economy, there are 50 of each of these in every generation. The savings functions for the borrowers are

$$s^{\text{borrowers}}(r(t)) = \frac{1}{2} - \frac{1}{r(t)},$$

so if we restrict ourselves to considering policies where the interest rate for those we call borrowers is not greater than 2, then they will always be borrowers. In stationary equilibria these individuals will always face the interest rate denoted r^L. The lenders will face the interest rate, $r^a = \lambda r^m + (1 - \lambda)r^L$. We can define two aggregate savings functions, one for the borrowers and another for the lenders. These aggregate savings functions are

$$S^{\text{lenders}}(r^a) = 50s^{\text{lenders}}(r^a) = 75 - \frac{25}{r^a},$$

and $S^{\text{borrowers}}(r^L) = 50s^{\text{borrowers}}(r^L) = 25 - \frac{50}{r^L}.$

In a more general form, both of these aggregate savings functions should be written as functions of both r^a and r^L, because both the borrowers and the lenders face kinked budget sets like the one shown in Figure 12.6. However, we restrict our discussion to equilibria in which the borrowers are to the right of the kink and the lenders are to the left of the kink on their respective budget lines. In this case the indicated interest rate is the relevant one.

In a binding stationary equilibrium, $r^L > r^m$, and the reserve requirement holds with equality; so

$$v = \lambda S^{\text{lenders}}(r^a).$$

From the discussion above,

$$\frac{v}{w} = \frac{p(t)M(t)}{p(t)P(t)B(t+1)} = \frac{m r^L}{r^m}.$$

From the first stationary equilibrium condition, aggregate savings equal the real value of government bonds and fiat money, or

$$S^{\text{lenders}}(r^a) + S^{\text{borrowers}}(r^L) = v\left(1 + \frac{w}{v}\right).$$

Substituting in the relationships we found above, we get

$$S^{\text{lenders}}(r^a) + S^{\text{borrowers}}(r^L) = \lambda S^{\text{lenders}}(r^a)\left(1 + \frac{r^m}{m r^L}\right),$$

which, using the definition of r^a, is a function in the two unknowns, r^m and r^L.

If we substitute into this equation the $S^{\text{lenders}}(r(t))$ and $S^{\text{borrowers}}(r(t))$ functions that we defined earlier, we can rearrange the equation to get a quadratic equation in r^L, with the exogenous variables r^m, m, and λ. In those cases where there are not very many government bonds relative to fiat money (m is large), there is only one solution to the quadratic equation in which r^L is positive.

Because r^m in a stationary monetary equilibrium equals $1/\mu$ (the reciprocal of the rate of growth of the money supply), it is possible to find Bailey curves for these economies with reserve requirements and with fixed ratios of money to government bonds, m. Figure 12.7 shows five Bailey curves for this economy when there are no government bonds, $1/m = 0$. In this economy, those we call borrowers are indeed borrowing and those we call lenders are lending. In a version of this economy without money, the competitive equilibrium with private borrowing and lending has a gross interest rate of $r(t) = 3/4$. There exists a stationary equilibrium with a fixed money supply with valued fiat money. The normal-looking Bailey curve (the lower solid line) in Figure 12.7 represents the case when there is no reserve requirement. The other four cases follow the normal Bailey curve until the reserve requirement kicks in, and then they follow the dashed line for the reserve requirement $\lambda = .1$, the dotted line for $\lambda = .2$, the dotted and dashed line for $\lambda = .3$, and the solid line for $\lambda = .4$.

Figure 12.8 illustrates the Bailey curves for the same economy, except $m = 1$. In this case the government is issuing equal amounts of bonds and fiat money. Because there is also a demand for private borrowing, when the reserve requirement is high, the rate of return on bonds is high and the returns from seignorage are low. The solid line that begins at -9 gives the seignorage (loss) when the reserve requirement is .4. The other λ's illustrated are 0, .05, .1, .2, and .3. With the high reserve requirements (above .2) and a fairly high ratio of government bonds to money (one to one, in this case), the government has a deficit in the monetary policy it follows if the rate of money creation is low. At low rates of money creation, the government is paying more in interest on bonds than it is making up from seignorage. At high rates of money creation, the seignorage becomes quite large.

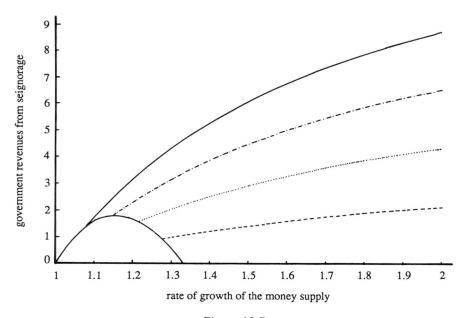

Figure 12.7

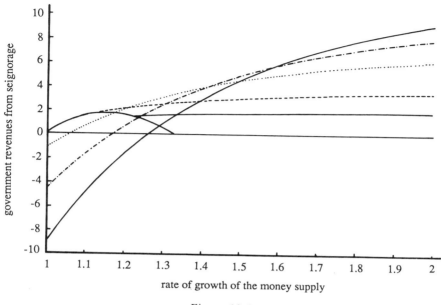

Figure 12.8

To illustrate the point that monetary policy can have different welfare effects on the borrowers and the lenders, we need to show how the interest rate on borrowing changes as the ratio of money to bonds changes for a fixed reserve requirement. Changing the ratio of money to bonds, that is, changing m, is our definition of monetary policy.

Figure 12.9 illustrates r^a and r^L and seignorage for three choices of m in the above economy with $\lambda = .1$. These interest rates are the same and their relationship with seignorage follows a Bailey curve until the reserve requirement kicks in. Point A in the figure is the point where the reserve requirement begins to bind for $m = 2$. Point B is for $m = 1$ and point C for $m = .5$. At each of these points, the line to the right is r^a and the one to the left is r^L. Consider the case where the government wishes to raise 2 units of the good each period by seignorage. Clearly, for each choice of monetary policy, r^L is greater than r^a. Note that as the ratio of government bonds to money increases (as we move from point A to C), both r^a and r^L increase. An increase in r^L raises the cost of borrowing to the borrowers, and an increase in r^a raises the return on lending for the lenders. The borrowers are made worse off and the

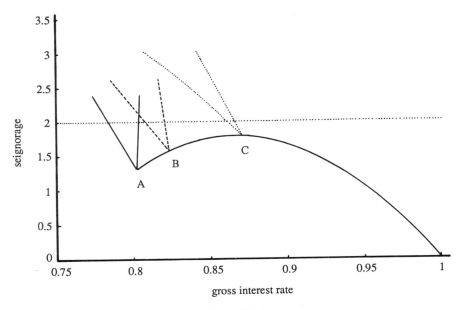

Figure 12.9

lenders better off by monetary policies with smaller m, that is, with larger ratios of bonds to money.

The next example shows that the addition of a reserve requirement can generate money holdings and seignorage in an economy in which no money is held without the reserve requirement. For this example, we need to have a market for private borrowing and lending that offers a rate of return higher than that of money (in fixed supply). Suppose, for example, that there are three times as many borrowers as there are lenders—suppose 150 to 50. Then the gross interest rate in the economy when there is neither money nor government bonds would be greater than 1. To see this, recall from Chapter 2 that a condition for equilibrium in an economy with no outside assets is that $S(r(t)) = 0$. For the economy with neither money nor bonds, the gross interest rate is

$$50\left(\frac{3}{2} - \frac{1}{2r(t)}\right) + 150\left(\frac{1}{2} - \frac{1}{r(t)}\right) = 0,$$

or $r(t) = \dfrac{7}{6}.$

Without reserve requirements, everyone will be in the market for private borrowing and lending and no one will wish to hold fiat money. Seignorage is not practicable unless a reserve requirement is added. Figure 12.10 shows the seignorage for this economy when the reserve requirement is .1 (the solid line), .2 (the dashed line), and .3 (the dotted line). In the example illustrated, no government bonds are issued.

The Bailey curve for a reserve requirement of 0 is the horizontal axis. Only with a reserve requirement can the government force individuals to hold money so that these holdings can be taxed.

EXERCISE 12.8 Find a stationary monetary equilibrium for the economy of Exercise 12.7, except the government is raising 3 units of the good each period by seignorage.

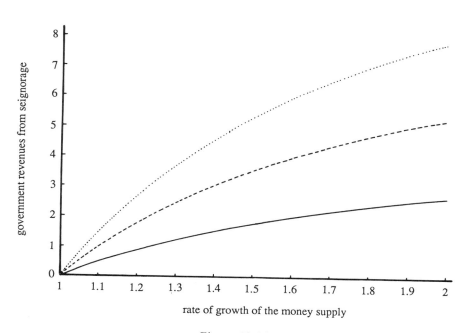

Figure 12.10

Large Denomination Bonds

In this section we assume a legal restriction slightly different from the reserve requirement, but one that can also give higher interest rates on bonds than those on fiat money. To do this, we really need two restrictions. The first establishes a minimum size for bonds; in other words, a bond cannot be purchased for less than F units of the time t good. A minimum size for bonds can be interpreted to represent the observation that government bonds come in much larger denominations than fiat money does. The second restriction is a prohibition on private intermediation (private borrowing and lending) or private division of bonds.

The two restrictions work together. If we restricted the government to large denomination bonds but allowed intermediation, then individuals could buy the bonds by selling portions of these bonds to other individuals. Intermediation could make the minimum denomination of the bonds meaningless. The large denomination bonds could, effectively, be broken up into bonds of almost any size. The imposition of these two restrictions can force the members of the economy to choose between bonds and fiat money as assets. When the denomination of the bond is large enough, there can exist equilibria in which individuals can choose either a bond or fiat money and the savings required to purchase a bond is greater than the savings one would wish to put into fiat money.

Consider a stationary version of the environment of Chapters 2, 3, 5, and 6. Suppose we rule out within-generation diversity, so all members of all generations have the same utility functions and the same endowments. Because we have not ruled out the possibility of lump-sum taxes, we can interpret these endowments as those the individuals have after the government collects any lump-sum taxes (endowments are net of taxes).

If fiat money and government bonds are the only assets, then the budget constraints facing a young person at time t are

$$c_t^h(t) = \omega_t^h(t) - p(t)m^h(t) - p(t)P(t)b^h(t),$$

$$c_t^h(t + 1) = \omega_t^h(t + 1) + p(t + 1)m^h(t) + p(t + 1)b^h(t),$$

$$p(t)P(t)b^h(t) \geq F \quad \text{or} \quad b^h(t) = 0,$$

and $m^h(t) \geq 0,$

where $p(t)$ is the price of fiat money in terms of the time t good, $P(t)$ is the nominal price of bonds, and $m^h(t)$ and $b^h(t)$ are the money and bond holdings of individual h of generation t. The third line of the budget constraint imposes the indivisibility restriction on bonds in terms of the time t good. The indivisibility constraint is expressed in real terms for expositional ease and because a nominal constraint would need to be changed over time if the government were using seignorage to raise revenues and to create inflation. Inflation could eventually make any fixed nominal restriction nonbinding.

Using this notation, we write the real gross interest rates on fiat money and bonds as, respectively,

$$r^m(t) = \frac{p(t + 1)}{p(t)},$$

and $\quad r^b(t) = \dfrac{p(t + 1)}{p(t)P(t)}.$

We can convert this set of budget constraints into constraints expressed in real terms. This conversion is useful because the indivisibility constraint on the bonds is also expressed in real terms. Let $q^{hm}(t) = p(t)m^h(t)$ be the real value of the fiat money held by individual h of generation t. Let $q^{hb}(t) = p(t)P(t)b^h(t)$ be the real value of the bond holdings of this same individual. The budget constraints can be written as

$$c^h_t(t) = \omega^h_t(t) - q^{hm}(t) - q^{hb}(t), \tag{12.21}$$

$$c^h_t(t + 1) = \omega^h_t(t + 1) + r^m(t)q^{hm}(t) + r^b(t)q^{hb}(t),$$

$$q^{hb}(t) \geq F \quad \text{or} \quad q^{hb}(t) = 0,$$

and $\quad q^{hm}(t) \geq 0.$

Even though it is not explicitly expressed in these budget constraints, all individuals of all generations have the same endowment pair.

The fact that everyone is identical and that we have outlawed intermediation means that no one can borrow. For all individuals,

$$s^h(t) = \omega^h_t(t) - c^h_t(t) \geq 0.$$

If, given $r^m(t)$ and $r^b(t)$, the amount of savings that an individual wishes to have is small—less than F—then our restrictions imply that this savings can only be done using fiat money. The rate of return a holder of fiat money gets is $r^m(t)$. If, on the other hand, the interest rate on bonds, $r^b(t)$, is so large that the individual wishes to save at least F, the choice is more complicated, but still simple. If $r^m(t) < r^b(t)$, then the individual chooses to hold only bonds. If $r^m > r^b(t)$, then the individual chooses to hold only fiat money. If $r^m(t) = r^b(t)$, then it does not matter.

There cannot be an equilibrium with any individuals holding bonds if $r^m(t) > r^b(t)$. When $r^m(t) = r^b(t)$, bonds are indistinguishable from money for both the government and members of generation t. The interesting possibility is when $r^b(t) > r^m(t)$. In this case, the budget constraint for a member of generation t can be illustrated by the broken line in Figure 12.11. The upper portion of the budget line holds when the individual saves at least F and holds bonds, getting a gross interest rate of $r^b(t)$. The lower portion of the budget line holds when the individual chooses to save less than F and holds only fiat money. This individual receives a gross interest rate of $r^m(t)$. Because everyone is saving

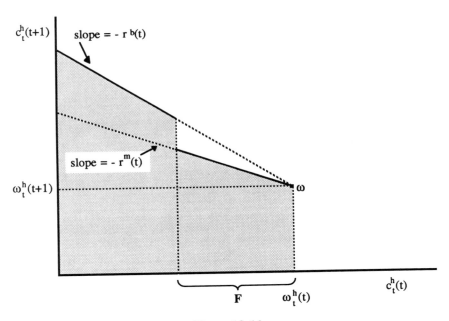

Figure 12.11

(or at least, no one is borrowing), the budget line does not extend to the right of the endowment point.

Suppose that we limit discussion to equilibria in which both large denomination bonds and fiat money are held. Under the assumption that all members of generation t are identical in tastes and endowments, we can say a lot about the conditions that must be true in such an equilibrium. If identical individuals have the options of holding either large denomination bonds or money and some choose to hold money and others choose to hold bonds, it must be because they are indifferent between holding one or the other. For these individuals to be indifferent, large denomination bonds and fiat money must yield the same utility. Given some identical individual preferences and endowments, the relation between $r^b(t)$, $r^m(t)$, and F must give rise to a budget line like the one illustrated in Figure 12.12.

Maximizing welfare constrained to either of the two sections of the budget line shown in Figure 12.12 yields the same level of utility. The highest obtainable indifference curve can be reached at consumption

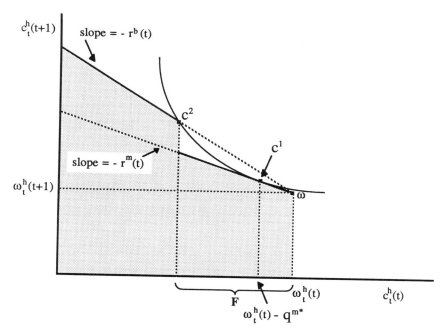

Figure 12.12

point c^2 by holding bonds with a real value exactly equal to F and no fiat money or at consumption point c^1 by holding q^{m*} units of fiat money and no bonds. For the $r^b(t)$ and $r^m(t)$ shown in the figure, if any other F were chosen, then everyone would either hold only fiat money or everyone would hold only bonds. The assumption that everyone is identical is crucial for this condition to hold. If there were diversity among individuals, the equality of utility condition might not hold.

There are several points worth mentioning about Figure 12.12 and therefore about what holds in an equilibrium with identical individuals. Notice that the indifference curve is tangent to the constraint set at point c^1, where the real value of money holdings when young equals q^{m*}. The first line of the budget constraints in real terms (Equation 12.21) holds with equality and

$$q^{m*} = \omega_t^h(t) - c_t^h(t) = s^h(r^m(t)).$$

Because these individuals are holding only fiat money, only the interest rate on money matters in determining their savings. Let

$$u[\omega_t^h(t) - s^h(r^m(t)), \omega_t^h(t + 1) + r^m(t)s^h(r^m(t))],$$

be the utility of any individual holding only fiat money. Figure 12.12 shows that any individual holding only 1 bond achieves the same level of utility. Notice that the indifference curve is *not* tangent to the portion of the budget line that represents bond ownership. Because any individual holding a bond spent F units of the time t good to purchase that bond, this individual's utility is

$$u[\omega_t^h(t) - F, \omega_t^h(t + 1) + r^b(t)F],$$

and because the holders of bonds and the holders of fiat money are on the same indifference curve,

$$u[\omega_t^h(t) - s^h(r^m(t)), \omega_t^h(t + 1) + r^m(t)s^h(r^m(t))]$$
$$= u[\omega_t^h(t) - F, \omega_t^h(t + 1) + r^b(t)F].$$

Equality of utility for holders of fiat money and holders of bonds implies that both can be held in equilibrium. Some members of each generation will hold bonds and others fiat money. Their consumption patterns are different, but the utilities that these consumption patterns generate are the same. One important implication of Figure 12.12 is that an equilibrium with both bonds and money is not Pareto optimal. The reader is asked to prove this conjecture in the exercise below. Although these equilibria are not Pareto optimal, an equilibrium with bonds may well be Pareto superior to equilibria without bonds.

EXERCISE 12.9 Prove that any equilibrium in which some members of generation t hold bonds and others hold fiat money, as illustrated in Figure 12.12, is not Pareto optimal. Recall the necessary conditions for a Pareto optimum from Chapter 2.

Stationary Equilibrium with Large Denomination Bonds

Consider an economy with a stationary environment. There are N members of each generation and all individuals are identical in preferences and endowments.

In a stationary equilibrium, the prices and quantities of fiat money and bonds can change through time, but the gross interest rates, price of bonds in terms of fiat money, consumption patterns, and the savings allocated to bonds and fiat money are constant. We restrict ourselves to equilibria in which both fiat money and bonds have positive prices. The number of large denomination bonds that the government issues is denoted by n.

Definition *Given* $\mathbf{g}, F, n$, *where* $0 \leq n \leq N$, *and* $M(0) + B(0) > 0$, *a stationary equilibrium consists of positive* $\{p(t)\}$, *positive and constant* P, r^m, *and* r^b, *and nonnegative* $\{M(t)\}$ *and* $\{B(t)\}$ *such that, for all* $t \geq 1$,

$$nF = p(t)PB(t), \tag{12.22}$$

$$(N - n)s(r^m) = p(t)M(t), \tag{12.23}$$

$$\mathbf{g} = (N - n)s(r^m) + nF - p(1)[M(0) + B(0)], \tag{12.24}$$

$$\mathbf{g} = (1 - r^b)nF + (1 - r^m)(N - n)s(r^m), \tag{12.25}$$

$$u(\omega_t(t) - s(r^m), \omega_t(t + 1) + r^m s(r^m))$$

$$= u(\omega_t(t) - F, \omega_t(t + 1) + r^b F), \tag{12.26}$$

$$r^m = \frac{p(t + 1)}{p(t)}, \tag{12.27}$$

and $\quad r^b = \dfrac{p(t + 1)}{Pp(t)}$ \hfill (12.28)

hold.

Notice that the h superscripts have been omitted from the savings functions, the utility functions, and the endowments. This omission is intended to remind the reader that all members of a generation are alike.

The first equilibrium condition (Equation 12.22) connects the real and nominal value of the bonds. It is a market clearing condition for bonds. The next condition (Equation 12.23) is the market clearing condition for fiat money. The next two constraints are the budget constraints for the government. Equation (12.24) is the government budget constraint for time 1, and Equation (12.25) is the government budget constraint for all other dates. The next constraint (Equation 12.26) equates the utility of bond holders and the utility of fiat money holders. This constraint was discussed extensively above. Note that this constraint can hold even if there are no bonds outstanding in the economy, $n = 0$, or if there is no fiat money in the economy, $n = N$. The last two equilibrium conditions (Equations 12.27 and 12.28) define the perfect foresight rates of return on money and on bonds, respectively.

Although some results about general stationary competitive equilibria can be obtained for this model (see Bryant and Wallace, 1984), the discussion here follows a particular example economy. The utility function we have been using for much of this book is $u_t^h = c_t^h(t)c_t^h(t + 1)$. This product utility function proves to be very tractable for studying the competitive equilibrium of an economy with large denomination bonds. In particular, it is possible to find a Bailey curve for this economy and to show this curve as a function of the number of outstanding government bonds, n. It is also possible to show that there exist equilibria with bonds that are Pareto superior to any stationary equilibrium without bonds for government expenditures, **g** > 0.

For the product utility function, the equality of utility condition (Equation 12.26) is

$$[\omega_t(t) - F][\omega_t(t + 1) + r^b F]$$
$$= [\omega_t(t) - s(r^m)][\omega_t(t + 1) + r^m s(r^m)].$$

If F is greater than $\omega_t(t)$, no one can purchase a bond. So restrict $F \geq 0$ to be less than $\omega_t(t)$. In this case, the above equation can be solved for $r^b F$, giving

$$r^b F = \frac{[\omega_t(t) - s(r^m)][\omega_t(t + 1) + r^m s(r^m)]}{\omega_t(t) - F} - \omega_t(t + 1).$$

The savings function for an individual with a product utility function has been illustrated many times before in this book. This savings function is

$$s(r^m) = \frac{\omega_t(t)}{2} - \frac{\omega_t(t + 1)}{2 r^m}.$$

The government budget constraint (Equation 12.25) is

$$\mathbf{g} = (1 - r^b)nF + (1 - r^m)(N - n)s(r^m).$$

Substituting for $r^b F$ (from above), we can find the government revenue as a function of r^m, n, and F. This function is

$$\mathbf{g} = (1 - r^m)Ns(r^m) + n\left[F + \omega_t(t + 1) - (1 - r^m)s(r^m)\right.$$
$$\left. - \frac{[\omega_t(t) - s(r^m)][\omega_t(t + 1) + r^m s(r^m)]}{\omega_t(t) - F}\right].$$

Because r^m equals $1/\mu$ for any combination of permissible n and F, we can construct a Bailey curve. Notice that when $n = 0$, the second term of the right side of the above equation equals 0 and the equation becomes

$$\mathbf{g} = (1 - r^m)Ns(r^m),$$

the seignorage equation for an economy with only money and with N identical individuals. When $n > 0$, the second term of the right side of the equation is the contribution to government revenues from having bonds outstanding. The sign of that term tells us the effects of issuing bonds on government revenues. A bit of algebraic manipulation gives the equation

$$\mathbf{g} = (1 - r^m)Ns(r^m) + n[F - s(r^m)]\left[1 - \frac{\omega_t(t + 1) + r^m s(r^m)}{\omega_t(t) - F}\right].$$

The contribution of bonds to government revenues is positive if

$$F > s(r^m) \tag{12.29}$$

and $\quad \omega_t(t + 1) + r^m s(r^m) < \omega_t(t) - F.$ $\tag{12.30}$

Government revenues from bonds are positive whenever the large denomination constraint on the government bonds is binding and the equilibrium looks like the one in Figure 12.12. Moreover, using the product utility function version of the individual savings function, we see that the inequalities (12.29) and (12.30) become

$$2F > \omega_t(t) - \frac{\omega_t(t + 1)}{r^m}$$

and $\quad 2F < \omega_t(t)(2 - r^m) - \omega_t(t + 1).$

We put these constraints together and find that if bonds increase government revenues from seignorage, then F must be such that

$$\omega_t(t) - \frac{\omega_t(t + 1)}{r^m} < 2F < \omega_t(t)(2 - r^m) - \omega_t(t + 1).$$

For an economy with a fixed money supply monetary equilibrium, savings at $r^m = 1$ are greater than 0. For these economies, there exist ranges of F for any positive r^m less than 1 where the contribution of bonds to government revenues is positive. One F that fulfills the constraints for any $r^m \leq 1$ is

$$F = \frac{\omega_t(t) - \omega_t(t + 1)}{2}. \tag{12.31}$$

Figure 12.13 shows the Bailey curve for this economy when endowments equal [2, 1] and the population $N = 100$. The solid line is the
Bailey curve when there are no bonds, $n = 0$. The dashed line is the
Bailey curve when $n = 50$ and F is determined by Equation (12.31);
that is, $F = \frac{1}{2}$. The dotted line is the Bailey curve when $n = 100$ and
$F = \frac{1}{2}$. The more people who hold these bonds, the higher the government revenues from seignorage at any rate of growth of the money
supply. Put another way, a given level of government deficits can be
covered at lower rates of growth of the money supply when there are
more bonds in the economy. The lower rate of growth of the money
supply results in a higher rate of return on holding money, r^m. Notice
that the Bailey curves in Figure 12.13 are not shown for μ greater than
2. For these μ, the gross interest rate on money is $r^m = \frac{1}{2}$; and for the
utility functions and endowments used here, the individuals who are
not holding bonds would wish to be borrowers. They are constrained
from doing so, hold no money, and consume their endowment. Because
this corner solution is somewhat difficult to illustrate, we restrict our
analysis to cases where the money holders actually hold money.

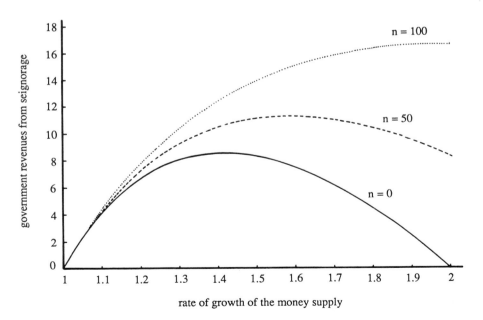

Figure 12.13

The following proposition holds for economies with the product utility function.

Proposition 12.1 *For an economy of identical individuals with the utility function $u_t^h = c_t^h(t)c_t^h(t + 1)$, if, for some $\mathbf{g} > 0$ there exists a stationary monetary equilibrium with $n = 0$, then there exists a Pareto superior equilibrium with $n > 0$.*

To see why this proposition holds, consider Figure 12.12. In an equilibrium the level of utility is determined by the indifference curve tangent to the portion of the budget line representing the rate of return on money, r^m. Higher rates of return on money mean that this portion of the budget line is steeper and that the resulting utility level will be higher.

Consider just one rate of return on money, r^m, and the rate of returns on bonds, r^b, that goes with it for some F. Figure 12.14 shows an exam-

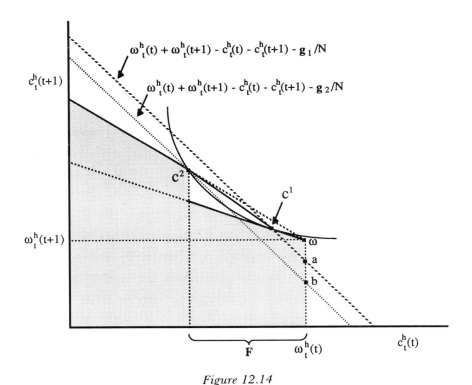

Figure 12.14

ple. The points c^1 and c^2 are the consumption points for individuals who hold either money or bonds, respectively. The 45-degree line running through point c^1 represents the set of symmetric allocations that are possible when the government is extracting $\mathbf{g}_1/N$ units of the good from the illustrated individual over a lifetime. The vertical distance from the endowment point, ω, and the 45-degree line at point a is $\mathbf{g}_1/N$. If there is only fiat money, the 45-degree line passes through point c^1 (the dashed 45-degree line in Figure 12.14) and the amount of government revenues is N times the distance $\overline{\omega a}$. As bonds are issued, individuals who purchase these bonds have the same utility as those with money but consume at point c^2. The 45-degree line through point c^2 can be used to find the amount of revenue that the government gets from each of these individuals. The distance $\overline{\omega b}$ is the revenue, $\mathbf{g}_2/N$, from each bond holder when the rate of return on money is r^m.

The line between points c^1 and c^2 indicates the average consumption points possible from some people holding bonds and some holding fiat money. No one actually consumes at one of these average consumption points, everyone is at either c^1 or c^2, but they can be used to find the revenues the government is raising from its financial policy. Increases in the number of bonds move the average consumption point, and the average government revenues, closer to those indicated by c^2 and $\overline{\omega b}$. Notice how this is consistent with the Bailey curves shown above. As the number of bonds increases from 0 to 50 to 100, the government revenues at each rate of growth of the money supply increase. Figure 12.14 shows why this occurs with the product utility functions. The consumption points with bonds give more revenue to the government, so the more individuals holding bonds, the more revenue the government gets. Note that it is possible that for some utility functions, the consumption point with bonds would be above a 45-degree line through the consumption point with fiat money. In that case, more bonds mean less government revenues from money creation. The argument is symmetric to the one given above.

For these equilibria with bonds to be Pareto superior to those without, the welfare of the old at date 1 must not decline. The old at time 1 either hold bonds or money. Those with bonds receive $p(1)b^h(0)$ and those with money receive $p(1)m^h(0)$. We use the following equilibrium condition (12.24) to find the price of money at date 1, $p(1)$:

$$\mathbf{g} = (N - n)s(r^m) + nF - p(1)[M(0) + B(0)]. \tag{12.24}$$

Because $F > s(r^m)$, for a given $\mathbf{g}$, $p(1)$ is larger as n is larger. The members of generation 0 also receive more where n is greater than 0. An equilibrium with bonds is Pareto superior to an equilibrium without bonds.

If some bonds are good, maybe more bonds are even better. There is a definite sense in which this is correct. Moreover, it does not depend on a particular utility function. The following proposition will be demonstrated by a combination of discussion and exercises.

Proposition 12.2   *If $\mathbf{g} > 0$ and there exists a stationary monetary equilibrium with no bonds, then there exists a Pareto superior equilibrium with $n = N$ that is Pareto optimal among the set of symmetric allocations.*

The consumption basket of each two-period-lived individual in a symmetric allocation where the government consumes $\mathbf{g}$ units of the good in each period is on the line

$$c_t(t) + c_t(t + 1) = \omega_t(t) + \omega_t(t + 1) - \frac{\mathbf{g}}{N}.$$

The superscripts have been left off to indicate that everyone is the same. With N identical individuals in each generation, the government ends up with $\mathbf{g}$ units of the good each period. This set of possible consumption baskets is illustrated in Figure 12.15. This line is the same 45-degree line that we saw in Chapter 10 when discussing seignorage and that we used above. The consumption point

$$c* = [c_t^*(t), c_t^*(t + 1)]$$

in Figure 12.15 is the consumption basket among the symmetric allocations that reaches the highest indifference curve. For the set of exercises below, we are always concerned with an economy in which the government raises (has a deficit of) $\mathbf{g}$ units of the good each period.

EXERCISE 12.10   Let $c' = [c_t'(t), c_t'(t + 1)]$ be the consumption allocation of any stationary equilibrium without bonds that raises $\mathbf{g}$ units of government revenue. Show that this basket is on the line in Figure 12.15 and is southeast of the point $c*$.

EXERCISE 12.11 Use the result of the above exercise to show that c^* is Pareto superior to the c' allocation.

EXERCISE 12.12 Show that there is no symmetric allocation consistent with the government getting **g** units of the consumption good each period that is Pareto superior to the c^* allocation.

EXERCISE 12.13 Show that the allocation c^* can arise as an equilibrium allocation if F and n are chosen appropriately.

The last exercise of the above group completes the general demonstration of Proposition 12.2. The denomination of the bond, F, and the number of them, n, are to be chosen so that the consumption of every individual ends up at point c^*. Because everyone is to be at the same consumption point (and not just on the same indifference curve but

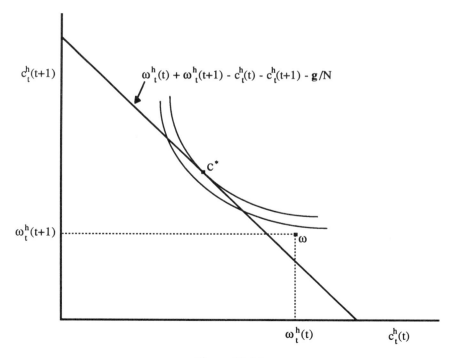

Figure 12.15

possibly at two different points on that indifference curve), it would be appropriate to have everyone making the same choice. One way to do this is to have the number of bonds be equal to the number of individuals and to have the denomination of the bond exactly large enough to make

$$F = \omega_t(t) - c_t^*(t).$$

In the next exercise, you are asked to find the appropriate number and size of bonds for a particular economy.

EXERCISE 12.14 Suppose the utility function is the product of consumption when young and consumption when old. Find an expression for $c_t^*(t)$ as a function of $\omega_t(t)$, $\omega_t(t + 1)$, and **g**. Also, express savings, $\omega_t(t) - c_t^*(t)$, as a function of $\omega_t(t)$, $\omega_t(t + 1)$, and **g**. Do

$$F = \frac{\omega_t(t) - \omega_t(t + 1)}{2},$$

and $n = N$

give rise to an equilibrium that is Pareto optimal among the set of symmetric allocations? Explain.

The above discussions tell us that choices of financing policies (choices of F and n) for a given economy have welfare effects both for the current old and for future generations. The legal restriction on private intermediation and the issuance of large denomination bonds allow the government, while covering some specified fiscal deficit, to achieve consumption allocations for the citizens of the economy that are superior to those where there is only fiat money. The restriction on private intermediation allows differential interest rates for fiat money and large denomination bonds. The government exploits this interest rate differential for welfare-improving monetary policies.

The ability of the government to exploit these differentials is not very different from the situation of a monopolist who decides to offer a lower price for her good if the consumer purchases some minimum quantity of her product. Choices of lower prices with minimum purchases can increase the profits of the monopolist. This monopolist can capture all of the consumer surplus if she chooses the correct size for these minimum purchases. If she captures all the consumer surplus, the equilibrium that results is a Pareto optimum. When the government acts as this monopolist in issuing assets, then it can capture more revenues (maximize profits) than it could with only fiat money. If instead of maximizing revenues, it chooses a fixed amount of revenues first, then choosing the proper mix of bonds and money can maximize consumer welfare while raising that chosen revenue.

As an example, consider an economy with $N(t) = 100$, $g = 6$, endowments of $[2, 1]$, and utility functions for all members h of all generations t equal to $u_t^h = c_t^h(t)c_t^h(t + 1)$. Let F equal .6. The solution of a stationary equilibrium for this economy is found from the two equations

$$g = (1 - r^b)nF + (1 - r^m)(N - n)\left(1 - \frac{1}{2r^m}\right),$$

and $\left[2 - \left(1 - \frac{1}{2r^m}\right)\right]\left[1 + r^m\left(1 - \frac{1}{2r^m}\right)\right] = [2 - F][1 + r^bF],$

where the first equation is the seignorage equation with both fiat money and bonds and the second equation assures that individuals will have the same level of utility when holding either fiat money or bonds. Substituting in all of the parameter values gives us two equations in two unknowns, r^m and r^b. If we let the number of bonds, n, be 50, these equations are

$$6 = (1 - r^b)(50)(.6) + 50(1 - r^m)\left(1 - \frac{1}{2r^m}\right)$$

$$= 30(1 - r^b) + 50(1 - r^m)\left(1 - \frac{1}{2r^m}\right),$$

and $\left[1 + \frac{1}{2r^m}\right]\left[\frac{1}{2} + r^m\right] = 1.4[1 + .6r^b],$

or $\frac{1}{2} + r^m + \frac{1}{4r^m} + \frac{1}{2} = 1.4 + .84r^b.$

Both equations can be solved for r^b as a function of r^m. Solving for r^b gives us the equations

$$r^b = .8 + 1.667(1 - r^m)\left(1 - \frac{1}{2r^m}\right),$$

and $$r^b = 1.190\left(r^m + \frac{1}{4r^m} - .4\right).$$

The above two equations can be solved analytically. Setting the right sides of these two equations equal to each other, which we can do since they both equal r^b, gives

$$.8 + 1.667(1 - r^m)\left(1 - \frac{1}{2r^m}\right) = 1.190\left(r^m + \frac{1}{4r^m} - .4\right).$$

This equation simplifies to

$$2.856(r^m)^2 - 3.776r^m + 1.1308 = 0.$$

Solving this quadratic equation gives r^m equal to .863 and .458. Using the second equation of our system to solve for r^b, we get r^b equals .896 (when r^m equals .863). The solution with r^m equal to .458 is a situation where those who are not holding bonds would be borrowing. Because they are constrained from doing so, this case cannot be an equilibrium.

Reprise

We have observed the equilibria that result when the government imposes three different types of restrictions on the economy. In the first case the government imposes a law restricting the amount of private borrowing and lending in an economy in which private borrowing and lending exist in an unconstrained equilibrium. This constraint on private borrowing and lending means that lenders will hold more currency than they would in an unconstrained equilibrium and permits the government to extract more revenue from seignorage. It should not be a surprise, therefore, that we observe credit controls arising in countries in which inflation is a major source of government revenues. The government actions in the Latin American countries of Argentina, Bolivia, and Brazil in the late 1980s and Chile in the late 1970s provide examples of this behavior.

In our model economy governmental restrictions are necessary to get bonds and money both being held and offering different interest rates. Imposing a reserve requirement of fiat money on all lending is one type of restrictions that works. When the reserve requirement is binding (when all money is used to fulfill the reserve requirement), the interest rate on bonds is higher than that on fiat money. One important observation from this model is that different monetary policies affect borrowers and lenders differently.

The third restriction we let the government impose is really a pair of restrictions. The government issues large denomination bonds (where the size restriction is in real terms) and prevents private intermediation of these bonds. Individuals can either purchase a bond or purchase fiat money. In binding equilibria, bonds offer a higher interest rate than fiat money does and can be used by a discriminating monetary authority to improve the welfare of all citizens (or to raise increased revenues) relative to welfare under policies using only fiat money. A policy of issuing only bonds is Pareto optimal if the denomination constraint is large enough.

References

Aiyagari, S. Rao. 1987. Intergenerational linkages and government budget policies. Federal Reserve Bank of Minneapolis *Quarterly Review* 11(2):14–23.

——— 1988. Economic fluctuations without shocks to fundamentals; or, does the stock market dance to its own music. Federal Reserve Bank of Minneapolis *Quarterly Review* 12(1):8–24.

Azariadis, Costas. 1981. Self-fulfilling prophecies. *Journal of Economic Theory* 25(3):380–396.

——— and Roger Guesnerie. 1986. Sunspots and cycles. *Review of Economic Studies* 53(5):725–738.

Bailey, Martin. 1956. The welfare cost of inflationary finance. *Journal of Political Economy* 64(2):93–110.

Barro, Robert J. 1974. Are government bonds net wealth? *Journal of Political Economy* 82(6):1095–1117.

Barth, John. 1966. *Giles goat boy: or the revised new syllabus.* Garden City, N.Y.: Doubleday.

Bernheim, B. Douglas, and Kyle Bagwell. 1988. Is everything neutral? *Journal of Political Economy* 96(2):308–338.

Bernheim, B. Douglas, Andrei Shleifer, and Lawrence H. Summers. 1985. The strategic bequest motive. *Journal of Political Economy* 93(6):1045–1076.

Bryant, J., and Neil Wallace. 1984. A price discrimination analysis of monetary policy. *Review of Economic Studies* 51(2):279–288.

Cagen, P. 1956. The monetary dynamics of hyperinflation. In *Studies in the quantity theory of money*, ed. Milton Friedman. Chicago: University of Chicago Press.

Cass, David, and Menahem Yarri. 1966. A re-examination of the pure consumption loans model. *Journal of Political Economy* 74:353–367.

Chari, V. V., Patrick J. Kehoe, and Edward C. Prescott. 1989. Time consistency and policy. In *Modern business cycle theory,* ed. Robert J. Barro. Cambridge, Mass.: Harvard University Press.

Devaney, R. L. 1986. *An introduction to chaotic dynamical systems.* Menlo Park, Calif.: Benjamin/Cummings Publishing Co.

Diamond, Peter A. 1965. National debt in a neoclassical growth model. *American Economic Review* 55(5):1126–1150.

Fisher, Irving. [1907] 1930. *The theory of interest.* London: Macmillan.

Friedman, Milton. 1960. *A program for monetary stability.* New York: Fordham University Press.

——— 1968. *Dollars and deficits.* Englewood Cliffs, N.J.: Prentice-Hall.

Grandmont, Jean Michel. 1983. On endogenous business cycles. *Econometrica* 53(5):995–1045.

Hicks, John. 1969. *A theory of economic history.* New York: Oxford University Press.

Kareken, John H., and Neil Wallace. 1981. On the indeterminancy of equilibrium exchange rates. *Quarterly Journal of Economics* 96(2):207–222.

Kondratieff, Nikolai. 1984. *The long wave cycle,* trans. Guy Danials. New York: Richardson & Snyder.

Kuznets, Simon S. 1961. *Capital in the American economy: its formation and financing.* New York: National Bureau of Economic Research.

Kydland, Finn E., and Edward C. Prescott. 1982. Time to build and aggregate fluctuations. *Econometrica* 50(6):1345–1371.

Long, John, and Charles Plosser. 1983. Real business cycles. *Journal of Political Economy* 91(1):39–69.

Lucas, Robert E., Jr. 1988. On the mechanics of economic development. *Journal of Monetary Economics* 22(1):3–42.

Murra, John V. 1980. *The economic organization of the Inca state.* Greenwich, Conn.: JAI Press.

Polo, Marco. 1946. *The travels of Marco Polo.* New York: Dutton.

Poma de Ayala, Filipe Huaman. 1613, trans. C. W. Dilke, 1978. *Letter to a king.* New York: Dutton.

Ricardo, David. 1951. Funding system. In *The works and correspondence of David Ricardo,* vol. 4, ed. P. Sraffa. Cambridge: Cambridge University Press.

Romer, Paul M. 1986. Increasing returns and long-run growth. *Journal of Political Economy* 94(5):1002–1037.

Samuelson, Paul A. 1958. An exact consumption-loan model of interest with or without the social contrivance of money. *Journal of Political Economy* 66(6):467–482.

Solow, Robert M. 1956. A contribution to the theory of economic growth. *Quarterly Journal of Economics* 70:65–94.

——— 1970. *Growth theory: an exposition.* New York: Oxford University Press.

Wallace, Neil. 1980a. Integrating micro and macroeconomics: an application to credit controls. Federal Reserve Bank of Minneapolis *Quarterly Review* 7(1):1–7.

———— 1980b. The overlapping-generations model of fiat money. In *Models of Monetary Economies*, ed. J. H. Kareken and N. Wallace, pp. 49–82. Minneapolis: Federal Reserve Bank of Minneapolis.

———— 1983. A legal restrictions theory of the demand for "money" and the role of monetary policy. Federal Reserve Bank of Minneapolis *Quarterly Review* 7(1):1–7.

———— 1984. Some choices for monetary policy. Federal Reserve Bank of Minneapolis *Quarterly Review* 8(1):15–24.

———— 1988. A suggestion for oversimplifying the theory of money. *Economic Journal* 98(390):25–36.

Index